THE FLETCHER JONES FOUNDATION
HUMANITIES IMPRINT

The Fletcher Jones Foundation has endowed this imprint to foster innovative and enduring scholarship in the humanities.

The publisher gratefully acknowledges the generous support of the Fletcher Jones Foundation Humanities Endowment Fund of the University of California Press Foundation, which was established by a major gift from the Fletcher Jones Foundation.

The publisher gratefully acknowledges the generous support of the Valerie Barth and Peter Booth Wiley Endowment Fund in History of the University of California Press Foundation.

Saints and Citizens

Saints and Citizens

*Indigenous Histories of Colonial Missions
and Mexican California*

———

Lisbeth Haas

UNIVERSITY OF CALIFORNIA PRESS
Berkeley   Los Angeles

University of California Press, one of the most distinguished university presses in the United States, enriches lives around the world by advancing scholarship in the humanities, social sciences, and natural sciences. Its activities are supported by the UC Press Foundation and by philanthropic contributions from individuals and institutions. For more information, visit www.ucpress.edu.

University of California Press
Berkeley and Los Angeles, California

Library of Congress Cataloging-in-Publication Data

Haas, Lisbeth.
    Saints and citizens : indigenous histories of colonial missions and Mexican California / Lisbeth Haas.
        pages cm
    Includes bibliographical references and index.
    ISBN 978-0-520-27646-8 (cloth : alk. paper)
1. Indians of North America—Missions—California—History.   2. Indians, Treatment of—California.   3. Indians of North America—Ethnic identity.   4. Indians of North America—Land tenure—California—History.   5. Missions, Spanish—California—History.   6. California—History—To 1846.   I. Title.
E78.C15H225 2013
    305.8970794—dc23   2013010524

23   22   21   20   19   18   17   16   15   14
10   9   8   7   6   5   4   3   2   1

CONTENTS

LIST OF MAPS AND FIGURES

MAPS

FIGURES

ACKNOWLEDGMENTS

I am grateful to the many people and institutions who supported this project from its start in the fall of 2000, with a fellowship from the Huntington Library, a University of California Presidential Research Fellowship, and a UC MEXUS research grant. They funded research in major archives, as did grants and fellowships from the Institute for Humanities Research and the Senate Committee on Research at the University of California, Santa Cruz. I appreciate a grant I received from the Hispanic Literary Recovery Project at the University of Houston. It provided funds for research trips to Rome and Bologna, Italy, to work with the manuscript of Luiseño scholar Pablo Tac and in related collections. I greatly appreciate a fellowship provided by the Davis Center at Princeton University that enabled me to finish the first draft of this book and to consider fear and other emotions in history.

This support opened doors to different and varied intellectual communities with whom I discussed the ideas developed herein. In particular I thank Steve Aron and Jeremy Edelman, whose conference on the comparative Americas at the Huntington Library in 2001 offered me the first venue for a lecture on the subject of Indigenous colonial painting in California. I thank the many scholars I met while in residence at the Huntington, especially Maria Lepowsky, whose knowledge influenced my work. I appreciate Steven Hackel's conference on identity in Alta California at the Huntington Library in 2006, and the important Early California Population Project (ECPP) that he began at the Huntington about the same time I commenced work on this book.

The year I spent at the Davis Center at Princeton University enabled me to elaborate many dimensions of this project. I thank Gyan Prakash, the director of the center that year, and the other fellows who made excellent intellectual companions: Alexander Etkind, David Lederer, Melanie McAlister, Ron Schechter, Marla Stone, and Ravi Sundaram. The valuable discussions with Arcadio Díaz-Quiñones, Christina Lee, Jussara Quadros, and Laura León Llerena from the Spanish and Portuguese Department, and with Tera Hunter from the History Department, enriched my thinking. I thank the late Sarah Hirschman for the long walks and discussions about life and literacy.

The archivists at the Huntington, Bancroft, and Santa Barbara Mission Archives and Libraries played an important role in accessing material and creating productive work environments. I found a rich trove of material at the Bancroft Library and benefited from the expertise of current and former archivists Teresa Salazar and Walter Brem, respectively. The Mission Archives and Library in Santa Barbara is a rich collection. In Santa Barbara, the collaboration of Chumash and non-Chumash scholars at the Natural History Museum and at the Presidio Trust created a distinctive context for research. I am especially grateful for the ample generosity of John Johnson from the Natural History Museum, with whom I consulted throughout this project. John carefully read the first draft and offered important comments.

Conversations with Ernestine Ygnacio-De Soto, a Chumash elder, and Niki Sandoval, from the Santa Ynez Band of Chumash Indians, influenced my approach. This book shares their emphasis on the perspectives and histories told by Chumash elders. Tribal histories in Chumash and Luiseño territory are generally embedded in specific geographies, and I am grateful to the San Luis Rey band of Mission Indians and to Mel Vernon, tribal chair, for conveying a sense of the persistent meaning of the former tribal space around Mission San Luis Rey. For his introduction to La Jolla reservation, I thank artist James Luna. I first began to think about these histories and tribal geographies in Baja California decades ago with Alejandrina Murillo de Meléndrez, an aunt through marriage. Though deceased, I remember her here for the knowledge she conveyed and for her strength, and to thank her children and relatives.

Some of my graduate students at the University of California, Santa Cruz, contributed valuable research assistance for particular aspects of this book. I thank them and express my admiration for the subsequent work that each has accomplished. In the early phases of this project Jessica Delgado and Michelle Morton did preliminary research for me in conjunction with their own projects, as did Marie Duggan. I thank Natale Zappia for his contributions at a later date, and for the pleasure of advising him as he studied for his degree and wrote an excellent dissertation. I appreciate Sarah Ginn-Peelo for her work on the ECPP and for the interesting years of discussion as she completed her graduate work. I also thank current graduate students Alicia Romero and Martin Rizzo who have taken some of the concerns expressed here in new directions. I am grateful to my undergraduate students at Santa Cruz, who have often heard this material as I wrote it. I especially appreciate the interactions with students from my senior seminars and from the university's mentorship programs. As a senior history major, and mentee, Carol Herndández used her intelligence and expertise as she played a critical role helping me to prepare the final manuscript.

I am indebted to the rich intellectual life and community created by the faculty in the Feminist Studies Department at the University of California, Santa Cruz. Their vitality enabled me to finish this and a related book while serving as chair of the department. For their consistently interesting ideas and company, I deeply appreciate Bettina Aptheker, Anjali Arodekar, Neda Atanasoski, Karen Barad, Gina Dent, Carla Freccero, Marcia Ochoa, and Felicity Amaya Schaeffer. My colleagues in Indigenous Studies at the university, especially Amy Lonetree and Guillermo Delgado, have made the environment for this work much richer.

I thank my colleagues in the History Department at Santa Cruz. Their perspectives on local and global histories, the expertise they bring to studies that frequently cross borders, and their abilities to incorporate popular voices and to write from a range of perspectives have inspired my own work. The Center for Cultural Studies has similarly offered inspiration throughout my years at Santa Cruz. I have appreciated the advice and critical spirits of Rosa-Linda Fregoso, Herman Gray, B. Ruby Rich, and Hayden White. For their astute comments on visual analysis, I thank Carolyn Dean, Cathy Soussloff, and Victor Zamudio-Taylor.

I also thank William Taylor for reading certain chapters, and for our many discussions throughout this project. I appreciate the influence of Rose Marie Beebe, Robert Senkewicz, and James Sandos on California mission studies. Bob Senkewicz twice provided a detailed reading of the entire work. I am extremely grateful for his excellent suggestions. I thank Andrés Reséndez for our discussions and his suggestions that I examine the trial Crespín and Carpio.

I presented some of my first writing on this subject at the International Institute for the Study of the Americas in Tepotzlán, Mexico. The place itself, and annual discussions among scholars who often work with harsh histories that have produced wounds and scars, has offered unique intellectual and spiritual sustenance for this project. The members of the Tepoztlán collective have been particularly important to me as I worked through this project, especially Josie Saldaña, David Kazanjian, Elliot Young, and Pamela Voekel.

Neils Hooper, my editor at University of California Press, extended an incredible quality of steady support as this project took its final form. He has an excellent eye for projects, as does Kim Hogeland, who offered her expertise in getting this book into production. This is the third in a trilogy of books I have written that address the deeper histories of places too often obscured. For all three books, the University of California Press has consistently provided high-quality editorial and artistic work. I thank the editors and design staff, especially Sandy Drooker.

My dear friends from my home in San Francisco have inspired me with their own writing and work in art, theater, and performance art. I especially thank

Carolina Ponce de León, Guillermo Gómez-Peña, Liz Lerma, Tim Keefe, Andrea Seuss, Elaine Katzenberger, René Yáñez, and Cynthia Wallis, who have offered love and tenderness that has sustained me throughout this project. Rebecca Solnit has been a friend and inspiration, as have Michael Schuster and Gail Goodman, who, as the others, are like family. Chip Lord has been an excellent companion as this project developed. We traveled through central Mexico as I pursued questions relevant to the book. His own work, his sensitive eye for form and spatial order, and his generous heart have offered incredible sustenance. I thank my daughter Sophia Zamudio-Haas for her adventurous spirit and love, and for our travel in Peru to view the work of colonial Andean painters from Cusco.

Writing *Saints and Citizens* has meant living for many years in the presence of the precarious and painful conditions of loss and devastation that pervaded Indigenous history during these years. For that reason, I am most grateful to the Indigenous writers, painters, storytellers, and historical actors whom I encountered in my research. Their visions moved beyond the colonial relations otherwise prevalent in the dominant archive of the era under study.

Introduction

Saints and Indigenous Citizens

A Chumash artisan at Mission Santa Inés painted the Archangel Raphael as a Chumash leader thereby attributing the powers of Raphael to the Chumash figure and Chumash authority to a Christian saint (See Figure 4 in chapter 3). Indigenous translators, writers, and painters in colonial and Mexican California left records like this one that invoked Indigenous leadership and native access to power. Collectively they created documents that expressed an array of political visions and demands.

The representation of this figure as a saint corresponds to at least one translation for the word *saint* in an Indigenous language of California. In Achachemem, spoken at Mission San Juan Capistrano, *nóonutum* ("saint") meant "any great men of the past in any line."[1] The church discouraged Indigenous painters from representing themselves or their histories and promoted a uniform iconography and consistent story of each saint. This painting of the Archangel Raphael is therefore unusual in that it defied church policies governing the religious image. It was painted at Mission Santa Inés sometime during the 1820s, perhaps after the reconciliation of the church and Mexican state with Chumash people at the end of the 1824 Chumash War. In representing this leader, the painting alludes to the strong system of Indigenous leadership that existed within the missions settled in Chumash territory.

The name and image of the Archangel Raphael and countless other saints' names and images formed an integral part of the imposition of Catholicism in the Indigenous territories along the coast from the Presidio (fort and military district) of San Diego to the Presidio of San Francisco. Their stories conveyed Catholic beliefs and history yet also became significant within Indigenous systems of

1

thought. The Chumash painting of the Archangel Raphael constitutes part of a wider colonial culture replete with Indigenous interpretations of things Spanish.

Within the eighty years, beginning in 1769, that are considered in this book, Indigenous people along the coast had been renamed for saints at baptism. A person would receive a Christian name that would often be written alongside his or her Indigenous lineage or family name in the baptismal registers and mission census records.[2] During the colonial and Mexican eras, one might have seen written or heard the names Juan Tajonalx, Antonia Atapal, and Juan Bautista Tepilchai at Mission San Diego; at Mission San Luis Rey, the names of Agustín Jayoc and Francisca Antonia Tobac; and at Mission Carmel, those of Amadeo Yeucharon and Salomé Signien.[3] In this book's title, Saints refers to these colonial practices of renaming and to Indigenous interpretations of Spanish concepts that fostered the survival of native communities during an era marked by dramatic loss. The book examines Indigenous histories and colonial relations, which made another dramatic shift after 1821, when Indigenous people would be declared equal under Mexican law. Citizens refers to the regional history of Indigenous citizenship and political visions.

MANY VOICES

California is an Indigenous space that has always spoken with "many voices." Approaching its linguistic and tribal history through the longue durée offers a narrative strategy that can capture, for a brief moment, a sense of these societies as they developed through millennia of continuous residence, and through histories of migration that took place thousands of years prior to Spanish occupation.[4] The language map, rather than reflecting actual spoken language, represents historically connected language speakers who often developed distinctive languages and dialects.[5]

California had a comparatively dense population of about 300,000 people and an extremely diverse array of spoken languages and autonomous polities and ethnicities in 1769, when the Spanish arrived. According to Victor Golla, seventy-eight mutually unintelligible languages were spoken. The majority of the languages had only "tenuous relationships" to languages spoken elsewhere. As Golla emphasizes, California Indian languages, like the cultures they emerged from, reflected "unbroken sequences of local events" that extended back to some of the oldest human settlements in the Americas.[6]

For Chumash people, human settlement on Santa Rosa Island can be traced to 12,000 years ago. Linguistic and geographic patterns shifted over time, but continuous residential patterns of habitation on the islands, and on the western shores of the mainland, can be traced back as far as 8,500 years ago. Those who spoke Chumashian languages formed part of a linguistically and ethnically diverse

MAP 1. California Indian Languages. Most of these language territories had more than one spoken language and dialect within them and many autonomous tribes. The language families suggest ancient origins and migrations and further highlight the linguistic diversity of California. Drawn by Benjamin Pease. Source: Victor Golla (2011).

coastal region that spanned from the Chumash territory southward to Tipai territory and had large and sedentary populations from around 5,000 years ago. Villages existed in most of the available niches near the shores, interior valleys, and
coastal mountain ranges.[7] Chumashian speakers prevailed in their territories,
while migrants who were speakers from the Takic language family (a branch of
Uto-Aztecan) moved into southern California. On the western side of the Santa
Monica Mountains, for example, Chumash villages persisted in ancient residential
sites. On the eastern side, in contrast, societies emerged in which new linguistic
patterns, influenced by Uto-Aztecan forms, predominated.[8]

The Takic speakers began moving west from the Mojave Desert beginning
approximately 3,000 years ago.[9] The languages of the Tongva or Gabrielino, the
Fernandino, Juaneño, or Achachemem, and Luiseño peoples reflect a relationship
to the Takic linguistic family and Uto-Aztecan forms.[10] That migration a millenium
ago also produced the societies of Cupeño, Cahuilla, Serrano, Tataviam, and Kitanemuk peoples in California.

A similar pattern of ancient migration and continuous settlement occurred
among Yokuts. At the time that the heat of the Mojave Desert inspired migrations
outward, the expansion of Penutian speakers of the Miwokan language expanded
eastward from the northern part of San Francisco Bay into the Central Valley.
Migration into the Sacramento Valley forced the existing population into the
southern San Joaquin Valley.[11] Their language came to be known as Yokutsan.

Nearly one-third of the Indigenous population at the time of Spanish settlement lived in the Central Valley, which extended nearly 450 miles long north to
south and 250 miles east to west. It had a vast interior that developed into "a jigsaw
of dramatically contrasting environments."[12] The Sacramento and San Joaquin Rivers converged in the Delta region, where their waters entered San Francisco Bay.
Yokuts resided in the central and southern parts of the valley and traded goods
with groups along the coasts and the Sierra foothills to the east. Ancestors of the
Yokuts and other peoples in the valley began to elaborate the "technological, economic, ceremonial, and socio-political characteristics" that became associated
with the California culture area around 4,500 years ago.[13]

As the diversity of languages in California suggests, Indigenous societies
emerged out of an intricate pattern of divergent and multiple histories. In the
places studied in this book, a matrix of villages sustained specific languages and
dialects. People often took the names of their villages as their own in Indigenous
societies that identified their ancestral histories through their connections to the
land. Villages ranged in size but commonly had 250–350 people, although towns
with more than 1,000 inhabitants existed in Chumash territory along the coast.
Linguistic and tribal differentiation took place among village groups that held
political autonomy from each other. Affinities between politically autonomous villages varied and involved ties forged through marriage and clan relations, trade

and ritual networks, and shared resources and ceremonial life. Common cultural practices often developed among people with neighboring borders even when they spoke distinct languages or dialects.

REPRESENTING COLONIALISM

Colonization involved a process that ultimately brought hundreds of tribal lands under Spanish control and initiated the violent restructuring of autonomous Indian societies even beyond the territories settled. By 1821, the Spanish had established twenty-one missions, four forts, and three towns on Indigenous lands along the coast. Eighty-one thousand people would be baptized in the missions between 1769 and 1834. Of those, 60,000 had died by 1834. Yokuts and other peoples on the periphery of these colonized spaces kept the limits of Spanish and Mexican settlement at a comparatively narrow range along the coast.

Spanish settlement shifted the geopolitics of an area. It introduced disease, livestock, weeds, and coercive practices that eventually produced a weakening or collapse of Indigenous polities nearer to the missions and then at greater and greater distances away. Scholars have represented colonialism in California as a "time of little choice," when Spanish settlement produced conditions that ultimately created a movement of individuals, and then whole villages, into the missions.[14]

Building on the understanding of the crisis within Indigenous societies that settlement produced, this book examines the particular histories of Chumash and Luiseño territories and the relationship Yokuts people established with the missions. Spanish objectives remained similar in each case, but Indigenous histories differed. This view of colonialism's impact points attention to how native societies defended and defined themselves under new and often traumatic conditions. They survived, and they found ways to thrive.[15]

To have ones' name placed on the baptismal register initiated movement into a condition of *neófia*. To be a neophyte meant losing freedom of movement and personal and cultural sovereignty. A temporary condition, it lasted as long as one was considered to be in training or a novice to Christianity and Spanish culture. A condition of unfreedom, it involved being renamed and the new name inscribed on the baptismal and census roles; unable to leave the mission without permission; required to work and live under mission regulations; and subject to the severe discipline of the missionary and guards. Neophyte labor built the entire colonial economy of California, and yet it was not their own to claim, as the law considered the neophyte's very person bound to the mission. Baptized people generally relocated into the mission proper unless they were children, who remained with their families until the age of adulthood at nine, when required to move into mission dormitories until their marriage. Once on the mission registry, a person could only move about with a permission pass that specified the time the

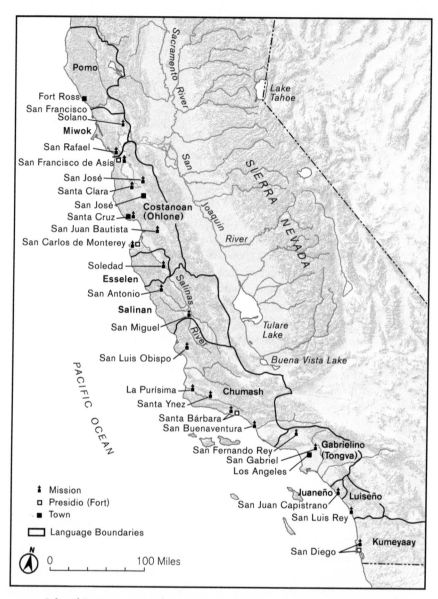

MAP 2. Colonial Institutions on Indigenous Lands. Sometime between 1769 and 1821 these colonial institutions were founded on the lands of specific Indigenous polities along the California coast. However, beyond those territories Indigenous polities remained autonomous and independent from Spanish and Mexican rule through 1848. Drawn by Benjamin Pease.

missionary granted the individual to visit relatives, cultivate foods, hunt, or to fish near their ancestral village. The lands of the Indigenous people on the baptismal roles would eventually be claimed by the missions as part of their extensive colonial domain. Indigenous geography would become obscured in the process.

Baptism marked conversion to a Catholicism often taught by Indigenous translators and interpreters and overseen by Indigenous godparents.[16] The missions became Indigenous colonial spaces as Indian people moved into them to join other members of their families and villages. Leaders and elders often assumed positions of elected authority.[17] Translators rendered Spanish belief and ideas into Indigenous languages.[18] Traditional elders taught dance and ritual and performed healing. At Santa Inés and San Luis Rey, for example, Indigenous elders translated Spanish catechism and prayer, and kin played the role of godparents, creating Indigenous reflections on and interpretations of the ideas encountered therein. Missions developed their own identities, languages, and practices based on their Indigenous populations.

This book argues that despite the physical dislocation and death the missions represented, they became sites of Indigenous authority, memory, identity, and historical narration. Becoming Indian in California involved being renamed and reclassified as *indio* and *neófito* and receiving the status of a minor under the law, confined to a mission except when given a pass. But within the missions, native translators, artisans, traditional, and new leaders used Indigenous forms of authority, knowledge, and power to seek redress and to sustain the community.

Painting formed part of the politics of conquest, as Serge Gruzinski has emphasized; the Spanish conveyed colonial ideas and relationships through their relationship to images.[19] The missionaries brought powerful stories about the past and present through their paintings and statues. Indigenous painters brought their own visual systems, iconography, and great figures into their interpretations of this visual order and created narratives of things Spanish and Catholic influenced by their systems of knowing. Despite the control the church and state attempted to impose on the production and use of images, Indigenous painters and artisans created work suggestive of the nature of Indigenous interpretation and belief. The missionaries' visual iconography and lexicon of printed and painted images expanded, rather than foreclosed, Indigenous visual practices.

This book considers Indigenous translation, writing, painting, oral history, and dance crucial elements of Indigenous means of taking control over how concepts entered Indigenous cultures. The colonial practice of misrepresenting and dismissing Indigenous forms of authority and knowledge gives Indigenous sources a particularly poignant significance. Scholars using them have created new ways of understanding Mesoamerica and the Andes.[20] In documents they created, native communities represented themselves as polities with their own histories and important people, undiminished, in many accounts, by the Spanish presence.[21] In painting and writing, Indigenous scholars left histories that depicted their lineages and geography and important people and events.[22] They produced documents that spoke to their own concerns.[23] The scholarship, as this book, gives prominence to Indigenous translators, interpreters, and cultural figures who moved between worlds in transition and came up with ideas that fostered their own and others' survival.[24]

Historians of California have developed a significant body of work in mission studies.[25] As a result of this work, the social history of the missions, and the conditions of life faced by their populations, has been thoroughly examined through the Spanish sources. In a recent study focused on Spanish–Indian relations, Steven Hackel has produced one of the most complete of such works. He elaborates and quantifies important dimensions of mission history and analyzes many aspects of Indigenous life, such as work, violence, punishment, marriage, and life expectancy.[26]

James Sandos has considered the relevance of song and music to Indigenous thought and understandings of Catholicism. He placed historical conditions like syphilis that became endemic at the missions at the foreground.[27] Sarah Ginn traces the emergence of specific practices that came to distinguish each mission, and emphasizes the Indigenous logic used to make new alliances and forge new communities..[28] Kent Lightfoot offers a sense of the comparative impact of colonial systems on Indigenous populations, and writes about Kashaya Pomo history at the Russian colony of Fort Ross in northern California.

More than other studies of colonial California, the one presented in this book situates this history in relationship to Mexico and the Indigenous histories of colonialism and empire in the Americas. The Spanish state and church viewed the conditions of unfreedom experienced by the neophyte as temporary. Relocation to the mission fell under the policy of *reducción*, a movement of people into the missions as part of the process of forming Christian communities. Within ten years or so, they were expected to repopulate the region in Indigenous pueblos, towns run by elected Indigenous authorities in charge of their legal and administrative life.

By the middle of the seventeenth century, as Indigenous populations began to recover from catastrophic population losses, the Crown had passed an extensive and growing body of ordinances to defend Indigenous communal and individual property, both ancestral property and improved property, like the missions.[29] Patricia Seed has emphasized that the connection between Indigenous land rights and tributary status in Mexico rested on Islamic-Iberian traditions that enabled conquered peoples to retain landownership and to persist in their communities but required them to fulfill tributary obligations. Rather than economic payment alone, "tribute symbolized vassalage ... subjugation and military defeat. Being Indian under Spanish domination in the New World meant continually being reminded of one's present conquered status by the payment of tribute."[30]

The missionaries classified California as a recent conquest, and rather than have Indigenous governance in tributary pueblos, they emphasized the idea that the population worked in common and formed a new community. The native people who affiliated to the missions of California could have, in theory, reclaimed their lands and also taken possession of the missions themselves. But California became part of a new republic that would claim Indigenous and church lands for the Mexican state.

INDIGENOUS EQUALITY AND CITIZENSHIP ON THE BORDERLANDS

One of the first things the Mexican state did upon announcing its independence from Spain was to abolish the inherited and legal distinctions among its population and do away with other colonial restrictions. The state would legislate the equality of all Mexicans, including Indians. Mexico declared the pending equality in its Plan de Iguala, published on February 24, 1821, months before Spain granted Mexico independence on September 16, 1821. The term *indio* became illegal for a period, and between 1821 and 1824, local ordinances across the new nation gave meaning to Indigenous equality. The Mexican constitution of 1824 granted citizenship to Indians and freed the majority of the Indigenous population from all forms of coercive labor, tribute, and service. The process of Indigenous politics in California formed part of the texture of Mexican history, defined as it was by "internally differentiated regional and national spaces" according to Claudio Lomnitz-Adler.[31]

Emancipation from the condition of *neófia* constituted the first step toward citizenship for Indigenous people in the California missions, and the process began in 1826. The government used the term *emancipation* in its official decrees, but the nature of unfreedom under *neófia,* and the smaller scale of emancipation, distinguishes this emancipation from emancipation from slavery. The important point is, however, that the process in California involved the problems raised in postemancipation societies elsewhere and produced similar political resolutions to questions concerning the organization of labor, land, and citizenship.

Native politics played an important role in the process, but consistent with the constraints commonly imposed by the state on the conditions of emancipated people elsewhere, the laws in California only offered "degrees of freedom."[32] The "problems of freedom" in California appeared in the earliest emancipations when government officials only talked of "emancipation" and offered licenses that the emancipated individual and their family members would each carry that acknowledged their right to leave the missions.[33] Those problems continued to assert themselves as the state established coercive conditions over the labor of former neophytes and restricted their rights to land, compensation for their labor, and the rights of citizenship.

Indigenous histories during these years were influenced by the way the Mexican Constitution created what Manuel Muñoz and María López identified as "the federalization of Indigenous spaces."[34] The tentative rights associated with Indigenous citizenship developed unevenly during these years in California. The outcome was consistent with what Florencia Mallon identifies as the Mexican republic's promise of equality. A promise that left entire groups of people "barred from access to citizenship and liberty" according to exclusionary criteria.[35]

At the local level throughout the republic, laws and custom often allowed for the persistence of colonial restrictions that limited the individual and collective rights of Indians. Though the Mexican elite did not reject the idea of Indigenous citizenship, "they intensely debated" the political rights of native people.[36] A group of Indigenous landowners and Indian pueblos emerged during the 1830s and 1840s in California, but they existed within a society in which Indigenous conditions of equality and rights remained uneven.

With Mexican independence in 1821, Indigenous politics took many forms, including the Chumash War of 1824. Chumash histories explained the war through Indigenous forms of leadership and thought and in relationship to the many types of cruelty and violence pervasive at the missions. More common than revolt, Indigenous leaders during this era sought a return to Indigenous ancestral territories, and to gain possession of the missions and the ability to move about, exercising their legal rights. A group of Indigenous citizens and landowners emerged in California during the Mexican era. But outside of native communities, much of this Indigenous colonial and Mexican history became obscured.

INDIGENOUS HISTORIES

The history of colonialism in California developed in the presence of another one: the Indigenous borderlands of Mexico's north where the Companche, Apache, and other peoples held dominion. Julianna Barr eloquently depicts a borderlands in which Spaniards had to use the geography and customs of Indigenous societies, and be alert to their desires, because they controlled the vast Texas borderlands through the early nineteenth century. Pekka Hämäläinen elaborates upon the emergence of the powerful Comanche nomadic empire that dominated the western plains and surrounding areas for hundreds of years, into the nineteenth century.[37] James Brooks vividly defines the regional economy and society that emanated from the colonial orbit of New Mexico and the multifaceted raiding and trading economy that involved a vigorous system of exchange in human captives.[38] Ned Blackhawk defines Ute dominance in the Great Basin and emphatically laments the web of violent colonial relations that enveloped the region, and the domination exerted by powerful Indigenous groups against non-equestrian tribes.[39]

That scholarship enables this book to situate California's history on the Indigenous borderlands of Mexico's north. It places California as a colonial orbit whose influence on autonomous tribes grew steadily. Yet it also points to the importance of those independent tribes who remained the majority population in California during these years. They never lived far beyond the boundaries of California's colonial sites. They remained autonomous and yet increasingly became intertwined with colonial and Mexican society.

The scholarship on Indigeneity articulates a set of concerns that inform this book. It has produced a clear insistence on the crucial role that Indigenous sources and categories of analysis play in the writing of history. This is in keeping with the recognition, in much contemporary work, of the validity of Indigenous knowledge and testimony as a basis for understanding California's colonial past.[40] That knowledge is crucial to make Indigenous people fully historical subjects, and is found, as Linda T. Smith emphasizes, in Indigenous stories, languages, and epistemologies.[41] Incorporating that material fosters "balanced narratives" that embrace a range of human truths that Devon Mihesuah identifies as one of the objectives of Indigenous studies.[42]

Those truths, Amy Lonetree emphasizes, must acknowledge histories of colonialism and its aftermath.[43] Framing Indigenous histories through native concerns allows historians to place people in "unexpected places" or outside the normative structures influenced by colonial and nationalist thought.[44] It allows historians to celebrate the knowledge and ingenuity involved in Indigenous peoples' ability to move between worlds in transition.

Hayden White's work on historical narration has been particularly influential in my writing of this colonial Indigenous history. White speaks to certain limitations in Western approaches to history that this book has navigated. White argues that insofar as written history is predicated on the idea that content alone has "truth value"; it limits access to a wealth of ways to understand the past. Instead, he points attention to the content of the form in "knowledge production." Limiting the notion of truth to narrow, legitimate truths excludes the "many kinds of narratives that every culture disposes of" to encode and transmit messages.[45] Most important, these messages point to particular kinds of truths that would otherwise remain obscure. He points to a method that gives importance to the role of imagination and culture "in the production of a specifically human truth."[46]

The first three chapters of this book elaborate on Indigenous colonial history in California that began in 1769. Chapter 1 traces the colonization of Chumash and Luiseño territories and the relationships that developed between the missions and Yokuts people. The Spanish imposed similar colonial institutions and structures, but Indigenous histories involved distinct encounters with these colonial impositions. The chapter argues that the missions were sites of displacement and grief, but also of Indigenous community, memory, and historical narration. Chapter 2 expands on those points. It examines what it meant to become Indian in colonial California, a highly Indigenous and Afro-mestizo world of soldiers and settlers. It traces the role of labor, particularly weaving, and the practice of "redressing" in defining colonial conditions. The chapter identifies native narration, including dance, as a means of community resilience and access to power.

Chapter 3 pursues this concern and focuses on native visual narration and the politics of the image in colonial California. The chapter examines the extraordinarily rich visual world the Franciscans sought to create and the colonial politics of the image that imposed restrictions on the representation of saints and other visual narratives. The chapter uses a methodology from Indigenous studies that encourages comparison between Indigenous groups around relevant experiences. It expands the field of comparison that previously only juxtaposed Indigenous and European painting. In this case, the comparison focuses on the process of visual interpretation and representation by a school of Andean painters in Peru and by Indigenous painters and artisans in California. The comparison illustrates the ways Indigenous iconography and visual practices are transformed when brought into colonial painting and sculpture and suggests how Indigenous artisans created meaning and influenced colonial narratives.

Chapters 4 through 6 elaborate on Indigenous politics in the Mexican era that began in 1821 and, in California and elsewhere in Mexico's north, ended in 1848. Chapter 4 concerns the dramatic history of the Chumash War of 1824 and reflects on the significance of the various histories that represent it. Chapter 5 discusses Indigenous emancipation from the missions and the native political visions that informed Indigenous politics concerning freedom, community, and property. The dramatic history of emancipation and the mission's secularization changed Indigenous peoples' circumstances in California. Their claims to their territories and mission sites reaffirmed the role of Indigenous memory, authority, and community during these years.

Chapter 6 focuses on the role of Indigenous citizens in Mexican California and places the unstable and changing conditions of Indigenous equality in the context of the Indigenous borderlands of northern Mexico. These borderlands increasingly linked the colonial orbits of Mexico's north. As Indigenous Californians petitioned for and received land, moved about, and otherwise created communities during this era, they showed the ability to negotiate their lives. They persisted in using an ingenuity, and an ability to move among cultures, languages, and worlds in transition, that long characterized Indigenous history within this region.

The Indigenous linguistic world that developed during the Spanish and Mexican periods changed again in the late nineteenth century. The representation of Chumash, Luiseño, and Yokuts languages in the colonial archive provides insight into an era when Indigenous languages changed and flourished alongside vernacular and formal Spanish. The traces of that world of multiple languages, and the subsequent integration of Spanish words into English, constitute important elements of this history and its legacies.

1

Colonial Settlements on
Indigenous Land

This chapter examines the processes of colonization in Chumash and Luiseño territories and identifies the relationships that Yokuts villages established with particular missions, even as they remained independent of colonial control. Not withstanding the specific history of each Indigenous territory, a colonial geography emerged that encompassed many independent tribes. Referring to the many who fled the missions, and to the independent native societies that stole and rode the horses, the missionaries spoke of *cimarrones* and an *Apachería*. These words identify colonial geographies that associated California with the Antilles and other areas of northern Mexico, respectively.

The missions formed part of a long-established colonial order. At the same time, they constituted very specific places. Sites where Indigenous people built communities in which deep ancestral ties and shared cultural, geographical, and political understandings still gave relevance to their lives.

The most recent explanation for how colonization developed in California rests on the idea that colonial settlement initiated changes that ultimately affected all aspects of native society and eventually propelled people into the missions nearest their land. That pattern is important to consider because it offers a general idea of the processes behind the fairly rapid settlement of California's coast. In the 1770s alone, the Spanish founded three presidios (forts), eight missions, and one pueblo (town). They placed the presidios at San Diego in 1769, Monterey in 1770, and San Francisco in 1776. Spanish soldiers protected the missionaries who founded eight missions, including the Missions of San Diego in 1769, San Carlos Borromeo and San Antonio in 1770, San Gabriel in 1771, San Luis Obispo in 1772, San Juan Capistrano in 1775 and again in 1776, and Mission Dolores in 1776. In 1777, the Spanish also established the first pueblo of California in San José. Nearby, they founded Mission Santa Clara that same year.

The Spanish military carefully strategized the site and pace of settlement according to their understanding of Indigenous populations and their appraisal of the potential for armed resistance. They selected sites with a viable water supply and abundant land for fields, orchards, and pasturage. Sometimes they negotiated with the leaders of the territories on which they settled; at other times, they simply selected the site and built a fortified mission.

For California Indians, the occupation of a single tribal territory by a mission, fort, or town undermined the political order that divided the land into specific areas for the cultivation of seeds, bulbs, nut groves, and other plant life. It disrupted economies governed by Indigenous thought, environmental practices, and seasonal change. Seeds, in particular, formed crucial daily sustenance because they could be ground into flour and stored for later use. This required the cultivation of fields through burning, selective weeding, and other practices. The ordering of the landscape sustained economic life and the power and privileges of elites who governed each territory. Indigenous political life rested on this production of wealth through acknowledged possession of land, oak groves, hunting sites, and other resource areas. Wealth in goods to gift and exchange fostered ceremonial activities and trade between tribes.

The Spanish economy undermined this political ordering of native society.[1] When the missions and presidios took possession of even a small portion of an Indigenous territory for buildings, and to create fields and orchards, foreign seeds and weeds easily invaded the habitats and compromised sections of the coastal valleys and western mountain ranges. The livestock they brought grew rapidly into immense herds that threatened to destroy seed fields, streambeds, and local trees.[2] These changes began nearest the mission first, but eventually they consumed village territories at greater and greater distances away. New diseases became endemic and defied traditional means of healing, thus producing tremendous losses in each family and village community.

Tribes divided over what to do: some people joined the missions, others refused to do so for one or more generations, and some found refuge in territories where they had connections through family relations.[3] Children, widowed persons, couples, and families from the areas nearest the missions entered first due to their greater vulnerability. Converts built the aqueducts and irrigation canals that brought water to the missions, fields, and orchards. They helped tend the livestock that found pasturage on the important seed fields that had produced so much of the native diet. The sheep and cattle gnawed at native trees like the oak and threatened the areas where they roamed. To expand and enhance their pasturage, the missionaries prohibited the burning of seed fields, eroding the management of traditional Indigenous crops. Soldiers severely punished Indigenous people caught stealing or eating livestock.

Native exchange and ritual networks began to shift under this duress as particular goods became scarce in some areas or a ritual leader or member of a family key to a particular ceremony became ill or died. These changes sometimes began long before people in a given territory had even affiliated with a mission. They could be initiated through contact with expeditions, the missions, and villagers who returned home from the missions to visit for the duration of their pass.

As a majority of people from any single village joined a mission, the tribe effectively lost control over their discrete territory, although technically they retained those rights under the Laws of the Indies, the body of law that defined imperial policy in the Americas. This political defeat of coastal societies from San Diego northward to Sonoma occurred in fewer than sixty years after the Spanish arrived. It was a period when the densely inhabited and linguistically diverse ancient societies along California's coast experienced devastation.

Randall Millikin identifies this process of settlement as one that produced a "time of little choice." His history of the encounter rests on "Spanish actions" and "Tribal actions" through a succession of encounters, mutual accommodation, and the social transformation of tribal life in the San Francisco Bay Area. Steven Hackel identified a similar pattern of environmental destruction that brought Ohlone people into Mission San Carlos. Hackel characterized the process as a "dual revolution" led by the destruction of the environment and the biological devastation of Indigenous populations by European diseases. For Hackel these two factors structured the encounter in Monterey, California. Once inside the missions, the prevalence of illness brought the further decline of Indigenous populations.[4] John Johnson found a similar pattern among the Chumash people, whereby the villages nearest to the mission experienced the devastation first and those at greater distances followed suit.[5] Johnson's model is important for Chumash history.

CHUMASH TERRITORY

In 1781 an expedition of settlers and soldiers arrived in California after marching north through the Yuma passing, prepared to found Los Angeles in Tongva territory, and to settle the presidio of Santa Barbara in Chumash territory. After they left the crossing in their movement northward, Quechan and Mojave warriors descended on the town of La Concepción and the remaining soldiers in the encampment of Rivera y Moncada. They killed 105 Spanish settlers and took 76 people, mainly women and children, into captivity. The captives and raided goods substantially enriched the Quechan nation "with slaves, horses, cattle, and firearms."[6] The war closed the overland route to California until after 1821. It meant, in effect, that comparatively few would settle after 1781.

The Spanish perceived Chumash territory to be too well guarded and populous to settle without military reinforcement, and waited for the Rivera y Moncada expedition before they founded the Presidio of Santa Bárbara in the most populous center, on the mainland off the Channel Islands. Over a decade earlier, in 1772, they had founded Mission San Luis Obispo in northern Chumash territory, but that remained quite distant from the center. With the arrival of the expedition, they began what the Spanish would view as the conquest of Chumash people.

About 15,000 Chumash lived on the mainland and on the Channel Islands off the coast by the time of Spanish settlement, and it seems the population had already experienced illness and loss after first contact began in 1769. Although densely inhabited as a region, the autonomous polities ranged in size from as few as fifty persons to more than five hundred, and sometimes more than a thousand persons.[7] They identified with, and usually called themselves by, the name of their autonomous territories and villages.

By 1782, the Spanish had reached an agreement with Yanonali, the most powerful leader in the vicinity of Santa Bárbara. He governed the town of Syuxtun, which held a prime position on the mainland coast to dominate the bead trade that linked the Channel Islands and inland Chumash communities. Syuxtun and Mikiw (Dos Pueblos) formed the two largest Chumash coastal towns, and both played important roles in the interregional trading system. By contracting Chumash workers, the military began to build the Presidio of Santa Bárbara in Yanonali's territory. According to the agreement, Yanonali would remain the autonomous leader of his town, and he and his people would not have to become Christians. They would work for the presidio in return for trade items.[8]

Governor Neve established strict guidelines, so that the missionaries would not turn the populations of this densely settled area against the presidio and planned missions. He prohibited soldiers from entering native towns except when offering protection to a missionary. Sergeants and corporals required a special order to go into the towns. Neve also hoped to implement a vision of settlement that avoided the *reducción* of the population into missions. His plan called for native people to remain in their own towns and villages after baptism. He wanted the missions that were being planned for the Chumash people to be religious sites. He wanted to avoid relocation and the building of farms, ranchos, and industries that other missions had developed. He anticipated that Chumash people would both continue to engage in their traditional economy and begin to work for the Spanish centered in and around the presidio.[9]

The agreement with Yanonali gave him access to new sources of wealth in trade goods. Similar agreements with other Chumash leaders began to affect the extensive exchange network that had fostered specialization in the pre-Columbian Chumash economy. Control of the bead trade had given rise to the chieftainship system centuries earlier. The political elite brokered these exchange relations among Chumash towns. They "fortified connections between politically autonomous territories and towns through feasts, ceremonies, and celebrations and the creation of federations during particular periods."[10] Gaining support of their leaders was crucial to Spanish colonization. At the same time, that elite confronted a new economy and set of circumstances that began to shift their regional power.

The ability to augment the wealth of leaders and villages remained key to Spanish policy. Chiefly wealth among the Chumash had involved the possession of beads and of the oceangoing canoes or *tomols*. The missions became part of the regional economy and technologies with their use of canoes and bead money. As late as the mid-nineteenth century one Chumash chief "supported elderly individuals who made bead money for him." The Mission of San Buenaventura negotiated with Gele, a chief of a Santa Rosa Island village of Qshiwqshiw, to purchase two *tomols* for the mission.[11] The mission used the canoes to trade with the islands and to fish and hunt sea mammals.

Beads produced on the islands and sent to the mainland remained the source of currency even into the mission era, but European beads also augmented the wealth of towns and individuals. They received them as gifts to forge alliances, and for their work at the presidio. During the first decade, the Presidio of Santa Bárbara placed orders with their supply ships for an ever-growing number of beads, with increasingly specific requests as to their size and color. They also ordered enormous amounts of needles and pita floss from the maguey plant, which provided new technologies for stringing beads.[12]

Trade goods such as beads, string, and needles entered the local economy during a period when the missionaries and soldiers founded the Missions of Santa Bárbara on December 4, 1786, and La Purísima on December 8, 1787. In contrast to the initial decision to settle the area but retain Indigenous village structures alongside modified mission sites and the military fort, the government again instituted *reducción* to physically remove the Chumash population from their ancestral sites.

It seemed especially difficult to reduce some of the coastal populations to Mission La Purisima, especially because many villages nearby "could still secure their subsistence eating fish," Governor Borica lamented in 1796.[13] He made a survey of Chumash settlements along the coast, named their leaders, and estimated the size of their populations. Emphasizing their strong identity with their towns, he noted that each group named itself after its place of origin.[14] These villagers had resisted being reduced to the mission because of the supply of fish, he argued. Yet he had no doubt about the eventuality. He identified which mission each village would ultimately be reduced to on his 1796 map. Two years later military commander Goycoachea reconfirmed people's identity with their towns and surrounding territory. He suggested that if they could "continue to live in their own towns," they would more easily become Christians."[15] But by 1798, villagers from other parts had begun to affiliate to Missions San Buenaventura, Santa Bárbara, and La Purísima. Their populations included 766, 796, and 915 persons, respectively. (See Appendix.)

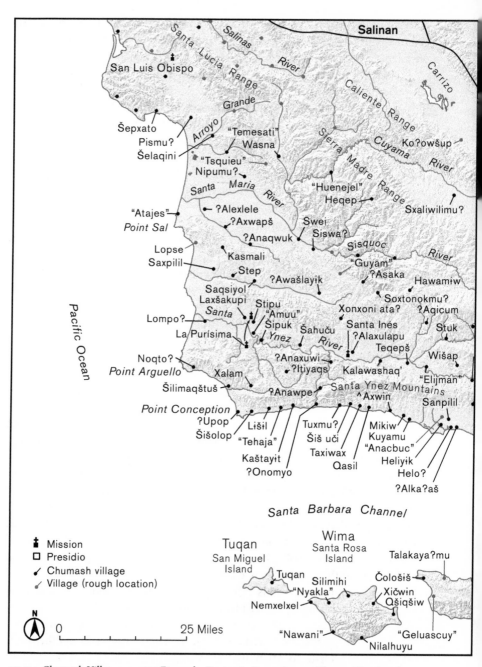

Salinan

San Luis Obispo

Santa Lucia Range
Salinas River
Carrizo
Caliente Range
Santa Madre Range
Cuyama River

Grande

Šepxato
Pismu?
Šelaqini

Arroyo

"Temesati"
Wasna

Ko?owšup

"Tsquieu"
Nipumu?

Santa Maria River

"Huenejel"
Heqep

Sxaliwilimu?

"Atajes"
Point Sal

?Alexlele
?Axwapš
?Anaqwuk

Swei
Siswa?

Lopse
Saxpilil

Kasmali
Step

Sisquoc River

"Guyam"
?Asaka

Hawamɨw

?Awašlayɨk

Saqsiyol
Laxšakupi
Santa

Stipu
"Amuu"
Šipuk

Soxtonokmu?
Xonxoni ata?   ?Aqicum

Lompo?
La Purísima

Ynez

Šahučɨ

Santa Inés
?Alaxulapu
Teqepš

Stuk

Santa Ynez River

Wišap

Noqto?
Point Arguello

?Anaxuwi
?Itiyaqs

Kalawashaq'

"Eliman"

Xalam

Šilimaqštuš

?Anawpe

Santa Ynez Mountains
^Axwin

Sanpilil

Point Conception
?Upop
Šišolop

Lišil
"Tehaja"

Tuxmu?
Šiš uči

Mikiw
Kuyamu
"Anacbuc"

Kaštayɨt
?Onomyo

Taxiwax

Qasil

Heliyik
Helo?
?Alka?aš

Pacific Ocean

Santa Barbara Channel

Mission
□ Presidio
✓ Chumash village
✓ Village (rough location)

Tuqan
San Miguel
Island

Wima
Santa Rosa
Island

Talakaya?mu

Tuqan

Silimihi
"Nyakla"
Nemxelxel

Čološiš
Xičwin
Qšiqšiw

N

0   25 Miles

"Nawani"

"Geluascuy"
Nilalhuyu

MAP 3. Chumash Villages, c. 1769. Drawn by Benjamin Pease. Source: Chester King (1975).

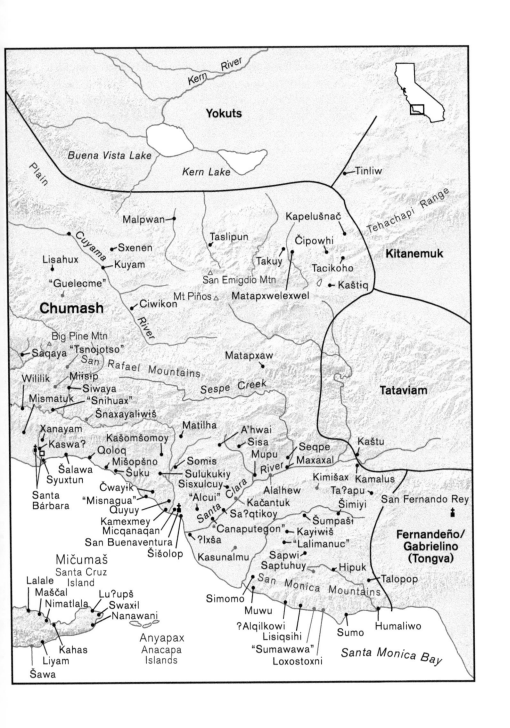

Kern River

Yokuts

Buena Vista Lake

Kern Lake

Plain

Tinliw

Tehachapi Range

Malpwan

Kapelušnač

Taslipun

Čipowhi

Kitanemuk

Cuyama

Sxenen

Takuy

Lisahux

Kuyam

Tacikoho

"Guelecme"

△ San Emigdio Mtn

⌂ Kaštiq

Matapxwelexwel

Ciwikon

Mt Piños △

Chumash

River

Big Pine Mtn

Matapxaw

△ "Tsnojotso"

Saqaya

San Rafael Mountains

Wililik

Miisip

Sespe Creek

Tataviam

Siwaya

Mismatuk

"Snihuax"

Šnaxayaliwiš

Matilha

Xanayam

A'hwai

Kaswa?

Kašomšomoy

Sisa

Seqpe

Kaštu

Qoloq

Mupu

Maxaxal

Mišopšno

Somis

River

Šalawa

Šuku

Sulukuiy

Kimišax

Kamalus

Syuxtun

Čwayik

Sisxulcuy

Alalhew

Ta?apu

Santa

"Misnagua"

"Alcui"

Kačantuk

Šimiyi

San Fernando Rey

Bárbara

Quyuy

Santa Clara

Sa?qtikoy

Kamexmey

Šumpaši

Micqanaqan

"Canaputegon"

Kayiwiš

Fernandeño/

San Buenaventura

?Ixša

"Lalimanuc"

Gabrielino

Šišolop

Kasunalmu

(Tongva)

Mičumaš

Sapwi

Santa Cruz

Saptuhuy

Hipuk

Lalale

Island

San Monica Mountains

Talopop

Mašcal

Lu?upš

Simomo

Nimatlala

Swaxil

Muwu

Humaliwo

Nanawani

?Alqilkowi

Lisiqsihi

Sumo

Kahas

Anyapax

"Sumawawa"

Liyam

Anacapa

Loxostoxni

Šawa

Islands

Santa Monica Bay

Borica's allusion to the importance of fish for coastal villages suggests the strains on the local economy and populations. By the late 1790s, it had become difficult to live in those towns. Since 1794, in the areas most heavily used by the Presidio and the Mission of Santa Barbara, which included territories well beyond the coast, the seeds that Chumash people processed as a staple element of their diet had become scarce. By 1800, the region did not produce any seeds.[16]

The absence of seeds had been especially pronounced because of a drought during the mid-1790s and the large number of livestock owned by the presidio and by the mission. By 1800, the presidio's ranches had more than 1,000 cattle, sheep, goats, cows, horses, and rams. The Mission of Santa Barbara similarly had 1,807 livestock at pasture by that date. Textile workers in the mission and presidio workshops transformed sheep's wool into blankets for *fresadas* or blanket-like cloaks. Native workers at the missions also raised 2,885 bushels of wheat, barley, corn, beans, and vegetables.

Many argue that migration into the missions enabled people to survive as traditional foods became more difficult to find and disease proliferated. In 1797, Yanonali received baptism with the stipulation that his people would remain in their village of Syuxtun after their conversions. But within a few years, his village had relocated to Mission Santa Barbara.[17] Indeed, during the decade after 1797, waves of Chumash people entered the missions. The Chumash missions would grow to have their largest populations in the first decade of the nineteenth century.

AUTONOMOUS REGIONS IN THE CHUMASH INTERIOR

The continuous movement of people back and forth between the missions and their villages of origin spread the influence of the mission well beyond the areas in the immediate vicinity. This created another way that the missions' diseases, goods, and ideas spread to autonomous territories. The missionaries at Santa Barbara reported in 1800 that one-fifth of their total population would commonly be away from the mission with a one-week or two-week pass, depending on how far away their territories remained. Every Sunday after mass at the door of the presidio, the missionaries or an Indian official read the names of the neophytes allowed to leave, putting their names in a book. No one got a pass during the wheat harvest, but at its conclusion, the missionaries gave all of those who worked in the harvest a two-week pass. If people did not return to the mission when their passes expired, other Indians were sent after them to bring them back. Runaways or delinquents were whipped, although the missionaries offered certain indulgences depending on the circumstances. The possibility of violent reprisal always existed.[18]

This *reducción* had affected the town of Soxtonokmu', a day's walk from Santa Barbara. By 1798, nearly a fifth of the village had already affiliated to either Mission La Purisima or Santa Barbara. Only 168 people remained in the village at that point.[19] Soxtonokmu' constituted one of the largest villages in the northern interior of Chumash territory, and it had extensive trade and marriage ties to coastal and island villages. Some people may have followed their relatives from other villages into the missions. Soxtonokmu' was located at the foot of the mountains, near where Mission La Purísima obtained pine wood. The town had integrated glass trade beads, metal objects, and mission pottery into its life ways during this extended period (1772–98) of contact and exchange with the missions. Earlier, in 1794, Indigenous Christians and non-Christians were invited to plan a war against Mission San Luis Obispo to the north, and four of the people from Soxtonokmu' had been incarcerated for "training to fight with soldiers."[20]

On a visit to the village in 1798, Sergeant Cota asked the leader if he and his people would become Christians. The chief remained noncommittal and said he would speak to the commander of the presidio.[21] This exploratory expedition to the interior took place on October 17 to 20, 1798, to further define the interior village territories with the intention of forging a new mission therein. Fray Tapis of Mission Santa Barbara, and a group of soldiers identified thirteen independent territories. He took a count of the houses. The largest towns of Soxtonokmu' and Kalawasak (*Calahuasa* in Spanish) had fifty and thirty houses, respectively. The majority of territories had villages with around twenty houses.[22] When the missionaries passed by Kalawasak they found a number of the inhabitants to be gone, some attending the Fiesta de Saspili and others in the mountains picking *yslay* (wild cherry). The political and economic life of these villages persisted together with the new material culture that villages like Soxtonokmu' engaged in. Just as the population of Soxtonokmu' already had relatives in the missions, individuals from all of the villages in this region had left to join coastal missions.

The missionaries located a spot for the mission near the town of Alaxulapu (also Lajulapu and Alajulapu). Alaxulapu had land to grow sufficient quantities of wheat and corn; trees for wood; excellent access to water; good stones for building; brown clay for tiles; and ample pastureland for livestock.[23] Though Fray Tápis decided where to place the mission in 1798, the Spanish did not begin to build it until 1804. In the intervening six years, the three coastal missions grew to their largest sizes.

By 1802, more than 60 percent of the coastal and interior Chumash had abandoned their traditional villages and lived in the missions.[24] In 1803 alone, more than 1,000 people joined one of the three coastal missions, abandoning still more villages. By 1803, Mission Santa Bárbara reached its largest size with 1,792 people. One year later, in 1804, La Purísima reached its population height of 1,520 people. The pattern identified previously—whereby the villages closest to the missions tended to be the first to be abandoned—could be found in Chumash territory.[25] When two missionaries and a few hundred native people returned to the site to build Santa Ines, many of those Christian Chumash had recently entered a mission in the wave of affiliations that took place in preceding three years.

MISSION SANTA INES

The founding of Mission Santa Inés on September 17, 1804, relied on 112 Chumash people born in villages in the vicinity of the mission site who had earlier affiliated to Santa Bárbara and 113 affiliated to Mission La Purísima. This large core of 225 people acted as interpreters, laborers, and godparents. They had placed the act of faith and the prayer for receiving the Viaticum, a ritual that often accompanied the Eucharist at death, in the Indian language of Santa Inés by its founding. The very formation of the mission at Santa Inés offers an example of how traditional leaders and others gave meaning to a translated Christianity, and offered, through many means, sustenance to their tribal and mission communities.

Fray Tapis initially called it "the Mission of Alaajulapu," acknowledging the native territory on which it settled. Three chiefs of the nearby villages of Kalawashaq', Soxtonokmu', and Hawamiw (Ahuama) attended. They "clothed themselves and were enlisted for catechetical instruction."[26] Five children from Hawamiw also received baptism, as did three from Kalawashaq' and four from three other villages. Raymundo Carrillo, from the Presidio of Santa Bárbara, served as their godparent.[27]

The first girl to receive the name of Ines, the patron saint of the mission, was baptized at the age of six. Born at Soxtonokmu', her father was one of the Chumash who came back to the region from Mission La Purísima to help establish the mission. Her mother had not yet affiliated with the missions. Francisca, wife of the retired Sergeant José María Ortega of Rancho del Refugio, one of the few ranches then granted to retired military personnel in the region, acted as the *madrina* or godmother of these first fifteen girls.[28] In the ensuing weeks and months, parents brought their children in from the surrounding villages. Baptized and renamed, they returned to the villages until their parents also affiliated. At the age of nine, considered adulthood, the missionaries removed them from their families to live in dormitories thereafter until their marriages.

The godparents assumed responsibility for the Catholic education and the spiritual and physical well-being of these new Christians, and almost immediately, the vast majority of godparents came from the Chumash population. These relationships created a strong bond in the new context that was often built on former relationships. They created a Christianity conveyed through Indigenous sponsors, commonly relatives of those baptized. The selection of Chumash godparents began within weeks of the founding. On September 24, 1804, a three-year-old girl would be baptized by her godmother Ana Victoria, who was married to Clemente, who had returned to the region from La Purísima.[29] For the next nine children baptized that day, Alhanasco, described as married to Catalina, assumed the position of godfather to the boys, and Catalina acted as the godmother of the girls.[30] On October 4, 1804, a recently born baby received the name Miguel at baptism. He was the son of Cesario Julucumaisset and Cristina Antonia; both had initially affiliated to Mission Santa Barbara. A man named María Momoguis, previously from Santa Bárbara, acted as their child's godparent.[31] (Note: The records rarely registered women's Chumash names.)

Similarly, on November 22, 1804, Alonso Huasucahuayol and Benita, who had returned to the region from Santa Bárbara, baptized their child María Gertrudis. The godmother was Ana, wife of Augustín Matiamahuilaut, both of whom had also returned to this region from Mission Santa Bárbara.[32] Of the thirty-two adults baptized in early to mid-December, Alonso, "married to Benita," served as godfather to the men, and Ana, "wife of Agustín," as godmother to the women. Both had relocated to Santa Inés from Mission Santa Bárbara.[33]

By December 16, 1804, adult relatives of Chumash people who had returned from Santa Bárbara and La Purísima were receiving Catholic instruction as wives, mothers, daughters, and fathers joined their relatives at the mission. Two relatives of Antonio de Padua, from Santa Barbara, joined the mission from the village of Kalawasak.[34] On December 28, 1804, the thirty-five-year-old captain of Silihuasiol of Soxtonokmu', father of Luisa, was baptized as Nicolás.

Within the first four months, 112 people from this region became baptized, and most of their godparents were from their villages, even family members, and recent affiliates themselves. During 1805 and 1806, fifty-two more people returned to live at Mission Santa Inés from Missions Santa Bárbara and La Purísima and reinforced this pattern. They too had come from the region. They returned at a time of mass baptism, when another 259 people joined from the surrounding territories.[35] An 1806 measles epidemic that spread throughout California cut into those numbers. Between 1806 and 1808, the number of people baptized at Santa Inés nearly equaled the number who died: the missionary baptized seventy-two and buried sixty-eight people.[36]

Within a few years of the mission's founding, people recently baptized at Santa Inés started acting as the godparents of new affiliates. They passed on a religion that their Indigenous godparents from the older missions had taught them. By 1810, the mission experienced its peak year of growth, when one hundred people affiliated from the surrounding towns and villages, and Santa Inés reached its largest size of 628 people (see Apendix).

After 1810, older people who had refused to join the mission started affiliating. They seem to have come only when they could no longer sustain themselves in villages that most of the young had left. Between 1810 and 1811 those baptized tended to be between forty and eighty years of age, and some came to the mission in their nineties. Sometimes their own children acted as their godparents, as in the case of a man from Kalawashaq' whose son had been baptized much earlier at

Mission Santa Bárbara.[37] Until around 1814, a handful of younger adults who had remained in their villages, or came in from more distant villages in the mountains to the east, continued to be baptized each year.

Until 1815, the mission population at Santa Inés came from the region around the mission and included older and newer Christians who sponsored their relatives and tribal members. Thereafter, the mission experienced an important migration from island communities that had survived more than thirty years, as the mainland Chumash with whom they had strong and steady economic relations became incorporated into the missions. The missionsaries began expeditions to the islands in 1815, and people, primarily from Wima or Santa Rose Island, began to affiliate to Mission Santa Inés.[38]The majority of the islanders migrated to Santa Inés in 1815 and 1816, which increased the mission population to its largest size of 768 people in 1816.[39] This diversifying of the origins of the mission population took place during a time marked by a tragically high number of deaths. Between 1816 and 1818, 154 persons died, including young children, new affiliates, and the longer resident adult population. Despite the influx of people, the population declined to 681 people by the end of 1818.[40]

Just two decades prior to this, the Spanish envisioned their founding of Santa Inés as part of the completion of a chain of coastal missions. It would "end the conquest of all the inhabitants from San Diego to San Francisco, between the mountains and the ocean."[41] During the 1790s the conquest had involved building a third town—the Villa de Branciforte, founded in 1791—and seven missions: Missions Soledad and Santa Cruz in 1791; San Miguel, San José, San Fernando, and San Juan Bautista in 1797; and, in 1798, Mission San Luis Rey. In 1804, Mission Santa Inés was the last mission in what is a tier of establishments influenced by Indigenous translators, interpreters, and godparents at their founding.

LUISEÑO TERRITORY

Without fear of being mistaken . . . none of the others have equaled these in grasping the purpose of our efforts.

—FRAY FERMÍN FRANCISCO DE LASUÉN, 1797

In 1798, as the Spanish began to explore for a site to establish Mission Santa Inés in Chumash territory, they also searched for a site to establish Mission San Luis Rey in Luiseño territory to the south. The Spanish had traveled through Luiseño territory for nearly a quarter of a century to reach all points north from the Presidio and the Mission of San Diego. Yet their records neither commented on the society they passed through nor the interactions and changes they witnessed due to the growth of colonial society to the north and south of Luiseño borders. The increase in disease in Luiseño territory, and the slow shift in power relations regionally, led some chiefs of Luiseño territories to welcome the establishment of a mission there by 1795, when the explorations for a mission site resumed, long after the first exploration in 1769.

During Governor Portolá's exploratory expedition in 1769, the population did not express a willingness to be settled. Instead, a group of about forty painted and heavily armed Luiseño warriors appeared to accompany the Spanish as they traveled uninvited through the territory. Juan Crespí, the missionary who recorded the journey and identified potential mission sites, described the valley as a "vastly large, handsome, all very green valley, seemingly all cultivated because it is so green everywhere."[42] He noted lush grasses and tall plants in a valley that measured about six miles from northeast to southwest, with a varying width from one-and-a-half to three miles. It had large, deep, spring-fed pools that watered the soil, but dry streambeds. The expedition camped on a level area, where two large villages, too distant to see from the camp, occupied each end of the plane.

Again, a group of about forty heavily armed and painted men from one of the villages approached the camp as they settled. The expedition went out to meet them as they approached. Their leader made a long speech to the expedition, which the translators claimed they could not understand. The translators presumably came from San Diego, and although many people in Luiseño villages might have understood their language, Luiseños' pronunciation and speech depended on deep traditions associated with their status and village.[43] Afterward the Spaniards and villagers sat down and placed their weapons on the ground. The governor brought out beads and asked the missionaries Juan Crespí and Francisco Gómez to distribute them. The Indigenous leader made Governor Portolá a present of four very good-sized nets used for hunting and fishing and made a "long speech to him inviting us, or so we understood, to visit their village."[44] Afterward, the fifty-two women and children who followed the men approached the gathering, and the women similarly accepted gifts of beads.

The next morning the people from the other village near their camp arrived and went through a similar ritual. Crespí named that site on the plane San Juan Capistrano. He identified it as a promising place for a large mission. The next day the expedition moved forward through a wide canyon that ran due north, finding again a cultivated environment where the population had burnt grasses "here and there" among the knolls and hills of sheer soil and dry grass.[45] Luiseño cultivation of these lands produced seed fields and bulbs and various greens and herbs that sustained their settled populations on semi-arid land. They entered another rich valley where again people from villages, painted for war, met them with diplomacy and gifting. They stayed near one of the largest Luiseño villages, called Topome, that had substantial territory and subsidiary villages. Crespí considered how this area would fit into his plan for a mission in Luiseño territory.

When the Spanish returned to survey the area in 1795, twenty-six years after the Portolá expedition, no armed opposition or curiosity greeted them. It is unclear whether the road on which they traveled remained cultivated and green after the heavy traffic that had passed through, but by their return in 1795, some individual Luiseños had already received baptism and affiliated to other missions, suggesting that dramatic change had begun. Father Juan Mariner wrote in 1795 that in the valley that the Portolá expedition had named San Juan Capistrano "the Indians say that, if a mission is established, they would become Christians." Before settling in that valley, Fray Mariner recommended the territory of Pala be explored, in one of the many interior valleys within Luiseño territory, with a river running through it, and about seven leagues from the Camino Real. The village population of Pala also "said the same, with much pleasure."[46]

The political discussions that took place within and between people in different Luiseño territories remain unknown, but the populations near the Camino Real again welcomed the Spanish in 1797, when Fray Fermín Francisco de Lasuén returned to find a site closer to the Camino Real than the territory of Pala. During his visit, a "numerous and amiable" population greeted them. He wrote of their "bravery and spirit of sacrifice to work and accommodate [the expedition] in the most courteous way." The population wanted the missionaries to establish a mission among them, "and we should attend them" he wrote to Governor Diego de Borica.[47] Having determined the valley along the coast sufficiently large to "reduce" the villages on the lower San Luis Rey into the mission, he placed a cross at the site "to be a signal" of their intent. His account suggests he had reached an accord with the population. But it also suggested he recognized a certain risk. He didn't bless the cross because he feared that it would be defiled.

Lasuén returned once more and, having baptized "some of their sick," he again emphasized their willingness and abilities. He wrote, "Without fear of being mistaken . . . none of the others have equaled these in grasping the purpose of our efforts." On this trip he examined the interior and coastal territories a final time, still in search of the best mission site. In the luscious valley near the Camino Real where the mission finally settled, the land could sustain only the population that then lived within the nearest coastal valleys. But when Lasuén could not find a place between the two missions of San Diego and San Juan Capistrano capable of supporting a *reducción* of 1,000, he settled on the site. Quechla (Pablo Tac's Luiseño spelling; the Spanish orthography is *Quechinga*) had been identified as a potential site by Juan Crespi in 1769, and the population's proximity to the road convinced him to proceed. In his estimation, the Luiseño population had an exceptional character. He wrote, "These pagans are such that, taking into account all the Indians who are subject to us, they are the ones who are outstanding for peaceful dispositions and for a friendly attitude towards our people. They are longing for a mission. . . ."[48] Lasuén's references suggest that colonial society had not yet touched

Luiseño society, but in fact, it had. In 1783, for example, the leader of the village of Guechi in the valley where the mission would settle sent his sons to Mission San Diego to ask the missionary to aid him by performing the Catholic ceremony of baptism.[49] By the late 1780s, individual Luiseños from coastal villages whose families may have been more severely affected by the Spanish presence had already begun to seek affiliation to the missions in San Diego, San Juan Capistrano, and San Gabriel. Most would return as the first translators and interpreters at the eventual founding of Mission San Luis Rey.

On a trip in 1797, Lasuén referred to baptizing "some of their sick," yet here, as in subsequent correspondence, he never followed up on the nature or type of illness that plagued the population. Moreover, a village near Pala had been attacked. Though Lasuén emphasized the extraordinary support that the valley population and those at Pala offered the mission, incidental notes in his correspondence suggest that some opposed it and that illness itself provoked the sense of need to affiliate to the mission. It formed one of the few recourses one would have. On that same trip in October 1797, Lasuén traveled through the interior territories from Temecula to Pala. They ate at a small, empty village of about eight houses in the territory of Pala (or Souquich). As they ate, someone from that village came along "painted in black." He told them that a few days previously, when the Spanish had camped around Temecula en route to Pala, "their enemies had carried out a raid and had killed a brother of his."[50] The raid could have concerned something else, but it wasn't uncommon for one village to attack another that favored Spanish settlement.

In February and March 1798, a few months before the mission's founding, the entire valley seems to have been taken ill by an epidemic of fever or flu that was spreading through the southern missions. Fray Lasuén recorded the illness only as incidental to the larger story concerning preparation for the mission. He had asked Fray Fuster at San Diego to go to the region and ask its inhabitants to build "four or five little huts . . . [and] do a little planting" at the spot around the cross. He told Fray Fuster to induce them to help "by distributing food to the pagans."[51]

The missionary contacted the leader of Quechla (or Quechinga) territory, the "chief of the district," to make labor arrangements. Too ill to meet with Fray Fuster, the leader sent a representative who reported that the population was "more or less incapacitated, and that for the moment nothing could be done." Fray Lasuén reported the incident after having been ill for twenty days, recovering because of "rather potent medicine."[52] He failed to express concern about the many Luiseños and other Indigenous people who attempted to recover without such medicine and perhaps without other remedies able to address the new illnesses.

The Spanish records are silent on any effects of the illness at San Luis Rey, but Luiseño writer Pablo Tac later recorded that "there were five thousand souls, with all the countries nearby; due to a sickness that came to California, two thousand souls died and three thousand remained."[53] Learning this by way of oral tradition, Tac remained the only one to suggest the devastation Luiseños suffered prior to the establishment of the mission. At San Diego, during its first twenty-five years, the mission baptized large numbers of orphans and widows due to the rise in death rates in the larger region. Epidemics and contagious diseases spread as people continued intervillage ritual, trade, and marriage.[54] They also spread through Luiseño territory because of the contact made on the Camino Real and through intervillage relations.

QUECHLA AND THE FOUNDING OF MISSION SAN LUIS REY

Lasuén founded the mission in the territory of Quechla, and the ceremony that accompanied settlement took place on June 12, 1798, at the place "known as Tacayame by the natives and as San Juan Capistrano by our first explorers" wrote Lasuén. The name *Tacayame* (or *Takayymay* in current orthography) meant, or came to mean, "volunteered" and "clearly heard."[55] Lasuén proclaimed the right of possession in the name of the king of Spain. Lasuén wrote about the logistics of the founding, the ceremony itself, and the first baptisms. He emphasized the importance of the "many neophytes who had come from San Juan Capistrano and San Diego Missions to do preliminary work here." Those Luiseños who had returned to their territory conducted much of the instruction that adults would receive before baptism. Lasuén also recorded the "great multitude of pagans" or Luiseño people who attended the mass. Some of them immediately made alliances through baptism with the missionaries by presenting twenty-five boys and twenty-nine girls. The next day Lasuén baptized these youth and accepted seven young men and twelve young women for instruction before their baptisms.[56]

Governor Borica attended the founding and referred to these young men and women as "seven adult Moors and twelve Moorish women."[57] The terms *Moros* and *Moras* that he used came from the reconquest of Spain and the many former Muslims and Jews who formed the ranks of new Christians in fifteenth- and sixteenth-century Spain. In this context, the term emphasized the way the reconquest of the Spanish peninsula had shaped the historical imaginary of those engaged in territorial and spiritual conquest in the Americas. The reconquest of Spain occurred in the centuries-old context of coexistence among Moors, Christians, and Jews.[58] In 1492, the Crown mandated the Moors and Jews of Spain convert to Christianity or leave Spain. Thereafter the new Christians faced public and clerical surveillance and the Inquisition Court if they showed signs of reversion to their original faith.

Borica brought this historical memory of difference, coexistence, and domination into play as he reflected on the founding of San Luis Rey. Lasuén brought a colonial imaginary. Certain as he was that Luiseños understood and agreed with his purpose. Luiseño scholar Pablo Tac brought the oral history he had heard about the founding to his rendition of the settlement and the catastrophe of so many deaths that preceded and ensued. Tac emphasized that Luiseño leaders allowed the Spanish to settle or it would not have been possible.[59] In this, his story concurs with Lasuén's rendition of village leadership willing to allow the Spanish to settle. But, unlike Lasuén and the missionaries, Tac emphasized that the land remained in the possession of discrete Luiseño villages and people, including the mission, built on Tac's paternal ancestral territory.

As many Indigenous writers from the Spanish Americas, Tac defined the Luiseño population according to the multiple designations that reflected their need to move between the realities established by Spanish dominion and the knowledge and group identities simultaneously alive among his people. Rather than the *Moros* and *Moras* prominent in Governor Borica's account, or the willing converts in Fray Lasuén's story, Tac defined the population as a Christian community of San Luiseños, as colonial subjects or *indios,* and through their own particular names and territorial designations such as Quechla, Pala, and Temecula. When he wrote of the founding of Mission San Luis Rey taking place on "our land," he meant quite literally the land of his family, kin, and village, as Tac's father's family came from Quechla.

A blind prayer-leader from San Juan Capistrano Mission who was a native of Luiseño territory worked with other translators to render Christian prayers and doctrine into Luiseño. He instructed the first adults who entered the mission "in their own language."[60] He and other instructors used the word *Chinigchinich* for the translation of "God," a reference to a personage who existed in the Indigenous belief system in the region for a long period of time. Fray Antonio Peyri, who had just arrived in California, welcomed the prayer-leader and those who joined him because they enabled the missionaries to begin their work immediately. They came from missions where native thought and cultural life was highly influenced by Chinigchinich belief and practice during the colonial era.[61] Their translations placed the Christianity Luiseños accepted in baptism into a framework that would sustain other precolonial practices and ideas.

Within a week after the founding of San Luis Rey, seventy-seven persons had been baptized and twenty-three others received instruction from the blind prayer leader. These twenty-three adults attended "punctually morning and evening from the very day of the founding." Lasuén testified that "larger numbers are not admitted to instruction for it is impossible to maintain them in the customary manner because of the grave and unavoidable inconveniences." They could not feed and clothe a larger group of new converts at that point, with just five soldiers, two missionaries, and thirty Luiseño translators and workers from Missions San Diego and San Juan Capistrano.[62]

As a result of the destructive aspects of contact and the need to gain a share of the new resources, people entered instruction for baptism in large numbers shortly after the mission's establishment, especially from areas most influenced by the decades of travel along the Camino Real. By August 1, 1798, three principal chiefs and their wives from neighboring villages were under instruction, together with twenty-nine others.[63] By early September 1798, Lasuén reported the mission "progressing in spiritual and temporal matters in extraordinary and admirable ways."[64]

REDUCCIÓN AND THE RELATIVE AUTONOMY OF LUISEÑO VILLAGES

One thousand, one hundred and fifty-eight people had been baptized at Mission San Luis Rey within the first eight years of its founding. The majority came from the towns in the immediate vicinity of the mission, such as Quechla, Pumusi, and others along the lower San Luis Rey River. Most of those baptized moved into the mission, but the mission could not adequately feed and sustain a larger population than the valley long had. At least half of the Luiseños who affiliated to the mission would never live within its confines. When Fray Lasuén made his decision to found the mission at that site, he planned to only "reduce" the people in that valley to the mission proper.[65]

The mission's ability to grow in size and wealth depended on extending its production beyond the coastal valleys and mesas immediately around it. To do so, missionaries secured agreements with local populations to establish fields, orchards, and grazing areas at Topome (or Santa Margarita), Uchme (or Las Flores), and at Pala, all of these identified as potentially good mission sites during early expeditions. To incorporate the rest of the coastal and interior populations, Lasuén adopted the model favored by Governor Neve (discussed earlier) because it affected the early settlement of the Chumash coast in Santa Barbara. The plan envisioned Indigenous populations living within their villages after baptism rather than in the colonial *reducción* of the mission, and it was put in place in Luiseño territory. The environmental conditions in San Diego, where many similarly lived beyond the mission after their baptisms, also favored this policy.[66]

Most of the people who initially planted and cultivated the mission crops did so in fields cultivated in Luiseño territories far from the mission. They worked in agriculture and tended the enormous herds of livestock, even while most would remain unaffiliated with the mission for decades. Some people in villages across Luiseño territory would never affiliate.

The existing structure of Luiseño society facilitated the agreements that enabled the mission to extend its economy beyond the valley. The precolonial Luiseño population had expanded over centuries within this region. As people forged new towns and claimed new spaces, they also developed a sense of ethnic territory and

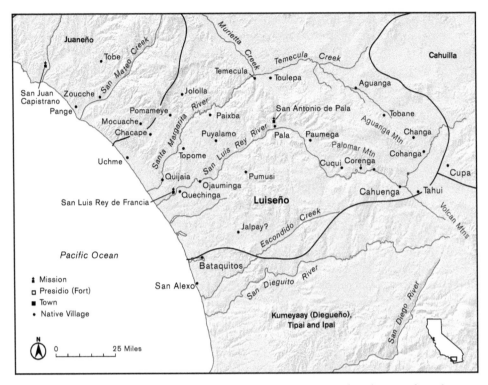

MAP 4. Luiseño Villages, c. 1769. Drawn by Benjamin Pease. Source: John Johnson and Dinah Crawford (1999).

a web of family and clan relations that connected different politically autonomous tribes or bands to each other. The relationships fostered by marriages that took place among people from Topome and Quechla, for example, probably made it easier for the mission to establish an agreement with village leaders to cultivate in the territory of Topome (Santa Margarita). Marriage ties also facilitated the use of resources of kin from different territories and reinforced the interconnections because some bands had agreements to share particular fishing, acorn gathering, and rock quarry sites.[67] The trails between discrete territories provided access to those areas, while a neutral route to the ocean, for example, ran from the interior along the San Luis Rey River channel, crossing through different territories.[68]

Well before most people had affiliated with the mission, the populations at Topome or Santa Margarita and neighboring Uchme (Las Flores) cultivated large fields of wheat, corn, beans, and barley for the mission. They developed a vineyard and grazed sheep and cattle, affecting the land of subsidiary villages within the political territory of Topome. An enormous increase in livestock took place in less than a decade. Rising from 162 to 4,025 head of cattle, 600 to 11,043 sheep, and 28 to 584 horses between 1798 and 1806, their grazing required the use of many ancient Luiseño territories. A total of 15,730 head of livestock grazed in different territories by 1806.[69] In less than a decade, the key Luiseño towns of Topome and Uchme, Pala and Temecula, had all become integrated into the mission economy with grazing areas and fields.

Since a majority of Luiseños from outside the area where the mission itself existed remained in their villages after baptism, affiliation to the mission could provide resources. During and after drought years, the number of baptisms increased at both San Luis Rey and San Diego as new affiliates sought to broaden their economic connections by gaining greater access to water and European goods.[70] This occurred during the early years of mission existence when the coastal populations in the large valley affiliated in great numbers until about 1806. It happened again in 1819, in the wake of an epidemic and a drought that might have affected native crops more adversely than mission crops.

Fray Peyri wrote that at Pala in 1819 "a large number of gentiles applied for baptism." Though some had been baptized, "many more could be admitted, if there were enough wool to weave into cloth," but many of the mission's sheep had perished.[71] Because of the drought, he had to ask those who applied to wait until enough wool could be produced to make the garments that would signify their status as Christians. After two years of extreme drought, and poor harvests in 1823, large affiliations took place, as they did in 1827, a year of a major epidemic, when the numbers of persons baptized again rose.[72]

The populations at Topome followed this pattern of affiliation during times of crisis as a way to optimize resources and find better possibilities for survival. In 1805 and 1806, in the face of a drought, a major wave of baptisms included ninety persons from Topome.[73] The next large wave of baptisms from Topome occurred five years later, in 1811, and another between 1818 and 1820.[74] Yet it took more than twenty years for most of the population of Topome to affiliate with the mission. Eventually 347 people did so. Topome became the single largest town and territorial population affiliated with Mission San Luis Rey, but as with many Luiseños, most of them remained in their home regions where non-Christians also resided. This pattern of Christians and non-Christians living in their Indigenous towns and villages was common in the Spanish Americas.[75]

More than one mission also served as the destination of Luiseños, especially in the interior, where villages included people affiliated to different missions. At Uchme, about four-and-a-half miles north of Topome, the mission established the rancho of Las Flores. But few of Uchme's population received baptism at San Luis Rey. Fifteen persons did so, while thirty-five affiliated with San Juan Capistrano. Near the borders claimed by each mission, villagers ran livestock and cultivated crops with relative autonomy from both missions. To conduct religious services for the Christians, San Luis Rey established a mission church at Uchme's center of Las

Flores, a center for the grazing region with granaries, corrals, and a house for the overseer. The native village of Las Pulgas (probably Chacape), about three miles to the north of Uchme, also became a sheep ranch of the mission.[76]

PALA AND THE INTERIOR

Through an alliance with the people at Pala, the mission began cultivation in the rich valleys to the east that were separated from the coast by the foothills of the Sierra Nevada Mountains' coastal range. Pala formed the colonial center in this interior, and the mission established a small chapel at Pala in 1806. During that year, the first wave of baptisms from interior villages began. Located seven leagues to the northeast of Mission San Luis Rey, Pala existed at the intersection of richly endowed and populous valleys. Streams fed the land around the village and created sufficient water for fields, vineyards, and orchards. In 1810, the mission built a granary for the wheat cultivated for the mission. It purchased vestments to perform more proper and elaborate masses and rituals in the chapel at Pala. The missionaries referred to it as an *estancia*, an area devoted to livestock grazing and farming, with an array of residential buildings, workshops, and storage areas.

Pala remained the mission's principal center in the interior and expanded to include a large apartment for the girls and unmarried women and another for the boys and unmarried men in 1818. This meant that some of the children baptized from surrounding villages would eventually live in the dormitories for unmarried youth at Pala at the age of nine. Although contacts remained close between the Mission San Luis Rey and Pala, missionaries did not reside at the *estancia* in Pala.[77] It remained governed mainly by the elders from the village of Pala and Christians who had authority to administer life and work related to the mission.

Some of Pala's population remained unaffiliated to the mission as late as 1825. There, as in surrounding towns, many remained unaffiliated long after their relatives affiliated, and as the mission's presence and influence grew around them. Ultimately, 134 persons from the Luiseño town of Pala affiliated to the mission through baptism, but only a generation after the first affiliation. In the territories surrounding Pala, most of those who affiliated to the mission also continued to live within their traditional villages together with non-Christians.

In the village of Paumega (Pauma), further up the lower San Luis Rey River, parents baptized a large number of their children in 1806, making an alliance with the mission and getting beads, cloth, and other gifts as a result. Yet people did not affiliate to the mission en masse; rather they did so over the course of twenty-five years after 1806. By 1831, 184 persons from Pauma had affiliated with the mission.[78] Cuqui, the second-largest town in Luiseño territory, had a vast political territory that included separate villages, including La Jolla and Yapicha. The first affiliations of Luiseños from Cuqui took place in 1797, and the last affiliation occurred in 1831, thirty-four years later. By that time, 270 people had affiliated to the mission.[79] The territory of Cuqui had an abundance of water, pasture, and large oak groves. Vast pine and redwood forests grew above the village on Palomar Mountain. Many clans composed Cuqui's large population, and marriages had long connected the district with large and small villages throughout Luiseño territory. Affiliation to the mission increased the material well-being of residents in Cuqui. There, as elsewhere in this interior, political autonomy persisted.

In the Luiseño village of Temecula, to the northeast, the mission had built rooms for an overseer in charge of livestock operations and who oversaw the livestock and cultivation of different kinds of beans and vegetables. The mission held its largest cattle ranch at Jaguara or Rancho San Jacinto to the far northeast, twelve leagues from the mission at the base of the Sierra Nevada range. Because most Luiseños remained in many of these villages after baptism, the interior population retained a larger degree of autonomy from the mission than did coastal villages in the immediate vicinity of the mission. Along the coast, many village populations had been reduced to live within the mission.

In the northern end of this long stretch of valleys and foothills that ran east to west along the base of the mountains, the boundaries of Missions San Juan Capistrano, San Gabriel, and San Luis Rey converged. To the southeast were the boundaries of Mission San Luis Rey and San Diego. Unlike in many areas, villagers in this interior tended to affiliate with more than one mission, creating a web of colonial connections throughout a region where autonomous villages thrived. To the southeast of Pala, in the Ipai village of Tahui, eleven people had affiliated with Mission San Luis Rey and many more with San Gabriel.[80]

At Cupa, 133 Cupeños affiliated with Missions San Juan Capistrano and San Luis Rey, while others affiliated with Missions San Gabriel and San Diego. From the large village of Aguanga to the north, most villagers affiliated with Mission San Luis Rey after 1810. In the Luiseño village of Pimixga, adjacent to Aguanga, in contrast, some villagers had affiliated to Mission San Juan Capistrano and another few to Mission San Gabriel before 1810. Thereafter most people from Pimixga affiliated to Mission San Luis Rey. In Temecula, some people affiliated to Mission San Juan Capistrano between 1803 and 1815, and others to Mission San Luis Rey from 1802 to 1823.[81] The interior villages changed as their populations became involved in these institutions, but overall these villages retained greater autonomy and often remained populated through the era.

EXPLORATION TO FOUND NEW MISSIONS, 1821

By 1821 the missionaries had devised a plan to establish a new mission by creating boundaries between Mission San Luis Rey and Pala. The new mission would enable the Spanish to reduce the many Luiseño, Ipai, and Cupeño people to live at

Mission Pala. The missionaries also hoped to expand into Serrano and Cahuilla territories farther east.

On September 10, 1821, Fray Mariano Payeras, head of the California missions, and Fray Sanchez set out from Mission San Diego with native interpreters and Mexican soldiers. They traveled northeast and founded a mission *estancia* in an Ipai village, which they named Santa Isabel. Payeras baptized villagers and others attending the ceremony from adjacent villages. At a place called Guadalupe, still in Ipai territory about seven-and-a-half miles from Santa Isabel, they raised a cross to mark it as the site of a prospective mission.

Upon entering Luiseño territory, they traveled through a countryside cultivated in places with mission crops that villagers grew for their own communities. After camping at Pala, Payeras said a mass the next morning during which he expressed the missionaries' intentions to found a new mission there. After mass, the Indian guides and translators who accompanied the expedition voiced multiple and strong objections to the establishment of a mission at Pala. Christian and non-Christian Indians attended the event and listened to the discussion. But Sanchez didn't record the content of their objections, implying they didn't need a record. He left silence on the subject, stating, "Having satisfied these [objections] and having baptized five children of neophytes, we had a pleasant rest of about two hours, watching the pagans and Christians enjoying themselves at dancing after their own fashion."[82]

Sanchez saw the dancing as something spontaneous and understood it as entertainment. Yet dance required preparation and had multiple purposes. It would have been organized in advance among the native communities in the region. Dance ritual generally involved the extension of invitations to other villages and gifting between the village holding the dances and those invited to dance. It also required the preparation of the proper regalia for each dance and notification to particular singers and dancers alike. Its performance on this occasion suggests the high degree of involvement in the discussion of and the serious concern over the prospective mission at Pala.

LABOR, WEALTH, AND LUISEÑO AUTONOMY

The Spanish never built a new mission at Pala because political objectives changed with Mexican Independence. Adults continued to affiliate with Mission San Luis Rey, especially from interior villages, during the 1820s and 1830s, and they generally remained within their villages. New affiliates and other villagers alike persisted with their traditional economic practices and contributed to a continuously expanding mission economy. Even within the mission community living at San Luis Rey, many of the economic practices and the taboos that protected the equitable distribution of goods and preservation of resources remained in place.

The Luiseño population continued to engage in systems of reciprocity and exchange that provided for the village and carried resources across many territories. For example, both the fisherman and the hunter refrained from eating what they caught. They gave it to their family and relatives engaged in systems of reciprocity. They traded fish from the sea for beads from the sierra. They traded most freely with relatives. Otherwise they engaged in an exact exchange, "so much for so much."[83] Luiseños also followed long-standing regulations governing birth and reproduction. Men abstained from meat and all fat for some days after the birth of their child, so the child would "not die." Women regulated the pace of their conception, often refraining from bearing a subsequent child until their youngest one could walk.[84]

The Indian village of Quechla at the mission consisted of "huts thatched with straw, mostly conical in shape, scattered or grouped on a large plot." One family occupied each hut. Initially, some of the houses were made of stone and "arranged regularly," but Luiseños considered the traditional huts, which they burned and rebuilt annually, cleaner and far more desirable.[85] The adjacent mission had an aqueduct that carried water to the mission proper and its buildings, small orchards and fields, textile and leather factories, hide and tallow workshops, residences for the guards, and dormitories for unmarried youth.

From Pablo Tac's description of daily life in the village, the household organized people's affective and daily life. Every household also belonged to a large tribal unit with its respective elders who held traditional knowledge and its linguistic particularities. Alcaldes, elected leaders who had attained the most fluent bilingual and bicultural status acted as mediators between the missionary and Indigenous community. Tac describes the mission village and Indian home with warm sentiments and foregrounds the authority of the father and the work of the mother to maintain the home. Each member of the household worked in traditional and new ways. Most family members worked at the mission, but the mother cooked to feed the family and the father hunted to fulfill his obligation to the mission.

Part of the well-being of the Luiseño population came from living within their villages where the authority and practices of traditional leaders prevailed. Healers persisted within and outside the missions, as did ritualistic practices such as dance and the use of *toloache.* The ingestion of which produced a trance state in which forms of knowledge and power could be derived, including the power to heal, to make rain, to produce better crops, and to rectify conditions. Astrologers remained active. They continued to hold feasts and dance at the time of the harvest of acorns and seeds. Despite the change to burial from cremation, Luiseños continued to follow many of their ritual practices around death.[86]

The large population of 2,603 Christian Luiseños in 1820 grew to 2,663 in 1827, and to 2,776 baptized Luiseños by 1830, but many other Luiseños had not been baptized. The large population created substantial wealth for the mission, and San Luis Rey had engaged in a vigorous trade in hides, tallow, and factory goods. By 1827 Mission San Luis Rey reached forty-five miles north to south, thirty-three miles east to west, and the size and wealth of the mission exceeded that of all other missions. The mission possessed 22,610 cattle, 27,412 sheep, 1,120 goats, 1,501 horses, and more than 500 pigs and mules. This livestock was scattered among the mission's four large ranchos established over a wide territory due to the scarcity of water and the ability to cultivate the many lush valleys. Livestock continued to increase through the 1830s, although agricultural production scaled back.

For decades, the Luiseño population had created the wealth that made San Luis Rey very important in the extensive trade with Spanish and then Mexican, American (north and south), and European ships. The government in California considered opening a port near the mission to facilitate this large degree of commerce. Luiseños also helped to support the military with their production of food from the mission fields and textile and shoe operations. In 1827, for example, Peyri sent a donation of "corn, beans, wheat, lard, soap, frazadas, serapes, and shoes" to the troops in San Diego.[87] At that point the missionary had developed elaborate trade relations with foreign ships and entertained parties that arrived on the Old Spanish Trail.

This productivity came, in large part, from the greater health and well-being of Christians living in their villages who could draw on their traditional and new economies. All three southern missions of San Juan Capistrano, San Luis Rey, and San Diego had lower death rates than the other California missions, but San Luis Rey's population had the lowest rate. When drought hit the harvest at other missions the rate of death tended to rise, but poor harvest did not affect San Luis Rey that way. Making use of diverse resources, Luiseños managed to retain more strategies for survival. Given the structure of affiliation, with more than half of the Christians living in their villages, Luiseños engaged in long-standing economic practices while also incorporating Spanish food production, growing grape vines, and peach, pear, apple, and fig trees. Individuals even held a few cattle and an occasional horse in their villages as family property. People who had affiliated to the mission by baptism, and some who had not, tended large mission flocks and incorporated other colonial products into their village life.

Where reducción had been partial, as at both San Diego and San Luis Rey, the populations reached their largest sizes in the Mexican era. Most other mission populations had reached their peaks and begun to decline by that period. The Chumash mission populations reached their height during the decade of the 1800s; they incorporated the island populations by 1816, but the overall size continued to decline. Missions San Juan Capistrano and San Gabriel reached their largest populations during the 1810s, with 1,361 affiliates at Mission San Juan Capistrano in 1812 and 1,701 neophytes at Mission San Gabriel in 1817. After these heights, their numbers slowly declined through the 1830s.[88]

At most missions, deaths became far more frequent than births during the 1820s, but not at Mission San Luis Rey, where the birth rate never declined. San Diego reached its largest size of 1,829 people in 1824. San Luis Rey's population continued to rise in the 1830s. During the entire mission period, San Luis Rey's baptismal and birth rate remained high in comparison to the population's rate of death. This contrasted sharply to other mission regions in California and was more in keeping with the populations who lived in autonomous villages connected to Mission San Diego.[89]

CHIEF TIISAC ON HORSEBACK: HORSES AND YOKUTS INDEPENDENCE

The troops only serve in the present system to inculcate respect, set good examples for the Indians, punish with prudence the excesses they commit, and prohibit their use or riding of horses.

—GOVERNOR FAGAS TO LASUÉN, 1787

In all the rancherías where I've been, I've encountered runaways.

—FRAY LUÍS ANTONIO MUÑÓS, 1816

Far north of Luiseño territory and east of Chumash territory, the Spanish established relationships with Yokuts people on whose lands they hoped to build missions. While the Spanish colonized Chumash and Luiseño lands, the Yokuts engaged in defending their Independence and increasing their power in relationship to the Spanish. Some Yokuts villages also established relationships with coastal missions who began to extensively recruit them during the decade of the 1810s. Yokuts territory became a region that gave refuge to people who fled the missions, with villages that had horses stolen from the missions. The area became one subject to increasing violence during these years.

In an interaction not uncommon among Yokuts and missionaries, in 1819 Chief Tiisac of Tachi, a large village in the San Joaquin Valley, arrived at Mission Soledad on horseback with a Christian Indian José María, three mounted assistants, and twelve men on foot. Though armed, they did not intend to fight. Rather, they rode horses and carried arms in order "to make themselves respectable" and for protection, as missionary Payeras later reported to the governor.[90] Chief Tiisac went to Mission Soledad in order to negotiate the status of fugitives from the mission who took refuge in his village and in other nearby villages. He sought to avoid Spanish aggression against his village, which the Spanish might attempt in order to retrieve those who had fled the mission. A year earlier, a group of forty-seven people escaped from Mission Soledad. About half the group came from Chief Tiisac's village of Tachi and another quarter from neighboring Eyotachi.[91] He and the missionary arrived at an agreement, the terms of which Payeras did not record.

Payeras sent the agreement and gifts to the brother of Chief Tiisac and asked Tiisac to wait at the mission for the answer. But Tiisac had sent for help, and when it arrived, he and his group escaped at night, undetected.[92]

That Tiisac and his party arrived on horseback in 1819 suggests the vast transformation that Yokuts territory had gone through in less than twenty years. In 1805 Fray José María de Zalvidea made a first major expedition to Yokuts country, setting out from Mission Santa Inés on July 21, 1805.[93] Within a decade, by 1817, the region of Telamni, opposite Mission San Miguel and about fifty leagues (or 150 miles) away, had been carefully explored and plans made to establish a mission and presidio there. The missionaries estimated about 4,000 people lived in the region.[94]

But during that decade nearly every village in Yokuts territory became a place for refuge from the missions and the villages now possessed horses. A new social geography had emerged in the valley. Particular missions made alliances with specific villages, and long-term relationships developed, especially with Missions San Miguel, Soledad, Santa Cruz, and San Juan Bautista. The contact involved the spread of epidemics and illness in Yokuts territory and the increasing presence of horses taken from the missions. It included the escalating violence Yokuts experienced from Spanish and Mexican expeditions to retrieve people and punish Yokuts for raiding and for abetting fugitives (or runaways from the missions).

Refugees from the missions brought knowledge of how to tame, care for, and ride horses that they had learned at the missions. Fugitives like the Christian Indian José María, who traveled with Tiisac's party, were often able to translate. Such translators helped devise a politics of negotiation and resistance from the understanding they had gained of the colonial world.

Chief Tiisac's desire to negotiate the fate of people from his village and to avoid conflict also speaks to the vulnerability of the many villages in Yokuts country. Violence and disease had increased within the region. The area had become subject to the recruitment of new converts for missions in the northern part of the central coast who sought to rebuild their populations due to the devastatingly high rate of death of the Esselin and Ohlone populations.

That Chief Tiisac and his party arrived on horseback with a Christian Indian also speaks to the limitations of colonial power in California. The region remained a land of independent tribes. Further, it illustrates the failure of one of the most important policies defining colonial relations. Since the early colonial era, the law strictly prohibited most Indians from riding horses while allowing exceptions for Indigenous leaders allied to the Spanish, native cowboys, and military auxiliaries who contributed to the economy and colonial governance. Governor Fagas reminded Missionary Francisco Lasuén of the prohibition, emphasizing that the soldiers "only exist in the present system to inculcate respect, set an example for the Indians, to punish with prudence the excesses they commit, and prohibit them from using or riding horses."[95]

Fagas accused Lasuén of allowing a notoriously excessive number of Indians on horseback at Mission San Luis Obispo, where he thought the number of riders exceeded the number of cowboys. Lasuén responded that Indians only rode horses and bore arms while in the service of the church or government and then in the smallest number necessary and according to all of the restrictions imposed by law.[96]

To the Spanish the horse was as important as soldiers for establishing their control over native societies and large spaces. For the Yokuts, the horse similarly offered a means to retain control of their region. Horses stolen from the missions became a new and important trade good. A regular trade in stolen horses had developed by the late 1820s with American and New Mexican traders who came to California on the Old Spanish Trail.[97] The Yokuts integrated horses into a tribal politics that increasingly demanded leaders able to negotiate with the Spanish authorities and missionaries. Horses also represented a new form of expressing status and a different way to move through space. The eating of highly nutritious horsemeat became routine for many Yokuts, and missionaries sometimes referred to the region as one inhabited by "horse eaters."

Access to horses increased as people entered the missions, and the missionaries disagreed over the effectiveness of the recruitment of Yokuts, whose villages generally took a three-day walk or longer to reach. In his most extensive correspondence on the subject, Payeras wrote, "The extremely fickle Tulareños are here today and gone tomorrow, not on foot like they come, but rather on horseback. . . . They kill the horses and eat them." He complained, "Any small altar boy grabs horses; kills cattle; goes about the mission chain terrorizing; steals tame and castrated herds, taking and selling them" in Yokuts territories.[98] To gain control over the region and its people, Payeras favored building a new chain of missions and presidios there. He feared that things would "get to the point of threatening the existence of this province and of transforming into a new Apachería a country that up to a short while ago was a center of tranquility."[99] The reference is to the geography of the Apachería, where native people with horses included Apaches, Utes, Navajo, and Comanches; they achieved substantial political control but were also caught in webs of violent colonial interactions.

YOKUTS VILLAGES AND COASTAL MISSIONS

Four missions in particular developed ties to Yokuts villages in the Central Valley from which they recruited populations for periods that sometimes expanded the course of decades. Substantial numbers of Yokuts affiliated to Missions Soledad, Santa Cruz, San Juan Bautista, and San Miguel. Many fewer Yokuts affiliated to the Chumash missions. Those who did came from the region around Buena Vista Lake.

Costanoan and Esselen affiliated to Mission Soledad between 1791 and 1807. But Yokuts people (designated as being from "El Tular," a reference to the entire region

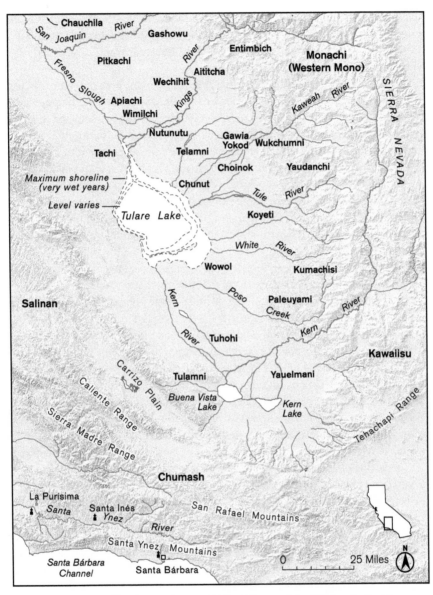

MAP 5. Tribal Lands of Southern and Central Valley Yokuts and the Missions La Purísima, Santa Inés, and Santa Bárbara. Many Yokuts tribes developed relations with the missions along the central coast, yet their territory remained independent. Drawn by Benjamin Pease. Source: Gayton (1948) and A.L. Kroeber (1963). Many more Yokuts tribes existed than appear on this map.

that included people from Chief Tiisac's village of Tachi and territories that surrounded it), began to enter the mission in 1806 and continued to do so until 1818.[100]
In the early 1820s, nearly one hundred people affiliated from Pitkachi and other
villages in south-central Yokuts territory.

Founded in 1791, Mission Santa Cruz attained it largest population in 1797 with
523 Indigenous people from territories surrounding the mission. The population
began to decline from 1797 until after 1810 when the missionaries turned to recruit
in two villages in the San Joaquin Valley: Tejey and Yeurata. In 1818 they drew in
another 150 people from different villages. Despite the recruitment of Yokuts, the
Santa Cruz Mission population declined to 358 people by 1817 because of death
and flight. When it began a concerted effort to rebuild its population once again,
the mission incorporated two hundred new affiliates from around ten Yokuts villages between 1817 and 1824. At that date, the Santa Cruz mission population had
risen to 519 people once again, and it had a multilingual and ethnically diverse
population.[101]

Mission San Juan Bautista, founded in 1797, reached a large population of 1,112
in 1805. It began a slow decline in its Ohlone population until it recruited 915
Yokuts between 1817 and 1822. The highly multiethnic population came from thirteen different villages.[102] Some wanted to join husbands and spouses who had affiliated to the mission, and some brought infants and children with them. By 1823,
Mission San Juan Bautista had a largely Yokuts population of 1,248 people.[103]

San Miguel, founded in 1798 in Salinan territory, had a large population of Sali-
nans by 1806, with 1,322 people. Thereafter it grew through recruitment of Yokuts
people.[104] The mission maintained enduring but fraught and violent relationships to
Yokuts villages, especially those of Wowol (Bubal) and Auyame.[105] Wowol figured
most prominently among them, and recruitment there sustained San Miguel's population between 1806 to 1817, when it reached its largest number of 1,025 people.[106]

The village of Wowol existed about seven leagues (or 21 miles) away from San
Miguel, and villagers from the territory established a relationship to San Miguel as
early as 1803 and through 1825, at which point more than a hundred people had
affiliated to the mission from Wowol, a territory with a population that ranged
from 250 to 300 people. Many more from Wowol joined the mission again between
1832 and 1838, when about 116 joined, as would other Yokuts during those years,
leaving villages that had recently been devastated by disease and warfare that
engulfed the territories in the valley at that time.

During these years, Wowol retained its independence but remained subject to
coercion and violence. In 1816 Mission San Miguel sent an expedition of soldiers
to recapture runaways, and they burnt down the village of Wowol when villagers
refused to give them up.[107] Yet people from Wowol continued to join their Christian relatives and compatriots at fiestas and other celebrations at San Miguel.[108] By
1826, Dolores Pico reported encountering "many Christians who were home on

vacation" in Wowol. Pico himself headed an expedition to bring fugitives back to the missions from Yokuts villages, and he checked the papers of everyone in the village of Wowol. His ability to do so emphasizes the repressive features of the relationship. Those from the mission presented him with their papers and passports issued at San Miguel to certify their right to take leave. Village leaders offered to supply Pico's party and help them "go and fight the Taches," who were another powerful Yokuts group.[109] Messengers from Mission San Miguel commonly moved back and forth between the mission and Yokuts villages to receive and convey messages about events in the colony and in Yokuts territory.

Smaller numbers of people also joined from Tulamni. Initially a handful of people joined the mission, but no one from the village did so subsequently. Mission San Miguel thrived, in part, through its connections to independent Yokuts tribes. Their populations continued to be integrated into Mission San Miguel through the early 1820s.[110]

Few Yokuts went to the Chumash missions, but a number of people from villages around Buena Vista Lake affiliated to Santa Inés, La Purísima, and San Luis Obispo. As happened at other missions, many of them subsequently fled back to their villages. Payeras wrote about one group of fugitives. The story suggests the connections forged with people who would later aid exiles from those missions during the 1824 war.

In 1817 a young man named Viquiet was baptized at Mission Santa Inés and given the name Sebastián. Missionary Urea transferred him to Mission La Purísima, where a few others from his region lived. His thirty-five-year-old father, Paulino Sualacia of Guasná, lived at Mission San Luis Obispo. Later that year, Viquiet fled La Purísima and returned to Yokuts territory with his father and four others. The village of Tulamni took them in. Three of the six fugitives were born in the village of Tulamni: a fifty-year-old woman named Marita and her two sons, twenty-five-year-old Felipe Amuchu, and thirteen-year-old Diego Chaiaui. They also took in Marita's fifty-five-year-old husband Sergioi Iaiachuit from the village of Esgeliulimu, Viquiet, and his father.

The missionaries thought Felipe Amuchu was the one fugitive among them who might resist capture. They sent Odórico, who was a friend of Felipe Amuchu, a former alcalde at La Purisima and considered a devout Christian, to bring them back. But upon Odórico's arrival, all six escaped by leaving the village via the lake. Unlike some of the native auxiliaries who traveled to capture fugitives, Odórico did not use force.[111]

The hostilities that arose in the next few months emphasize the bitter resistance developed among Yokuts leaders against the sexual violence of the soldiers. Soldiers had attempted to rape the daughter of a man named Ecsanonauit, who defended her with his brother-in-law and a group of armed Yokuts. Afterward, many Yokuts leaders refused to have relations with the Spanish for a period. Their leaders threw back the beads offered as gifts to negotiate the return of the fugitives. By May, Fray Payeras wrote that the Yokuts were "establishing in the interior a republic of Hell and a diabolical union." He insisted that, if the situation was not "promptly dealt with, a missionary soon will have nothing left to do in the Province."[112]

Tulamni had taken in fugitives from all the missions in the jurisdiction of the Santa Bárbara Presidio, and the villagers protected Felipe Amachu and the others. By May 1818, two expeditions had been sent out with Yokuts among them. Despite their promises that the missionaries would forgive rather than punish them, the fugitives refused to return. Moreover, one of the Indigenous envoys sent to retrieve Amuchu, "in whom I had placed the greatest trust," wrote Payeras, refused to return to the mission. He too took the "protection and safety" offered by the people at Tulamni.[113] In October 1818 Payeras again sent Odórico to capture the fugitives; this time accompanied by native archers and cowboys who had "26 bows and 500 arrows."[114] Of the group who escaped La Purísima, Felipe Amuchu never returned. Only the father of Paulino Sualacia eventually did so.[115]

Fray Muñoz complained about the often unrestrained violence against those who resisted the orders of the military to burn villages. He noted the conditions of general warfare as an aside, in warning of the "deceptive friendliness" of villagers who, he insisted, could not be trusted.[116] They had very little legal protection, but their environment offered the conditions that enabled them to resist, negotiate with, and raid from the Spanish.

Swampland and marshes existed near the most densely inhabited parts of the valley, areas where the cavalry could not enter. When a person risked being captured or a village faced invasion, they retreated into the swamp where horses could not go. Although such an escape might precipitate the burning of a village, the fish, plant growth, tule roots, and various freshwater shellfish such as clams existed in the lakes and swamps in abundance. This environment made it possible for Yokuts populations and fugitives to hide and subsist in places inaccessible to their pursuers for long periods of time.

INDIGENOUS TRADE: YOKUTS AND MOJAVE TRADERS AT THE MISSIONS

Historical trade routes ran from the coastal tribes through the Yokuts territories and beyond, extending into the mountains and the Colorado and Mojave Deserts. Yokuts acted as intermediaries linking the trans-Sierra and coastal regions.[117] Every Yokuts village had individuals and families of professional traders. They covered great distances during their trading expeditions. From their trade with Gabrieliño, Chumash, and other coastal tribes who lived in the missions, they procured horses, glass beads, and other Spanish and Mexican goods. They introduced these products into their trans-Sierra trade with Eastern Miwok, Monachi, Tubatulabal,

Kawaiisu, Mono Basin Paiute, Owens Valley Paiute, and Coso Shoshone people. East–west trails followed the primary waterways within valley and foothill regions and reached the coast via a few low passes that cut through the coastal range.[118]

Yokuts and other traders from tribes along the Colorado River followed their trade partners to the missions, where annual and seasonal exchange persisted. Indians within all the missions remained part of long established and newer trade networks. Yokuts traders went annually to San Fernando, San Gabriel, and Chumash missions. They often arrived in large numbers, perhaps for ceremonial occasions that included gifting and dispersing goods otherwise shared through trade. Their visits probably included dancing and speeches and may have deliberately coincided with traditional events and the Christian calendar. The Spanish seemed to know little about the trade. They recorded the presence of some of the traders and their own fears about their proximity. The mission often increased the guard while traders were present.

The missionaries expressed their strongest reservations against the Mojave tribes who traded at the missions in cloth, dyes, beads, blankets, and other things. In both 1807 and 1808 the missionaries at Mission San Fernando attempted to stop the trade. The governor asked the traders to withdraw from the mission and ordered the guards not to admit them and to jail those who persisted.[119] In March 1811, officials wrote of their fear that all the Indians from the mountains and the desert would join together and attack Mission San Gabriel.[120]

Rumors of Colorado River tribes offering to help stage a rebellion echoed again in 1813, with reports that Indians from the Río Colorado went to San Gabriel to invite the population to live among them after they rose up against the mission.[121] The problem persisted. In 1816 the governor decided to "prevent the Indians who came from the Colorado from bartering cloth and dyes." He threatened to punish them if they should return.[122]

The growing fear of the Colorado River tribes erupted into a major disaster against Mojave people at Mission San Buenaventura in 1819, when a group of Mojave traders came to the mission to trade "and have social relations with the neophytes of these missions," as one later stated. They also stopped for trade and socializing at Mission San Fernando. The sergeant at San Buenaventura had received orders not to allow the Mojave traders to stay at the mission but to direct them northward to the Presidio of Santa Bárbara. They were to be sent off with the warning that they were not to return. Instead, the guard at Mission San Buenaventura placed them in the jail. The Mojave traders got control of the guns and shot at the soldiers. Unfortunately, a few of the Mojave died in the battle. Others escaped. The soldiers captured four and put them on trial.[123]

At the trial these traders described themselves as Amajaba Indians, who bartered old blankets for beads and traded beads for the ochre dye they brought. Mojave people functioned more as a nation of interrelated tribes than most

California groups who lived in politically autonomous tribes. They traded widely and had a long history of sending traders to the California coast. From a nation divided into sixteen villages, each of the captured men had been born and lived in a different village headed by a chief, and they worked together trading. They estimated their territory lay fourteen days by horseback and fifteen to sixteen on foot.[124]

Trade relations became less frequent between the Mojave and the missions after this violent incident and deaths. Missionaries continued to express their fear of a united opposition against them that would include the Mojave, other autonomous tribes and groups, and Christian Indians from the coast. By 1821, the authorities at San Gabriel and San Fernando planned to "wall the missions" in order to "ward off the attacks of the savage Indians" and "prevent all trade and communication" between indigenous people in the missions and Yokuts and Mojave traders.[125]

CIMARRONES AND THE APACHERÍA:
A COLONIAL GEOGRAPHY BEYOND SETTLEMENT

A colonial geography emerged that encompassed Indigenous territories on which the Spanish settled and that extended far beyond the coast through the spread of a set of relationships, technologies, horses, illness, and goods that brought independent Indian societies into the colonial orbit. In part this happened because of the many Yokuts people who affiliated to the missions and then fled. Those who had escaped formed a visible and significant part of Yokuts society. By 1816, Fray Muñoz said that *cimarrones* inhabited every Yokuts village he visited.[126] In the 1819 encounter with Chief Tiisac and his party at Mission Soledad, discussed earlier, Fray Payeras referred to the party as "those gentiles and perverse *cimarrones*." Nonetheless, Fray Payeras extended an invitation to Chief Tiisac to have people from his village join the mission, trying to further deepen the connections between the village and Mission Soledad.[127]

These references to *cimarrones* and the *Apachería* brought together two distinct dimensions of Spanish colonial and native history and situated them within a long-established colonial geography. *Cimarrones* associated California with the Antilles, where the word *cimarrón* was already in use during the first third of the sixteenth century. Of Antillian Indigenous origin, it applied to Indians, blacks, and animals that took flight to the hills and mountains by 1535.[128] In Spanish, *cima* refers to the geography created by those who fled across "summits" or the peaks crossed and mountainous villages inhabited by the runaways. It carried into the French and English as *marrones* and maroon colonies, places throughout the Americas to where individuals and groups who had been enslaved escaped, and set up their own villages or integrated into native villages that would accept them.

The *Apachería* was connected to northern Mexico, where groups of Apaches, Comanches, Navajos, Utes, and other tribes vied for dominance in the system of raiding and trading in goods and human captives. The most powerful tribes adopted the horse and expanded and transformed their economies. The Quechan and Yuma tribes that closed the Yuma Pass to military and settlers bound for California in the 1781 war formed part of the Indigenous borderlands or *Apachería*.

A notable number of *cimarrones* lived within the southern part of the San Joaquin Valley and toward the Colorado and Mojave Deserts to the east of Mission San Diego. Established communities of Yokuts and other societies took in fugitives even before the missionaries began to recruit in the region. As early as 1799 a man named Agustín reportedly fled Mission San Antonio to Yokuts territory.[129] In 1806 Fray Estevan Tapís organized a large expedition that left from Mission San Diego intent on retrieving and bringing back the many *cimarrones* missing from that mission.[130]

Violent conflict sometimes erupted between the *cimarrones* and Indigenous people at the missions. In 1807, a group of Indigenous people, including *cimarrones,* killed between eleven and thirteen Christian Indians. Fray Abella reported that an alcalde probably had "a divided heart, with the better part probably inclined to sympathy" for the *cimarrones* rather than the mission population. As will be seen, that alcalde would not be alone. Another group of *cimarrones* stole thirty-one horses from a native *vaquero* (cowboy) and had among them native men who had escaped prison.[131] Soldiers and some Indian auxiliaries sent to capture fugitives from the missions frequently clashed with *cimarrones* and Yokuts villagers. But many of the auxiliaries from the mission retained familial or favorable relations with Indigenous people who fled, as alluded to by the missionary's insinuation about the alcaldes' sympathies.

The missionaries almost always saw *cimarrones* as thieves, integrating their knowledge of horses and other livestock into the trade economy of the interior. In 1822 Missionary Ruiz identified *cimarrones* from San Gabriel who lived in an Indigenous village in the hills. They formed an illicit venture in "stealing cattle and horses that they eat and trade with those from the Colorado." Here he alludes to the larger network of trade relations that would become significant during the 1820s. *Cimarrones* and non-Christian tribes nearer to the missions would raid livestock and trade with the Cahuilla, Yuman, and other tribes in the desert region to the southeast.[132] From Mission Dolores, Father Ygnacio Martínez declared the Christian Indians Apolonio Sebastian and Hilario to be "*cimarrones,* confirmed killers of cattle and robbers of horses." Martínez said they would serve prison terms. One of them made his defiance clear, stating the punishment would be pointless, since, he insisted, they had long been in the business of killing and stealing livestock.[133]

Any alliances the missionaries forged with autonomous Indigenous groups remained somewhat tentative and unstable. Such tensions can be seen in the interactions with the Coco-maricopa of the Yuma Desert, who aided with delivery of the mail between the missions and northern Mexico. In 1824 the missionaries compensated a group of Coco-maricopa for their service by giving each of them a horse. Yet later, when the missionaries could not locate the whereabouts of these mounted Coco-maricopa, they exchanged desperate correspondence that suggested the messengers had gone to the mountains with "el Capitancillo José" and wouldn't return or send information.[134] The missionaries frequently seemed nervous that native allies would become enemies. The dominance of independent tribes that began at the boundaries of colonial institutions created a space missionaries would speak about with fear, as will be discussed at a later point.

A geography of colonial sites on Indigenous lands emerged in California in the decades after 1769, and it reflected the rapid restructuring of Indigenous societies along the coast as they addressed new conditions during a "time of little choice" produced by Spanish colonization. The varied geography of colonial California reflected the distinctive histories of colonial encounters and gave rise to colonial imaginaries long used to define geographic areas of independent and autonomous Indigenous societies. The next chapter explores the meaning of becoming Indian in California and the framework of native thought and ritual practice that addressed such things as military defeat, relocation, and massive deaths. After being renamed and dressed in new cloths, the chapter suggests, leaders sought their own redress through Indigenous means, to recover dignity, and to acquire new knowledge while living in the missions.

This chapter has looked at Chumash, Luiseño, and Yokuts people to establish a sense of the distinct histories involved in the formation of each mission. Missions Santa Bárbara and La Purísima had large populations by 1804, when the missionaries, soldiers, and some Chumash people affiliated to those missions founded Mission Santa Inés. As Indigenous translators and godparents, they interpreted the significance of the massive change and new ideas to their relatives and tribal communities.

In the years when the missionaries explored the independent villages in the area of the prospective mission of Santa Ines in 1798, they also founded five missions, including Mission San Luis Rey. Unlike the policy of *reducción,* under which many people lived estranged from their ancestral lands when they relocated to the missions, more than half of those baptized at Mission San Luis Rey remained in their own villages. In this way, the mission spread its economy across Luiseño territory in advance of significant baptisms. This degree of autonomy facilitated the persistence of the traditional economy as well and sustained a greater degree of wealth and well-being than in missions where *reducción* led to a slow and uneven pattern of decline due to death.

In contrast to the situation of coastal tribes, Yokuts people lived over the Sierra Nevada mountain range around lush marshlands, major rivers, and lakes. They were able to remain Independent, even as particular Yokuts villages developed relationships with certain missions. Yokuts villages had diplomatic and antagonist relationships with the Spanish. Though they engaged in conflict, retreat into swampland proved their most effective means of evading deadly violence. The Yokuts economy became part of the raiding and trading Indigenous borderlands after 1800. That borderlands becomes particularly significant to this book in later chapters.

2

Becoming Indian in
Colonial California

The vernacular Spanish that Indigenous people learned at Mission La Purísima in 1800 was spoken by the troops in California and contained elements of other Indigenous languages in Mexico. Fray Gregorio Fernández wrote that the common Spanish vernacular spoken by the missionaries, soldiers, and Indians consisted of "a mixed language of Otomite, Mexicano, Apache, Comanche, Lipan." The vernacular, he emphasized, "is what is used by the troops."[1] In defining the vernacular as such, Fray Fernández identified a language that had traces of Indigenous speech and experience from the long colonial history of conquests that the military had undertaken.

Fray Fernández used "Otomite" in reference to Otomí Indians who had allied with the Spanish in the sixteenth century. They had migrated to particular areas of Mexico, and some Otomí formed part of the Spanish army. "Mexicano" brought in the influence of Náhuatl speakers of central Mexico. The missionaries made both Náhuatl and Otomí the lingua franca of the colony of New Spain. Some Náhuatl-speaking communities had traditions of military service. Lipan was an Apache language. Different groups of Apache, including Lipan Apache, settled in peace camps in northeastern Mexico. From there, they joined the Spanish army, as did some Comanches.[2] Despite their Indigenous pasts, within California society during the colonial era the status of Indian referred to Indigenous people from the Californias who the Spanish considered conquered, and who lived within the missions. In constructing the relocated mission of La Purísima, for example, they built two water fountains: one for Indians, and the other for the rest of the population, including missionaries, soldiers and their families, town dwellers, and the religious and governmental personnel who traveled through.[3] The fountain used by the Purísimeño population was right beside the infirmary where so many Chumash people would die.

Indian people from the missions in Lower California formed part of the Indigenous population at the missions, although they often held positions of authority that acknowledged their longer history as Christians and their role in establishing the colonial regime. The missions in Lower California had staged major rebellions to expel the Jesuits some twenty-five years previously. The reach of the missions had grown under the Franciscans, however, and many came from the newer and northernmost missions to California. Those who survived the journey north aided in building the first missions in Alta California, and still more migrated during the early years of settlement. They included people of Guaycura, Pericu, Monquis, Cochimi, and Laimones tribal affiliations, but they were known as *indio*. Most of the Indigenous population who settled in California from the missions of Baja California worked as cooks, tortilla makers for the soldiers, and skilled workers. Although they held the status of *indio*, they tended to have higher social standing.

The status of *indio* emphasized people's tributary obligations, but Indigenous people did not always share the same status under the law. Whole communities of Indigenous people in the Spanish Americas negotiated and attained special rights and privileges that removed them from tributary status. Because of their alliance with the Spanish, and the favorable relations they maintained with Franciscans, the Tlaxcalan elite petitioned for privileges for their entire group. Because of a royal mandate in 1591, Tlaxcalans received rights not shared by most Indigenous people in Mexico. The decree freed Tlaxcaltecos from the tribute and personal service required of Indians without their having to pay compensation.

Unlike other *indios*, Tlaxcalans had the right to bear arms and to ride horses with saddles. They had marched with the Spanish army to colonize regions since the sixteenth century. Tlaxcalan communities became common in the mission and mining frontiers of the northeastern Mexico, where Tlaxcalans worked as farmers and in livestock, mining, and as administrators and teachers at the missions. Tlaxcalans commonly found employment in the military, in commerce, and as artisans. To protect Tlaxcalans' autonomy and privileges, laws made it impossible for Spaniards, other Indigenous groups, or *casta*s to buy property or live within Tlaxcalan communities.[4]

The system of *casta*s established a legal and social framework that defined the rights and status of each *casta,* attributing status to colonial people of African, Asian, European, Indigenous, and mixed descent. The legal framework for the *casta* system emerged in New Spain during the mid-seventeenth century. *Casta* identities emerged through a series of local and ecclesiastical court rulings and decisions.[5] *Casta* standing would be determined by a number of factors, including racial and ethnic descent, legitimate birth, Christian heritage, and family background, including wealth and comportment, degree of education, and regional conditions. Because of the localized nature of these deliberations, *casta* categories could differ by place within the Spanish Americas and over time. Though *casta* standing theoretically defined the privileges and restrictions individuals faced, people could also negotiate their *casta* status through various means to arrive at a higher standing for their families. Within this system, Indians and Spaniands were favored for their purity of blood (*pureza de sangre*). But Indians held a low social status because of their non-Christian heritage and because they emerged out of a situation of conquest. Through marriage with non-Indians and migration out of their communities, many Indigenous people moved out of the condition of being tributary Indians, and they or their descendants assumed one of the many *casta* designations that developed in the Spanish Americas.[6]

Many Indian and African-descent *casta*s migrated to California, and African-descent people formed an important part of the *casta* system. A forced migration from Africa began in the mid-sixteenth century, and before about 1700, more Africans than Europeans had migrated to Mexico.[7] Men predominated in the forced migration as slaves. As a result, as Aguirre Beltrán and others have argued, African slavery effectively lost its importance in Mexico by 1742, as Afro-mestizo and Indo-mestizo populations rose in nearly identical numbers to those of the Euro-mestizo *casta*s. African slaves and free people of African descent initially dominated the skilled and unskilled workforce in market-oriented agriculture, mines, and workshops in sixteenth- and seventeenth-century Mexico. Enslaved people of African descent constituted an important part of the early colonial population, but during the eighteenth century, free people of mixed African, Indian, and Spanish descent came to dominate in most of these sectors of the economy, although the transition varied by place and time.[8]

By 1769, the enslaved remained so only in small numbers and particular places. In the Yucatán, for example, a total of 169 free and enslaved Afro-Yucatecans worked alongside other workers. Those enslaved had been born in Africa (primarily the Congo, Guinea, Mandinga, and Mina). Many Afro-Yucatecans married Mayan women, and their Afro-Yucatecan world was connected to the larger Caribbean region that brought together Belize, Jamaica, Havana, and Cartagena.[9] Though the African-descent population had declined in Mexico by 1810, it remained only slightly smaller than the European-descent population as a percentage of the total. However, the *casta*s that included African-descent people often found themselves in the "least desirable situation" in Mexico because of prejudice against them.[10]

Most of the soldiers and settlers who went to colonial California migrated in two major expeditions, and a majority came from northeastern Mexico, where there was a large variety of Indigenous societies and *casta* populations. People with least status tended to move north, where they could become more securely part of the dominant group on that frontier. In 1776, Juan Bautista de Anza moved north with about two hundred soldiers and men, women, and children who intended to settle the pueblos and presidios.[11] Upon their arrival in California, they more than doubled the population of colonists. The second expedition, led by Fernando Rivera y Moncada, came in 1781 with twelve settler families and some sixty soldiers. Many came from mixed Indian, African, and Spanish descent.

Because *casta* definitions had emerged as categories through discrete rulings, *casta* status could more easily be negotiated and changed during one's lifetime and as one moved about. This would happen in California. A majority of the people who married in Alamos, Sonora, and then went to California—thirteen of twenty couples—changed their status from lower to higher *castas*. Especially prominent was the assumption of the highest position of Spaniard by those previously identified as *mestizo* or *mestiza* (of mixed Spanish and Indian descent).[12]

The rights the Spaniards held continued to give them the ability to hold the highest offices and expect universal deference. Louise Pubols eloquently shows how José de la Guerra y Noriega, a noble Spaniard who arrived in California as a military *alférez* (officer rank) in 1801, had to learn how to properly assume and use his authority in California. She writes that elite families were "headed by men who moved up through the ranks, and probably 'whitened' themselves as they did so."[13] Pubols shows how lower classes with ambitions had the ability to rise through the *casta* system on this frontier and secure the necessary documents to qualify as white, or as a higher *casta*, and to marry the elite. Through the web of family relations they could gain access to wealth, military authority, and eventually to land.

Within the highly Indigenous and African-descent population of soldiers and their families at the Presidio of San Francisco in 1790, Spanish *castas* formed a minority of the population.[14] Barbara Voss traces how the process of ethnogenesis shaped this presidio population as it created Californio identities and material practices.[15] Spanish *castas* constituted a larger portion of the Monterey Presidio population than that of San Francisco in 1790. Of the Monterey Presidio's 525 people, half included Spaniards and the other half were composed of *indios* and *mestizo, mulato,* and *coyote castas*. These settlers favored the adoption of categories such as *gente de razón* that distinguished them from conquered *indios* and regional identities such as Californio that disregarded *casta* standing altogether in favor of a common identity with the region as settlers.[16]

Castas formed the majority of the presidio population of San Diego. Soldiers in the Presidio of San Diego identified as Spaniards, Indians, *mestizos*, and a range of African-descent castes that fluctuated during the years 1782, 1785, and 1790.[17] In the Presidio of Santa Bárbara, in contrast, more than half of the population listed their *casta* status as Spaniard in 1790. Indian soldiers formally constituted a little less than 10 percent of the Santa Bárbara population, and *mestizos* well over one-quarter. Together with African-descent *castas*, they probably used the vernacular

Spanish spoken by the soldiers and identified by Fray Gregorio Fernández in 1800 at Mission La Purísima.[18]

At Santa Bárbara Presidio, as at so many, the population moved away from *casta* identities and their legacies altogether as they adopted the term *gente de razón*—people of reason—to distinguish themselves from the *gente sin razón* or the Indian populations at the missions. In Santa Bárbara, for example, the missionary argued in 1814 that it could not be known for certain how many *castas* existed within the presidio population. "Even though it is well known that everyone is not legitimate European or American Spaniards . . . it causes grave agitation if one says they are not." Everyone passed for Spaniards born in the Americas. "For them, all of them, not being Indian, they are *gente de razón*."[19]

In the late eighteenth-century towns of Los Angeles and San Jose, many African-descent *castas* lived among a handful of Spanish and *mestizo* residents. In 1781, African-descent *castas* and Indians formed the single largest population among settlers in Los Angeles. In the pueblo of San Jose, nearly half the population in 1777 considered themselves *castas* of Indigenous descent, including one "Apache." Slightly more than half listed themselves as Spanish.[20] Both populations considered themselves far more Spanish by 1790, when about half the population of Los Angeles also came to identify as Spaniard.[21]

The movement from lower- to upper-class *castas* remained important to a group whose families had become quite distinctive within the region. Because of the lack of migration, by 1830, 85 percent of the adult settlers in California had parents who both had been in the territory by the 1790 census.[22] They had the deep sense of regional belonging and interconnected practices that brought local and historical traditions together.

For most Indigenous Californians in colonial society, their legal identity as *indio* referred to their conquered status. A few also became part of the settler population of *gente de rázon*. In Monterey, just under 10 percent of the 191 *gente de rázon* marriages between 1773 and 1833 took place between a *gente de rázon* and a California Indian woman.[23] That figure was a bit higher in the colonial period, when they accounted for 15 percent of all marriages.[24] But Rosemaría Tanghetti found that in the settler world, in which people sought status and upward mobility through marriage, the racially mixed men who married California Indian women "did not occupy elevated positions" in the presidio company.[25]

One of the most well-known cases of a marriage between an Indigenous woman and a soldier took place between the religious leader and elite Gabrieliño woman Toypurina and a soldier from the Monterey military district. Toypurina's father and brother held the position of village/lineage chiefs in her town of Japchivit.[26] She used her influence to enlist the support of leaders of affiliated villages to join a planned revolt at Mission San Gabriel on October 25, 1785. Villages and individuals from a more than 40-mile radius intended to join, but someone revealed the plot and the leaders were caught.[27] The court sent Toypurina into "perpetual exile" from Mission San Gabriel, and "she would not have hope to reunite with her relatives, nor cause new disturbances with her influence, power, and tricks." Sometime after the trial ended, but while still in captivity, Toypurina decided to be baptized. She assumed the name María Regina.[28] Once in exile, she married a soldier at Mission San Antonio and had children with him. Her children persisted as *gente de razón* integrated into the world of settlers in the northern California region.[29]

REDRESSING AS INDIAN: TEXTILES, CLOTHING, AND STATUS

New ways of dressing constituted an intricate part of colonization, as fabric and style of clothing designated *casta* standing. In colonial California, Indigenous dressing involved extensive textile production using weaving techniques common elsewhere in Mexico. The missions' workshops often made the cloth that their mission populations wore and the vestments and cloth used in religious ceremonies. Some missions also produced higher-value textiles and hides for clothing worn by military personnel at the presidio, and products used for export.

The missionaries required that Indigenous populations redress, meaning that they adopt new clothing to symbolize their status. The affiliates wore a *fresada*, or a full piece of cloth worn over the shoulders and draped over the body, worn by both men and women. All wore the *cotón*, a hand-woven shirt produced as a single piece of material, sometimes closed at the sides with sleeves attached. But when left open, as was common at the missions, it would be pulled together at the waist with a cord or belt (and also called a *gabán* or *manga*).[30] It reached just below the waist or, in variation, down to mid-thigh, extending the width of the shoulder. The men and boys wore a *sapeta* (a term used in Sonora) or *taparrabos*, a loincloth made of cotton or wool. The women wore the *cotón* and *fresada* and a skirt; the skirt, referred to as *naguas, enagua,* or *saya,* was wrapped around the body rather than sewn, and was made at the mission in the textile factories or from imported cloth.[31]

Baptized children living in their villages with their parents also received a *cotón* and a *fresada* annually.[32] Among Chumash, Luiseño, and Ohlone people, the men and women often wore capes made of animal skin. After baptism, they often continued to wear the capes with the wearing-blanket and shirt, a loincloth for the men, and *naguas* for the women. At San Diego, everyone used a cord tied at the waist over their wearing-blanket for modesty. At some missions, cotton and hemp production enabled the weavers to weave softer fabrics, but in all the missions, the sheep's wool predominated in the cloth spun and woven by laborers.[33]

In every mission, some Indigenous people wore clothing that portrayed their occupation at the mission. The Indigenous political elite often wore attire that looked more Spanish. The newer elite of *vaqueros* (cowboys), alcaldes, and *mayordomos* (overseers) rode horses and wore attire that signified their jobs and positions. Fray Ramón Olbés noted that certain Indians, whose work or service called for it, "are given some of the clothing used by the *de razón*." That placed them in a higher-status category.[34]

Textile production at the mission reflected the larger history and economy of textiles in Mexico. The *fresada* and other draped outer garments of cloth corresponded to precolonial clothing in Mexico that came to be associated with the lower classes during the colonial era. Náhuatl documents sometimes equated the *fresada* and *tilmatli*, a long cape worn by nobles made of *manta*, or plain white cotton Indigenous to the Americas, that was open at the sides.

In colonial Mexico, the pre-Hispanic technology of the backstrap or stick loom, and the single Spanish treadle loom, were used in small shops, and they commonly supplied cloth to families and to local markets. Many Indigenous communities grew enough cotton to supply local needs. Each household grew cotton to produce most of the fabric and clothing their inhabitants wore. They formed part of the "web of weavers" in Mexico who contributed to local and regional self-sufficiency.[35]

Missionaries strove for self-sufficiency in the production of cloth and clothing for their missions and to supply the presidio. Early mission textile workshops probably looked like either the *telar suelto* or the *trapiche,* a single-loom shop found across Indigenous Mexico where the weaving was done as a supplementary occupation. They grew to resemble the *obrajes,* textile factories of various sizes and degrees of capitalization where the workers generally lived. Most of the various stages of the production of cloth occurred within the mission workshops and *obrajes:* from cleaning, carding, and spinning of the wool or cotton, to dying the yarn or cloth and weaving. Vast differences existed in the quality of the cloth made.

At San Juan Capistrano, the government contracted a weaver in 1797 to improve the skills of the textile workers there and to produce a better quality blue dye, a common color worn in the clothes of Indigenous people at the mission. It turned out that after twenty-one years of the missions' engagement with cloth production, Achachemem weavers possessed skills at least as good as the artisan's. During the year the artisan was in residence, the mission spinners, weavers, and dyers produced a carpet for the church; twisted cording for the *mangas* or the long, open shirts of the Indian cowboys; and eighty shorter wearing-blankets. For the presidio they made 120 shawls or wraps in three different fabrics, and two large pieces of cloth: one in cotton, the other white flannel. The friar said that the missions' weavers and textile workers could have produced as good or better-quality fabric without the artisan. The artisan also failed to help create better fabric dyes at the mission, but, the friar lamented, a weaver usually did not make flannel or dyes.[36]

In Mexico the colonial textile industry began when entrepreneurs and the Crown established *obrajes* during the sixteenth century in the Puebla-Tlaxcala Basin and the Valley of Mexico. Enslaved Africans and tributary Indians made up much of the labor force. By the end of the seventeenth century these workers had been largely replaced by servants, operatives, convicts, and day laborers who worked either as apprentices or in a state of peonage.[37] African workers, Indians, mestizos, and Afro-mestizos began to fill the ranks of the workforce, but "free wage labor and market incentives could not bring sufficient labor to most *obrajes*." Local power and influence formed a major part of the procurement in a system in which "some owners got labor, some officials got rich, and some workers got protection."[38] Attempts to regulate their conditions were made, echoing attempts to reform and regulate the missions; institutions that did not engage in free wage labor practices

The mission at Santa Barbara had three separate treadle looms with sixty Indians producing textiles. In about half a year they had made 728 yards of material for shirts and loincloths, and some 637 yards of material for wearing blankets, and another 366 yards of material for skirts. They dressed those who arrived to receive baptism in shirts made of plain white cloth from Puebla, a common import that indicated, in this case, their separate status as initiates.[39]

At the three-loom textile works at Mission Santa Bárbara in 1800 the weavers wove fairly constantly from March to October commonly making *sayal*, a kind of sackcloth, for shirts, breech clothes, and women's skirts. Every weaver made ten *varas* (27 1/2 feet) in five days, a labor compensated with additional food rations and two *reales* for every ten *varas* of cloth. After finishing a piece, the weavers received a day of rest and one *reale*-worth of beads or wheat. The market placed a high value on the quality of the cloth, and weavers occupied a privileged place within the textile rooms. Those who wove wearing-blankets also produced a given quantity of cloth. The carders cleaned and prepared three pounds of wool for spinning. The spinners made specified daily pounds of the wool yarn for the shirts, loincloth, and skirts. The work hours decreased during the months of November to February.[40]

Given the continual demand for clothing and the tradition of establishing small workshops when there was available labor, Santa Bárbara Presidio Commander Felipe de Goycoachea started one in 1797. He put up a single-loom workshop in the area of Montecito about 3 miles south of the presidio. The use of Indian labor in his single-loom operation caused problems between the missionaries and Goycoachea. One interaction in particular brought up the issue of the firm control over Indigenous labor that the missionaries exerted and their use of surveillance and punishment to control the workforce. At Mission Santa Bárbara, the friar went to the textile operations in the morning to read the roll of workers to see if any of the threaders, carders, spinners, or weavers were missing. If missing, they might be found in the textile rooms of Commander de Goycoachea or washing wool to prepare it to weave into a particular piece, the missionaries reported.

Agapito, a weaver from Mission Santa Bárbara, had been weaving for Commander Goycoachea for five days without a pass. When the missionaries discovered his absence, "they brought him to the mission and gave him eight lashes," declaring emphatically, "That is what we always do when we know one is going to work in the textile rooms of Don Felipe." By 1800, the presidio had its own textile works in the compound proper and continued to use mission weavers and other textile workers. Skilled textile workers from the mission used their passes to work at the presidio, and they commonly received food and cloth for their labor.

The exchange items that Indigenous workers received for their labor at the presidio revealed the sharp inequities in the society. When contracted, the mission received the pay directly. The military gave Indigenous workers, both men and women, compensation in the form of a piece of watermelon or a corn *tortilla*. Soldiers ate those foods, but they were not made available to Indigenous people at the mission. Older women from the missions often sold wool they had produced at the presidio on Saturdays. Other goods would also be traded for labor, but the system of payment remained informal and effectively unregulated. [41]

The missions also ordered materials and clothing, including fabrics and shirts, wearing-blankets, and skirts, from Mexico for dressing their populations. The vast majority of people in the mission wore fabrics and articles of clothing associated with Indigenous people and lower-status Mexicans. They would be given lesser-quality fabrics, with the single largest requisition being sackcloth called *jerga* and *sayal*. The cloth usually came in blue and white stripes but sometimes arrived in woven plaids or checks. The missions commonly ordered sackcloth, also used for clothes for the poor in Mexico, for sacks and carpeting. It arrived in lengths or bolts. Cloth from Puebla, *manta poblana,* had declined in value, and the missions frequently ordered it. The Puebla-Tlaxcala region had diminished in importance in woolen production by 1800, as internal competition from places like Querétero increased, but the region still produced large quantities of coarse woolen cloth and lower-quality cottons.[42]

Broadcloth constituted a common requisition, as did blue flannel, and occasionally *pita azul,* a cloth made from fibers of the maguey cactus plant. "Cloth made at the poor house" arrived in some orders, a reminder of the difficult conditions of production that cloth entailed. The mission ordered the materials used for the wearing-blankets and shirts according to their width to adjust them at the shoulders. Fabrics came wide for wearing-blankets and narrower for the shirt.[43] They also ordered fabric already cut for wearing-blankets, shirts, and skirts.

In the desire to modernize Mexican apparel, the viceroy José de Azanza issued an edict in 1799 that encouraged guild workers to give up many of the very clothes also worn at the mission and to adopt a more modern form of dress. He referred to "*mantas, sábanas, fresadas, jergas,* or what they call *chispas* or *zarapes,* or any other similar shred or rag."[44] The *sarape* represented a more modern form of wearing-blanket, made of two pieces of cloth instead of one and joined together with a slit for the head. By the middle of the nineteenth century, the middle and upper classes wore elaborately designed *sarapes* made of fine cloth.

The dress of Indigenous people at the mission sometimes reflected a rise in their status and a certain modernization of their appearance. At Mission La Purísima, Fray António Payeras discussed the "customary relief in clothes" attained annually by imports of skirts for the women and blue woolen cloth for wearing-blankets, trousers, shirts, and underdrawers. With that and domestic production, in 1810 they clothed from thirty to forty men and women a year "from head to foot" and mended other clothing.[45] Here some of the men were also wearing trousers, which, with other imported goods, "cause them much joy." [46] Pants marked a more elevated status than did the loincloth, and many Indigenous men adopted pants early in the colonial period in the style of Spanish clothing. At Santa Bárbara, the missionaries imported skirts to augment the clothing staple in 1800, and in a short period of months they had distributed 165 skirts among the women.

More commonly, mission textile shops made the more modern garments for the troops. The *sarape* first appeared in the records of the late eighteenth century in the nascent textile industry of northern Mexico. A workshop with convict labor in northern Mexico, near Patos, west of Saltillo, made "*mantas, sarapes,* wool cloth, sackcloth, flannel" and other provisions for the poorest workers on a huge nearby *hacienda* that employed 600 people and had 200,000 head of livestock.[47]

The mission of La Purísima produced seventy red *sarapes* for presidio soldiers at Santa Barbara and the six guards at the mission in 1817. A total of two years' worth of work, Fray Payeras said. Twenty-five of them were woven in red and worth 5 pesos each; the rest cost 4 pesos, 4 *reales.* The mission also sent four white leather jackets produced at the mission, worth 24 pesos "without a discount."[48] Mission San Antonio made shoes for soldiers. In June 1825 San Antonio sent an Indian trader with eighty pairs of shoes to the presidio. It sent another sixty pair in September 1825, seventy in 1826, and another seventy-nine in 1827.[49]

The difference in the quality of goods purchased for distinct *castas* remained prominent in relationship to the world market. Military commander and Governor Felipe de Neve, for example, ordered fifty-nine short jackets of blue Querétaro (Mexico) wool, fifty-nine wool flannel breeches, eight dozen shirts for men of Pontivy wool (a textile center in France), and twelve dozen "fine domestic stockings and ten dozen under stockings from Genoa (Italy)."[50] The next year, in 1781, he made another order of jackets and breeches. The shirts were to be made of fine linen from domestic production with eight dozen black hats from Texcoco (Mexico). Cuffs and lining were ordered for clothing of lesser quality or "second-class" wools in reds and blue (the color of the Bourbon monarchy).

The dress of the military families and settlers who accompanied them to California also distinguished them from the Indigenous population in California. For the women the presidio ordered six dozen fine Puebla shawls, four dozen women's silk stockings, and, in much smaller quantities than domestic fabrics, pieces of linen from Brittany, France, and thirty pieces of blue silk and wool blend from China. But some soldiers also wore the draped clothes commonly worn among the lower classes in Mexico over their uniforms with two types of material cut for wearing-blankets, one far more crude, and one finely woven.

The Presidio of Santa Bárbara ordered large quantities of *jerga,* cheaper wool, to give to Chumash people as gifts and in return for their work at the presidio. In 1779 the presidio ordered 173 yards of *jerga* and in 1781 another 136 *yards*.[51] Notably, soldiers did not wear the striped fabric common at the missions. This *jerga* would begin to be produced at the missions during the 1780s and became part of a varied textile production that abounded at all three missions by the 1790s.

Unlike the orders from the missions, those for the presidio reflected changing tastes in fabrics. The rise in the popularity of cotton in the Atlantic trade occurred in Mexico as well. In Tlaxcala in 1780, for example, 3,000 *telares sueltos* produced cottons and only 1,000 produced woolens.[52] The orders from the presidio reflected the shift in preference for cotton. Silk, fine woolens, imitations of European linens, and *sarapes* also became important.

In 1796, for example, the presidio ordered three dozen blue shawls of embroidered Sultepeque (Mexico) cotton and one and a half dozen black shawls of the same; another one and a half dozen of Sultepeque cotton in a checkered, embroidered pearl color along with four pieces of multicolored calico. In 1797, ten dozen blue cotton shawls for women and thirty-six pieces of calico in lively colors were ordered.[53] In 1810, twelve pieces of multicolored calico with small flowers, printed cotton, and imitation Brittany linen, along with huge amounts of dark blue cloth from Panzacola, Tlaxcala, Mexico, for uniforms, which had been made at the presidio for about ten years. The clothing and the fabrics drew wide distinctions between the population of soldiers and settlers and that of Indigenous Californians.

But despite the drop in the prices of European and Asian textiles from the late seventeenth century through 1780, Mexican textiles accounted for most of the fabric worn in the colony. Fewer than 20 percent of Mexicans purchased luxury cloth as late as 1817.[54] The Mexican market never relied heavily on imported textiles. Mexican textile operations remained the most important source for cloth. At the missions, different woolens constituted the most common cloth made, although some missions also produced cottons and hemp in a variety of fabrics and colors.[55]

Colonization meant new forms of dressing changed the visual culture of Indigenous society. Native people within and outside the missions primarily wore low-quality mission and Mexican-made woolens. Often dressed in striped cloth, they wore the *cotón* instead of shirts, and a wrapped cloth instead of a sewed skirt;

the loincloth instead of pants; draped fabrics rather than shawls; bare feet rather than socks and shoes. The exceptions marked the distinctions in status that existed within the Indigenous populations at the missions.

BEADS AND TATTOOS

The important role of the bead trade forged in the Channel Islands in promoting a prosperous society among Chumash people prior to conquest probably augmented the importance of beads and bead technologies in colonial trade. The Presidio of Santa Bárbara placed orders with the supply ships for things that rapidly transformed bead technology and culture. The presidio placed orders for an enormous amount of needles, and for pita floss made from the maguey plant, both of which offered new technologies for stringing beads. In their orders for beads the presidio made increasingly specific requests as to their size and color. In 1783, for example, the presidio's order included four bundles of blue and green glass beads and four bundles of deep red garnet-colored beads, 1,000 assorted needles, and 25 pounds of pita floss.[56] In 1789, the presidio ordered twelve bundles of glass beads, 4,000 assorted needles, and two pounds of assorted silk floss to string beads. In 1792, they requested the largest purchase yet: forty bundles of blue and green beads and thirty-six bundles of red glass beads. In 1793, they insisted on receiving thirty-six bundles of the "largest deep red beads" that could be found.[57]

Beads and cloth served as the most important gift and trade items distributed by the missionaries and at the presidios. Chumash people influenced the choice of beads and continued to string their own with the thousands of needles and pounds of thread the presidio secured. These items began to change the visual order of Chumash society and Indigenous societies within all the missions. In 1792, Longinos Martínez wrote of Chumash territory, "The men wear strings of their beads and ours on their heads and around their necks, woven in various patterns. Each man displays his wealth on his head, from which he removes it for gambling or trafficking."[58] Ethnic markings persisted in the combination of beads used, the amulets or talismans worn around the neck, and the tattoo designs people wore on their bodies. Von Langsdorff wrote that Indigenous people at Missions San Francisco and San José made heavy use of beads and jewelry and elaborate bodily ornamentation when he visited those missions in 1806.[59]

In the early years of the mission, the Purísimeño population wore shell beads three times more frequently than glass beads, suggesting both that they had the beads before entering the mission and that they probably still traded for them. The mission continued to place large orders for imported beads and, in the later years, the population wore European glass beads twice as often as shell beads.[60] Within

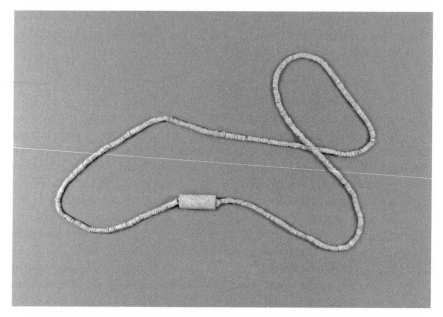

FIGURE 1. Chumash Shell Beads. These strung beads are mostly Olivella callus cup beads that first came into use as high-valued currency about A.D. 1000. The large cylinder bead is from Pismo clam. Courtesy of the Santa Barbara Museum of Natural History.

that mission, the value of European and shell beads remained high as currency, gift, and diplomatic exchange items throughout the mission era and often thereafter.[61]

The women at Missions San Buenaventura and Santa Inés "had glass bead necklaces in considerable variety" and some shell beads.[62] They wore small necklaces of Spanish beads, "which had the color of the beginning dawn sky."[63] At San Buenaventura, Fray José Señan listed six beads that may have been the most commonly worn there, or the most desired, in a confessional book in the section on stealing. As a prompt for other confessors, he noted the translations for big white beads, white bone beads, colored bone beads or seashells, small spotted beads, and garnets. The deep red beads or garnets insisted upon in the orders from the presidio and the spotted beads are the two most closely identified with European beads.[64] The substantial presence of Channel Island beads in the confessional questions might reflect the value those beads maintained, or their augmented value by the first decades of the nineteenth century when the island population began to move to the mainland. The beads must have been increasingly scarce.[65]

Indigenous production of beads within and outside the missions persisted, as at Mission Santa Cruz, which became a center for the manufacture of shell beads after its founding in 1798. The Ohlone (and possibly some Yokuts) artisans exchanged them for imported clam beads from Coastal Miwok people of Bodega Bay and obsidian tools from the Napa Valley. Here, as elsewhere, they often appeared in necklaces along with imported glass beads. The population at Mission Santa Cruz probably also used the trade networks to exchange abalone shell and dried shellfish meat for native goods.[66]

Tattoo designs created a specific colonial Indigenous aesthetics, although tattooing constituted one of the Indigenous spiritual-political rites that the missions attempted to suppress. At San Juan Capistrano, and perhaps among most groups all the way south to Cape San Lucas in Lower California, girls were tattooed "from their eyebrows down to their breasts, some from the chin only, and covering the arms." The application and style varied. Elder specialists used a cactus to prick spots on the girls' skin until they bled and then applied the mezcal plant to produce a blue color.[67] A sketch that Louis Choris made in 1816 defined tribal differences among some groups of Indigenous people at Mission Dolores through their tattoo design. Tattooing constituted more than design and tribal practices; it was also a way the body produced knowledge. Bodily designs oriented individuals to the universe.[68]

FORMAL SCHOOLING

To be an *indio* in the Spanish Americas never precluded formal learning. On the contrary: the Laws of the Indies called for the education of the Indigenous elite from the sixteenth century forward, and native and *mestizo* scholars during that century recorded precolonial thought, visions, and texts in painting and writing. Indigenous education initially focused on the elite, to develop colonial subjects and administrators with the ability to write and speak in Spanish. Indeed, an archive of legal documents, community histories, and other writing in Náhuatl created a substantial set of records about colonial society in New Spain.[69]

In 1691, the Crown amplified the educational program, passing an order "in all the cities, rural settlements, places, and Indian towns or villages [*pueblos de indios*] of the provinces and Islands of both Kingdoms of Peru and New Spain that they should establish schools with teachers to teach the Indians Castilian." The Crown asked for two schools: one for boys and the other for girls.[70] The decree emphasized that Indians who did not understand Spanish would be unable to assume official positions in the República de Indios, an administrative and legal structure governing Indigenous people in the Americas. Province by province the Crown insisted upon establishing schools at which Indians would learn to read and write in Spanish. In 1700, for example, the Crown ordered the bishop of Guatemala to establish schools in all areas and *pueblos de indios* "where the natives learn to read and write in our language and Christian doctrine."[71]

By the end of the eighteenth century, that mandate took on a particular urgency as the Crown attempted to modernize and rationalize governance and society, and the missions, presidios, and pueblos of California were directed to form schools. The government expressed specific interest in the Indians learning Castilian and soldiers and settlers learning to read and write. Military Commander Goycoachea responded from Santa Bárbara that some children were enrolled in schools in San José and Santa Bárbara, but the difficulties of getting and keeping teachers remained. The government emphasized through 1795 that teachers needed to be sent to the province and that the Indians had to be taught Castilian.[72]

In the Mexican era that insistence continued, as did the relative absence of sufficient teachers. In 1827 Fray Vicente Francisco Sarría sent out an order that in every mission of the territory primary schools must be established, especially in the missions of San Francisco, Santa Cruz, San Juan Baustisa, San Carlos, San Luis Obispo, Santa Bárbara, San Buenaventura, San Fernando, San Gabriel, and San Juan Capistrano. Insisting that they attend to the matter, he sent a copy of his order to the new governor, José María Echeandía.[73] By the end of 1829, when Pablo Tac was growing up at Mission San Luis Rey, eleven schools existed in California, seven of them at missions, including one at Mission San Luis Rey. Mission San Miguel, with three students, had the only school north of Mission Santa Bárbara. The mission of Santa Bárbara had a school with forty-four students; Mission San Buenaventura educated thirty-six students; Mission San Fernando, another twenty students; the school at Mission San Gabriel had eight students; Mission San Juan Capistrano educated seventeen students; and thirty-five students attended the school at San Luis Rey where Pablo Tac studied.

These numbers reflect fractions and small percentages of the total mission populations and indicate that only a select group of students received formal education in those mission schools in the late 1820s. The pueblos and presidios also seemed to have a selection of students rather than comprehensive education. The town of San José had thirty students, and Los Angeles had sixty-one students. Eighteen studied at the Presidio of San Diego, and the largest group, sixty-seven students, studied at the Presidio of Santa Bárbara.[74] Nearly all the missions, presidios, and towns had established schools at some point, but California lacked instructors.

As Governor Echeandía explained, although previously there had been some schools at the presidios, they hadn't been permanent "for lack of money" or because of the "lack of teachers." Similarly in the missions, "almost all have had schools, but few have conserved them and now in others they have established them again." The decadence that they have had in these parts was due to lack of instructors who could teach basic things to the young neophytes, true also "for

FIGURE 2. Basket Made by María Marta, Mission San Buenaventura. This basket is one of six woven with the design of colonial coins. The inscription reads, in translation. "Maria Marta, Neophyte of the Mission of the Seraphic Doctor Saint Buenaventura, made me." Courtesy of the Pheobe Hearst Museum of Anthropology.

those called *de razón.*" In all the schools, the students generally made very basic advances, obtaining only minimal instruction in doctrine, reading, and writing. At the mission the young students were similarly taught Catholic doctrine, how to read, to sing masses, and to play instruments. Affirming the absence of teachers, Fray Juan Sancho wrote to Mexican Governor Echeandía in 1829 from Mission San Antonio to say that he received the order about the schools and the mandate to provide instruction in science, but, at present, they hadn't found a teacher.

At each mission, some of the Indigenous population could read and write. Their written documents exist in the Spanish and Mexican archives. They wrote in the official genres of the day, but they often delivered a unique content. Following the tradition of writing on paintings to dedicate or title them, Chumash weavers inscribed a number of baskets that became gift items. Previously the design elements had been "purely geometric," but weavers left names on sewing baskets with lids and on bowls, and they made commissioned items like hats for the padres. Six baskets exist with Spanish colonial coins woven into them. Three of those baskets had inscriptions written around the brims. María Marta, Juana Basilia, and María Sebastiana, Chumash women weavers, each produced one of the baskets. All had been baptized as adults at Mission San Buenaventura between 1788 and 1807.[75]

The Indigenous elite at La Purísima were the first to learn the Spanish language. As holders of cultural rites and transformative knowledge, they could exert some control over how Spanish ideas and knowledge were brought into their language as speakers of the language. To be able to translate and interpret offered people a greater ability to negotiate the new system for themselves and others. Many of the elite already spoke Spanish "quite well" at the missions established by the end of the eighteenth century.[76] Speaking Spanish provided a means to maintain their power by moving between worlds.[77]

To write gave individuals a particular leverage; it was a technology of those in power, and the missionaries maintained strict control over the means to write. In one case, a man named Raymundo, affiliated to Mission La Purísima, stole a pen. The colonial government took the act so seriously that they intended to deterritorialize him by placing Raymundo in permanent exile from his family, village, and Indigenous lands. They intended to move him to another military district and mission without the chance of return. Writing in favor of a lighter sentence for Raymundo, Fray de la Cruz made a plea for him.[78] De la Cruz suggested that Raymundo's offense was not that severe, as he stole only "a pen, but not my heart (and that was to amuse his friend)." Fray De la Cruz wrote in his defense that Raymundo "doesn't even seem to be Indian," showing the accepted and shared disdain for things Indigenous. He strengthened his appeal by pointing out that Raymundo had a son at the mission, whom the missionary said he felt compassion for, and he noted that Raymundo was a good worker, which may have been Raymundo's best defense.[79]

Comparatively few people of any background read or wrote with fluency in California. An oral culture prevailed among Indigenous people and settlers alike, although the missions would import large numbers of printed images and written material, as is discussed in chapter 3. Native people at the missions may have had a similar degree of introduction to the printed word and writing, as did many of the soldiers.[80] The missionaries, military, and business elite tended to write, although even some elite employed an *escribano*, or a person who wrote for hire and knew the formal genres associated with correspondence and legal documentation.[81]

KNOWLEDGE, LIES, AND SILENCES

Knowledge remained an important consideration in the missions, and the missionaries generally believed that Indigenous societies lacked knowledge, history, and figures of learning. When answering questions concerning mission populations, nearly all the missionaries reported that Indigenous societies did not have any knowledge of their own origins or histories with great individuals and learned traditions. Frays Estevan Tapis and Xavier Uría wrote that at Santa Ines, for example, Ineseños did not have any knowledge of their ancestors nor traditions about where they came from.[82] Fray Peyri echoed many missionaries in frequently affirming his inability to understand Indigenous ideas and practices. Peyri complained about the lies and deception that he thought Luiseño elders practiced, and about the obscure references made when he asked for clarification about the meaning of Indigenous rituals, ideas, and relationships.

Attempts to obscure information and the reluctance to reveal beliefs may speak to Indigenous resistance to Spanish authority, but it also addresses an Indigenous relationship to knowledge and its possession that was widely shared in California. Cultures had specialized knowledge and sacred languages. As in many areas of California, the *puplem* or council of ritual elders among Luiseños spoke a ceremonial language that the majority of people did not understand. But understanding the language did not solve the problem of translating it. Castilian did not have adequate words or concepts to express certain Luiseño ideas about the sacred world and the enactment of power. The Luiseño concept of knowledge, for example, had varied and specific meanings that were difficult to capture in their multiplicity.[83]

Certain things could not be conveyed without specialized language, and some knowledge remained the possession of the individual who had acquired it. Fray Gerónimo Boscana commented, "A veil is cast over all their religious observances and the mystery with which they are performed seems to perpetuate respect for them [the council of elders] and preserve an ascendancy over the people." Boscana also commented on all he did not know because he could not understand what he was told. He found the ideas obscure and himself "unable to penetrate their meaning."[84]

Secrecy protected access to many forms of knowledge and power so that it could not be misused. In certain ceremonies, elders could take back the power or knowledge from someone judged unable to use it properly.[85] Secrecy also allowed for specialization and for the compensation of individuals who focused on acquiring and properly using specialized knowledge.[86] Those with specialized knowledge of plant and land management could work most effectively with that world of living things through ritual practice.[87] Only those who had specific rights and abilities could exercise the specialized knowledge found in songs, dance, and other forms of oral, visual, and corporeal communication and ritual. People paid specialists to pray for the production of seed and acorns and continued to do so in the mission era.[88] Missionaries' lack of access to knowledge about the culture left Luiseño and Chumash religion and belief systems beyond their grasp. Though they imagined that the ritual and historical knowledge they sought was available to everyone, many forms of knowledge in these societies had specific connections to individuals and to specific groups alone.

INDIGENOUS THOUGHT AND RITUAL PRACTICES
WITHIN THE MISSIONS

In Luiseño and Chumash territories and beyond, Indigenous systems of thought and ritual practice found vivid expression in the colonial era. Specific practices have been documented in one form or another among the Chumash, the Tongva at Mission San Gabriel" and among the Achachemem, Luiseños, and Kumeyaay.[89] The practices persisted alongside Catholic ritual and among the Luiseño and Chumash people who had separately been identified as the most able to grasp Christian ways and purpose. The Indigenous elders at these missions had specialized knowledge and continued to direct rituals such as dance and healing. Ritual knowledge and Indigenous political-ritual organizations played a critical role in the life of people within mission communities, even as Catholic belief, literacy, and writing offered access to new forms of power. So did everyday practices that had to do with the use of seeds, beads, shrines, and healing.

One detailed ethnographic account by Fray Boscana discussed Indigenous belief as he found it at Mission San Juan Capistrano between 1814 and 1826. Prior to going to that mission, Boscana had lived at other missions where similarly strong and potentially related Indian practices and ideas prevailed. He began his missionary work in California at Mission La Purísima in December 1806 and stayed there until 1811, a period when there were a number of prophecies and collective actions generated by Indigenous thought and leadership.[90] He was at Mission San Luis Rey between 1811 and 1814 and saw the authority of traditional elders and rituals at the mission and in the many Indigenous villages there. From San Luis Rey he made a short move to the north to Mission San Juan Capistrano, where he stayed from 1814 until 1826. He lived at Mission San Gabriel from 1826 until his death in 1831. His experiences in Chumash and Luiseño territories, where these Indigenous structures of thought and politics can be most clearly identified, had given Boscana a set of experiences and questions he brought to the study at San Juan Capistrano. He wrote in the tradition of Franciscan ethnographers who, since the sixteenth century, were similarly interested in understanding Indigenous belief and practice in order to better convert the populations they lived among.

Boscana wrote about Mission San Juan Capistrano after it had been established for more than forty years, yet the life of the community remained organized in fundamental ways around Indigenous beliefs and practices. At San Juan Capistrano, native spiritual and cultural life revolved around Chinigchinich belief and practice, and the first translators and interpreters active in founding Mission San

Luis Rey, including the blind prayer leader who taught the catechism, came from Mission San Juan Capistrano.

The point of interest here is the way Indigenous power persisted through the practices Fray Boscana describes. In the origin story as related by Boscana, Chinigchinich, the creator of all things, first appeared at the funeral ceremony of a great but cruel leader named Ouiot. Chinigchinich arrived and made the descendants of Ouiot into Indians. He invested particular individuals and their descendants with specific kinds of power and knowledge. These became the chiefs and elders. At the end of these ceremonies, Chinigchinich created the men and women from whom the Indians of the present day descended.[91]

During the mission era, the population "frequently consulted [these elders] as to their harvests, and gave in return for their advice a gift of some kind, either in money or clothing." Boscana found "the result of their harvest depends entirely on the maintenance given to these sorcerers."[92] Chinigchinich belief dominated the rearing of children and the general ordering of the spiritual and political life of the Indian population at Mission San Juan Capistrano.[93] The temple or *vanquech* structure that Chinigchinich specified be built also formed part of the ceremonial architecture at San Luis Rey mentioned by Tac. The dancers emerged from the *vanquech*.[94]

Some say Chinigchinich thought entered Luiseño territory from the north. It traveled to Santa Catalina and San Clemente Islands and from there to San Juan Capistrano and then to San Luis Rey. From the coastal area of San Luis Rey, "they brought the ceremonies and 'gave *toloache*' to all the upland Luiseño places, such as Rincón, Potrero, Yapiche, and La Jolla, and carried the ritual to the Diegueños of Mesa Grande and Santa Ysabel."[95] Missionary Salas recorded closely related beliefs held by the Cupeño peoples who lived to the east of Luiseños and Diegueños: belief in a creator god, several similar ceremonies, shamans for each seed, food crop, and the specialization of and control over knowledge by individuals.[96]

Chinigchinich songs, myths, and ceremonies formed a core of Luiseño sacred practice, but they also held beliefs that existed before and independent of Chinigchinich thought.[97] Pablo Tac's dictionary in Luiseño–Spanish is full of words related to Indigenous thought and belief that he grew up with during the 1820s at Mission San Luis Rey. The word *chappicat*, for example, refers to "the person who makes the rain stop." *Aluiis*, which meant "to look up," included sixteen possible forms of looking up related to dance practice and the relationship established between movement, astrological knowledge, and song.[98]

In Chumash territory a political-ritual organization called the *'antap* brought together the elite: all Chumash chiefs and their families, shamans, and other high-status members of the community joined. The members were initiated as children, and their families had to pay to have the children inducted. They served apprenticeships during which they learned about the "acquisition of power, use of cult objects, esoteric language, sacred songs and dances, oral history, mythology, and poetry."[99] The organization may have had antecedents during the era when hereditary village chiefs, inherited ranking, and specialized craft production emerged after 1100. Members included the political leader of each town who had inherited the position and his assistant, the *paha* or ritual leader who presided over all of the ceremonies, astrologers, and healers. The duties varied, but each held ritual knowledge and exercised it for the benefit of the community.[100]

When people went into the missions, they took these political structures, beliefs, and practices with them. The *Wot* functioned as a supra-village leader who ruled over a larger district of villages. The council functioned at the village level. Healers traveled between villages to cure, receiving pay for their work from the families of the sick. The degree to which the structure changed is unclear, but it is very clear that leaders with specialized knowledge performed rituals and made and used sacred objects in the mission communities. They remained prominent as individuals.

In 1810, Fray Antonio Payeras discussed the widespread belief in non-Christian ideas among the large population at Mission La Purísima. He found "superstition, fallacious and even idolatrous observances" and pervasive ceremonies for the adoration of "their Achup" (*sup* or *chupu*). Yet he also represented the mission population as very adept at every task and demonstrating reverence at prayer, singing, and music. He notes their success in creating a new sung mass in 1810 and reported their high level of religious training in Catholicism. It enabled many to participate in the sacraments of confession and communion.

He warned that the frequent participation of Purísimeños in the Catholic rites of communion and confession had to be understood carefully. "The land is so steeped in it," meaning Indigenous beliefs and practices, that taking the sacraments had a different significance for Indians than for Spanish Christians.[101] Just that year most of the pregnant women, particularly the younger ones, at the village had given birth to dead babies, two and three a week. This was a year when adult baptisms of people in the region had virtually ended. Most village populations had moved to the mission, where more than 1,000 people resided. Many came from villages in crisis due to sickness. At first the missionaries attributed the deaths to disease or other physical problems, but then they started to suspect that it formed part of a collective action deliberately undertaken by the women.

The movement, they discovered, was related to the advice of elders who attempted to halt births to change the high rate of illness and death that had plagued the population for years. In response to these actions, the women "were chided, preached to, and maybe punished (leniently) but so far all has been to no avail," Payeras complained. He said the missionaries were "unable to prevent the origin and motive for such deplorable happenings."[102]

Indigenous practices at Mission San Buenaventura received attention by Fray José Señan, who arrived among Chumash people at Mission Santa Bárbara in 1797 and took charge of Mission San Buenaventura sometime thereafter. He learned Ventureño and wrote a confessional manual *(confesionario)* in that language and Spanish, probably during the 1810s. He died at San Buenaventura on August 24, 1823. Señan probably wrote his confessional after the one produced in Barbareño at Mission Santa Bárbara. It had the standard doctrine and the Lord's Prayer, the Angelic Salutation, the Apostles' Creed, the antiphon Salve Regina, the Twelve Articles of Faith, the Ten Commandments, the Five Commandments of the Church, the Seven Sacraments, and the Seven Capital sins.[103]

Señan's writing contains ethnographic information, but its major importance is the way it documents the practices of cultural wounding at San Buenaventura and, by extension, elsewhere in the missions. Señan's instructions to other missionaries performing confession involved silencing the confessant; asked the confessant to disavow his ideas and the meaning behind his actions; and replaced the Chumash narratives about their cultural practices with new ones suggested by the confessor. Confessions were taken only once per year, yet the attitudes behind the interaction pervaded others throughout the year.

Señan's confessional is particularly interesting because he breaks into instructions to other missionaries, making it clear how they should convey their questions and direct the answers of the confessants. Señan warned other missionaries that the Ventureños would ask question and want to discuss the questions that the confessor posed. He insisted that theological debates with them should be avoided at all costs, especially because they liked to talk about the questions raised. Señan informed missionaries who would use the book that discussion "wastes time," produces little benefit, and would be confusing to the confessor who did not know the Ventureño language. In essence, he sought to silence the confessants and render their questions irrelevant. He suggested the response should be, "Look, I don't understand what you are telling me. Just tell me how many times." In addition, he placed numbers in Ventureño and Spanish as prompts next to that statement.[104]

The *confesionario* discusses the many cultural practices shared by Indigenous societies in California, including their use of dance, seeds, beads, and shrines. Here, again, Señan's many prompts were directed toward making people produce a verbal disavowal of their beliefs, which constitutes a kind of wounding of the spirit. Señan suggested that the confessor ask, "When you danced, did you believe it to be true you wouldn't get sick?" And offers the acceptable response: "I saw others dancing, that is why I danced." Señan expressed concern with the power associated with seeds and beads. Señan asked, "Did you believe that by scattering seeds, etc. you would kill fish?" That, if you did so, "there would be plenty of seeds, and deer, and rabbits and jackrabbits?" Again, he supplied the acceptable answer, which emphasized that the person committed the act because "I saw the others doing it."[105] The answer was intent on making the confessant deny his or her vision and volition in scattering seeds.

Concerned with the power of the shamans and other elders in the missions, Señan fashioned a series of questions about the power of individuals who "make it rain," "make acorns grow," and "heal the sick." He spoke against those individuals and groups paid for their specialized knowledge of the elements, of plants, seeds, and acorns. He also elaborated distinctions in Ventreño among "the quack healer," "to heal badly," "the good healer," and "to heal well." He considered it acceptable if a healer used herbs; that was "good" healing, thought of as "well." But he otherwise considered belief in Indigenous knowledge about healing, and the rituals themselves, unacceptable.

Señan emphasized the evil involved in believing in and paying for traditional shamanic rites and identified the widespread use of *toloache* or jimsonweed in Indigenous rituals at Mission San Buenaventura. *Toloache*, when ingested, produced a dream state desired for rituals related to the production of knowledge. During their initiation ceremonies, boys and girls also took *toloache* prepared by elders, and they learned the related songs and dance. Taking *toloache* formed a cornerstone of shamanic practices in a wide range of cultural areas. In general, the missionaries rarely wrote about that and other Indigenous practices except in passing. As did Señan, they focused on renarrativizing the experience and seeking to get a disavowal of beliefs. They couldn't prohibit many cultural practices and sometimes incorporated them into the Catholic calendar of celebrations.

Fray Señan described a community at San Buenaventura in which Indigenous patterns of kinship made it difficult for him to delineate even the most simple family relations. "It is very difficult to understand blood relations among these people," he wrote.[106] He found it exasperating that he could not ascertain simple things like brother and sister, first or second cousin, close or distant relative. Señan lamented their practice of using these terms even when people were not related by blood. To "get clear even such an obvious relationship as that of brother and sister," he offers guiding questions such as "Is your aunt the mother of your sister?" "Do your wife and the other woman have the same father and the same mother?" These familial relationships established an intertwined set of obligations to each other among the Indigenous community. As with the godparent structure defined at Mission Santa Inés, close relatives played a fundamental role in sustaining the spiritual and material well-being of their godchildren at the missions.

DANCE AND ACCESS TO POWER

The redressing of Indigenous populations formed part of the definition of the new colonial subject, but it coexisted with longer-enduring modes of dressing worn to perform dances and ceremonies. While the one reflected Indians' relative loss of power in a new imperial setting, the other—such as dressing for and enacting dance practice—constituted a foremost way that Indigenous communities at the missions continued to access power. Dance produced and sustained particular kinds of knowledge and addressed the new conditions faced at the missions. Dance formed a critical part of mission life such that, Fray Boscana emphasized, "hardly a day passed without some portion of it being devoted to this insipid and monotonous ceremony." Dancing "was the principal ceremony" occurring "on all the feast days of the Indians," referring to the saints' days and other occasions such as birth, marriage, and death. Fray Boscana spoke of dances that lasted for days on end and emphasized dance's constant presence.[107] Fray Peyri, too, emphasized its presence at nearly all occasions and its performance for healing and before and after the harvest of native foods.

Pablo Tac wrote about dance twice in his history of Mission San Luis Rey. He would have seen dances and been keenly aware of the boy's coming-of-age celebration, which he wrote about twice. He would have seen it before and after he reached adulthood around the age of nine in 1830. Fernando Librado Kitsepawit, born at Mission San Buenaventura in 1839, described dance practices he heard about from the community of Chumash people he knew from the five Chumash missions. He also saw the last great flourishing of dances from the era of the 1840s-60s in his youth and young adulthood.[108] Librado and Tac offer an Indigenous way of talking about dance and speak to its significance within Luiseño and Chumash communities, respectively, and about changes in dance practice that took place at the missions and among people from former mission communities.

Fray José Señan and Fray Juan Cortéz talked about dance practice at Missions San Buenaventura and Santa Bárbara in their confessionals, and Fray Boscana returned to dance many times in defining Chinigchinich belief and thought at Mission San Juan Capistrano. Fray Peyri wrote about the many kinds of dances and related forms of knowledge, regalia, and ceremonial time. Foreign travelers also described dancing as they saw it in the missions. G. H. von Langsdorff, while on a trading and diplomatic voyage to the presidio and missions of San Francisco and San José in 1806, wrote, "Among all their amusements there is none in which they take so much delight as in their dances." He said that the missionaries "liberally indulged" this "amusement" as it took place with regularity.[109]

European writers relegated dance to entertainment and celebration. They did not see the body as capable of producing knowledge through dance. Yet in Indigenous dance, the songs and the movement that conformed to the sound could generate new understandings of things and transform conditions. European writers on dance spoke from cultures in which bodies had long been "divorced from their capacities to theorize" and could not be conceived of as able to produce the kind of knowledge or power associated with shamanic dance practice.[110] Spanish lacked the language and concepts to describe it. In Polynesia, where dance also played a central role in life, languages did "not have a word, phrase, or concept that precisely covers the English concept of dance." The Polynesian words for structured movement often reflected "context, function, and level of formality," differentiated between sacred rituals and nonsacred contexts, and indicated such things as style, rhythmic motif, movement motif, and gender.[111]

Native writers' descriptions of dance drew the relationship between power and dance to the foreground and showed how it was structured through a concern for the astrological order and divine animation. In contrast to European accounts, Tac and Librado emphasized the relationship between sound and movement in dance. They wrote out or described the sounds. Their accounts indicated the time of year and the time of day that the dance took place. They specified the direction of entrance of the dancers, the direction of their movements and their faces. The importance of time and direction reflected the concern of Luiseño and Chumash astrologers that structures, ritual areas, and ceremonies "conformed to their perception of the cosmos."[112]

Librado emphasized that the older dancers insisted strictly upon proper movement and design painted on the dancers' bodies and that the specific feathers and regalia be utilized. The exactness of representation conformed to the requirements of "divine animation." It made the dancers recognizable to supernatural beings and animal spirits by presenting the visual cues associated with them and inviting them into the dancers' spirit.[113]

Boscana emphasized how Chinigchinich conveyed the laws and established rites and ceremonies for the preservation of life through dance. The different names for Chinigchinich derived from different states related to dance: *Saor,* the period in which Chinigchinich could not dance; *Quajuar,* when he was enabled to dance; and *Tobet,* when he danced enrobed in a dress composed of feathers.[114] He danced before the people, painted in black and red, and referred to himself when dancing as "Tobet." After dancing, he selected the chiefs and elders and said, "They alone should wear the kind of dress which had adorned his person, and then taught them how to dance." Chinigchinich gave those elders the name of *puplem,* who would "know all things and relieve the infirm and diseased."[115] Healers, as others with shamanic power noted earlier, continued to be sought out and paid by Indigenous people in the missions.

Dance sustained traditional forms of knowledge held by Indigenous elders. They possessed most of the chants and sounds made during dance. Each culture had specific rules by which elders passed down their *awekeli,* or specific knowledge or power, to a successor; often the person chosen would be from within the family lineage, but those who demonstrated special qualities could also be selected.[116] In describing the boys' coming-of-age dance, Pablo Tac emphasized the importance of the village elders in teaching the song and movement. "No one can dance without the permission of the elders, and they have to be of the same people, ten years or older." Tac repeated and emphasized that elders "of the same people" governed the song and ceremonial knowledge. The religious leaders from each village included singers who possessed the songs and taught the dance according to the song and those who made and kept the dance regalia. The elders selected each dancer, choosing boys for puberty initiation whom they determined ready from age ten onward. The singers, "who are the old people," might include younger ones, "but of the same people." Tac emphasized the learning that went on. "Before doing the dance publicly the elders teach them the song and make them learn it perfectly because the dance consists in knowing the song, because according to the song it was done."[117]

His description makes clear the persistence of traditional knowledge and elaborate preparation involving the cultivation and trade of feathers and other materials related to the dance regalia as well as the many different skills required to make everything for the dance. Feathers in the thousands had to be gathered, and elders possessed the skills of feather work to make the regalia worn and carried during the dance. They also held the knowledge about the production and application of body paint. Elders wove the baskets that were often used in dance ceremony. They cultivated techniques for gathering, preparing, and administering the potentially deadly hallucinogenic *toloache* that dancers sometimes used.[118] Thus the knowledge, authority, and skill of many people sustained dance practice.

Von Langsdorff also wrote in 1806 about the masterful dance regalia that he and other explorers gathered all along the coast. In exchange for European glass beads and things such as silk ribbons and knives, he acquired one headdress that consisted of 450 feathers of the golden-winged woodpecker. The headdress used only two middle tail feathers, which had brilliant vermilion color on their shafts, from each bird. Von Langsdorff couldn't figure out how feathers from 225 woodpeckers could be gathered in a place without much forest, but Indian trade networks often supplied the material needed for the regalia. Woodpecker feathers, for example, stood out prominently in the goods sent south from tribes to the north of San Francisco Bay.[119] The regalia could have also been brought into the mission when people relocated. Beads and other ceremonial objects continued to be made at the missions. Some Indigenous baskets, for example, were made specifically to trade for European goods.[120]

Understanding dance as a fundamental part of Indigenous culture, some missionaries encouraged dances and festivals to be held to commemorate the anniversary of the baptism of village leaders and thereby affirm the bonds with the church. Fernando Librado had heard, for example, that a missionary at Santa Bárbara asked the captain of each village to hold a baptismal day anniversary party to commemorate the leaders' baptism every year. The missionaries also thought it could attract nonconverts to the mission. Barbareños complained that it cost too much to do so annually. Fray Antonio Ripoll ordered shell money be made to help pay for some of the celebrations.[121] The dancers would be invited, other invitations extended, and long preparations ensued that involved time off work at the mission.

The guests also prepared gift items to support the big celebration; during these celebrations different villages traditionally exchanged valued goods.[122]

In the 1840s and 1850s, Librado saw many dances performed at festivals that drew people from various Chumash mission communities. He had seen the fox dance performed about nine or ten o'clock in the morning at Missions Santa Inés, Santa Bárbara, and San Buenaventura. About this dance he noted, "A captain of a group or of the Indians at the mission might save up some money" to pay for the ceremony "so that his subjects, when in distress, could be assisted by him." It was also performed at weddings or baptisms "if a family had enough money to pay for it." The dancers at these events "received presents and more money than they otherwise would receive."[123] Librado spoke of these celebrations at Mission Santa Bárbara and at Cieneguitas, a rancho of the mission. He spoke of the fox dance performed at Cieneguitas in which either an old man or an old woman sang for the dance. When performed at "Marcelino's fiesta at Santa Inés," Librado recalled that the fox dance involved two whistlers, two singers, and four dancers.[124]

Librado saw the blackbird dance performed at Santa Bárbara during the fiesta of Captain Francisco Solano Seqpeweyol, in the Indian quarters, near three rows of adobe houses. He later saw it performed at Mission San Buenaventura, sometime before 1859, by the side door of the mission, after the last tile had been placed on the mission roof.[125] At "Santa Bárbara Day" on December 4, Librado recalled the devil dance, bawdy and profane, performed in the morning; a bullfight after mass in front of the church; and then the blackbird, rabbit, barracuda, swordfish, seaweed, and the Santa Rosa Island Wi'ma dance, among others.[126] People came from six former mission communities to participate, emphasizing a set of interactions around dance and culture that reflected the strong ties among the larger regional Chumash community into the second half of the nineteenth century.

European dance had few parallels in conceiving the relationship between dance and the sacred, and Tac drew broad distinctions between European and Indian dance. "Europeans only dance for happiness. We dance for happiness, for sadness, to make war, for the good harvest."[127] In one version of dance he added, "But now that we are Christians we only dance for ceremony, and to remember our forefathers because they died, and because they have been beaten in war."[128] The dances he described, however, have a range of purposes and include the more traditional boys' initiation dance, in which the young men took *toloache,* and the eagle dance, which is one of the Chinigchinich dances.

Dance had the power of "conceptualizing, reinforcing, or addressing political systems or situations."[129] In two of the three dances Tac describes, the dancers looked to the sky where the ancestors resided and presumably retained "all their great, ancient *ayelkwi* power unimpaired."[130] In both the boys' puberty dance and the eagle dance, the two elders named "Pajaom" emerged from the house or temple carrying with them large wooden sticks and yelling. They stood in front of the place where the dancers would move and looked at the sky "for a long time" while the crowd fell into silence. Afterward they went in and the dancers came out.

In the initiation dance, the boys took *toloache*, entered into an altered state, and came out and danced for three hours during the heat of the day. As the dance ended, they took off their *cheyat* (dance regalia worn on the head and made of feathers) and raised it to the sky. The singer made the sound of a mare looking for her colt. After the dancers went back in, the two Pajaom began to smoke "and all the smoke they threw to the sky, three times before ending the dance."[131] It is interesting that the dance incorporated a horse. Used by the Spanish for domination, a mare's voice in this dance brought it into an Indigenous system of meaning.

The eagle dance related to Chinigchinich belief. Tac illustrated it in a drawing he made in which the Pajaom came out and began yelling toward the sky as they had in the first dance. The dancer emerged and began to run around a circle of people about 80 feet in diameter. The dancer looked at the sky the whole time, with one foot raised in the air and the other on the ground, one arm in the air and the other extended toward the earth. That is how he went around the whole circle. The dancer's entire body was painted. Elders stood at different points to catch the dancer if he fell. Tac represented the dancer in still motion and one of the elders in his picture. This dance again called upon divine energy to enter the dancer.

A final dance that Tac wrote about incorporated Spanish motifs and, in contrast to most dances, was performed by women with the men; many people, mostly older women and men, danced this together.[132] It used a traditional instrument; an elder sang. People would throw the new foods of wheat and corn on the dancers.

While highly choreographed according to the singer, dance practice also involved continuous innovation. The ability of dance to innovate and incorporate new elements enabled it to address larger social and cultural changes that could have otherwise simply created great despair. Dance spoke to traditional knowledge and to new things: the sound of the mare, new foods, and new form, with men and women dancing together.

Dance played the role of a social text that signaled and enacted "social identities in all their continually changing configurations."[133] For Tac, dance took place "in many ways according to the type of Indian." He writes that the Yumans, the Apaches, the Christian Diegueños, the Juaneños, Gabrieliños, Fernandiños, and those from Monterey "also have their dances different from one another."[134] That Tac identified broad tribal identities through dance is consistent with a role it played in many cultures, in which dancing constituted a "site of confrontation and negotiation of identities."[135]

In a drawing that represented one group of dancers at Mission San José in 1806, von Langsdorf captured dancers painted in distinct ways one from the other, each with particular regalia. The dancer at the extreme right wears a uniform of a Spanish soldier. In the multitribal community of San José, dance defined group

FIGURE 3. Dance of Indians at Mission in San José, New California, 1806. Sketched by Georg Heinrich von Langsdorff. The day of his visit to the Mission of San José, the missionary allowed people to dance. G. H. von Langsdorff noted that one dancer in this group was painted as a soldier. Courtesy of the Bancroft Library.

identities under new conditions, affirmed valued skills, and provided intercession with the sacred over daily life and political existence. The dancers performed many different scenes of battles and domestic life; they ate glowing embers as they danced in what would have become a trancelike state around a fire; and they staged a dance related to the hunt. The dance they saw related to the hunt was intended to establish a particular relationship to the animal and the right conditions for hunting. Similarly, the creation of the figure of the soldier in the dance, and represented in the painting, could alter the relationship to soldiers. Dance could affect the balance of forces more generally.[136] Here, as elsewhere, the women had their own particular songs and movement. They tended to remain less visible in representations of dance.

In 1816, Louis Choris also wrote about dances at Mission San Francisco that took place every Sunday after mass. He described what could have been one or many dances, with half the men dressed in feathers with belts of feathers and shell money and others painted with regular lines of black, red, and white. The men danced in groups of six to eight, carrying lances, all making the same movement. They danced to the clapping of their hands and to the sound of what he called "a horrible cry." The women danced among themselves without making violent movements.

The multilingual character of the missions also brought change in dance practice. Many of the songs Fernando Librado discussed demonstrated the range of interethnic engagement that Chumash dance came to embody by the mid- to late nineteenth century. Dialects had come to predominate at each Chumash mission, and dance also included the language of the Yokuts who maintained relationships to the Chumash during the colonial and Mexican periods. The songs for the bear dance, for example, were "in part Cruzeño," from Santa Cruz Island, "and in part all places and dialects, for the bear is powerful and goes everywhere."[137] The coyote song was in part Barbareño and in part Ventureño. Other songs, such as the fox dance sung in "the Santa Rosa Island language," were performed in languages that found fewer and fewer speakers over the course of the nineteenth century[138]

Other dances, such as the barracuda dance, were in "the language of the old people, known only to themselves, and they never taught it." Frequently sung in a sacred language, their significance remained tied to the song or chant and to the knowledge produced in the process of movement. Because of the private nature of that knowledge, and semi-private nature of the language, some knowledge was lost because of the high rate of death at the missions and the use of new languages. Librado recalled two Chumash bards named Benjamin and Mileton who knew the words to songs, but "no one else understood them." Changes in the population by the late nineteenth century meant that fewer people could perform some dances.[139]

The very changes in language use, and the widespread ability to speak Spanish among younger generations, made it difficult to correctly perform some of the songs. Librado attempted to learn the *wansak* Tulareño bear song, but after a period of time, the old man named Juan who taught him gave up. He said that Librado had a voice that could not "intone it right"; because his voice had become more adapted to Spanish. Librado "just could not sing these songs in the way that the old Indians did." [140]

In other dances, part of cycles of songs became lost and the songs fragmented. The swordfish dance, for example, was only one of a cycle of dances, but Librado remembered only some of the cycles, not the rest. Others, such as the arrow dance, in which bowmen shot at each other, were lost as particular skills receded in the late nineteenth century. Although specific kinds of esoteric knowledge could die with a shaman who had not passed them on, practices fundamental to Indian religion persisted throughout the mission era and beyond.

Dance practice also changed to better address human intentions and spirit under uncertain circumstances. "The ancient Indians, before eighty years ago" [c. 1835], for example, performed the seaweed dance distinctly, without the addition of the Santa Cruz Island bear song. "More recent believers" thought that "if anybody was sick for love or for any other reason . . . adding this dance would bring them out of that state of melancholy." They performed part of the seaweed dance at night under the constellation of Pleiades. The lyrics of one of the last songs suggest possible responses to the history of settlement that persisted with the dance. "In the land where I was born/never does a foreigner dare/to say that this land is his."[141]

Luiseño translators brought dance practice into the daily life of the mission in the Luiseño word they offered to identify colonial dressing. Wearing the clothing made at the mission and purchased through trade constituted a symbol of being Christian. They translated the verb "to dress" as *cheiis*, which also meant "to dress with a *cheiat* for dance."[142] The *cheiat* (variant spelling of *cheyat*) was made of fine feathers and worn on the head during certain dances such as the boys' puberty dance. The verb *cheiis* contains the reference to the sacred enactment of dance. The use of that verb brought the presence of dance and sacred regalia into the daily practice of dressing at the mission. To dress (*cheiis*) and to make clothing constituted a significant part of the material culture and labor under colonialism. People produced clothing for themselves, and the missionary traded for clothes with mission products. The Luiseño verb brought the Christian practice of dressing and traditional dance practice together. That colonial reference ceased to have meaning by the early twentieth century, when Luiseño speakers once again used the word *cheiis* only to refer to dance regalia and no longer used it as a verb related to daily dress.[143]

VIOLENCE AND REDRESS

An incident at Mission San Buenaventura in 1829 that involved people from different Chumash missions emphasizes the potential restrictions on Indigenous thought and practice within the missions that healers and others had to be aware of. The incident involved three Chumash healers arrested for divination and creation of a healing ritual. Soldiers beat the men with a stick, incarcerated them, and ultimately sentenced two of them to a public whipping.

One of the men named José came from Mission San Buenaventura, and two men, Anastasio and Apolonio, came from Mission Santa Inés. Anastasio confessed that the devil had told him to dance in order to heal the sick or everyone would die. He also said the devil had given him seeds and then disappeared. José, he reported, had said he would begin dancing that same night and threatened Anastasio with death if he did not do the same. Though the devil had appeared to Anastasio, he blamed José for carrying out the ritual. José and Anastasio called everyone to bring their sick to the house of José at San Buenaventura. People carried their sick relatives and friends there for healing.

The two of them, and Apolonio, prepared about thirty different herbs to administer to the sick during the healing ceremony, and. danced for three successive nights. Some of the sick who attended the ceremonies also danced. People paid the healers in beads, seeds, and other objects.

Someone reported the prophecy and dancing to the soldiers who arrested the three. Four months later, a military court tried and sentenced them. The liberal governor Echeandía, who had arrived from Mexico in 1826 with the intention of emancipating Indians from the missions and encouraging their treatment as citizens, signed the judgment against them, thereby accepting the terms of punishment. The judge set Apolonio free. Anastasio and José were sentenced to twenty-five lashes after mass on Sunday in front of the entire mission population. The ruling emphasized that everyone be told the men received this punishment for witchcraft. After the public whipping with enough lashes to create substantial physical harm and pain, they were to be set free.[144]

The humiliation of being whipped, the fear created by the whipping, its treatment as a public spectacle, and the viewers' responses to their leadership and loved ones being physically hurt to the point of potential death emphasize the violent and traumatic circumstances ever possible at the mission. The acceptance of the punishment by Governor Echeandía, who had spoken favorably of Indigenous citizenship, suggests the limits of liberal reform and thought.

This incident reminds one of the claustrophobic nature of living in a condition of *reducción* during an era when illness and loss had predominated for more than two generations. It also recalls Señan's insistence that it was acceptable to dance in imitation of others, and to heal with herbs, but not to participate in divination or rituals related to Indigenous knowledge and power. When not dismissed as entertainment, those practices could be prosecuted during the colonial and Mexican eras. Yet Indigenous healers continued to engage in practices of healing, even in the face of dire repression. The public whipping on Sunday produced the kind of trauma among the population that, as will be seen later, remained seared into Indigenous memories of irrational and deathly violence during the era.

BEING INDIAN IN CALIFORNIA

The Spanish brought the category of *indio* to California with their arrival, and the term identified a legal and social condition for the Indigenous population introduced by the Spanish. By no means did the term identify everyone of Indigenous ancestry. Instead, in California, the status of *indio* largely related to Indigenous people at the missions. The visceral representation of *indios* was drawn through the type of clothing and cloth people wore, their own use of beads and tattoos, and the status of minor and colonial requirement to have a pass in order to leave the mission. The use and production of textiles in the missions connected their populations to the colonial Mexican world of production and exchange in which workers made cloth under arduous, often coercive conditions of labor. This labor, and the products that circulated in the missions, deepened the connections among California, Mexico, and the world market. The nature of work done at the missions also shaped the meaning of *indio* as a historical category that coexisted together with tribal identities. Each mission had specific languages and cultural life and distinctive historical communities.

Indigenous leaders and communities cultivated forms of knowledge and power at the missions to seek redress for humiliating conditions and to help people survive in the wake of shattered worlds. How people adjusted to this world of constraint, and the loss of loved ones, ancient territories, and political power, is partly addressed by pointing to the significance of dance. Dance offered a means to knowledge and the means to try and rectify unfavorable circumstances. It situated people within Indigenous places and practices of healing and redress. It helped affirm the life-giving elements that the community shared under the new conditions of being Indian.

3

The Politics of the Image

Writing about colonial Mexico, Serge Gruzinski argues that images were preeminent in the Spanish politics of colonization and cultural mestizaje. He elaborates on the intensity and significance of the visual world Spanish and Indigenous painters created during the sixteenth century in Mexico.[1] David Freedberg emphasizes the inherent ambiguity of images. Despite restrictions placed upon them to control their meaning, from the perspective of the viewer, there are many ways images can be received. W. Mitchell emphasizes the life that images acquire as they are viewed.[2] These scholars reflect on the critical and multifaceted role visual culture plays in the structuring of ideas and perception.

The visual culture the Spanish brought to colonial California elaborated on the stories of the saints whose names were assumed at baptism, thus situating converts within a new historical narrative represented in the proliferation of paintings and figures. In this setting, where few soldiers, settlers, or native people read and wrote, the visual image was an especially poignant form of narration. The baroque visual splendor that the missionaries sought for their churches in California formed a crucial part of Catholic ritual. As Gruzinski, Freedberg, and Mitchell point out, images created communities of viewers with a shared experience and fostered interpretive responses.

Prints rather than paintings enabled images to circulate in great numbers in the early days of Spanish settlement. Prints would either be framed and hung in the mission chapels or be passed out to the Indigenous population. They arrived in quantities the missions could afford, often consistent with the size of their populations. Mission San Buenaventura requested four hundred prints in 1807, and specifically many sets of the archangels.[3] In the early years at Mission San Luis Obispo, the missionary ordered three dozen prints of saints and pounds of different colored pigments for painting the church and surrounding buildings, thus deriving most of his early decoration from painting done on site. They acquired a painting of the patron San Luis Obispo, another of Saint Joseph, a painting of paradise, and another of hell, but they didn't acquire a painting or a sculptured piece for several years thereafter. The church was decorated initially with the prints in frames made at the mission and hung on walls painted by native painters and decorated by gilded tissue, crosses, and paper decorations. The friars at the Mission San Luis Obispo ordered another thirty prints in 1778.[4] Sixty-six religious prints circulated within a small-built space less than eight years old and among a native population of around two hundred.

The missionaries distributed prints among new converts and families associated with the mission who were living in their villages, sometimes sending the images out of the mission proper. San Diego acquired one thousand prints of virgins, saints, archangels, and biblical scenes in 1791. This quantity gave the missionaries enough prints to distribute among the entire adult population of the mission.[5]

Quite a number of these prints were of seventeenth-century paintings whose themes were explicitly developed for export to the colonies from Sevilla, Spain.[6] Apart from paintings of the Virgin Mary, whose number was rivaled only by representations of the cross, the other imported images during that era tended to be less common, sometimes absent, in Sevilla, Spain where collections proliferated and offer a comparison to the exports.[7] Angels constituted the second largest category of exports, yet they were infrequent in Sevilla during the period. The patriarchs, the third largest category of imported paintings, represented the twelve sons of Jacob found in the Old Testament who became identified with the twelve tribes of Israel. Their popularity in seventeenth-century imports is connected to the theory that Indigenous populations descended from these lost tribes. In contrast, paintings of the patriarchs did not exist in Sevilla. Child martyrs and missionary martyrs similarly appeared among New World images but infrequently in Sevilla. New World themes and martyrdom stood out in these imported paintings and would be conveyed in the prints and favored images that the Franciscans brought.

Prints "were not merely illustrations or sources for the creation of new imagery," but they had "tremendous power in affecting how the world was understood" and how individuals connected to that world by creating "a common visual experience."[8] With thousands of printed images at the missions and circulating within Indigenous territories, the missionaries established a proliferation of Christian narratives that encompassed a visual vocabulary and set of historical events. Print culture played a role in establishing a community of viewers who shared the literacy they derived from those images.

Images also predominated because the missionaries and settlers sought compelling images to enhance the intensity of their own devotional experience and to represent and affirm their religious purpose. After 1805, when the extensive phase of conversions ended for many missions because the populations in their vicinities had affiliated, missionaries began to spend ever-larger sums on religious goods. Economist Marie Duggan wrote of "spiritual capital" when she identified the purchases as investments made to "raise the level of faith which they aspired to instill" and noted the desire for those goods and the large amount spent on them rather than on machines and other innovations related to economic production. In the larger missions, "statues, paintings, vestments, monstrances, chalices, and ornaments for the church such as rugs and candelabras" often cost more individually than the entire annual subsidy the government provided to the establishment.[9] Duggan attributes the missionaries' ability to acquire these goods to their increase in trade with the military and, especially after 1810, to their engagement in legal and illegal export trade.

Smaller missions like Santa Inés and San Fernando relied more heavily on the work of Indigenous artisans and craftsmen than did the larger missions, and Indigenous artisans at both missions produced important paintings. But at every mission the missionaries imported tons of pigments for painting and decorating churches and imported objects that hung on walls and stood in niches. Decoration and painting offered a way to contribute to the narration of Christian stories and create other potential meanings.

The images that Indigenous painters and artisans made formed part of a multifaceted politics of the image in the colonial era. The missionaries established powerful stories about the past and present through these paintings and statues. Indigenous painters brought their own visual systems, iconography, and great figures into their interpretations of this visual order, and they created narrative interpretations of things Spanish and Catholic in their painting and artisanal work.[10]

THE ARCHANGEL RAPHAEL AND A CHUMASH SAINT

One of the controversies about understanding Indigenous colonial painting has revolved around interpreting the image in relationship to the European figures that served as the basic models. For too long images like the Chumash painting of Raphael were dismissed as "poor imitations." Art historian George Kubler, whose influential work is typical of the older approach, argued that preconquest visual forms "became extinct, save for a few weak after-images, during the sixteenth century" when speaking of central Mexico. He elaborated, "The extirpation of native observances by the religious authorities was so vigorous that the last gasps of the bearers of Indian rituals and manners expired unheard" during the seventeenth century.[11] For years art historians ignored colonial Indigenous painting, while colonial statutes often treated Indigenous artisans as "untrained and unlicensed" status as painters.[12] Art historian Kurt Baer echoed this attitude when he dismissed the Chumash painting of the Archangel Raphael, as a "crude" work.[13]

FIGURE 4. A Chumash Painting of the Archangel Raphael. Painted at
Mission Santa Ines, c. 1825. The painting currently hangs on the walls
of Mission Santa Inés. Courtesy of the Santa Bárbara Mission
Archive-Library.

Today most scholars have abandoned the assumptions that Indigenous
people soon forgot their culture and world views, and instead ask how precolonial visual systems, iconography, and cultural knowledge found their way
into colonial painting. Art historians like Carolyn Dean identify Indigenous
colonial painting as having "both/and" qualities, meaning that they reflect
elements of each culture they are working with, and offer something new.[14]
Others identify "converging and diverging" cultures and devotional practices,
and emphasize the multiplicity and diversity of meanings that Indigenous

societies in the Americas came to attribute to Christian objects such as the cross.[15]

As first discussed in the introduction, the painting of the Archangel Raphael offers an extraordinary image of a Chumash leader as a Catholic saint. With his relatively dark coloring, wearing a cloak typically worn by Chumash men, and holding an effigy of the killer whale used by the 'Antap leadership in Chumash territory as a ritual icon, with its black fin extending upward into the creases of the archangel's clothing, this image is unique. The cross at the center of the headband suggests Spanish dominance, but the painting as a whole presents a Chumash concept of angel, leader, and healer, thereby contesting the erasure of history, memory, and political structures sought by the missionaries. The painter created an image that brought Chumash symbols and visual logic into the rendition of Raphael.[16] The image assigns the power of the archangel as both healer and guardian to a Chumash figure, while attributing Chumash authority to a Christian saint. It speaks to the strong Indigenous leadership within the Chumash missions, and gives form to the Chumash Catholicism that emerged as translators and godparents rendered Catholic ideas in their own languages and through their own interpretations.

The Chumash painting of the Archangel Raphael constitutes one of the rare figurative canvas paintings executed by an Indian at the California missions. Though trained in European-style painting, the painter (unsigned) does not seem to master the different elements of European technique in representing the archangel. The figure of Raphael takes up the entire canvas. He stands on clouds and his feet are buried in them. There is no scenery or backdrop. The painter did not use underpaint, and his order of approach differed from that of a guild artist. He painted the whale first, with the foreground and background around it; both elements would normally have been painted first and the fish afterward.[17] The figure is two-dimensional and not anatomically correct. The archangel depicted does not have shoulders or a neck, his knees and feet are sideways, and the painter left little room for the two arms. The painter boldly outlined the body and cape. The cape stands straight out and stiff, and the strokes of applied paint are uneven.

Raphael means "God heals," and, according to the Old Testament, the archangel came to earth dressed as a pilgrim. He dispelled devils and cured illness and blindness using different parts of a fish. The church determined that Raphael's representation should include a fish, humble dress, and wings, and other paintings commonly include a healing pouch on a staff. This image of the archangel is probably based on a painting, print, or tin representation of the Archangel Raphael.

Yet many of the formal elements in the painting come from Chumash iconography and style, lending the image specific and figurative meaning: making reference to a specific leader and talisman and offering a larger image of Chumash leadership and religious authority. European painters generally portrayed the fish as small and thin and dangling from a string, but the Chumash painter used

FIGURE 5. Chumash Whale Effigies. Two whale effigies from the archaeological site Las Llagas. The site dates to 700–500 B.C. Courtesy of the Santa Barbara Museum of Natural History.

instead a local fishlike icon, based on a mammal or dorsal whale, cradled in the archangel's arm. The flat tail, rounded face, large eye, mouth, and dorsal fin resembled one of the many kinds of whale effigies or ritual objects that were carved in stone for centuries in Chumash territory.[18] People carried these effigies as personal talismans. In painting and as effigies, they represented one of the many dream helpers or spirits who guided the shaman through his or her ritual experience and aided the shaman in accessing the knowledge and power previously attained in trance states.[19]

The fact that the depicted archangel carried this effigy relates the figure back to the 'Antap religious-political organization. Its members governed ritual life, healing, and politics in Chumash territory. The same leaders who formed the 'Antap council often held high positions within the missions as cantors, skilled artisans, painters, alcaldes, and translators. Their work contributed to the rendering of Catholic belief into Chumash languages and cultural frameworks.

The painted archangel, with his direct stance and serious gaze, suggests the strong claim to authority held by this figure and affirms the presence of Chumash leadership, ritual, thought, and culture within the missions (discussed in the previous chapter). The painting presented the things required to identify Raphael, yet the overall image conforms to Chumash visual logic. The painter used a Chumash painting technique found at painted rock sites when he outlined the image and cape in red and black. The archangel's cape does not fall in a way that imitates fabric, but stands outward, with no conceivable model in European fashion. (Chumash men, especially those in leadership positions, wore hide capes.) The area within the cape is composed of visibly uneven painted strokes and may indicate a geographic region, such as that governed by an 'Antap tribal leader or the Wot.[20]

Many elements link the painting to the Chumash concept of the sacred. They include the headband; the whale as effigy held by this archangel; and the use of outline technique and colors common in Chumash painting. The image of the Archangel Raphael appears in the final inventory of goods at Mission Santa Inés in 1845 with the reference "painted by an Indian" *(pintado por indio)*.[21]

Chumash society had a long and specific tradition of painting. That may explain this rare representation of these favored saints on canvas. In the precolonial era, artisans devoted their work to making pigments for paint. These traditions fostered the canvas painting and vivid artisanal work done at Santa Inés and other Chumash missions in the colonial era. Chumash painting tradition created a particularly vivid visual world and narrative depictions of events. Chumash territory had a spiritual geography of painted rocks and caverns, shrines of rocks and of stone figurines adorned with plumage, red wooden seafaring canoes, decorated bowls, bright arrows, bows, and spears for hunting, and vibrant cemeteries with images and color on wooden planks, poles, and whalebone.[22]

From the first Spanish expeditions through Chumash territory in 1542, writers reported pictures painted on funeral posts in the cemeteries. More than two centuries later, members of the Fagas expedition again noted the grave markers or boards that recorded events and the person's affiliations and status through various pictures and figures.[23] They sometimes painted the personal talisman and charms that the individual wore for protection and luck. They helped create the painted world in which colored canoes took beads to the mainland and trade goods to the islands, and painted flagpoles with feathers and narrative markers identified gravesites and the social position of the dead.

The Chumash worked from a visual narrative tradition, and among Chumash people and other tribes in California, painting also contributed to create the sacred world with painted bodies, painted rocks, and the painting of sand during ceremonies. Yet these painting traditions differed from Spanish canvas painting and conventions. Colonial Luiseño indicates that European painting and writing had been placed in a separate category from Luiseño design and form. Ñautí meant to "signal or signify," and to paint and to write. Ñauicat meant one who makes the sign, the painter, and the writer.[24] In giving writing and painting the word *ñautí*, Luiseño translators placed Spanish painting and writing in the realm of a particular kind of narration and distinguished the process from Luiseño design (referred to as *eskan-ish*), embracing the creation of figures, markings, basketry, woven patterns, and tattoos. Sand painting was called *eskanish tarchayish,* words that bore little relationship to *ñauíi* or colonial painting and writing.[25] The word *ñauíi* placed Spanish-inspired painting in the narrative realm of writing.

A final reflection on the Archangel Raphael as the subject of this painting: the church encouraged the adoption of these archangels as patron saints in missions and in Indigenous confraternities and parishes. Saint Michael became the patron saint of the California missions in 1779. The Archangel Michael also held a special place in Chumash territory, especially at Mission San Buenaventura. The missionaries named the Indian chapel at San Buenaventura after Saint Michael.[26] The important post-harvest festival of *Hutash,* which took place sometime in September in the precolonial era, began to be held at San Buenaventura on Saint Michael's Feast Day, September 29. Christian and non-Christian Indians came from all around for dancing and other rituals that lasted for days.[27] Saints were avengers of God; they cast out the bad angel Lucifer from heaven and protected the heavens. As patron saints, they protected and defended their followers. As militant figures, Michael and Raphael offered a particularly multivalent image for resistance and native power.

THE POLITICS OF THE IMAGE

The Chumash painting of the Archangel Raphael is especially rare because it defied the Spanish politics of the image that had predominated since the late sixteenth century and held sway thereafter in church policy that was upheld by the colonial state and that guided practice in the early nation. But initially, for the first half-century of the Spanish presence in Mexico, the native elite learned Spanish, sometimes Latin, and European conventions of writing and painting in monasteries built from the stones of Aztec and other Indigenous sacred and governmental structures. Using new and pre-Columbian methods, they recreated codices that embodied the sacred scriptures and the historical, religious, genealogical, and tributary information recorded in precolonial times on deer hide and *agave* bark.[28] Incorporating long-standing practices such as feather work, they absorbed the European image into another sensibility.

They created painterlike images made of delicate feathers of many colors, thus making the European figure speak to their own tactile relationship to sacred objects. Those early works could be understood from multiple perspectives. It was an era when Nahuas and other Indigenous elite had a closer relationship to, and a more direct role in, the transposition of Christianity to the Americas.[29] Even during that era, it was very rare that a painting or image of one of the virgins, crucifixions, or saints around whom regional dimensions of Catholicism developed appeared with Indian features, as found in the Chumash painting of the Archangel Raphael.

By the late sixteenth century, the church had changed its policies governing the image. During the Council of Trent that met between December 13, 1545, and December 4, 1563, the church adopted regulations to avoid the influence of heretics and popular religiosity in Europe and elsewhere. The council decreed that religious painting must demonstrate iconographic accuracy whereby particular symbols, objects, and colors identified each virgin, saint, angel, and the representation of events. Persons and scenes had to evince "stylistic realism" by conforming to three-dimensional representation and European likeness. Following these same aesthetic conventions, the regulations demanded that paintings be "spiritually uplifting" with poses that showed devotion, religious ecstasy, and appealing scenes of martyrdom. They discouraged paintings that recounted popular legends or history. They encouraged biblical stories.[30] When applied to America, the council's edicts discouraged Indigenous artists from introducing pre-Columbian iconography, visual practice, and history into their paintings. Religious architecture had to similarly conform to the edicts rather than embrace vernacular forms.[31]

The edicts privileged the position of European master painters who began to settle in urban centers in Mexico and Peru by the mid-sixteenth century. The first guild in Mexico City, established in 1557, brought the "correct practice of their art" to the colony.[32] The *Ordenanzas de pintores y doradores* (Statutes of Painters and Gilders) allowed master painters to establish workshops, employ apprentices, and examine them in figure drawing, classical interpretation, and in three-dimensional perspective. Passing the exam enabled the apprentice to become a master of his own workshop or head of a monastery workshop.[33] The master painter's name appeared on the paintings, and he negotiated the contract, thereby determining the selection of clients, subject matter, form, and terms. Most New World guilds allowed only Spanish, Creole, and, with less consistency, *mestizo* artists to attain the lucrative rank of master. Indians, blacks, and *castas* constituted the majority of journeymen.

The Mexican guilds never allowed Indian apprentices and journeymen to become master painters, and Indigenous painters were restricted from the position of master painter elsewhere in the Americas. The work of most native painters remained anonymous. Even where Indigenous painters received notoriety and prominence, they "were seldom given adequate credit or recognition by their patrons."[34] Mestizos and African-descent *castas,* in contrast, rose in the ranks and could attain the status of master painter by the late seventeenth century, when Juan Correa became well known.[35]

Although workshops run by guild masters produced a proliferation of images with a European form and aesthetic, Nahua communities of central Mexico demonstrated the ways those images could be used to sustain their connections to the sacred. They incorporated a patron saint to guard their town and used images of the saints in their household and religious activity in a way that showed the images' persistent potential to give expression to devotional practices and beliefs that orig-inated prior to the introduction of Catholicism. They did so despite the control exerted over the representation of the saints through the guilds, the Inquisition court, and the persistent wariness of the clergy against the creation of idols.

Colonial documents written in Náhuatl reveal that "no other aspect of Chris-tian religious belief and ritual had a remotely comparable impact" on as broad a range of activity as did the devotion to the saints.[36] Wills, testaments, and city archives written by native scribes from the mid-seventeenth century onward, with the demographic recovery of the Indigenous population, show most Nahuas in the Toluca Valley "worshipping the holy images on private altars, providing candles, flowers, and incense, and embracing the honorific job of sweeping around them."[37]

Sweeping for the saints remained consistent with the precolonial practice in which women swept as an important act to purify the home among their highly patterned and ritualized housekeeping activities that were "surrounded by taboos and linked to the gods."[38] When they could afford to, households built oratories to house their precious images. Within a century after the Spanish invasion, many Indian towns had patron saints around whom the entire population unified to celebrate the saint's calendar day or feast, prayed to in times of disaster, and forged religious brotherhoods to guide and protect that devotion. Every household sought to possess one or more saints of its own. Parents named children after the town patron, but even more frequently, they named their children after family saints, many of whom they passed down to their descendants for generations.[39]

Sweeping for the saints constituted a daily activity that women asked others to pursue for them after their deaths, and men and women both bequeathed "saints' land" with instructions to cultivate maize and maguey on it. The proceeds pro-vided for the saints' care, including the purchase of wax for candles, flowers, and other objects of veneration, and paid for ceremonies and feast days in their honor.[40] The population exerted control over Catholic images by bringing them into more ancient devotional practices.

Village and family saints varied among the extensive number of Náhautl com-munities, while for the large and equally diverse communities of ethnic Otomí, veneration of the cross or crucifix developed early in the colonial period. For the Otomí, the cross carried "a bundle of meanings for social and personal well-being" and continued to hold the central place in household shrines over other family saints through the colonial period.[41] Veneration among the Otomí developed for one cross in particular—the *cristo renovado*, a large crucified Christ—that became known as a miraculous image after it began to show signs of life, to perspire, make noise, shed blood, and perform miracles. As ethnic Otomí migrated for work dur-ing the colonial era and established new communities through a large area of the present states of Hidalgo, Querétaro, and Guanajuato, their devotion to the cross migrated with them.[42]

The church imposed a politics of the image meant to control its meaning, but the use of images conformed to both old and new practices within communities. It is important to understand how Indigenous painters worked their own visual vocabulary and iconography into colonial painting when they could, as in the Cuzco school of painting that flourished in the Andes from the 1650s through the 1780s. Indigenous and colonial societies differed within and between each other in Peru and California, but Andean painting offers a counterpoint: a view of Andean representations of things Spanish, or the study of painting by comparing interpretive processes.

In colonial Cuzco, the pre-Columbian center of the Incan Empire, there had congregated extraordinary craftsmen. Andean artists, who had labored for a century in painters guilds that assigned them a lesser status, began to break out of their roles as journeymen and to establish their own workshops.[43] They achieved greater and greater degrees of commercial independence through the commissions they received from the bishop of Cuzco and from Indigenous parishes in and around Cuzco. The Andean elite, composed of landowners, colonial administrators, and others of noble Incan or Andean background, similarly offered their patronage, as did the occasional Spanish administrator. Merchants commissioned these paintings in large numbers to sell to a wide range of customers across the Andes. They ordered pieces by the dozens for the less affluent customers. By the early eighteenth century, La Paz, Bolivia, had become a second center of Andean painting, and the style and form of the work traveled through the Andes as painters adopted it and paintings were sold into Argentina and Chile.[44]

Cuzcueño painters infused their work with Andean representations of the sacred while conforming to the subject matter imposed by Spanish convention and law. Images of the Virgin Mary and of the archangels constituted characteristic subjects of Andean painters. Andeans didn't have a painting tradition prior to the Spanish. They incorporated into painting the iconography of textile design and metal work, producing elaborately clothed saints and gilded paintings.

The paintings remained unsigned, characteristic of guild restraints. Yet they offer a visual vocabulary that conveyed historical, aesthetic, spiritual, and social significance to the Andean viewer. For example, the Virgin Mary was commonly painted as a flat two-dimensional statue whose triangular figure resembled a mountain in ornately designed dress. The design on the dress, together with the planar approach to the physical body, created the effect of tapestry. Richly woven cloth inscribed with symbols constituted a critical way of conveying the status and lineage of the wearer in Andean society. The elaborate clothing of the painted images spoke to the sensibility developed in the Andean textile tradition.[45] The prominence of representation of Andean textile design in paintings of the Virgin, angels, and other figures made sense in a society that stored knowledge through the tactile and visual system of the Incan *quipu,* a nonlinear structure made of cotton and wool cords, colored, spun, twisted, and knotted in particular ways, rather than in writing or painting.. The *quipu* held and conveyed various kinds of information through the abstract system of twists and knots. The one who made the *quipu* delivered the stored information orally when called upon.[46]

The planar figure of the Virgin replicated the quality of *wak'as* or *huacas,* household deities venerated daily. As sacred objects, they embodied a power that could be transferred to the Christian saints and images. The deities predated Inca imperial domination, and their worship as domestic or household gods persisted into the colonial period. Representations of the Virgin also referred back to female deities in Andean ritual and belief such as Pachamama (earth mother). The choice and placement of Native flora and fauna filled the background of these paintings, and the type and placement of flowers and the decorated garment represented specific female deities.[47] The scenery itself sometimes referred to specific Andean sacred places.

Some of the same design elements entered a series of paintings of angels that gained wide popularity after 1660 across the Altiplano from northern Peru to northern Argentina. The paintings, called *Arquebusiers,* tamed the angel soldiers, who commonly carried *arquebuses* (Spanish guns that inspired the name of the series) by making them into playful, highly decorated figures. The presence of arms seemed to contradict the extraordinary splendor of dress, intensity of presence, and air of freedom and delicacy with the proliferation of lace and rainbow-colored wings that distinguished the Andean painting. Though initially imitating the series of angels sent from Europe, these Andean images found no parallels in European depictions.[48] The paintings of the Archangel Raphael would accompany those of Archangels Michael and Gabriel in every series. Raphael could also be found alone, a playful figure who, in one work, dragged a big fish behind him. In another, he threw it over his back.[49]

Marie Timberlake has argued, "The painted image in colonial Peru acted as a stage upon which the political pretensions of different institutions and social groups (religious, civil, wealthy residents of diverse ethnic backgrounds) were displayed for public consumption, veneration, and affirmation." As in California, the walls of the church constituted the most prominent public interior space. They "provided the principal locale for the exhibition of one's status within the community."[50] Andean patrons commissioned paintings of religious scenes and events that often gave expression to specific rivalries and long-existing ethnic tensions between Andean communities.[51] The crowd scenes represented in a series of Corpus Christi paintings, for example, constituted a kind of rivalry to gain or assert contested status.[52] Cuzcueño painters also made portraitures of Andean elites who served as the link between the Andean communities and colonial authorities. Represented in Andean embroidered clothing, replete with its lavish meanings, those paintings offered a means to codify the elites' status within colonial society.[53]

These paintings had the subversive potential of narrating a colonial world under terms that loomed out of authorities control, and after the Tupac Amaru II rebellion of 1780, the government prohibited this genre of painting. It also restricted the use of traditional native garments, especially the elaborate textiles worn by the nobility. The government insisted, instead, that Andeans wear Spanish dress. Painters were henceforth required to follow the established guidelines governing painting, including those concerning perspective and realistic form.[54]

FRANCISCAN-FAVORED IMAGES AND THE DICTATES FOR PAINTING CALIFORNIA

At a time when the authorities in Peru began to restrict Andean painting and representation, Franciscans were bringing their saints to California in 1769. In the Andean world, contending groups vied for narrative representation on the walls of the church, and in California that process had a distinct history. It began during the first years of settlement, when the prints and imported goods introduced a new vocabulary.

Images of the Virgin Mary, the cross, and the archangels were among the first things sought by the missionaries, together with the image of each mission's patron saint. Every mission eventually displayed paintings that represented heaven, hell, and paradise, and saints who represented the themes of evangelization, martyrdom, and Christ's death on the cross. Each Franciscan mission possessed representations of the fourteen Stations of the Cross, which held a special significance for the Franciscans. In 1342 the pope made the Franciscan Order guardians of the site of Calvary, and in 1686 Pope Innocent XI granted them the sole right to hang the paintings of the Stations of the Cross in their churches. In 1731 the papacy extended that right to all Catholic churches, placing the Franciscans in charge of hanging them.[55]

The images used to establish the mission at San Diego remained fairly representative of the core visual vocabulary of the Franciscans in California. Fray Junípero Serra brought a set of the fourteen paintings of the Stations of the Cross to the mission in 1769. He also brought paintings representing Christ's judgment, death on the cross, and resurrection, emphasizing separately some of the scenes found in the paintings of the Stations of the Cross. Reflecting the veneration shown for the Virgin throughout Latin America and Spain, eight of the mission's eighteen original paintings represented the Virgin Mary. The cross, ever present in Christian iconography and among common gifts to new Christians and their families, formed one of the most repeated images found in each mission. San Diego had three representations of the cross.[56]

Mission San Carlos, headquarters of the California missions, early accumulated the largest collection of images that documented the Franciscans' own connections to the divine. Within a few years the mission acquired a silver cross adorned by little crystal crosses that contained a relic of the cross on Calvary, where Jesus Christ hung and died. A paper guaranteed its authenticity. A large engraving represented the genealogy of the Franciscan Order via portraits hung on a tree. Three sets of prints on "fine paper" displayed the saints, popes, and cardinals and the "Most Reverend Generals of the Order."[57] The Franciscans used the walls to display pictures of their own hierarchy and to affirm their connection to the sacred.

They also emphasized the story of the new convert and the missionary martyr. Santa Inés, patron saint of Mission Santa Inés, offered the example of a child convert who lived among gentiles, like many youth at the mission who continued to reside with their parents in Indigenous villages after their baptism. A virgin martyr, she accepted death at the age of thirteen rather than deny her allegiance to Christianity by giving up her faith.

Santa Bárbara, another virgin martyr and patron saint of a mission, had a similar story. A young woman who converted to Catholicism without the consent of her pagan father, she refused to marry the non-Christian chosen by her father. When her father killed her with his own hands in anger, lightning immediately struck him down. Guilds of workers such as those who made fireworks took her as their patron long before the church recognized her as a saint. For populations living within highly evangelized situations, however, she and similar martyrs spoke to the long history of conversion that sometimes situated the convert against their family and society, and celebrated those who gave up their lives in defense of the new faith.

The paintings and prints offered multivalent meanings about the world of Spanish and Catholic objects, history, and the sacred. Images and sculptures of the saints gave a form to the Christian names given to or chosen by every convert upon baptism. While each name could be linked to a biblical story, the visual representation of the person bearing the name provided a way to imagine the story. They also placed things the Spanish brought, such as sheep, into a narrative framework. The number of sheep rose more rapidly than that of cattle in California. Their foraging destroyed thousands of acres of seed fields over time, but their wool provided an essential material for the textile factories and production of clothing at the missions. To represent the Virgin as shepherdess tending the flock visually related things Spanish to the divine.

Soldiers, settlers, missionaries, and trade ships carried favored local saints from Mexico to California, as happened with the Virgin of the Agave Mexicana (maguey cactus plant). The image is common in central Mexico among Otomí Indians and other communities represented among the soldiers in California. A painting of the Virgin at Mission Dolores in San Francisco depicted a large cactus from the middle of which rose the Virgin instead of a flower stalk. In central Mexico, the Virgin Mary came to be associated with agrarian rites. "In some colonial Indian villages there were fields of maguey named for the Virgin Mary," and in the late eighteenth century, people sometimes referred to the Virgin of Guadalupe as the Mother of Maguey.[58] Guadalupe, and other images of the Virgin of Immaculate Conception, also exerted strong appeal as patrons of hospitals and guardians against illness. The Virgin's association with growth, abundance, fertility, and healing situated her images among the most common miraculous figures. At Mission Dolores in San Francisco, the missionary told von Langsdorf that she had performed many "extraordinary miracles" for those who had prayed to her.[59]

The missionaries distinguished between the devotional image of great beauty and inspiration, which they found crucial to their own devotion and to generate, they believed, greater devotion in others, and more common images. Some they used explicitly to teach about Catholicism. Serra ordered some things "directly concerned with the spiritual side of the missions . . . a little statue, a painting, or a holy picture for teaching the gentiles." [60] Such images for pedagogy included a canvas of "the Judgment, Heaven and Hell with Indians" ordered by Mission San José in 1807–08, a time when the mission also acquired extremely valuable paintings, a monstrance (used to display the host for communion and often elaborately designed in gold), a chalice, and other goods to enhance devotional practice.[61] High-quality paintings constituted a common acquisition.

Serra struggled to get good images from the Franciscan monastery headquarters in Mexico because of the greater devotion they might inspire. In commissioning a painting of the patron saint of each mission for their main altars, he asked that they be made with the ability to inspire. About San Juan Capistrano he wrote, "It should not be painted by any kind of painter. . . . They should find a good engraving and have Páez paint it, or some other good artist."[62] Two years later he again desperately sought someone who could paint an inspiring image. Serra suggested that "Father Castro might get together with the painter Páez and arrange for both paintings," including one of San Francisco. [63] Serra referred to the painter José de Páez a well-known painter in Mexico, known for small formats, delicate tones, and prolific work that he often painted for convents. He painted at least eleven escudos, beautiful and elaborate devotional badges worn by some orders of nuns.[64]

Aware of how easily the images lent themselves to interpretation, Serra attempted to control their message, emphasizing time and again that the saints' clothing not be painted in blue, the color of the vestments worn by Indian sacristans who assisted at masses and other liturgical ceremonies. In December 1774, for example, Serra ordered "two cassocks of blue cloth . . . for the sacristans" and four of the same in red for big feast days. Blue also constituted the most common color used for Indian clothing. As Missionary Payeras wrote from Mission La Purísima, their looms produced "five lengths of blue cloth and an equal amount of hemp cloth similar to coarse brown linen."[65]

Friars of the Apostolic College of San Fernando used grey habits, which predominated in California, but many friars in Mexico wore blue habits. Mexican painters therefore frequently sent paintings of the saints and members of the order represented in blue.[66] Serra expressed his frustration about the use of blue clothing and repeatedly requested painters to avoid blue cassocks for the saints.[67] In his request for paintings by Páez of San Francisco and San Juan Capistrano he added, "His habit should not be blue, as in other pictures which have come here."[68] At a later point he again pleaded that San Juan Capistrano and San Francisco be painted in colors similar to the Franciscans' clothing. "Above all things," he wrote, the "scheme should not be a blue habit but of an ash gray."[69]

The missionaries' behavior conveyed the importance religious images and objects held for them and how to properly interact with them. To announce the arrival of special paintings, statues, or other religious objects, the missionaries held religious festivals and processions and provided extra or special food to the native population attending and residing at the mission. When a statue of the Virgin of Dolores arrived at Monterey, Serra "made arrangements with the officers aboard ship and the crew of the boat to hold solemn festivities for the blessing of a new statue."[70] The gift of an expensive monstrance, which Serra welcomed to raise the "dignity of divine worship," also arrived in that shipment. In his sermon during the celebratory mass, he mentioned the gift sent to what he called "these new Christian lands," boldly redefining the geography of a region still organized and possessed by tribal society.[71]

As Serra sang mass, cannons shot to celebrate the monstrance far and wide, announcing the triumph of Christ over the new land. The missionaries also greeted religious objects and paintings with gun salutes whose sound extended the missions' spatial possession through sound beyond the boundaries they could claim in the early years. (By 1775, the mission in Monterey had acquired a big bell and twenty-four guns for religious celebrations.) The Indian population at Monterey received an extra portion of meat during the celebration of the monstrance, perhaps meant by the missionaries to encourage an alliance with the host that became Christ's body when blessed.[72]

The Franciscans themselves coveted beautiful images and objects for their own devotional practice. They sought images that spoke to their aesthetic and emotional sensibility and to create a world around them and within the church that mirrored their purpose and place in history. The missionaries consistently conveyed their belief in the sacred power embodied in the image through their ritual interaction with it. Because there were few paintings in Monterey initially, Serra borrowed one belonging to the inspector general while his boat rested in port. "That day and the next, they sang in Spanish (rather than Latin, so all soldiers and sailors could participate) the Salve Regina, in harmony, in front of the wonderful painting of Our Lady, which was on the altar."[73]

Serra writes vividly about his relationship to images that he imagined could offer him protection, guidance, inspiration, and intercession with God. He showered them with devotion and protected himself with paintings and crosses. During a small attack by warriors on Mission San Diego in its initial months of existence in 1769, Serra sought recourse in prayer and images. He held the picture of the Virgin Mary in one hand and a cross that he identified as "her Divine Crucified Son" in the other as arrows rained everywhere around him. He believed "that with such defense either I would not have to die, or that I would die well, great sinner that I am."[74]

Serra expressed a personal, intimate, and emotional relationship to certain paintings, a stance that formed a fundamental part of Catholicism and would have been shared by other missionaries. For a Corpus Christi mass held in a half-finished warehouse, the soldiers decorated the place so "tastefully" that, Serra wrote, "In me it excited devotion." Serra placed a strongly devotional image of Mary on the altar and described her active agency and presence. He writes, "She stood on guard over the church, whilst her Most Holy Son passed" through the crowd in the monstrance that Serra held high as he walked in the procession through gathered Christian and non-Christian Indians, sailors, and soldiers.[75]

Shortly thereafter Serra discovered the first shipments of three paintings and wrote, "My delight knew no bounds. We took my saints on shore to remain there. We put them on the altar, and there was the Blessed Virgin surrounded by Cardinals and her lay sacristan, seemingly as pleased as could be."[76] When a painting of Saint Anthony was presented to the friars at the mission, they similarly reacted with intimacy and emotion. They "kissed, over and over again, their holy patron saint" and expressed their enthusiastic admiration for it and another painting that Serra carried.[77]

AN INDIGENOUS SACRED LANDSCAPE

An elaborate visual vocabulary of abstract and representational painting and design existed in precolonial California. It was present in the missions with tattooing and body painting for dance. The particular form and colors lent meanings that varied by place. In the Chumash swordfish dance, for example, the dancer's face was painted in green and then spotted with red, white, and blue dots to signify a swordfish and draw that spirit form into the dancer.[78] Painting on rock, sand, and wood formed part of the visual logic present throughout the state, although again, distinct forms held discrete meanings according to the region.

Painted images formed part of the sacred geography that existed throughout southern and central California. Petroglyphs painted on rocks and in caves existed within each territory and at some shared sites. Shamans and, to a lesser extent, people undergoing puberty, healing, and other ceremonies created the rock and cave painting after ritually taking *toloache,* the most common hallucinogen that produced an altered state of consciousness. It enabled a person to enter a trance state and to begin a vision quest in the realm of the supernatural. During the quest, they encountered spirit helpers, also referred to as dream helpers, shaman's familiars, and *?atishwin*. These spirit helpers would guide them through the experience and help them attain the specialized knowledge or power they sought. It might have to do with healing, astrology, or with influencing such things as harvests, luck in hunting, fertility, and the weather. The petroglyphs depicted one or more of the spirit helpers whom the person encountered in his or her trance. After the trance, or sometimes while still in it, the individual would paint the spirit helper.[79]

The motifs included representational images, abstract images, and anthropomorphic and zoomorphic figures, all of which represented spirit guides encountered during a trance.[80] Zigzag and diamond chain motifs commonly referred to the rattlesnakes who acted as guardians of the portals to the sacred space. People throughout the region considered the rattlesnake to be one of the first beings seen upon entering the supernatural world and to be a protector of that world. Concentric circles or spirals represented the concentration of supernatural power in the whirlwind. Other geometric designs included vulva-shaped motifs. One of the images, a mandala-like figure, represented the sun as spirit helper.[81]

Some paintings depicted the shaman himself in trance. Some theorize these painted images embodied the memory of the trance experience. One could return to the sites in order to renew the power and knowledge received in the altered state or to revitalize the knowledge gained. The powers could also be embodied in *?atishwin* or talisman. *?Atishwin* also "refers to supernatural power in general, as possessed not only by spirits, human beings, and animals, but even by things and places."[82] Effigies and *?atishwin* represented the spirit helpers and became the personal talismans of the shamans. The people who sought a particular shaman would often carry or wear the shaman's talisman for luck and protection.

An intimate relationship existed between the talisman and the dream helper who guided the shaman and initiates through their ritual experience.[83] Sculpted in bone, rock, or wood, the objects were sometimes painted. These images proliferated in the large and socially stratified villages where Chumash men and women specialized in craft production. In nearly all Indigenous California societies involved in these practices, people wore talismans that identified their particular affiliations to a shaman or a community protected by particular powers. The effigies might be representational like the whale held in the painting of the Archangel Raphael. They also would be made in the zoomorphic and anthropomorphic figures found painted at rock sites.

Rocks played an extremely significant role in spiritual life, and their cracks, crevices, and holes served as portals to the supernatural. "Entering a rock" constituted one of the metaphors for going into a trance. These sites often could be found near permanent bodies of water; water also served as a metaphor for entering a trance state. It transported individuals between the sacred and profane. Other metaphors for entering the trance state included words and images involving death and killing, going underwater or drowning, flight, and sexual intercourse.[84]

Shamans owned most rock sites for their private vision quests, but throughout southern California communal initiatory painting also created a collective set of images as sites of memory of the knowledge gained by the young in their puberty rites. The puberty ceremonies associated with Chinigchinich thought and ritual have been studied especially among Luiseños, where painting during puberty ceremonies occurred after the ingestion of hallucinogens. Girls and boys painted the images of the spirit helpers they acquired during the trance on rocks near their villages. Gendered distinction in motifs and color existed at these sites. The female initiates tended to paint zigzags and diamond chains, referring to the rattlesnake helper who assisted them in their trance. They painted in red, the color associated with women. The boys' sites tended to be painted in black. The intertwining of red and black suggested the joining of the sexes.

Sand or ground painting involved both the creation of ritual space and a sphere in which the shaman could interact with the sacred. Luiseño and Kumeyaay peoples made ground paintings, as did some other societies in California.[85] The shaman painted by sprinkling colored sands, powdered charcoal, or pigment in a space dug out and shaped for the painting. The paintings represented elements of the universe via the colors used, geometric patterns, and tactile differences such as the creation of mounds within the painting. Among Luiseños, sand painting was used in at least four ceremonies, all connected to the idea of initiation into particular kinds of knowledge and becoming prepared for various stages of life, such as in the girls' and boys' ceremonies.[86]

Among the Kumeyaay, there appears to have been a single or most common type of sand painting. It involved representation of local topography around the village where it was painted and abstract representations of sacred figures. But here too, the painting both represented the universe and allowed shamans and others involved in the ritual to act upon the world.[87]

MISSION CHURCHES

The iconography and colors of native California often influenced the painted design of the churches, something most clearly seen in the early churches and in the poorer, smaller missions. In every mission the painting of native artisans influenced the visual order. Large caches of pigments to produce paint accompanied each shipment of imported canvas paintings. Native artisans painted the elaborately designed churches. Even as the imports increased, such as in 1792, when Mission San Diego received twenty-three paintings; Mission San Gabriel, nineteen paintings; and Mission San Juan Capistrano, ten paintings, the shipment still included pounds for painting: red lead, white lead, ochre, and vitriol.[88]

A book to teach painting without an instructor constituted one of the first things ordered by missionaries at Mission San Gabriel in 1771.[89] In the many missions with elaborate baroque design elements, the missionaries and native painters worked without master craftsmen. Instead they made their own stencil cutouts and took designs and drawings from books. Some churches had painting and wallpaper imported from China. To build the churches and other parts of the missions, the government brought artisans from Mexico to teach techniques of plastering, painting, carpentry, and weaving. The missionaries also hired itinerant European painters when available to create elaborately designed and painted walls.

Despite the predominance of European images and themes in the highly painted churches of California, the baroque designs of mission chapels lent themselves to representation of Indigenous iconography with its attendant meanings. As Norman Neuerburg pointed out, the "checkerboard motifs, zigzags and diamond chains, dentates, sun-wheels, mandalas, and simple circles" found at rock art sites had counterparts in European design.[90] Shamanic painting offered the iconography and conceptual framework for a convergence of Indigenous and European traditions. Petroglyph-like images could also be found painted covertly on mission walls, especially at Mission San Juan Capistrano, where Indian painters placed many petroglyph images on the church walls. Painted principally in black, some images also appeared in green and a few red. One seems to be the figure of the Tobet (one of three representations of Chinigchinich).[91] Sometimes these petroglyphic figures formed part of the larger composition, as in the chapel at Pala, founded in the valleys interior to the coastal range. At Mission San Fernando, a painter depicted the image of a bowman in the act of killing a deer. The bowman represents a metaphor for entering a trance state such as produced in a vision quest.[92] Placed over a threshold of the door, it offered a continual memory of the space of the supernatural as lived in shamanic practice.

In the early years at Mission San Luis Obispo, the missionary ordered three dozen prints of saints and pigments for painting the church and surrounding buildings. They derived most of the mission's early decoration from wall painting and Indigenous painted frames and niches that held imported prints and small carvings. Between 1776 and 1778 the mission also acquired four canvas paintings, including that of the patron San Luis Obispo, one of San José, and a painting of paradise and of hell. These hung on the painted walls with framed prints, and with crosses and paper decorations. The walls glittered from the gilded tissue that hung on them and over the rafters.[93]

Like Mission San Luis Obispo in the early 1770s, other early chapels had a few paintings and many prints in frames painted by Indigenous painters: they had crosses and painted walls that glittered from the gilded tissue hung on the walls and over rafters.[94] At Mission San Francisco, one of the earliest *reredos* (altarpiece or painted screens behind the altar) remained intact after the mission built a wall in front of it to support the altar screen imported in 1797. The older, painted *reredos* followed a Spanish pattern common for the era with sacred hearts struck through by a sword and design embellishment around it. Painted by Ohlone artisans, it incorporated the *nichos* or carved spaces in the wall that held sculptures of saints. The embellishment stands out for the featherlike quality of the design. It seems to speak to the multiple uses of feathers in sacred regalia and the particular sensibility toward texture in painting produced by working with feathers in other contexts.[95] The rafters of the adobe church were painted in a chevron design and the colors of red and yellow ochre and white and indigo blue. Rawhide held the rafters together.

The painted walls in the baroque floral and geometric patterns at Mission San Francisco are now hidden under layers of lime, plaster, and whitewash. This largely erodes clear evidence of the different periods and types of design one might find there.[96] The mission's imported work from the Philippines added to the quality of the art and to its baroque and popular (versus elite) dimension, as Filipino colonial artisans often worked from within a translated Catholicism of their own.[97]

Native painters created the internal walls of the church in broad swaths of decorated color and whitewashed surfaces with floral designs, vines, Franciscan cockle shells, painted draped cloth, architectural motifs, and crosses. They stenciled patterns and reproduced decorative design at varying levels of elaboration and complexity and created a combination of abstract geometric and figurative patterns along walls, over doorways and window arches, on the altars and ceilings. This painting, and the designs they placed in the niches where statues stood and on the frames of imported images, influenced how native audiences familiar with such iconography would have understood this European work distinctly.

The missionaries had the outside of mission churches plastered in deep reds and pinks. They imported mirrors to bring greater light into interiors that became more and more elaborate, with silk, brocade, and gilded vestments added to perform particular masses and rituals. All of this was meant to increase, in their conception, the quality of the sacred experience and to augment the belief and reverence expressed by parishioners. Though built in a uniform design, each mission church looked different, according to the history and size of its population, the particular visual histories the Franciscans and Indian populations brought into it, and the way the missionary decided to spend the funds available to him.

Some mission churches changed location in the earlier years; earthquakes destroyed others (especially the major quake of 1812), some burned, and many were expanded. The missionaries replaced some of the earliest adobe structures with large stone churches. This rebuilding makes it difficult to reconstruct anything but fractions of the interiors of the earliest mission churches. Scholars have begun to explore the way some mission and presidio churches seem to be

geographically situated by master craftsmen and missionaries according to the solstice calendar, as found in other parts of Latin America.[98]

At Santa Bárbara the population built three adobe churches. They lengthened
and then replaced the original chapel with a second adobe church in 1789. With
population growth, they began to build another one just four years later in 1793.
Father Tapís, perhaps the only missionary with that skill, painted the church; he
sometimes made patterns to stencil the walls in other churches.[99] By 1820, the
stonemason José Antonio Ramírez finished a second large stone church at Santa
Bárbara. At both missions the mason found a high level of craftsmanship among
the native apprentices who worked with him.

Celebration and patronage marked the opening of new churches. Indian musicians sent from Santa Inés and San Fernando traveled to Santa Bárbara to perform
during the three days of music for the mass, dancing, and other festivities that
accompanied the dedication of the church on September 10, 1820. The missionaries invited Salvador Béjar, a soldier at San Diego Presidio who was a skilled rocket
maker, to prepare fireworks for the celebration.[100] They invited Governor Solá to be
the *padrino* or sponsor at the dedication, which secured his patronage for the
upkeep and further additions to the church and elicited his financial contributions
to pay for the expenses associated with the celebration. From the tower waved flags
of various colors. One of the bell towers from that era fell, and the church replaced
it in 1833, when the Chumash artisan sculpted the solar figure with the cross, flag,
and rattlesnake motif discussed earlier.[101]

Astrology played an important role within native thought, and it would be
common to have a shaman-priest and astrologer learn the trade of mason.[102] In the
bell tower constructed in 1833 for the Santa Bárbara Mission Cathedral, a Chumash mason carved a plaster relief. He had positioned it to be seen from the
ground in front of the church at particular times of day and season.[103]

The image is of a simple, unpainted cross that rested on a pedestal between
slanted spears bearing diamond-shaped points on which triangular flags hung.
Double ribbons flittered on the bottom on the spears. In religious processions, full
flags such as these would be carried and symbolized the victory of the church.
When the newly built stone church on which the tower stood was commemorated,
an Indian carried flags with streamers such as these. Underneath the cross, a band
with zigzags formed a triangular motif in dark and light, and below that, another
zigzag motif was carved at the base of the sculpture. As stated earlier, zigzags often
signified rattlesnake protectors of the supernatural.

The entire motif is open to different readings. It suggests the victory of the
cross, flanked with flags, but the zigzags or rattlesnake protectors ultimately provided the edifice for the victorious cross, thus casting the larger meaning through
Chumash icons. The image suggests that the cross itself rested on Chumash
concepts of sacred power and protection and that Christianity rested on the

FIGURE 6. Chumash Plaster of Paris Image, Bell Tower, Mission Santa Bárbara, 1833. This image was hidden in the bell tower of the mission church except for particular hours and days of the year, when the sun made it visible from the ground. Courtesy of the Santa Bárbara Mission Archive-Library.

foundations of Chumash belief. Perhaps the times that it becomes visible from the ground marked specific dates in the solar or lunar calendar.

In the smaller missions, where the population did not produce enough surplus wealth for the purchase of expensive goods, the Indian choir and orchestra, elaborate vestments, and Indian painting played a larger role in creating inspiration, adornment, and ceremony. Such was the case, for example, at the chapel at Pala at Mission San Luis Rey and the mission churches at San Miguel, Santa Inés, and San Fernando. In these places Indian painters contributed to a vivid aesthetic of painted walls and painted or printed images framed by geometric motifs. Missionaries purchased less expensive objects that had vivid and tactile qualities like mirrors, wax images, and cloth. The missionaries themselves composed music for the masses and Indian orchestras, choirs, and choristers. The missionaries also purchased novenas or ritual prayers.

FIGURE 7. The Chapel at Pala, Mission San Luis Rey. Luiseño Painting of the chapel at Pala. Courtesy of Santa Bárbara Mission Archive-Library.

Native painters decorated the chapel of Pala, a Luiseño village that began to raise crops for Mission San Luis Rey and to maintain a chapel and Christian community as an extension of the mission in 1806. Native artisans painted the chapel virtually without the supervision of a missionary. Although only one or two of the motifs within the painted chapel appeared entirely unrelated to conceivable European prototypes, most had multivalent meanings. The sundials and zigzags that framed the statues and *nichos* constituted very important and frequent images in rock painting. The painters of the chapel also utilized colors common to the smaller missions such as San Miguel and Santa Inés, with a predominance of red, black, and green.[104]

Spanish painter Estevan Carlos Muños, working with native artisans, painted the church at Mission San Miguel from 1818 to 1821. The altar area, with a painted *reredo* in wood, exploded with intricately patterned floral and shell designs elaborately painted in repeated patterns in pastel greens and pinks and included painted draped cloth. At San Miguel and elsewhere, "all-over repetitive designs were inspired by imported fabrics, wall papers, or traditional tile designs."[105] Yet what this imitation of fabric meant to the native population who received fabric as gifts and wore imported and mission-made cloth may have been different from its significance to other viewers. Given its primary role in dress and production at the missions, fabric may have taken on multiple meanings when used as decoration.

The pastel design at Mission San Miguel continued for three-fourths of the church, while the back wall of the church, where the native population stood, squatted, and kneeled, was painted in deep red and black design in bold strokes of rattlesnake or diamond motif outlined in black. Muños "gave leeway to the painters." He "allowed free expression" with designs they copied from books.[106] The red and black pattern carried upward to the choir loft, where the Indian choir performed. The ceiling carried the same black line and thicker red line found on the lower half of the wall in the back. Black also framed the black-red design on the back wall or entrance and on the upper choir loft. The incongruity in the overall painted design and color scheme suggests the character of the California baroque: one infused with a native sensibility.

Unlike many California missions that spent enormous amounts on imported goods for the churches and rituals, Santa Inés began with an inventory brought from other missions or acquired for it prior to its opening. It had mostly unsigned, lesser-quality paintings and sculptures from the monastery workshop in Mexico. Some of the imported paintings suggest they were done by "Indian students or apprentices of art" in Mexico, emphasizing the relative poverty of the mission in its decision to purchase what would be considered lesser-quality paintings.[107]

The mission early directed its resources to procure building materials, pounds of pigment to paint the church and other buildings, and musical instruments to create an orchestra and choir. They spent a large portion of their stipend on gift items to build alliances in the countryside and for the new converts who came in. In 1806, for example, the missionary ordered cloth, tobacco, and mounds of blue beads and purchased masses: three masses for San Felipe de Jesús and others for Santa Inés.[108] With spending focused on attracting affiliates, as with other early missions, the missionaries here spent a significant amount on expensive and elaborate imported vestments and cloth for the altars.

The mission population itself created the rest of the ceremonial splendor through Indian wall painting and carving, the quality of song and music at the mass, mission-made vestments for the priest, and cloth for the altar. Art historian Kurt Baer argued that Santa Ines became a repository of colonial art not because of its acquired paintings but due to "the decorations on the walls and in the carving of wood and leather."[109] In addition, Santa Inés had a choir known for its exquisite sung masses, many of which were written at the mission.[110] The musicians from Santa Inés were well known throughout California, and they traveled to play and to help train others.[111]

The Indigenous quality of the décor at Mission Santa Inés is emphasized in the few purchases made for the newly rebuilt church dedicated in 1817, after the earthquake of 1812 destroyed the original one. The missionaries acquired a gold-plated chandelier and eloquent vestments decorated in silver and gold threads and others made with the finest linens and silks. The missionaries purchased only one set of paintings: the Stations of the Cross. Otherwise they relied on native workmanship. Native artisans painted two *reredos* for the altar in green and purple in 1819, and mission weavers made two sleeveless vestments in colors that matched the *reredos*.[112]

The mission acquired nothing between 1819 and 1825. In contrast, in 1823 alone, nearby Mission La Purísima purchased expensive cloth and vestments, crystal fixtures, four large mirrors, candlesticks, and six oil canvas paintings of various saints.[113] La Purísima had a longer history and a larger population. It accumulated far greater wealth due to the size of its labor force and its long-established trade with the Presidio of Santa Bárbara and foreign ships. The mission church was largely burnt in the Chumash War of 1824; in the ensuing reconciliation, native artisans repainted the church in highly stylized floral and baroque design, faux marble, and Franciscan shells. They repainted new *reredos* and gilded three paintings. Using "Indian coloring" with "reds, yellows, greens, browns, and black predominating," the overall aesthetic suggested the influence of Chumash visual preferences.[114]

The painted church of 1825 at Santa Ines demonstrated the mastery of Spanish technique by the artisans and an Indigenous sensibility in the colors and overall execution of form.[115] The mission also acquired in this era of reconciliation twelve rugs to offer warm seating on the floor to the congregation and twelve cushions of silk and brilliant colors to adorn the altar area. It purchased exquisite vestments and altar cloths. Some Indigenous artisans painted designs on pieces of canvas stretched over wood and bound to the choir arches with strips of rawhide.[116] A piece of that canvas could well have been used for the Indian painting of the Archangel Raphael discussed at the beginning of this chapter.

From within this environment of native painters and artisans who dominated the lexicon and interpreted European material, an Indian painter executed the painting of the Archangel Raphael, the most important figurative work in California. In light of the history of colonial painting, it seems likely that the archangel represented a particular leader in Chumash territory. In general, Indigenous artisans shared the interpretive process with other colonial Indigenous painters. Their work formed part of the colonial visual culture in California.

PERSPECTIVE: THE PAINTINGS OF THE STATIONS OF
THE CROSS FROM MISSION SAN FERNANDO

The San Fernando Mission, founded in the same era as Missions Santa Inés and San Luis Rey, also developed an Indian aesthetic by relying substantially on Indian painting and carving and the use of decorative objects that had pronounced tactile qualities. The mission church had fourteen Stations of the Cross painted by Indian painters at the mission. Though painted by different artisans, they demonstrate a similar representational style. Some Chumash people had affiliated to San Fernando, but the mission stood at a crossroad of Indigenous territories, and the painters' tribal origins are not known.

FIGURE 8. Christ in a Dance Skirt Hanging on the Cross, Mission San Fernando. This is a sculpted figure of a crucified Christ in a dance skirt such as those worn in the Indigenous cultural area of the vicinity. Courtesy of Santa Bárbara Mission Archive-Library.

The mission church used an extensive number of wax figures that evinced a tactile quality and constituted a less expensive purchase; some were perhaps made on site at the tallow factories. By the 1820s, artisans had painted the church facade red, a color that favored the Virgin. Indian painters reproduced European style and themes while they created a highly decorated mission that spoke to particular renderings of Christianity at this mission.

One sculpted image represented Christ in a dance skirt hanging on the cross. This sculpture brought Christ into the vital world of dance and transformed him into someone who could embody the aspirations and visions found in native systems of belief and practice. A sculpture of the Virgin Mary also had attributes

FIGURE 9. Statue of Virgin with Bare Breasts and Feet, Mission San Fernando. The Virgin has strong arms, bare feet, and bare breasts hidden by long hair. Anonymous sculpture. Courtesy of the Santa Bárbara Mission Archive-Library.

relating to an Indigenous woman. Depicted in bare feet with her breasts cloaked by her hair, her arms have the muscles developed from hard physical labor. The image stood in a large niche in the mission church.[118] These two sculptures brought Christ and Mary into Indigenous frames of reference and contemporaneous native thought.

The Stations of the Cross adorned a particularly tactile church in which mirrors, cloth, wax, and intense color predominated. Four large mirrors and four smaller ones about half a yard high served as the *reredos* behind the altar. They reflected images and action back to the main body of the church, and their glimmer replaced the usual painted altarpiece. Cloth was lavishly placed as canopies for statues and for dressing particular saints. Its ample use suggested a vernacular meaning in that cloth was crucial to the dressing of Indigenous converts and a cornerstone of mission production. Indicative of this extensive use of material, a statue of Saint Joseph dressed in a colored garment stood in the front of the altar's wood railing with a canopy of red cloth framing it.[117]

Sometime around 1820, native artisans at San Fernando painted the fourteen Stations of the Cross on canvas, offering a unique interpretation of an event that is central to the origins of Catholicism. The stations depict the story of the death of Christ from his judgment before Pontius Pilate, through his walk to cavalry where he was crucified on the cross, died, and was buried, and then resurrected from the dead.

The stations at San Fernando offer a particular perspective on that story. The fourteen paintings have inconsistencies in scale and in the representation of the clothing worn by the same individual from scene to scene. This and the varied brush strokes indicate more than one painter accomplished the work. The direct source of painting or print from which the painters derived the scenes remains unknown, yet the special features it held, especially the portraits of the horses, offer insight into the painters' understanding of things Christian.[119]

Norman Neuerburg examined the paintings' relationship to possible European prints that might have been used as models. He could not find the exact model, but did find that the painters presented the historic characters in the paintings based on the people they saw around them. The soldiers' uniforms resembled the clothing that men, rather than soldiers, wore between 1800 and 1819.[120] The soldiers' range in color resembled the multiethnic force of European, Indian, African, and mixed-race descent soldiers and colonists who went to California. These scenes also included Indian alcaldes from the mission who carried sticks, often dressed as soldiers, sometimes rode on horseback.[121] Neuerburg could not find any parallels in European work for these elements. Nor for the single feather that emerged from many of the soldiers' helmets.

Other elements that stand out strongly contribute to the paintings' Indigenous form and sensibility. Striking is the representation of the enormous cruelty the soldiers used in their treatment of Jesus. The women are portrayed with jewelry and through their affective manner. The many horses in the series consistently look directly at the viewer. These elements suggest an interpretation of the Christian story from a position that the painters held as *indios* and through an Indigenous sensibility around feather work and the relationship established to horses.

Most of the soldiers have a single feather, in a variety of shapes and sizes, rising from the backs of their helmets. The paint strokes also resemble the texture of feathers. This seems to add an Indigenous iconography related to war. The extensive use of feather work for war and ceremonial regalia in California may have inspired this rendition of an event carried out by the military. Perhaps these feathers make the soldiers into more manageable figures, as did the angelic figures in military uniforms with guns represented by Andean painters. Reimagining their

FIGURE 10. Indian Painted Stations of the Cross, Station Nine, Mission San Fernando, c. 1820. This painting forms one in a series painted by Indigenous artisans at Mission San Fernando. Courtesy of the Seaver Center for Western History, Natural History Museum, Los Angeles.

actual power is especially important given the extreme cruelty in the missions and as demonstrated against Christ.

The soldiers and alcaldes in these prints administered cruelties to Christ more severely than found in most European depictions. In the painting of Station Nine, the soldiers pulled Jesus by a rope tied around his neck from the front and the back and pushed him with one foot on his back. One soldier kicked him on the top of his head once he had fallen. Another pulled his hair from behind. While cruelty exists in the story itself, that particular representation of punishment appears to be very specific. The painters could have easily witnessed soldiers pulling native people at the missions along with a rope, dragging and kicking the person if he resisted, and whipping him sometimes beyond endurance.

The more diminutive female figures of the Virgin Mary and Mary Magdalene wear the jewelry that Spanish and *casta* women wore at the missions and at the presidios.[122] In Station Five a small crowd of women of varying hues of color stand at the side and weep. Where groups of soldiers crowd together in scenes of leading, whipping, pulling, kicking, and crucifying Christ, the women mourn and aid Christ, as they do in biblical accounts of the crucifixion. But unlike the generally vapid expression found on the faces of the soldiers, these women express sorrow, as they do in Station Nine. Present at the mission as wives, widows, and unmarried

FIGURE 11. Indian Painted Stations of the Cross, Station Twelve, Mission San Fernando, c. 1820. The series was painted by more than one Indigenous painter and hung on the walls of Mission San Fernando. Courtesy of the Seaver Center for Western History, Natural History Museum, Los Angeles.

workers, the women did not administer punishment as did the soldiers. In their memoirs, Eulalia Pérez and Apolinaria Lorenzana, who lived and worked at Missions San Gabriel and San Diego, respectively, expressed a sense of Indigenous equality when they discussed training and working with Indian people that is rarely found among settlers.[123]

The effusive amount of blood seen in Stations Ten and Twelve represent the kind of visceral rendition of the bloodied Christ that especially characterized work found in heavily Indigenous parishes. It brings traditions of ritual bloodletting into imaginings of the piercing of Christ's side and may have specific local meaning. The prominence of the sun and moon in Station Twelve can also be found in both medieval Christian work and other Indigenous colonial work. As discussed earlier, in California the sun and moon formed an important part of Indigenous astrology and thought.

Horses are present in eight of the fourteen paintings and, unlike any of the other figures in these scenes, they consistently look directly at the viewer, with varying intensity of gaze. Even when the horses' bodies are depicted sideways, the painters placed the horses' two eyes and heads looking at the viewer. They painted almost every other figure in profile, but never the horses. When other figures looked outward, their eyes would be cast elsewhere. The horses' gaze suggests a

FIGURE 12. Indian Painted Stations of the Cross, Station Two Mission San Fernando, c. 1820. Horses are represented in portraiture, looking directly at the viewer, in eight of the fourteen paintings. Courtesy of the Seaver Center for Western History, Natural History Museum, Los Angeles.

human quality, consistent with native narrative traditions in which animals share all the attributes of humans.

The great number of horses in these paintings reflects the prominence of the horse in establishing colonial power. The colony strictly enforced the law that prohibited Indigenous persons from riding horses except in particular circumstances. The horses the Spanish brought to California had grown into enormous herds. There were more than a thousand horses at San Fernando in 1808. The law only allowed the Indigenous alcaldes, *vaqueros* (cowboys), and militia to ride them. The horse remained a principal form of military domination, and the skill to ride horses in the mission community led to higher status and better dress. The prominence of horses in these paintings seems to emphasize their impact on native California.

Other Indigenous communities in Mexico similarly placed the horse as prominent in religious work and thought. Santiago el Caballero, or Saint Santiago with his horse, became an extremely popular saint in the Americas. Santiago stood for the Spanish reconquest of the Iberian Peninsula. In the Americas, Spaniards invoked Santiago Matamores to defeat Indigenous populations. But Indigenous communities appropriated the image for themselves. In the process, the horse often took on greater significance than Santiago himself. William Taylor argues that Santiago's attraction for native Christians "was due partly to his horse."[124]

Varying Indigenous beliefs attributed animals with the power to help shape human destiny. By the late eighteenth century, a shift occurred in some Indian communities away from veneration of Santiago the man to veneration of the horse. Santiago's horse became a focal point for offerings and ceremony. In the dance of Santiaguitos, forbidden by colonial administrators, participants adorned and venerated a pony.[125]

The comparatively large number and the stance of the horses in the paintings of the Stations seems to allude to the way Indigenous people in California appropriated the horse into their systems of meaning and power. A symbol of colonial authority, military strength, and social status, the horse became something else in native sacred thought and iconography. Recall that in colonial Luiseño, the word *as* referred both to domesticated animals and to the "shaman's familiar" or "spirit helper" who constituted one of the many beings that appeared during a trance to impart specific knowledge. During the colonial period the horse and cow became synonymous with *as,* the shaman's familiar.[126] As with other "spirit helpers," the horse could be incorporated into the shaman's very being. This metamorphosis of livestock so closely associated with political defeat into shamanic spirits augmented Indigenous power that had been otherwise diminished by Spanish rule. It drew the horse and cow into the world of the Luiseño sacred.

Horses and horse riders also appeared on painted rocks during the colonial era, suggesting an extensive incorporation of the horse as a spirit helper beyond Luiseño territory.[127] As will be seen in the next chapter, Chumash accounts of the 1824 war featured the ability of Chumash leaders to jump on a horse and disappear, and to reappear on a mountain out of the range of Spanish bullets. In another aspect of the war, Indians at La Purísima took full control of the mission herd and rode the horses at will during the four-month period of revolt. Others found refuge in Yokuts communities in the Central Valley who maintained their autonomy from the Spanish and Mexicans because of their activity raiding, trading, and eating horses.

The horse, along with representations of saints, martyrs, and biblical events, entered the iconographic and imaginative landscape of Indigenous people in the missions. Where they could, Indigenous painters interpreted the visual narratives of the Spanish through their own iconography and set of meaningful subjects. Despite the control the church attempted to exert over interpretations of the image, Indigenous painters and artisans help create a visual world in which they established narrative influence.

4

"All of the Horses Are in
the Possession of the Indians"

The Chumash War

*Those whom I sent to Taché to warn the heathen Indians not to join with the
rebels have returned from their mission. They say that the Purísima Indians
sent two sacks of beads to persuade all the villages to join them in annihilat-
ing the soldiers.*

—FRAY JUAN CABOT TO GOVERNOR ARGÜELLO, FEBRUARY 28, 1824

In 1824 Chumash leaders at Missions Santa Inés, La Purísima, and Santa Bárbara
organized a major war against the missions and government. In preparation, the
leaders sent beads to the Yokuts villages of Tachi, Telamni, Nutunutu, Wowol, and
Suntaché and asked them to join. The people of Tachi and Telamni refused the
beads. The village of Nutunutu accepted them, but apparently did not join the war.
The people of Wowol and Suntaché took the presents and headed for Mission La
Purísima on the day that the war began.[1] During the four-month period it lasted,
more than one thousand people from Mission Santa Bárbara would go into exile
in Yokuts territory, in villages around Buena Vista Lake and beyond. The support
of many Yokuts and other Indigenous people sustained the war. Within this larger
geography defined by an emerging *Apachería*, maroon societies, and the elusive
"Rió Colorado" and Mojave (Amajaba) groups, discussed in chapter 1, the revolt
drew on interethnic and intertribal alliances.

The revolt thrived due to a unity between mission populations and Independent
tribes that the missionaries had long feared. The timing was important. The 1824 war
took place about two years after official news arrived from Mexico about the country's independence from Spain. With it came pending changes, such as Indigenous
legal equality. Those rights began to be discussed and debated in Indigenous communities, and the changes in government seem to have brought a marked decrease
in Yokuts affiliation to the missions in the year before the 1824 war. The moment
for alliance might have been optimal, but it had to be planned and negotiated

through appeals and gifting. This history of the war begins the focus on Indigenous politics during the Mexican era that is also pursued in subsequent chapters.

INDIGENOUS CITIZENSHIP AND EQUALITY

The missionaries and prominent Californios who wrote about the causes of the war refer to the political events that preceded it to explain Indigenous motives. In Spain and the Americas, revolutionary ideas, such as legislating the full equality of Indigenous people as citizens before the law, were circulated. The constitution passed by the Spanish Cortes of Cádiz (1810–14) established the precedence for Indigenous equality. After 1810, independence movements raged in the Americas, and Napoleonic forces occupied Spain and replaced the Bourbon monarchy with a more liberal regime. The Spanish government called a special session of its legislative body, the Cortes, in 1810. The Cortes would democratize the Spanish Constitution and address the disintegration of the empire that threatened. It initiated changes in the colonial status of Indigenous people that would have great significance in Independent Mexico.

In an extraordinary action, the Cortes of Cádiz invited delegates from all over Latin America and the Philippines to participate on an equal basis with representatives from Spain. The Cortes produced the 1812 Spanish Constitution, a document heralded throughout Europe as one of the most prized visions of political rights produced during its era. The constitution rode in a carriage through the streets of Naples and St. Petersburg and influenced political thought throughout Europe, the Americas, and in California.[2]

From unequal colonial subjects of various ranks, the constitution made Spanish and Indian people and their descendants born in the colonies legal Spaniards.[3] Indigenous people from throughout the Americas became Spaniards with the full rights of citizenship. Passed on September 13, 1813, the constitution ended Indian tribute, special taxation, and all forms of coercive labor and corporal punishment.[4] It terminated missions, such as those in California, that had been established for ten years or more.

For Mexican delegates, the major dispute concerned Article 22 of the draft of the 1812 constitution, which excluded African descent people from citizenship. They argued that the *castas* of Mexico deserved citizenship on the basis of the historic role they played in building the wealth of the Mexican colony. As Catholics and free subjects of the king, African-descent Mexicans should not be excluded from citizenship. José Beye Cisneros, a Mexican delegate, said that excluding African-descent people effectively disenfranchised 10 million of the 16 million residents of Mexico.[5]

The Constitution of 1812 affected California for a brief period in 1815, when Governor Solá arrived from Mexico intent on putting the new provisions into place. When he later learned that the Bourbon monarchy had been restored and had already rescinded the constitution on March 24, 1814, Solá talked instead about executing the spirit of that law. He wanted to make the missions account-able to the state for all of their fiscal affairs and make their assets public. He had planned to secularize the missions and oversee the formation of Indian pueblos. Revising his plan, he proposed that the most educated Indians from all the mis-sions be placed together in two new pueblos or be allowed to live in the pueblos of *gente de razón*. The focus of the constitution on Indian equality and the forma-tion of Indian pueblos remained a constant in the plans California would put forward in the 1820s and 1830s.[6]

Mexico published its declaration of independence and its vision for the gover-nance of the new republic in the Plan de Iguala on February 24, 1821. The plan abolished all distinctions among Europeans, Africans, and Indians. Echoing the liberal principles favoring equality that many delegates had articulated at the Cor-tes, Article 12 stated that all citizens could pursue professions according to their merits and virtues. In newly independent Mexico, a decree passed on September 17, 1822, eliminated the term *indio* from use. It had to be replaced with the term *citizen*.

The Plan de Iguala and the news of Mexican independence reached California in March 1822 with a special mail shipment, and the citizenry learned of the for-mation of an empire (1822–23) under Augustín Cosme Damián de Iturbide y Arámbara. A Mexican commissioner, Commissioner Agustín Fernández de San Vicente, arrived later in March 1822 to preside over patriotic celebrations and fes-tivities and institute new governmental bodies and practices. On April 11, 1822, Father Payeras, head of the Alta California missions, and ex-prefect Fray Vicente de Sarría went to Monterey and swore their allegiance to the new government in a very public ceremony. Afterward, the troops and general population heard the decree read and a patriotic speech given by the commissioner, who asked soldiers and ordinary citizens to similarly swear their allegiance to the new nation.

Commissioner Agustín Fernández de San Vicente stayed through November 1822, circulating along the coast to announce the liberty and equality of the Indian population and their impending emancipation from the missions in coastal settle-ments. Emancipation from the state of *neófia* that bound people to live within their missions established the precondition for Indians to assume their new status as citizens. The commissioner held a meeting of military officers and missionaries to discuss the new legal condition of the Indian population.[7]

Through circulars and meetings, he announced and emphasized the prohibition against flogging and corporal punishment, acts similarly prohibited by the consti-tution of the Cortes of Cádiz. Payeras sent his own circular to every mission announcing independence and the policies of the new government concerning Indigenous rights. By order, each mission held masses and patriotic festivities to celebrate the occasion of independence and to announce the new mandates.

Fray Payeras reported that about one-fourth of Indigenous people in the Cali-fornia missions expressed enthusiasm for the changes, or, as he put it, they had been "corrupted with ideas of liberty, [and] emancipation." These promises would initiate a growing and heterogeneous Indigenous politics in California.[8] The missionaries generally stood in opposition to the new state, but Fray Escudé from Mission San Luis Rey stood alone when he refused to sign the oath of allegiance to the new government. The commissioner took him back to Mexico, and from there, they shipped him to Spain.[9]

The missionaries signed the oath, but most also signed a petition requesting permission to leave California as soon as possible. Many awaited word of their transfers when the Chumash revolt occurred. More than half the missionaries wanted to go; only fifteen of the thirty-five expressed their desire or willingness to stay in California. Of those who petitioned to leave, both missionaries from the Missions of San Luis Rey, San Juan Capistrano, San Juan Bautista, and San José asked to go. The sole missionaries of Santa Inés and Santa Cruz expressed their fervent desire to leave California. One of the two missionaries from San Buenaventura, La Purísima, San Antonio, Santa Clara, and Soledad wanted to leave California. At the other missions, the missionaries in charge intended to stay. Some of the old and infirm missionaries wanted to remain rather than travel great distances. Only a few missionaries expressed an interest in taking a role in the new nation.[10] Some wanted to retire in Spain, and others to found new missions elsewhere in the world. In California, they now faced the prospect of laws that undercut their authority at the missions and the eventual replacement of the Franciscan Order by regular Catholic clergy.

The commissioner attended ceremonies and conveyed the ideals and visions then articulated by the Mexican federal government, and he oversaw the establishment of democratic governmental bodies. He created the California Territorial Deputation, an elected body entrusted to develop the legal framework for Indigenous equality and citizenship in California. He also established elected *Ayuntamientos* (town councils) in each pueblo.

After the commissioner's visit in 1822, Fray Payeras wrote that at least one-fourth of the mission population had been "corrupted by the ideas" of the new republic. The new legislative bodies that would determine the meaning of Indigenous freedom locally began to convene in California and throughout the nation. Meanwhile, the Mexican nation debated the new constitution, which was enacted on October 4, 1824. The constitution ended all *casta* designations and noble titles. It affirmed the citizenship of *indios* and of African-descent *castas*.

WAR AND EXILE IN 1824

Months earlier, on February 21, 1824, the population of 554 Ineseños at Mission Santa Ines became involved in a war planned by leaders at Missions Santa Inés, La Purísima, and Santa Bárbara. The men took up bows, arrows, and rifles stolen from the soldiers' quarters. They set fire to the mission, destroyed the workrooms and girls dormitory, the houses of the five guards and their families, and the Indian quarters. The toll in human life reflected the vulnerabilities of the entire population. Nineteen Ineseños died in the insurrection and subsequent exile, the majority being fifteen women and children from Mission Santa Inés. Four men unfortunately burned to death in the fire, and one Mexican soldier died.[11]

The majority of the population fled to Mission La Purísima where the 722 Purísimeños had taken up arms. Purísimeño leaders gained control of the mission's firearms, and killed José Dolores Sepulveda and three other settlers passing by La Purísima seemingly by chance. The rebels welcomed the population from Santa Ines, who brought canons, more arms, and bows and arrows.

As many as 1,270 Ineseños and Purísimeños participated in the occupation of Mission La Purísima for nearly a month. They kept the soldiers and their families at the occupied mission for three days. Some Indians sorted through their possessions and wore their things, flaunting in front of the soldiers and their families the clothing that had long connoted their elevated status of this frontier. They had to leave behind their goods, and they still sought compensation for them a year later.[12]

When the rebels eventually allowed the soldiers and their families to leave the mission with Fray Blas Ordaz, they sent along a message warning the soldiers who had returned to the ashes at Santa Inés that they would defend La Purísima by force. Fray Ordaz cautioned other officials against communication with Fray Antonio Rodríguez, who remained behind. Some Purísimeños knew how to read and write, he warned, and they would intercept any message.[13] The occupation would be long and almost without precedence on Mexico's vast northern frontier, where rebellion and war commonly occurred.

In coordination, the population at Santa Bárbara took up arms and fled the mission at dawn the next day. The women, children, and some of the men ran into the hills in the early morning hours. Others stayed to fight the presidio soldiers who arrived in force from their fort near the mission. As people fled, they drove livestock and carried other provisions and goods with them. The leaders needed to feed and shelter more than a thousand women, men, and children who moved into exile. They also used these things to gift the many allies they sought as they headed to the area around Buena Vista Lake in Yokuts territory. (See map 5, chapter 1.)

Andrés Sagimomatsse, an alcalde at Mission Santa Bárbara and one of the leaders, chose three Yokuts men, all *cimarrones*, to be envoys for the group to get help from Yokuts villages. Hilarión Chaaj had been born at a Yokuts village on Buena Vista Lake. He affiliated to the mission after he moved to Najalayegua, a large and politically important town on the upper Santa Ines River. He became one of 105 persons from that village who affiliated to Mission Santa Inés. Hilarión had fled the mission earlier. José Venadero came from Siguaya, a village on a stream in the higher mountains of the Santa Ynez mountain range. His wife grew up in a village near the southern San Joaquin Valley where the rebels headed. Luís Calala, the third messenger, had a brother who was the chief of Taxlipu, a Chumash village in San Emigidio Canyon, just south of Buena Vista Lake. Luis Calala and his wife had escaped Mission Santa Bárbara a few years earlier and lived in the southern valley in the region of Luis Calala's birth.[14]

As the leaders moved towards Buena Vista Lake, Andrés Sagimomatsee sent messengers and gifts to Yokuts leaders and requested their presence at a meeting. At the village of the Pelones, for example, a messenger of Andrés's arrived, inviting them to come and fight the troops. Half the people in Pelones said they would join the revolt; others refused.[15] After a five-day walk, they reached Buena Vista Lake, from where Andrés sent out additional envoys to each village in Yokuts territory. They held an initial meeting between Yokuts leaders and rebels and slaughtered twenty-five steers to divide up and to feed the exiles and their Yokuts allies and send gifts back to the villages of their allies.[16]

Villages around the lake had long been a center of trade linking the coast and tribal areas to the east. As discussed in chapter 1, Yokuts had maintained trade ties with the missions, and some people from the area of Buena Vista Lake had affiliated to, and then fled from, Missions La Purísima and San Luis Obispo. Many villages had long taken in *cimarrones* from various missions, including their own villagers who returned home.[17] Tulali, a large village on Buenavista Lake, took in eighteen Santa Bárbara Indians and seven fugitives from the missions of San Diego, San Miguel, and San Luis Obispo. Julala, a nearby village to its north, took in sixteen Santa Bárbara Indian families. Most villages had given some individuals and families exile.[18] But the problem of addressing the needs of a thousand people, when Yokuts villages normally supported around 250 residents, meant that many different villages took in Chumash people.

For the majority of the Santa Bárbara population and the few from Santa Inés and La Purísima who joined them, exile placed their lives in jeopardy. It also strained the resources of the entire region. Relatively few possessions could be carried. The ill, frail, young, and old fared poorly on the difficult and long journey. The precarious food supply created perilous situations. Physical accidents on the road might be fatal. Without allies, the rebellion would not have endured.

OCCUPIED SITES

As individuals and families found their specific places of refuge in and around Yokuts territory, more than 1,200 people occupied La Purísima, in full possession of the horses, livestock, fields, and orchards. On March 14, 1824, 109 soldiers with artillery, infantry, cavalry, and a cannon left Mission San Luis Obispo with the intent to reoccupy La Purísima.[19] En route, they ran into two Indian couriers who had illicitly left Mission San Luis Obispo before them and had delivered the news to La Purísima of the pending attack. On the morning of March 16, the military contingent arrived at La Purísima and began firing at the rebels about 8 A.M. The rebels fought back with musket fire, a cannon, and arrows. During the two and a half hours of battle, soldiers cut off the passages of flight out of the mission.

The four hundred men who fought from within the mission asked for a cease-fire after sixteen Ineseños and Purísimeños lost their lives and others had been wounded. They asked Fray Antonio Rodríguez to negotiate the truce. The troops seized two canons, sixteen muskets, 150 lances, six machetes, and an incalculable number of bows and arrows. In contrast to the high casualties among the rebels, only one soldier died and two were wounded.[20]

Nine days later the military held a trial against "the revolutionary rebels." José de la Guerra, commander of the presidio; José Estrada, commander of one of the Monterey contingents; and second subtenant Francisco de Haro acted as judges. Hardly an impartial court, two of the presiding judges, Estrada and de Haro, headed military forces against Indigenous people at La Purísima and Santa Inés. They tried twenty-five men, finding nine of them guilty in the death of José Dolores Sepulveda and his three companions on the night of the insurrection, February 21, 1824.

The judges sentenced all nine accomplices in the murders to death: Baltasar, Pacífico, Estevan, Gines, Antonino, Felipe, José Andrés, Martiniano, and Camilo. The court found four men guilty for being the principle agents of the revolution: Marciano, Pacomío, Benito, and Bernabé. The court sentenced them to ten years of work at a presidio in exile from the Santa Bárbara district. Seven men received the sentence of eight years work at the Presidio of Santa Bárbara for being "thieves and rebellious": Aiccomeiles, Felipe Fumu, Agustín, Germán, Isaac, Pisco, Guille. The judges declared five other men free and absolved of all accusations: Frutos, Jaime, Narciso, Pedro Antonio, and Melchor.[21]

The military retook the mission, but they could not regain control of a region in which so many remained in exile. The defiant population continued to ride on horseback. General José de la Guerra complained about this, accusing Roberto Pardo, the soldier left in charge of the troops at Mission La Purísima, of not doing his duty. The general wrote that he had heard "all the horses are in possession of the Indians, and that most of the time they are on horseback."[22] Pardo responded with indignation at being treated "as though I did not know anything about the countryside and the horses, and am unable to execute the orders that I get." He refused to address the accusation, and rejected the idea he had been negligent in his duties.

Pardo wrote with a bite to his words. His last name referred to the *casta* term *pardo,* meaning of mixed African and Indian ancestry. The missionary from Santa Inés had identified many *pardos* among the soldiers of that region.[24] Under Spain, that *casta* status would have limited his advancement in the military. Pardo wrote as a man from newly independent Mexico, a nation that had declared it would end the regime of *castas* and other hereditary distinctions. He had requested an elevation in rank prior to receiving the letter from de la Guerra, and in his response, he again insisted on being advanced. If not, he asked to be relieved of his post to avoid what he called "further insult," including de la Guerra's accusation. That the Indigenous population at La Purísima remained in control of the horses during this period is not surprising, but Pardo's response suggested the limits of military power in the region with so many in exile.[24]

The missionaries feared the spread of the revolt to San Luis Obispo, where they tried three men whom they declared guilty of attempting to organize an uprising. The Obispeño man G. Sonaleta attempted to mobilize people to join on the basis of prophetic voices he heard favoring revolt. Lorenzo Puyala lied to three soldiers in the course of organizing the population. Feliciano Cuynayet was one of the two messengers who left San Luis Obispo and notified those occupying La Purísima about the advancement of the troops against them in March. They also accused Cuynayet of being incorrigible, and a horse thief.[25]

The military attempted to reassert control by spreading the fear of severe retaliation against the rebels. The governor sent General Ignacio Vallejo to Missions San Luis Obispo, San Miguel, San Antonio, and Soledad and all central coast missions with Yokuts populations. He had orders to punish those who favored the revolt and to put pressure on delinquents.[26] But his tactic was to threaten massive reprisal against the entire population.

At San Luis Obispo, Vallejo gathered everyone together and spoke through an interpreter. He used violent and accusatory language. Though he acknowledged that they had been incited to revolt and congratulated them for being firm against it, he warned, "Maintain yourselves vigorously in this state; if you act contrary I will take action with fire and blood." He threatened to "do away with not only the neophytes of this mission, but with all of those who are under my responsibility when they give me a motive" and asserted that he "had troops and arms sufficient for that and much more." To "do away with" all the Indians meant killing everyone. After violently threatening them, he asked them to prove themselves loyal to their religion and to the authorities. Vallejo emphasized he would punish anyone who disturbed the "peace and quiet" of loyal neophytes.

At Missionary Fray Martínez's request, Vallejo left ten soldiers at Mission San Luis Obispo to increase surveillance.[27] Built close to a route into Yokuts territory, the mission lay on the other side of a piece of the coastal range that separated it from Missions La Purísima and Santa Inés. Though Vallejo could not find signs of revolt in any of the missions from San Luis Obispo northward, he repeated his violent threats to crowds gathered at each of five successive missions.

Writing from mission San Luis Obispo, Fray Martínez was among the missionaries whose correspondence created the greatest specter of fear of a war being organized by independent tribes against the coast. He foresaw them joining with the mission populations. He reported to Governor Argüello on reconnaissance to the village near San Emegidio to seek Chumash rebels. The party went to Taluhilimu, Tulu, Hilimu, and Cuihamu, villages most immediate to San Emegidio. They saw horses from the missions but not one of the Indians, which made him think "that without doubt they will seek protection with the Mojave and those at the head of the Tulares to make raids on the coast with the troops who, with little work, they could destroy by falling here and there."[28]

Fray Martinez continued to warn of widespread threats through May.[29] He sent the Indian Verano to Yokuts territory for news. He returned from Buena Vista Lake in the company of one of the Purísimeños who had been sentenced to death, and who then sought refuge in the church at Mission San Luis Obispo. Verano purportedly told Fray Martínez that Indians planned to attack Mission San Buenaventura to do away with the soldiers and Christian Indians and go on to the presidio to do the same. Leaving Missions Santa Inés and La Purísima in the hands of the rebels, he feared another group of rebels would take over San Luis Obispo. He insisted their contingents included more than a thousand warriors who would join with Indians from Missions Santa Bárbara, San Buenaventura, San Fernando, and San Luis Obispo.

Fray Sarría echoed the fear that "an infinitude of Barbareños, Bentureños, Fernandinos, and Obispeño" Christian Indians would be joined "by another thousand composed of the gentiles of the Tulare on the route to the Amayahuas" (Mojave) in a massive attack on the Californios.[30] Fray Gil y Toboada wrote about the impending danger. He believed rebellions would occur frequently if they could succeed.[31]

Fray Blas Ordaz, who remained in the region living among the ashes at Santa Inés, warned of the possibility of a province-wide revolt organized by leaders from Missions La Purísima and Santa Bárbara. They had all the non-Christians in Yokuts territories "on their side," he warned. They had ample arms, and the Christian Indians "taught them to shoot at Whites." They would join with the population of San Buenaventura and do away with the guard. He insisted they would be determined to kill all the *de razón* or settlers in the province. According to Fray Blas Ordaz (but not consistent with other records), very few of San Fernando's population remained at the mission because they had fled to Yokuts territory.[32]

A larger uprising never occurred. The missionaries' fears created the specter of a coordinated revolt that had little to do with any real possibility: the task was out of reach, even if leaders hoped to plan the action. The missionaries' recourse to "liquid fear," an irrational sense of a limitless and amorphous enemy, obscured the very specific conditions under which the revolt had been organized and made possible.[33] Mission Santa Inés had been founded in 1804 with Indigenous people affiliated to the older missions of La Purísima and Santa Bárbara. Many had been born in the region of Santa Inés and had family ties there. They had built connections to people in the older missions and created the community at Santa Inés. Connections made stronger by the Indigenous political and ritual structures they shared among themselves. Those connections made it possible to plan such a massive action and could not be generalized to other missions.

Their fear also obscured the difficulties involved in organizing a province-wide revolt. Compounding the problems attendant on agreeing upon strategy, gathering and making sufficient arms, and creating the necessary alliances, Chumash and Yokuts people had the problem of survival itself. Villages that had supported around 250 people faced the serious problem of addressing the needs of more than a thousand exiles. That, and the anticipation of military reprisal, created difficult conditions in all the villages that participated.

The missionaries' expressions of fear seemed to sanction the violence of the state. The first military expedition to enter Yokuts territories in pursuit of the rebels headed off on April 11, six weeks after the rebellion had begun. Led by Don Narciso Fabregat, the expedition took five days to reach the proximity of Buena Vista Lake. As they traveled, they seized and later decided to kill an Indigenous man from Mission San Fernando. They subsequently killed others. Governor Argüello responded to the killing of rebel Indians and the injury of patriotic Indians with the same disinterest: the expedition, he wrote, "recaptured thirteen horses and killed four of the rebels, with the sole casualty of three auxiliary patriots wounded, two of them rather seriously."[34] Before they reached Buena Vista Lake, a wind and dust storm arose and made it impossible to see any distance. Unable to proceed, they turned back.

THE PARDON

The population of exiles in Yokuts territory grew during April and May 1824. As groups of ten and twenty people made their way back to Mission Santa Inés from La Purísima beginning in mid-April, others headed for Yokuts territory, where the rebels had encouraged people to join them. Those who remained in the vicinity of the mission seem to have experienced a heightened state of violence. At Mission Santa Inés a soldier murdered an Indian cook, which represented an extreme violence that commonly threatened Indigenous people. Their vulnerability increased during a time of war.

Scarcity began to be felt in the kitchens and in the production of resources due to the lack of workers and greater demands in the region. The Presidio of Santa Bárbara requested seeds from Mission San Luis Obispo, but the mission couldn't comply. It had to give seeds to the populations of La Purísima and Santa Inés and feed ten additional troops. "I can't give the presidio any seeds," Fray Martínez told Governor Argüello. The Indian women *tortilla* makers at San Luis Obispo also asked Governor Argüello for extra corn to feed the additional ten troops stationed at the mission.[35] These women asked for corn so as not to decrease the amount of corn meal they had for the stews and thick porridges they made to serve the Indian population at the mission. Only the *gente de razón* (including soldiers, missionaries, and visitors) would be served *tortillas*.

During these months the president of the California missions, Fray Vicente de Sarría, supplicated the governor to be lenient with the rebels and excuse their actions. But in early May 1824, Missionary Ripoll of Mission Santa Bárbara made the decisive appeal that shifted the course of events. Ripoll wrote a long explanation for the revolt that emphasized the innocence of the Indians at Santa Bárbara. He insisted they had suffered wrongdoing and lacked recourse to justice. Their fear of retaliation drove them away from the mission.[36] This official explanation enabled the governor to extend a pardon to everyone who participated in the revolt, with the exception of those condemned at the March trial at Mission La Purísima.

Governor Argüello announced the pardon on Sunday, May 16, 1824, and, that very evening, Fray Sarría sent two Yokuts messengers from Mission San Miguel with a card to announce the indulgence. Sarría immediately began his own campaign to secure complete amnesty for the nineteen Indians sentenced earlier.[37] He requested amnesty three times, including in his correspondence with Californios in Santa Bárbara, who also pleaded for a pardon to be extended to those sentenced to die in March.[38] The Purísimeño who had taken asylum in the church at San Luis Obispo received Sarría's special attention. He asked that the governor pardon the man "in a very public way." He wanted to use the incident "in order to declare and make it clear how comprehensive the indulgence is."[39]

Fray Sarría requested that the Indian leadership spread the message about the pardon and be involved in the negotiations. He especially asked that an alcalde named Camilo, a leader and a translator, be sent with Antonio del Valle's part of the expedition into Yokuts territory from Monterey. "With this you'll save expeditions and work."[40] The expedition to extend the pardon and bring the population back included three separate military contingents headed by Pablo Portillo, Antonio del Valle, and Mariano Estrada.

Pablo de la Portillo headed the major expedition, accompanied by Frays Sarría and Ripoll, who had actively agitated for leniency and pardon for those in revolt. They left Mission Santa Bárbara on June 2, 1824. On the fifth day of the journey, Portillo sent a messenger ahead to ask for the principal men among the rebels to meet at a camp set up outside the region of exile. The next day armed Chumash and Yokuts leaders met the expedition outside the swamplands around Buena Vista Lake at a place called Mitochea.[41]

According to Portillo, "Seeing my intentions some of them came to greet me, among them one named Jaime who had some authority among the Indians. I delivered to him the pardon which I brought them from the Governor."[42] They agreed to accept the pardon only after explaining their reasons for the uprising and their apprehensions about turning over their weapons. Though Portillo wrote about the crucial role of the native leadership in accepting the pardon, he did not record their reasons. Portillo only noted that they expressed them, but kept them out of his extensive written record.

After a preliminary meeting with some of the leaders, they agreed to call a mass meeting at which many hundreds of exiles gathered on June 11 at the main headquarters of their camp. Portillo read the pardon "at their request, and it was explained in their language." They took up the flags of peace and shot the cannon and guns to announce the pledge. During that meeting an Indian arrived from Mission San Miguel and spread the rumor that they should not trust the pardon because troops were on their way from Monterey, referring to the expedition of fifty men who had left Mission San Miguel under Lieutenant Antonio del Valle. They intended to join the Portillo expedition at the lake. Upon hearing about the troops, many families again escaped into the villages around the lake, although others brought their belongings and joined the camp to await the walk back.[43]

On June 13 they held a fully sung Corpus Christi mass and celebration, and Portillo appointed three new alcaldes: Lázaro Huiyalamuit, Juan Pablo Aguilar, and Andrés Sagimomatsee. Sagimomatsee had been very prominent in organizing the revolt. That afternoon, and for the subsequent week, soldiers and Indian alcaldes and *vaqueros* moved through the villages around the lake to find those who had taken exile and refused to return. It took more than a week for the reconnaissance to bring back hundreds of people. In the process, the soldiers confiscated firearms and horses. Some of the alcaldes remained behind, continuing to persuade those who had been reluctant to return.[44]

The first contingents to leave Yokuts territory arrived in Santa Bárbara on June 16. Exhausted from months of exile and in precarious conditions that caused a number of deaths, they moved slowly and in a staggered fashion. Some leaders remained armed to protect their groups from any hostile encounters on the road. For weeks parties arrived. Pablo de la Portillo noted, "Families that remained behind are arriving daily by twos and threes, for some of the people are very old, some infirm, and some have died."[45] Some stayed behind to gather seeds in the countryside because the mission had few provisions left. Of the initial population of nearly 1,000 at Mission Santa Bárbara, the missionaries counted 816 people having returned from exile, and 163 still in the Yokuts territories as of June 28, 1824. Of those who returned, 353 people took up residence at the mission, 10 returned to the islands temporarily, and 453 resided in the mountains and valleys of the mission to help resume production on the mission *ranchos* (ranch lands) and farms.[46]

The missionaries and military leaders commemorated the pardon and truce with masses, festivities, and ceremonial pageantry to which they invited some of the Yokuts who had been allies in the war. Fray Martínez writes that Don Maríano Estrada's expedition arrived at San Luis Obispo with a formal march into the mission.

Music, festivities, and food created fanfare and ceremonial closure to the event. A similar commemoration took place at Mission La Purísima with Yokuts in attendance, who received a warm welcome from the population.[47] On June 28 Fray Sarría commemorated the pardon and return in Santa Bárbara by celebrating a mass at the presidio and another at the mission. Fray Martínez sent a barrel of wine to Governor Argüello to thank him and to "alleviate his headache."[48]

Some people remained in the countryside. By July 23, 1824, Governor Argüello told General de la Guerra to give the Indians eight more days to present themselves, or they would be considered troublemakers and the troops would move against them.[49] Most returned. One year later, in June 1825, a group of twelve fugitives who had been promised indulgence also came back, and only "four men and two or three women" remained in Yokuts territory from the time of the war.[50]

CHUMASH HISTORIES OF THE WAR

The Ineseños were all saying something like this: "If they shoot at me, water will come out of the cannon." Another would say, "If they shoot at me, the bullets will not enter my flesh." etc.

—MARIA SOLARES, 1914

Maria Solares, who was born in 1842 and whose father had been a baby during the revolt, explained that Ineseños were willing to take up arms because a prophecy existed that they could rectify their conditions while having immunity from the power of colonial restraint. The accounts of Maria Solares, Lucrecia Garcia, and Luisa Ignacio narrate the causes for the event, the event, and its meaning with some parallels and marked distinctions.[51] In all the accounts, Chumash leaders share an ability to be impervious to bullets and to the normal control exercised by soldiers.

These stories, told in the early twentieth century, offer community memories of the 1824 revolt passed down to relatives by those who had been involved. They were written down as ethnographic field notes about history and language. Like other Indigenous histories, these "differ most markedly" from Western ones "in their narrative structure" and, as Joanne Rappaport found, they involve histories "encoded in physical space."[52] They address specific communities and places. Maria Solares spoke of events from the perspective of Missions Santa Inés and La Purísima.[53] Lucrecia Garcia and Luisa Ignacio spoke of events that transpired at Mission Santa Bárbara.[54] Their accounts focus on Indigenous leaders, including those who held forms of power that aided individual and group survival, and others who betrayed the community. They identify high levels of violence and despair. Where they intersect with the Spanish accounts of the revolt, they cast the same persons and events in a different light, one grounded in Indigenous forms of power and political vision. None of them use the language of fear so frequently attributed to Indigenous people in Spanish writing.

Maria Solares begins her account describing a Chumash sacristan at Mission Santa Inés and immediately turns the focus to a group "more learned in Indian religion." The men prepared *pespibata,* one of the plants that produced an altered consciousness. Most could only take a few sucks of it before they "staggered down." As this transpired, they entered the altered state. The sacristan arrived and said, "Do you know what is going on? All of you will be punished next Sunday." He told them the priest said he would punish all of the women and the men. Then he went and told the priest that the Indians were going to "shoot priests with arrows the following Sunday." The priest was alarmed; he didn't hold mass that Sunday and got the soldiers to guard the church. The sacristan then told the men not to go near the church or they would be killed. They stayed up all night and "began to prepare themselves to fight."

Some of the Indians said, "The priests can't hurt me." They divided between "those who said that the priests could not hurt them and a group who said that they wished to investigate if there was any truth in the report." When one in the latter group passed by the church, he was shot in his left thigh. "Then the Indians revolted." An Indian messenger went to La Purísima "to announce that there was to be a war."

The power of the Chumash as told by Solares and Garcia resided in their access to the supernatural via ritual objects. According to Solares, when people took up arms at La Purísima, the Spanish soldiers captured seven Purísimeños, blindfolded them, tied their hands behind their backs, and shot them. "One of them got up after they were shot. The soldiers shot again and he fell. The priest prayed while soldiers shot." When that Indian did not die, the soldiers examined him. He wore an *ʔatishwin* "of woven *(tejido)* human hair about his neck and that was the reason he did not die." When they broke it and shot him again, he died.

Lucrecia Garcia represented the power of the *ʔatishwin* necklace by the fact that a shaman could be called an *ʔatishwinic.* If a person had on an *ʔatishwin* and "a whole crowd of men" takes after him, "if you have your *ʔatishwin,* they are like a pack of babies, and nothing will happen if they catch him." *ʔAtishwins* varied. "The Indians each had a different kind of *ʔatishwin.*" Some could carry a person over the mountains, others protected one from a bear; still other *ʔatishwin* enabled a person to disappear.[55] The *ʔatishwin* formed part of shamanic practice involving the dream helper, an entity encountered in a trance induced by taking a hallucinogen to help transport the shaman into a different realm of consciousness.[56] In that altered state, the dream helper gave particular powers and knowledge to the person, and the *ʔatishwin* embodied those. A person might take on the *ʔatishwin* of a shaman he or she associated with as a personal talisman.

In Lucrecia Garcia's account, the *ʔatishwin* protected the person who wore it. According to her, three old men responded to the call to attend mass at Santa

Bárbara unaware that the rebellion had begun. As they approached the mission, the one who wore the *¿atishwin* charm felt it "throbbing on his neck and he knew something would happen." Shortly thereafter they came upon soldiers who shot and killed the other two, but "the one with the necklace was fired at but became invisible for a stretch, and ran most swiftly." He disappeared two more times, and then "they never saw him again. He got away into the mountains."[57]

In the stories of Solares and García, the horse also appears as a means of escape and forms part of the supernatural world they could inhabit. It allowed its rider to jump on, disappear, and reappear at a safe distance, or to disappear altogether. A messenger went from La Purísima to Santa Inés to warn everyone that soldiers had killed seven Purísimeños. He met a Spanish soldier on the way. Thinking the soldier was on his way to join the other soldiers at La Purísima "to kill us," he "commanded him to dismount from his horse and take his clothes off." The Indian killed the naked Spaniard, clothed himself in the dead man's uniform, and rode to Santa Ines on the Spaniard's fine horse. On approaching Santa Inés he lassoed a fresh horse and saddled it.

"Among [the] bravest of soldiers was a man named Valentín," whom the Indian came upon in the corral. "Who ordered you to take this horse?" Valentín asked. The Indian told him, "My horse is tired and I have to get a new horse. I have to go back." Valentín ordered him to take off the soldier's clothing so that it wouldn't get stained with blood. The Indian told him, "I have killed a man." Valentín had a leather shield in his hand and again told him to take off the suit. The Indian jumped on the horse. Valentín had the horse by the bridle and soldiers were all around the corral. As the Indian jumped on the horse, he disappeared, giving a cry as he did so. At that point, "Valentín was holding pure air." Moments later, the "Indian and horse made an appearance on the hilltop and yelled, 'Here I am. *Quítenme*' (Take it from me!)"

The Wot at La Purísima (or a religious leader who held authority over many villages) sent another Purísimeño to Santa Inés at the beginning of the revolt to ask the Ineseños to go to La Purísima so that "if they were all to be killed, they would all be killed together." The message told everyone at Santa Inés to go to La Purísima "as there was no hope for them." Someone responded that it wasn't right to go without the seven men who had been captured and put in jail at Santa Inés earlier that day, and suggested it was better if they all stayed at Santa Inés to die with those men.

But they assembled to go to La Purísima, and as the Ineseños waited amid a large amount of chaos, two Chumash men named Marcos and Andres entered the jail door through a keyhole in order to release the imprisoned men. At the jail, they met the soldier Valentín guarding the prisoners. When he looked up and saw the two brothers between him and the prisoners, "Valentín trembled but did not say a word. Valentín opened the door and went out silently." In the battle between soldiers and Chumash, Valentín, a brave soldier, was a good match undone by his Chumash opponents.

Solares also spoke of another sacred object that Marcos and a man named Estevan used to devise what would happen in the war: the *takulsoxsinas* or "woven band such as Coyote used." The Indians "used to have many of these for Indian religion." Estevan had it "guarded away in his house." It was worn on the head when Indians went to war. Marcos asked Estevan to give half of that "magic string" to him, but Estevan refused. As Estevan's *?atishwin*, it was incorporated into his person. Estevan told him not to cut it as "it would be like stabbing Estevan's heart." Estevan lent it to Marcos and told him to take good care of it, because "to cut it," he repeated, "was like the veins of his heart." But something happened to it, and Estevan told Marcos they would die.

Though María Solares said that a belief existed at Santa Inés that people thought they were impervious to the bullets of the soldiers, she also recounted a pervasive sense of deep vulnerability. Though people were "saying like if they shoot at me, water will come out of the cannon," time and again she related their expectation that they might face death and their desire to die together if that occurred. When Marcos took the ropes off the hands of the prisoners in the jail, Solares said that he expressed this uncertainty. "Go. We are all going to die together. As soon as we arrive there [at Purísima], we shall know whether we are to live or not."

Solares recounted the great despair people felt during the revolt, especially on the journey to La Purísima, when many women left their children by the roadside. "In those days a good many threw their children away on the journey. Mothers said, 'I am suffering and they are going to kill the child and me. I will throw the child away.'" In order to find one of the lost children, a man named Marcos turned to magic. He sought a *Saxlaps*, or a person "who divines where a child is by means of arrows." Marcos "went over to a place where there was quite a gathering of *hechiceros*" (sorcerers). But Marcos "made a mistake." Andres, his brother, noticed it and got worried. "My brother, I don't want to live alone. We will both perish or die." They placed the string on the ground and Marcos told Estevan, "Brother, we are lost; we'll perish."

Luisa Ignacio also spoke of this despair. She told a story drawn from the experience of her mother-in-law, María Ignacio, who took part in the revolt and the long walk to exile as a child.[58] She vividly remembered the death of one child and the sadness they felt for having to leave everything behind. She recounted the welcome they received from the Yokuts, one that resounded in Yokuts territories and beyond. "The Tulareños received the Santa Bárbara Indians well." Another group of Indians who she identified as living "further east" offered even more extensive aid. They "gave the Santa Bárbara Indians many things and treated them finely, even better than the Tulareños did."[59]

María Ignacio recounted to Luisa the day of the pardon how "the women cried, thinking they would all be killed."[60] She emphasized the role of the mission official Jaime, whom Luisa identified as "a doctor, singer, and teacher" at the mission.

He "took hold of them and persuaded them to return." But she insisted, "The women cried, thinking they would all be killed." To weep as an expression of sorrow and loss recalls Indigenous writing from the period after the conquest of Mexico, when sorrow, grief, anger, and lament for the dead predominated in the expression of emotion.[61] She, too, emphasized the dangers. "Many Indians who went to the Tulare died on the way."

Solares spoke of the revolt as a war and of the desire the Chumash had to revenge the killing of Indians. She mentions the vow one father made to "revenge myself by killing every woman and man of [the] Spanish race" if something happened to his son. She emphasized how the rebels humiliated the Spaniards by taking off their clothes and leaving them naked and redressing themselves in the clothing. Solares's story ends with the mutual agreement to end hostilities made between the Mexican and Indian forces when General de la Guerra arrived at La Purísima from Mission Santa Bárbara the next day.

María Solares is the only one of the three who identified a crucial element of Indigenous political consciousness in the revolt in speaking about the belief that Spanish bullets could not kill them. This reference to invincibility has formed part of the visions held by movements that respond to long histories of colonial violence.[62] Yet in all three cases, the stories identify the initiators and main actors from within the Indigenous community. All three identify the duplicity of an Indian sacristan as the cause of the revolt when he conveyed a message about the deaths purportedly threatened against the Indian community.[63]

Luisa Ignacio stated that the sacristan spread the rumor that "they were going to kill the Indians when the Indians entered the church next Sunday."[64] Lucrecia Garcia stated the rumor threatened that the missionary would "call them out [of mass] into another room one by one and put them to secret death." In Maria Solares's story the sacristan told Indians that the missionaries planned their death on the following Sunday, recalling the whipping of Indian healers on Sunday after mass, with everyone present (discussed in chapter 2). The stories invoke the frequent utilization of the public space for punishment. For his duplicity, the sacristan ended up in jail at the end of the revolt, according to Solares. He faced a brutal death by burning according to Luisa Ignacio and by burning and dismemberment in Lucrecia Garcia's account.

The story of the sacristan reveals the etching of violent murder, death, and dismemberment in collective memory. It emphasizes that violence formed an intricate part of life in the mission. Random death at the hands of the soldiers could occur at any time and especially during a revolt. All three Chumash accounts and military records allow one to see the prevalence of violence against the native population. That part of their stories also speaks to the way someone who fell outside the ritual and political life of the Indian community at the mission, and who played a duplicitous role as mediator, could suffer a terrible fate. But the overall focus of the Chumash stories is on the powers held by Indigenous leaders and the precarious state of things they experienced during the war.

MISSIONARY AND MILITARY ACCOUNTS

In the whole province there are not more than 3,000 souls, scarcely, of the Gente de Razón, whereas the Native Indians existing in the Missions exceed 22,000.

—GOVERNOR ARGÜELLO TO THE MEXICAN GOVERNMENT, APRIL 21, 1824

Despite the correspondence generated during the revolt, the missionaries remained curiously silent about its cause and the details of what happened. They never wrote about what transpired during the uprising at Santa Inés or about the occupation of La Purísima. The silence of Fray Uría, the missionary at Santa Inés during the uprising, remained absolute. Fray Rodríguez, who stayed at La Purísima during the entire occupation of the mission by people from La Purísima and Santa Inés, never breached a word on the subject. Fray Blas Ordaz, who had been at La Purísima for the first few days of the revolt and then left with the soldiers and their families, similarly said nothing about the cause of the revolt, nor did he reveal how the rebels actually ran the mission during its occupation.

The military similarly revealed nothing about the cause of the revolt, although they expressed little surprise over its occurrence. In his first official report to the Mexican government on April 21, after about three months, Military Governor Argüello simply provided a sketch of the "facts": they revolted, killed various individuals, and destroyed and reduced to ashes Mission Santa Inés, with all its furniture, provisions, and goods.[65] Governor Argüello seemed to assume that specific causes remained irrelevant, because the threat of insurrection always existed. In the same letter he wrote, "In the whole province there are not more than 3,000 souls, scarcely, of the *Gente de Razón,* whereas the Native Indians existing in the Missions exceed 22,000." The troops, he argued, are "in constant campaign in order to secure us against their plots."[66]

Fray Sarría echoed this sense of inevitability. In his first letter about the revolt, written on February 25, 1824, Fray Sarría reminded the governor that the law anticipated the rebellion of those whom the Spaniards had conquered and reduced. Time and again he wrote for leniency. Even as he expressed his fear of a massive, coordinated attack on the coast, he cited Indians' status as minors under the Law of the Indies and the paternal responsibilities toward them that their position entailed.[67]

Fray Ripoll finally identified a specific cause of the rebellion on May 5, 1824, more than two months after it had begun; it formed the basis of the churches' appeal for the pardon and offered a legitimate reason for the governor to issue it.

Fray Ripoll stated that a whipping of a Purísimeño Indian by the soldier Valentín Cota precipitated the revolt. The whipping infringed upon the Indian's rights under Spanish law.[68] When the captain of the guard and the missionary failed to level charges against Cota, as demanded by the alcalde of the mission and his people, the Indians revolted. They had long suffered under the disregard of Fray Uría, he contended.

Fray Ripoll based his account of the revolt on what he had purportedly heard from Andrés, Jayme, and Cristóval, three Chumash men whom he considered the "best Hispanicized among the Indians and who are persons of great intelligence." The injustice of the whipping and lack of recourse reflected, he emphasized, the many humiliations and despotic actions that characterized the behavior of the soldiers. The circumstances that provoked the revolt included daily humiliation, suffering, theft of their crops, general mistreatment, and labor without pay. Although they had long endured these abuses, he said, they spoke without anger. Since the Mexican era began, he argued, these problems had greatly increased. In one of his many quotes of purported Indigenous voices, he said they asked, "Now that they should treat us with even greater kindness, they act in a worse manner."[69] He emphasized their childlike humility: they brought up this and many other things "but with the submission of a son speaking to his father."

Fray Ripoll's account is replete with stories that would give the governor rightful cause to issue a pardon: the Chumash revolted on the basis of their fear. One of the alcaldes from Santa Bárbara named Andrés told Fray Ripoll about the revolt at Santa Inés and "came to me a second time to tell me that the women had already left the mission, that he and all his people were in a great state of fear." They had been "assured that the soldiers were to come and kill them while they were at Mass." Fray Ripoll went to the presidio and summoned the three Indians to come and settle "the issue," but they answered "they were afraid." Before they moved across the mountains, he again "called them back but they replied that they were afraid to come." Fray Ripoll expressed his own fear that the military policy of retaliation would create terrible violence. His defense portrayed the Chumash as meek, fearful, under paternal authority, having just cause to rebel, and having committed comparatively little harm. These reasons favored a pardon, which was granted.

Fray Sarría wrote his own account of why the revolt transpired only after it had ended. He identified two causes. Citing purportedly Indian voices, as did Fray Ripoll, he described the principle cause as their opposition to the new laws the territorial government debated, which would enable soldiers and settlers to gain mission land.[70] The second cause was the great amount of work imposed on the native population by the missionaries to feed and cloth the soldiers.[71] Though presumably representing Indian voices and political ideas, both missionaries articulated the churches' opposition to the new laws imposed by the Mexican government. Neither missionary addressed the Indian politics identified in native accounts but, rather, they attributed political motives consistent with the ideas of the church.

Some of the military and missionary records referred to the Indigenous leaders as revolutionaries and rebels. Those references may have arisen because leaders expressed political visions and goals that claimed the political rights offered by the new nation. But if so, their demands remained unrecorded. Those writing the reports frequently silenced their ideas. They did not, and perhaps were not able to, represent them.

CALIFORNIO ACCOUNTS: INDIAN HEROISM

The great Indian leader José Pacomío organized a revolution that had killing all of the de razón *as its objective.*
—GENERAL MARIANO GUADALUPE VALLEJO, 1874–76

In his five-volume history of California, former Mexican General Mariano Vallejo, a member of the California landowning, military, and political elite, contributed yet another story to the *rashomon*–like series of accounts of the 1824 revolution, as he and the military court at mission La Purísima referred to it.[72] Interested in leaving a history of California that demonstrated its elevated civilization before the American invasion of 1846, Vallejo began writing what became a 900-page history in 1867. The manuscript burned, together with his large library of more than 12,000 books. The five-volume history discussed here resulted from his dictation of a narrative he defiantly called "his story" to Henry Cerruti, an assistant of Hubert Howe Bancroft between 1874 and 1876. In the style of the rest of his history, Mariano Vallejo wrote about the revolt as "memories and stories of an irretrievable past."[73]

Vallejo organized the story of the revolt around a single leader, "the great Indian boss, José Pacoméo." Pacomío [the spelling used in the Spanish records and today] was one of four leaders of the revolt sentenced in March 1824 to permanent exile from Mission La Purísima and ten years labor at Monterey Presidio.[74] Vallejo attributed Pacomío with such extraordinary intelligence that Fray Payeras of Mission La Purísima had selected him out from the others, taught him to read and write, and placed him as an apprentice with a Spaniard for four years to learn carpentry and plaster work. The carpenter suggested Pacomío go to Europe, where he could make a good life free from the prejudice that would keep an Indian with skills earning less in the Americas. Pacomío responded that he had "a mission to complete" in California.

With the apparent rift growing between the white population and the missionaries after Mexican independence, Pacomío "resolved to prepare a coup that in one day could do away with the *de razón* established in the country."[75] For a "work of revenge," Vallejo stated, without evidence to back it, Pacomío brought together native people from as far south as San Buenaventura and as far north as the Missions of San José and Santa Clara. "Two thousand Indians arrived from other missions to attack and take prisoner the guard at La Purísima." Pacomío, he elaborated, also promised to open the road to the missions to the "wild Indians" and "in one well-combined blow put an end to their slavery."[76]

His divided loyalties constitute the core of Vallejo's drama: Pacomío felt torn between gratitude to the missionaries and his desire for revenge. After recounting the retaking of Mission La Purísima and the truce secured through Portillo's expedition to extend the pardon to the exiles in Yokuts territories, Vallejo focused on the celebration and citizenship extended to Pacomío by Governor Argüello. Vallejo ends his story by recounting that Pacomío never broke the laws of the country again. The California settlers felt so appreciative, he argued, that they elected him as a member of the town council of the capital in Monterey.

Vallejo's history presented an extraordinary leader who rose out of enslavement to set his people free. That is a powerful nationalist narrative that presents Mexico as a liberal and enlightened nation capable of producing heroic Indigenous citizens. His focus on Pacomío emphasized the success of the civilizing dimension of California history. As narrator, Vallejo was not alone in selecting an Indian hero for this purpose. In his history of California, Juan Bautista Alvarado also represented Pacomío as a hero and the Chumash revolt as an attempt of Indians to gain liberty from an oppressive church.[77]

Identifying one individual as the most important leader of the revolt is consistent with the notion of the masculine national hero. Pacomío was one among many convicted leaders in the 1824 war. Identifying his sole leadership ignores the many political visions, aims, and objectives that the Chumash sought in the rebellion. In fact, many leaders of the revolt worked together as a group, and they allied with Yokuts leaders. Other Chumash men and women could read, write, and had been trained in various kinds of skilled labor. Pacomío was not alone in being able to move between worlds, although he made extraordinary gains in his civil status in the years immediately after the revolt.

Pacomío went to Monterey to serve his sentence of eight years of labor at the Presidio, but at some point in the reconciliation process, Pacomío and the others were pardoned. The 1829 census listed Pacomío as a *vecino* and citizen. He had the right to vote.[78] Previous to his exile he had worked as a carpenter in Monterey, and he resumed that job. Pacomío lived in Monterey with his second wife and stepson, and his daughter and son-in-law. His daughter, María de Jesús, had married a Chumash man named Gregorio from Mission Santa Inés, whom she met in Monterey. The ties to their Indian community offered Pacomío and his family bonds of kinship in Monterey.

Pacomío stayed active in Indian politics. In 1833, he petitioned Governor Figueroa for his portion of the property of Mission La Purísima. At that date, the government was formulating plans to secularize the missions. Pacomío's demand articulated a radical vision of right to mission property as Indigenous land. Other Indigenous leaders shared that vision in 1833. But at no point did government policy recognize that as a right, or allot individuals parcels of mission land on that basis, and Pacomío did not receive any of the land.[79]

Pacomío lived within a larger Indigenous community in Monterey where people remembered him for his ability to sing and perform dances. María Viviana Soto recalled seeing him dance painted in red, white, and black, with feathers on his head and a breech-cloth.[80] An Indigenous citizen, he participated in native political, religious, and cultural life as an important figure. Active in dance practice, he had also been involved in revolutionary activity at the mission and formal political participation in Indigenous and civic politics while living in Monterey.

A final word on Californios' stories about the revolt is needed. Antonio María Osío wrote a history of California in 1851. In his account, purportedly uncivilized Indians rose up against heroic missionaries and military officials. He called the rebels "devil followers" who seized the moment when conditions for revolt appeared. Those conditions arose, he reported, from the large number of Indians "reduced" into the missions in 1823 (yet the mission's baptismal records do not show any mass baptisms).[81] He argued that the mass murder of whites constituted the major objective of the revolt.

Osío wasn't in California at the time of the revolt. He moved to Monterey in 1826 from Loreto, Baja California. His account reflects what he heard from other Californios, for whom many Indian people remained minors, lacking reason and rights. Those attitudes would make Indian equality difficult to achieve in California in the years subsequent to the revolt.[82]

CAUSES AND SIGNIFICANCE OF THE WAR

The Chumash stories offer information about the forms of power and political visions that Chumash leaders held during the revolt, and a focus on Chumash actions suggests impressive coordination and strategy on the part of the leaders. Chumash leaders from Santa Bárbara drove cattle and other livestock with them as they fled the mission. They gifted the meat and other things while seeking refuge, safety, and space for ceremony and ritual. They successfully made those alliances, and the revolt drew on an enormous amount of support from Yokuts and other Indians. At the end of the war, some of those Yokuts leaders went to Chumash missions in the reconciliation ceremonies. They were invited to participate in order to acknowledge and celebrate the reestablishment of peace.

It seems clear that Chumash leaders thought they could engage the support of at least some Yokuts allies. They made excellent use of their connections with *cimarrones,* who been baptized earlier at one of the three missions involved and then fled. The *cimarrones* made important connections for the rebels with village leaders in their own villages, and in villages where they had formed connections through marriage or clan relations. The alliances made with people from Tulamni, the area of Buena Vista Lake, proved very significant. Many of the villages around the lake offered critical help to the Chumash during the war. Chumash leaders strategized to secure help as they moved into exile from the missions.

The forms of power and political visions held by the Chumash leaders are elaborated in community memory. For Solares, the story involved Indigenous belief that they would be impervious to Spanish bullets. This would be one of many prophecies that took place in Chumash territory (as discussed in chapter 2). Indigenous thought involved the transposition of human beings into other forms, such as the ability of the men to move through the keyhole discussed by Solares. She suggested the presence and power of revitalization thought at Mission Santa Inés when she said that people believed "the bullets will not hurt me." In Ripoll's story Valentín Cota's actions spurred the revolt. In Maria Solares's account, Valentín served as a soldier whom Indigenous leaders confused and defeated.

The image and power of the horse in Chumash histories spoke of non-Western structures of knowledge and power involved in the revolt. Horses appeared in relationship to the power of the ¿atishwin. Those who wore it could jump on a horse and be transported, invisibly, to reappear "on the hilltop." As with the Indian paintings discussed in chapter 3, the ethnographies brought the horse into shamanic thought just as Solares, Garcia, and Ignacio relate elements of it in their accounts.

These stories resemble other native narrations of the past that offer a framework to understand Indigenous authority and the many sides to it, including the story of Indians who became "too close" to the missionaries and betrayed the rest of the community. They express the vulnerability that all felt in the face of persistent violence, and the importance of facing death together, as stressed by Maria Solares. They speak to the power native leaders invested in ritual objects. Rather than describing communities living in fear or overwhelmed by the Spanish conquest, Indigenous writers and oral historians left records that emphasized Indigenous sources of power and native solutions.

Joanne Rappaport emphasizes that "history is a question of power" as she traces how Indigenous writers navigate the conventions of official documentation to produce their own histories. Those histories told within Indigenous communities, she argues, differ from others "in their narrative structures." They are usually "encoded in physical space."[83] Native historians tend to address their own pasts. They often condense time frames and relate their histories through myth, ritual, and other oral and performative mediums. Native documents tend to make local claims.

In recovering Indigenous stories, languages, and epistemologies, Indigenous histories speak to "oral ways of knowing." They often involve "contested stories and multiple discourses" to establish "a range of truths."[84] The Chumash narratives about the revolt relate to the plurality and multiplicity of family stories and pasts. As other native narrations about history, they offer ways to understand and reconcile painful events with other kinds of truths, like the importance of community and Indigenous leadership. As Ashis Nandy writes about histories formulated outside the Western concept of "objective, hard history," they are intended to produce a more reliable, ethical, or reasonable way of constructing the past. In the case of Chumash histories of the war, they simultaneously recognize loss, anger, vulnerability, and the viability of Indigenous ways of seeing and forms of power.[85]

The many stories and archival sources converge in a vivid history of the war that opens an era of native politics ignited by diverse demands and structures of leadership. In identifying an Indigenous citizen as hero, Vallejo kept an important part of the history of this era in sight. Pacomío, like other leaders in Chumash territory, was knowledgeable about the formal legal rights Indigenous people held. He provided leadership in traditional Indigenous ritual and politics and had been involved in formal politics. Pacomío knew Chumash dance and song and sacred language. He claimed his rights as citizen and claimed his rights as a former colonial subject. He lived in a community of Chumash, Ohlone, and Indigenous people of many origins in Monterey. After 1826, many others would begin to seek the conditions of Indigenous citizenship that Pacomío ultimately exercised.

As will be seen in the next chapter, Indigenous people began to attain legal rights during the late 1820s in California, but that was not yet the case in 1824. Two years later, the first provisional emancipation decree was passed. It opened the way for a change in the colonial status of neophytes under the law, and would initiate other aspects of Indigenous politics during this era.

5

"We Solicit Our Freedom"

Citizenship and the Patria

Emancipation from the state of *neófia* constituted the first step in attaining citizenship. Emancipation from that condition of being bound to the mission began in California on a provisional basis in 1826. It continued long after the final Decree of Emancipation and Secularization passed the California Legislature on August 9, 1834.

Emancipation was a process unique, in the Mexican Republic, to California. Prior to Independence, the colonial government had secularized the missions in the colonial center of Mexico, and then in Mexico's north, including Sonora and Texas. During the colonial period, the government referred to the process of releasing Indigenous people from the status of neophyte as secularization, whereby priests, rather than the missionary orders, assumed charge of the mission church. The state and church claimed the rest of the mission's property and wealth, which was partially redistributed among former neophytes. Their populations formed Indian pueblos or became part of the society of *castas*. With Mexican Independence and the new condition of Indigenous equality and citizenship, the government talked not only about secularization of the missions, but about emancipation itself, a process that acknowledged the new political rights of Indigenous people. The process of emancipation began in California before the secularization of the missions. Yet historians rarely acknowledge this history of emancipation, or talk about the history of Indigenous political visions and demands.

The government used the term *emancipation* in its official decrees, and the process raised questions over the meaning of freedom and the organization of labor, land, and citizenship that other post-emancipation societies debated. The nature of unfreedom under *neofía,* and the smaller scale of emancipation, distinguish California from the emancipation of African-descent peoples from slavery in other young republics. Yet emancipation in California raised the same questions. In addition, the political debate about emancipation and secularization in California formed part of the Mexican national discussion of the rights of Indigenous citizens. California had not yet been integrated into the Mexican national story of Indigenous citizenship, yet it formed an intricate part of that era and those political struggles.[1]

PETITIONING FOR EMANCIPATION AND SEEKING FREEDOM

From your generous goodness, we solicit our freedom.
—VICENTE JUAN AND GASPAR, INDIANS OF THE MISSION OF SOLEDAD TO GOVERNOR ECHEANDÍA, 1826

José María Echeandía, the first governor of California appointed by the Mexican nation and a liberal in favor of Indigenous citizenship rights, initiated a provisional emancipation shortly after he arrived in California in 1826.[2] He sent out a circular that enabled self-supporting Christians (from birth or for fifteen years) to apply to be disaffiliated from their mission. In this same document Governor Echeandía told the missionaries to provide information on runaways from each mission, and to give the runaways who qualified a license to disaffiliate from their mission. He instructed the missionaries to find and force the return of those who did not qualify. In acknowledgment of the 1812 Spanish Constitution and the laws of Mexico, Governor Echeandía restricted punishment to incarceration. But, in parentheses he said that whipping adults would be tolerated for the moment, restricting it to fifteen lashes per week per individual.

The new law required that each missionary (except in the San Francisco district) identify neophytes ready for emancipation. Some native petitioners wrote their own requests. Others had petitions written for them by the missionaries. A statement by a missionary or military officer in charge of the district had to attest to the Christian education and conduct of the petitioner and affirm his ability to be self-supporting. If granted permission, the petitioners would "segregate themselves from the condition of being a neophyte with their family, if they have one, and go to where it is most advantageous as a member of the Mexican nation. . . ."[3]

Men alone shared the full rights of citizenship under Mexican law, including the vote. Women tended to be named in the petitions of their husbands and related men, and the wives and children of male petitioners received their licenses to leave the missions along with their husbands and fathers. But, women's work related to the preparation of foods and the labor that sustained daily and material life, as well as women's skills in manufacturing products, remained unrecorded. As women, they stood outside the definition of citizen.

Emancipation petitions began to be written almost immediately after the circulation of the decree. One of the first would refer to Indigenous citizenship, the tentative nature of which is suggested by its virtual absence in subsequent records. Written on April 30, 1826, the petitioner identified himself as "the citizen Gil" from Mission San Diego. He worked as a carpenter. With that skill, he stated, he could "go where he is able to exercise it and enjoy the benefits that it can bring."[4] Echeandía sent the short petition back to the missionaries with questions written in the margins, asking whether Gil had been a Christian since childhood and about his conduct and matrimonial status.[5]

The missionaries at San Diego responded that Gil Ricla (now with a last name) had been a Christian since his infancy. A child of Christian parents and born at the mission, he was twenty-nine years old (born c. 1797). He was married to Pia, who had been baptized at Mission San Luis Rey, and they had three children who would leave the mission with them.[6] Granted a license that allowed them to live outside of the mission and move about, the missionary scratched their names off the mission roll. As with others who received permission to leave their mission during this era, each person in the Ricla family would need to carry his or her license in order to prove their emancipated state.

Ricla's father had come to San Diego from Baja California to help found the Alta California missions. As such, he translated the project of colonialism to the population at that mission. Gil had already served in the capacity of being a godparent to many new converts and had sponsored a number of marriages by the time he applied for his emancipation. With their *licencia* to leave the mission, Gil Ricla's family moved to the Presidio of San Diego where he worked as a carpenter. Ricla, like Pacomío, one of the Chumash leaders from Mission La Purísima, ultimately enjoyed the status of citizen. [7] Others would join them.

Ricla's emancipation seems straightforward, but its terms were fraught with potential problems that arose with land, tools, and goods for subsistence, none of which he received. Yet, even under these precarious conditions, Ricla and many others would seek their licenses. The previous years of public celebrations of the new republic and discussions of equality seemed to have generated a sense of hope and possibilities visible in these early petitions.[8]

A group of early petitioners from Mission San Buenaventura carried the intent of provisional emancipation a step further, making a collective request on behalf of 125 men from the mission. This was a number that included a substantial sector of the entire male population at San Buenaventura on October 23, 1826 (see the Appendix). As Fray Señan had written more than a decade before, the population at San Buenaventura fostered close ties of kinship among them that conformed to long histories and an interwoven tribal and mission past. The petitioners Pacífico,

Mansueto, and Francisco Xavier wrote in the elaborate language of respect used in the formal Spanish of the era. They drew a design on the petition that was similar to those on baskets the mission sold to trade ships.[9] The petition included their signatures at a time when many settlers and Indians could not sign their names, identifying an Indigenous leadership that could read about their new rights.

The petitioners followed the requirements Echeandía had set forward for emancipation petitions. The petitioners elaborated the occupations found among self-supporting citizens: they represented cowboys, weavers, tile makers, soap makers, and laborers, among other skilled workers. In a second petition that they wrote five days later, Pacífico, Gervasio, and Peregrino María requested that Echeandía convert the mission into a pueblo. This request followed the premises of the 1813 law formulated in the Cortes of Cádiz and widely pronounced a decade earlier in California during the governorship of Solá. In a third petition that they carried to Echeandía while he was stationed in San Diego, they asked him to redistribute the mission's land, money, seeds, livestock, and tools among them. That request also conformed to their rights under the Constitution of Cádiz.[10] Though the idea of forming Indian pueblos from mission land and redistributing mission goods among their populations had long been discussed, Echeandía's emancipation plan did not include those rights, and Echeandía denied their requests.

Other petitions followed. A man named Jacobo Niacopal presented himself before Echeandía and asked to be "disaffiliated to support himself with his wife outside this mission."[11] Echeandía wrote a brief petition on his behalf, and the following day the missionaries affirmed that they gave a license to Jacobo Niacopal and Christina Samanan to disaffiliate from the condition of *neofía* and earn their living with their labor.[12] A petition made on October 30, 1826, asked for the release of Jacome de la Ulorca and his wife Beata Rosa. Born at Mission San Carlos, both had been Christians from birth. They included in their petition a widower named Loreto. The petition confirmed that Loreto, baptized at six years of age in 1791, knew the Catholic ceremonies and how to pray. The missionary removed Jacome de la Ulorca, Beata Rosa, and Loreto from the mission rolls. All three people, Fray Abella wrote, applied themselves diligently to their work and could support themselves.[13]

Manuel Ventura asked for his "segregation" from the mission of San Carlos. Written "with the most profound respect that is owed," he referred to the law that allowed Indians whose religious conduct made them eligible to "segregate themselves from their mission to freely use" their abilities and skills to support themselves. It is not by chance that Ventura brings the word "freely" (or *libremente*) into his petition; the word remained absent from those written by the missionaries but formed a common parlance among Indigenous people.[14]

The word *freedom* did not form part of the official vocabulary of the California government when they decreed emancipation or approved petitions, yet Indian people wrote and spoke of freedom repeatedly. They referred to *libertad* or liberty, and to emancipated individuals as *gente libre* or free people. Santiago Argüello emphasized this difference when referring to people emancipated during this time. He wrote about "some of those emancipated who they call free." Argüello emphasized the different language and called attention to the different visions it expressed. Pablo de la Portilla noted the same distinction when writing about "the emancipated whom they call free."[15]

The government documents referred to people being "released from *neófia*," "scratched off the mission roll," or allowed to "disaffiliate" from their mission. That language stands in sharp contrast to the idea of "freedom," itself open to interpretation. As in other areas in which governments emancipated people from conditions of slavery and coercion, emancipated populations defined, gave meaning to, and attempted to shape the conditions of their freedom despite the many constraints imposed upon them.[16]

Indian petitioners such as Manuel Ventura used the official language and the word *freedom*. Vicente Juan and Gaspar from Mission Soledad wrote their own petition to Echeandía. Describing themselves as married, workers, and Christians who had been born at the mission, they also used the word *freedom*. They wrote:

> Vicente Juan and Gaspar, Indians of the Mission of Soledad, married, and workers: we present ourselves before you with the most profound respect and we say that, having been born in this mission, and knowledgeable about the Christian Religion, according to our abilities and the instruction that we have been given by the missionaries, we consider ourselves capable of maintaining ourselves with our work. We put ourselves before your wisdom [asking] you, if you find it just, to segregate us from said Mission and missionaries.

In a postscript, they added, "From your generous goodness, we solicit our freedom."[17]

Governor Echeandía sent a note back to Mission Soledad requesting more information about the petitioners. Fray Francisco Xavier Uría (who had worked at Mission Santa Ines at the time of the 1824 revolt) wrote a favorable response. Vicente Juan had been baptized at the mission at the age of three months and trained as a cook. Gaspar worked as a *vaquero*. Fray Uría considered both men skilled workers. Vicente Juan's wife Vanerada and Gaspar's wife Antonia had been baptized as eighteen-year-old adults. The women's status, particularly the comparatively short number of years these women had spent in the mission, did not seem to be of great concern to the missionary. Uría extended licenses to all four to leave the mission.[18]

By 1829, the petitions became shorter, as if the process had grown routine. Petitions often included nothing more than notices that a license had been given. A note from Fray Sánchez at Mission San Gabriel, for example, simply announced that Juan Agustín and his wife Casimira were segregated from the *padrón* (census) of the mission. Fray Sánchez wrote that he placed a note in the respective mission censuses to that order.[19]

Persons thus emancipated left the missions without land, animals, or tools to cultivate the land and carry out their craft, and without any recognition of their rights to their tribal territory. Despite being able to move where they might find jobs to use their skills, being disaffiliated under these terms created an incredibly precarious existence. It set those emancipated at odds with the most normal precedents in which settlers and soldiers alike initially received seeds, tools, and livestock as they set up their households in the towns and presidios of California.

Patricio, who petitioned for his own emancipation from Mission La Purísima, attempted to avoid utter poverty when he asked for the land that he already cultivated at the mission in his emancipation petition. He did so at a time when many former soldiers and settlers already petitioned for and sometimes received pieces of mission land. Yet, Fray Marco Antonio de Victoria wrote a strong letter against Patricio's request. "In no way can I agree that a neophyte be given particular land of the mission," he emphasized.[20] Fray Victoria articulated the position held by all the missionaries at that point. They considered that the mission land belonged to the new community of Christian Indians that had been created at each mission, rather than to the tribes whose lands the missions now claimed.

In the colonial and early Mexican period, the state gave settlers and retired soldiers in California plots of land to grow table food, more substantial plots for field crops, and orchards. As vecinos or town dwellers who shared responsibilities to maintain the town and church and rights to use common areas and resources, they had access to common land and water for their livestock. They assumed a shared responsibility to maintain the common good, and to sustain their own fields, orchards, and households. To conduct a trade and meet basic needs, every individual needed tools, livestock, and land. Few owned substantial property upon their migration northward, and even fewer carried goods away from the mission. Without a plot of land in the California territory, individuals and their families lacked the material means to exercise their sovereign status as citizens.

Local practices generally failed to extend the rights of vecino to those emancipated. Rather than being allowed to settle as vecinos with land and water rights in the towns of San José, Los Angeles, Branciforte, or in the presidios and emergent pueblos of San Diego and Monterey, the majority of emancipated families found it difficult to find a secure place to live during this period. They resided in the households of non-Indians as servants and in communities on the outskirts of towns where Indian neighborhoods existed. They established small farms near the missions they left on land the missionaries allowed them to cultivate. Some moved to the ranchos (ranch lands) that settlers, soldiers, and new migrants from Mexico began to be awarded by the state. Others returned to their villages where that possibility existed, but the law would not protect their tribal land. In formulating emancipation and secularization law, neither the California Territorial Legislature nor the Mexican Congress acknowledged Indigenous rights to their ancestral lands. Without land, and in the face of limited conditions for sustaining their livelihoods, many people eventually returned to the environs of their missions. The missions remained Indigenous communities, and held many Indigenous territories and ancestral sites within their boundaries.

As waves of emancipations occurred in response to subsequent government mandates, many people would be crossed off the mission rolls and allowed to leave the missions with little more than their passes. A decree sent unsigned from Monterey, for example, simply read that Fausto, Dionicio, Antonio, Ignacio, Jacobo, Manuel, and José Antonio were segregated from Mission San Luis Rey. Another segregated José Conrado from the condition of *neofía* at San Gabriel.[21] At Mission Soledad, the missionary erased Pasioc Maioc, Simeon, Santa Ana Unquigo, and their families from the mission rolls.[22] In a separate document also from Soledad, Agapito and his son received their license to leave the mission.[23] In contrast to the initial petitions, these examples of abbreviated ones left off the petitioners' formal names, status as Christians, occupations, and references to their family circumstances.

Pablo de la Portillo emphasized the precarious conditions faced by those emancipated during the first seven years of the process when, in 1833, he wrote about "the time of Don José María de Echeandía." He recalled it as a period when "the emancipated who they call free" would only be given a license to leave. "Without anything else they were given the paper and they had to leave their mission with their families to accommodate themselves as servants to subsist." Despite the many skills they had, popular practice left many in the social position of servant. Portillo said the majority had to return to their missions in order to support themselves.[24] When advising the government, both he and General Argüello stated that these first *licenciados* emancipated before the final decree and distribution of land, should also be granted rights in the final Emancipation and Secularization decree. Yet, no such provisions would be made.

Some Indigenous people worked within the law as they gave their own meaning to emancipation, and increasing numbers of people took their freedom outside the law. In February 1828, the entire community from Mission San José had been released on week passes so that they could return to their native territories, visit relatives, hunt, and gather seeds and other goods. After the end of their time, people from the village of Lacquisamnes refused to return. Others from that territory at Missions Santa Clara, Santa Cruz, and San Juan Bautista joined them, and they took many horses with them. "They have declared themselves rebels *(alzados)*," the missionary wrote. He went on to note they did not fear the soldiers because, in a statement meant to imply he quoted their words, the soldiers numbered very few and they "don't know how to shoot." The missionary blamed their insurgence on two leaders, Estanislao from Mission San José, and Cipriano from Mission Santa Clara. Missionary Durán asked for troops to be sent after them before the rains and requested Estanislao and Cipriano be brought back dead or alive.[25]

The group continued to accumulate horses, and one year later, they began to take a more aggressive stance by raiding the missions for goods as they built their base of power in the countryside.[26] By August 1829 Missionary José Viader at Mission Santa Clara promised those who had revolted from his mission a full pardon if they returned. The group demanded the pardon be extended to Cipriano as well. Cipriano sought confirmation that the government would comply with that agreement and warned they could not expect the group to return without it.[27] In the climate of change and growing rights, the missionaries extended the pardon to Estanislao and Cipriano, who remained visible leaders at each mission. It is striking here that this group returned to their territory from various missions under a strong leadership, and yet their life there did not seem to offer a viable long-term solution. The continuous threat of military intervention and harassment and the difficulties subsisting in an environment that had undergone change from traders, trappers, warfare, and illness for decades left them unable to reassume life in their village by 1829.

MAPPING NATIONAL TERRITORY AND LOSING SITE OF THE *PATRIAS*

The nation wanted the lands of the missions that were forged from native territories and identified as *patrias* in the baptismal records. In 1822 and again in 1827 the Territorial Legislature asked each missionary to draw up the boundaries of his mission. The legislature wanted to know about the size and wealth of each mission, whether it could support its population, asked for figures on the quality and quantity of production, and solicited ideas about how to increase the output of goods. But of central concern here is the question of mission boundaries. One of the objectives of the inventory was to determine what land the state intended to claim. It read, in part, "What quantity of land does the mission recognize as its own?"[28] Very few missionaries attributed mission land to the Indigenous populations, or referred to the Spanish laws that guaranteed Indigenous land rights to their original and improved land. Some did. But in each of these inventories, the Indigenous territories that the missions had enveloped disappeared from the records. The land became firmly identified and mapped as mission or church property.

Only the missionaries at San Luis Rey and San Juan Capistrano, and Frays Sarría and Abella from San Juan Bautista, defended Indian land rights. Fray Peyri repeatedly claimed San Luis Rey's land to be the possession of the Luiseños population. He also spoke of the mission's vibrant economy. He described the production of Spanish seeds, by which he meant the colonial foods of wheat, corn, and a large assortment of beans that, he said, "in an occasional year supports the entire population." He also emphasized that the Luiseños, or "the *Naturales*" as he called them, harvested "wild seeds and fruits, and fish from their beaches."²⁹ "Their" beaches remained a crucial reference to ownership and reinforced his instance that the land belonged to the Luiseño community as a whole.

But Fray Peyri's language obscured the nature of Luiseños' claims to land that identified specific and historic territories that belonged to different groups. In Luiseño geography people held affinities to specific tribal and mission spaces. Yet Peyri wrote as if everything had always been shared rather than highly demarcated and carefully ordered with rules as to who could use what. Moreover, more than half of the mission population still lived in their villages among non-Christians. Peyri wrote, "The natural citizens *(ciudadanos naturales)* have various parcels where they fish," but he obscured tribal claims when he wrote of "parcels," bringing a tribal system of tenure into an incompatible notion of place. His reference to *ciudadanos naturales* contained colonial and early national references. "Naturales" had noncivilized properties. *Ciudadanos* acknowledged the official policy under Emperor Iturbide when the law mandated that the word *indio* be replaced by *citizen*. But, if affiliation to the mission could denote being a member of a single community, Luiseños also had different historic communities and multiple ways of identifying the territories and specificities of ownership claims.

Peyri seemed to erase the larger socioeconomic and political system integral to Luiseño land tenure in his definition of Luiseño territory. Though he defined mission land as Luiseño land, he did not acknowledge village possession and differentiation. In effect, the concept that all of Luiseño land belonged to the entire mission community went against the political structure that organized tribal society.

The missionaries at San Juan Capistrano proved the most exacting in their defense of Indian land as they drew the boundaries of the mission. Like Peyri, they insisted that the mission land "legitimately belonged to" the entire Indigenous community.³⁰ Speaking against the encroachment on the land that pertained to Mission San Juan Capistrano by Mission San Luis Rey, they articulated the most common defense: "All have been baptized in this church and some of them who were born there are still alive." And again, in reference to San Luis Rey's substantial *rancho* of San Jacinto, they claimed, "All the lands that are on the other side of said hill, towards the west, are San Juan Capistranos" because people baptized at the mission were born there. People from those territories had affiliated to both missions. The villages did not simply pertain to one mission or another. The idea of these territories forming a single mission space obliterated claims to ancestral land made during this era by Indigenous communities.

The missionaries from San Juan Capistrano cited the colonial laws discussed earlier, which declared no one could take away lands originally possessed by the Indians when they relocated to new Indian pueblos or missions. Nor could Indigenous villages and land be given away to Spaniards or others. The missionaries cited other laws including the ones that defined the needs of each Indian pueblo or mission, such as water, land for grain fields, and land for cattle that would set the mission herds apart from other herds. At the end of the inventory, they asked that the "privileges and favors" the Spanish dispensed to the Indians be conserved, amplified, and extended by the Mexican state. Their defense of Indigenous lands remains a welcome intervention. Most of the inventories ignored altogether the legal precedents established by Spanish law.

From Mission San Juan Bautista, Frays Sarría and Abella wrote about Indigenous claims to land that had become mission *ranchos,* but they still identified the land as church property. Referring to the Rancho de San Bernardino or Los Sanjones, he stated that it had been the "birth place *(sitio nativo)* of the majority of the neophytes living at the mission" in 1801. He emphasized, "They recognize it as their own" and recorded the Indian name of *Ensen.* They also identified the sheep ranch La Salinas as the original site and birthplace of some of the Indians who lived at the mission in 1798.[31] But they only identified two of the missions' ten *ranchos* with Indian names, part of the erasure of the Indigenous geography of the region in this document, as in other inventories.

THE POLITICS OF INDIGENOUS CITIZENS

They have sent me to ask. . . . They want to know the truth.
—TOMÁS TAJOCHI TO ECHEANDÍA, 1833

The California territorial government voted in favor of implementing emancipation and secularization in 1831, but the arrival of Governor Manuel Victoria, newly appointed from Mexico to replace Governor Echeandía, stalled the process. A rebellion against Governor Victoria left Echeandía in power over the southern portion of the territory between 1831 and 1833.[32] During that period he had a room of his own at Mission San Luis Rey, although he made his headquarters at the Presidio of San Diego.[33]

The missions in the south were the largest, with populations of 1,004 Christian Indians at Mission San Diego and 2,122 at Mission San Luis Rey. Their populations were mobilized politically and, by February 1833, demanded emancipation. In both places only part of the population lived at the mission and others remained in their villages. San Gabriel, with 1,330 persons, had the second largest population in 1833. Sizable communities also existed at San Juan Capistrano, where 872 Achagemem and Luiseños lived. Mission San Fernando had a population of 775 people. Most missions tended to have around 500 Indigenous persons living in them by 1833.

A large group of Indigenous people from the Missions of San Luis Rey and San Diego gathered in northeastern San Diego in a meeting also attended by non-Christians among whom they lived in native villages. They met to discuss emancipation in February 1833. The group asked Tomás Tajochi, an Indigenous overseer of the Rancho Santa Mónica of Mission San Luis Rey, to represent them before former Governor Echeandía. Tajochi wrote in Spanish:

> My very esteemed José María de Echeandía Comandante General,
>
> Tonight we have had a large gathering of all the Neofites small and large, joining the people and also the Captains of the gentiles and the Captains and Alcaldes of Santa Isabel and Santa Mónica. They have sent me to ask. . . . They want to know the truth.
>
> *Tomás Tajochi February 6, 1833.*

In response, Echeandía wrote a note congratulating them for acting as citizens, stating "as Mexicanos you have done well to unite."[34] He then told them that he now obeyed Figueroa, the incoming governor, "who will act for you." He signed, with the familiarity of an egalitarian statesman, "Greetings to all. God protect you."[35] In the ensuing days, a stream of neophytes and gentiles passed by the missions to speak to Echeandía in San Diego and to inquire of the commanding officer at Mission San Luis Rey when the new leader would arrive.[36]

Four days after that meeting, rumors spread that the populations of Missions San Gabriel, San Juan Capistrano, San Luis Rey, and San Diego planned a major uprising to force the distribution of "the land and goods." They also wanted to proclaim Echeandía rather than Figueroa political leader of the province.[37] The mobilization continued within Indigenous communities, and the government took action against those they considered the leaders. On July 15, 1833, some *vecinos* from San Diego captured Christian Indians as they came from the Indian village of Tecate that now pertained to Mission San Diego. The Indians purportedly had a letter written by Tomás Tajochi to invite mission Indians and autonomous tribes to join a rebellion. Tajochi addressed people from Tecate to Mission San Gabriel and beyond. The messenger, a non-Christian named Cartucho, said he had been given a letter in which Tajochi had called all of the non-Christians together in a large rebellion. He revealed a meeting planned for July 20 in El Cajón, some 30 miles to the east of Mission San Diego.[38]

To head off a feared attack, fifty armed militia of *vecinos* and ten Indian guides set out to surprise those attending the meeting. They had orders to use their weapons with moderation, and to avoid killing women, children, and anyone who surrendered. The militia found little to reinforce their fears. They heard that the Yuma and other non-Christian groups decided against the plan once they realized someone disclosed it. Meanwhile, a conflict had arisen between Tomás Tajochi and the leader Capitán Coyote of the village of Santa Ysabel. The expedition to stop the rebellion turned into one that was asked to cultivate peace among those bitter against the Mexicans. The military strategy changed. They decided to ask the militia to encourage those who might join the rebellion to join the nation instead.[39] That gesture to non-Christian tribes remained a fundamental part of the diplomacy of the Mexican government on the northern frontier.

On July 1, 1833, alcaldes from Santa Ysabel, a historic village and part of Mission San Diego, turned Tomás Tajochi and four accomplices over to Captain Portillo. In the November trial that followed, six men were accused of trying to instigate a general uprising and an assault on the Presidio of San Diego, to "do away with the whites" and become "independent and govern themselves." Tomás Tajochi and José Antonio Molina were sentenced to two years of labor on public works. Román, Gregorio, and Peregrino received one-year sentences, and the court set a man named Domingo free.[40] Yet, the specter of fear of a united opposition of non-Christian Indians from the Colorado River and other places fluttered through the correspondence between the military leaders in 1833 as it did during the 1824 revolt. They feared Indigenous armed aggression against Los Angeles and other rapidly growing population centers in Mexican California. Their fears would be echoed in government communications throughout 1833 and 1834.[41]

Meanwhile, at Mission San Luis Rey, the missionary had become "melancholic and half-desperate" because the large population of Luiseños would not obey the orders of the missionary or soldiers. Fray Durán reported to the governor that the missionary in charge was afraid and "said yes" to everything the Luiseños demanded. He said he could not make people work without offering them compensation, nor could he punish them because of their resistance to the conditions that existed within and outside the mission.[42]

VISIONS OF AZTLÁN

No country in the Republic is better to make a fortune for the poor than Alta California.

—FIGUEROA TO HIS TROOPS, LA PAZ, CALIFORNIA, 1832

As General José Figueroa moved with his troops into California to take over the governorship, he invoked the image of Aztlán, a country "of our progenitors." He promised the troops that "they would visit the mansions where the Aztecs lived before they left for Tenoxtlán where they established the empire of Moctezuma." This reference to the Aztec empire replaced the Indigenous societies that existed in California with what had already become one of Mexico's foundation stories as a nation. Figueroa promised the troops that as Mexicans they would soon end their labors and "arrive in the privileged land . . . of our compatriots the Californios," placing the soldiers' stakes with the region's settlers. He insisted that the troops served to "accomplish the will of the heavens" and promised them that upon completing their task they would "attain the benefits" they deserved in terms of land and wealth. Figuroa's speech to the troops emphasized once and again that Alta

California offered the best country in the republic "to make a fortune for the poor."[43] His attitudes reflected the government's intention to colonize California with Mexicans and foreigners who would build a national patrimony in an area still largely unsettled.

Figueroa supported the Federalists, as did Echeandía, and not the Centralist that Governor Manuel Victoria had represented. Victoria had returned to Mexico in January 1832. Figueroa's first act was to make peace with those who supported Governor Manuel Victoria and to bring the territory back into political union. Echeandía prepared the way for Governor Figueroa's arrival, speaking "to the Californios" in San Diego, calling for patriotic unity and promising they would enjoy "the general rights of our República Mexicana and the particular rights of Alta California."[44] Figueroa spent his first months in Monterey, where he presented a general amnesty for the participants in the 1831 rebellion. He promised soldiers and settlers alike a redistribution of land from mission property.[45]

To build patriotism Figueroa sent out orders for a large celebration of the Mexican Republic. He mandated that the order be sent to every small place so that they could observe the day. In Monterey, the festivities would include a run of bulls, fireworks, and a dance. Figueroa would make the most concerted effort to build national sentiment that had been undertaken in California.[46] He emphasized the need for constitutional order and unity and initially seemed to be concerned with completing the mandates of the nation in terms of recognizing Indigenous citizenship.

DEFINING FREEDOM: INDIAN TOWNS VERSUS LA MISIÓN AND PATRIAS

. . . to elevate them to the dignity of free men . . .
—SANTIAGO ARGÜELLO, SEPTEMBER 27, 1833

In response to the demands for emancipation emanating from Indigenous communities in southern California, in July 1833 General Figueroa drew up "Provisional Steps for the Emancipation of Mission Indians," which allowed those emancipated to step out of the condition of being minors under the law and to assume citizenship. The plan warned officials to be sure to extend to the emancipated their rights of citizenship and to ensure that Indigenous men "receive equal treatment during voting."[47]

The many rules the plan set forth made this citizenship an altogether unstable condition. The provisional emancipation law required the emancipated to form self-governing pueblos. Following Mexican land law, the private allotments could not be divided or sold, but they could be inherited by wives, sons, daughters, and their descendants. The villagers were obliged to build the town through their common labor, including the construction of dams, irrigation ditches, corals, places to round up the cattle, and a church in their new pueblos. In this plan, citizenship involved the assumption and management of private property. Article 23 established the tentative nature of the legal condition of emancipation. If the emancipated did not attend to their work or care for the cattle, failed to cultivate their land, or abandoned their houses to move around like vagrants, "they will again be subjugated to the missions they left."[48]

With the intention of putting a provisional emancipation into effect in the three southern missions where the political agitation for emancipation had been strongest, the government hoped to create exemplar Indian pueblos of productive citizens that could be models for others during emancipation. Figueroa ordered General Santiago Argüello to identify those among the mission populations "who have good dispositions" and to distribute "land and some goods" among them so they could cultivate the land. The decree also stated that the pueblos "should adopt measures to govern themselves" that are consistent with forms of governance in the republic. As elsewhere in Mexico, the pueblos would have an infrastructure of water and land that they would hold as a corporate entity. The decree emphasized that the emancipated needed to value the private property distributed to them.

As he began to implement the plan, General Argüello expressed his conviction that, above all, mission Indians needed experience with autonomy and instruction in how to build a town. This idea of initiating a "practice in freedom" would be used in Jamaica during these same years by instituting an "internship" program of three years for emancipated people. The idea would be part of emancipation laws in other places too.[49] On September 27, 1833, General Argüello began to select people for emancipation from among those identified as the "most civilized." He intended "to elevate them to the dignity of free men."[50] When they were emancipated to form the pueblo, General Argüello asked the adults to swear their allegiance to the Mexican nation.

With the aid of the missionaries, he identified 109 adults and their families— approximately a fifth of the mission population—for emancipation, but when he gathered the group together, most refused his offer. Argüello proposed that they accept emancipation and form an Indian pueblo at San Dieguito, an Indigenous territory renamed by the Spanish. But when he did so, only those from San Dieguito and the person appointed as the leader of the group accepted the emancipation. The others refused. Yet, people at Mission San Diego and vicinity had been among the most militant in demanding emancipation. Why did they reject the offer?

Speaking against forming a pueblo in San Dieguito, one man spoke up and said that water and good land existed in his territory. Eager to set the process in motion, Argüello responded favorably to what he though he understood and said that the pueblo could be established in that leaders' territory instead. The man responded, "No sir, those from San Dieguito won't go to my land." He repeated it several times and ended by saying, "We will stay in our mission."[51]

Of the initial 109 people in the group, four related adults, all from San Dieguito, accepted the terms of emancipation that Argüello offered, as did the relatives of Ligorio María Yeutec, whom Argüello selected as the leader of the pueblo. Ligorio María Yeutec, a fifty-four-year-old carpenter, had been born at the mission. His forty-five-year-old wife María Antonia Tecala came from a village named Pomo. Their two children and Yeutec's older son Zeferino, all born at the mission, would join him, as would another probable relative named Armando Ligorio. The family of six from the territory of San Dieguito included a man aged seventy-one who had been a Christian for fifty-six years, and his forty-nine-year-old wife, a Christian for twenty-nine years. Their adult children had been raised at the mission, as had the two relatives: a man aged forty-four who had been a Christian all of his life and worked as a shoemaker, and his thirty-one-year-old sister.

Two things stand out prominently: although they had lived all or the better part of their lives at the mission, those from San Dieguito sought to return to their territory with families and relatives from a larger mission community that had been forged over decades. Twenty-four other adults from that tribal territory would soon join them. This group immediately petitioned to "leave" the condition of *neófia*, be emancipated, and return to their territory with their families.[52] Between the ages of twenty-one and fifty-eight, the group included ten couples, nine children, and four single men. Of the fourteen employed men, most listed their specific skills: five worked as fishermen, three as carpenters, three worked with livestock, and one was a shoemaker. Once situated at San Dieguito, some of the men and women might also engage in work on ranches and in the towns as domestic laborers and seasonal workers in livestock and farming.

Among those people who said they preferred to stay at the mission, nearly half had either been born at Santa Ysabel, a historic village to the northeast of the mission that some people still inhabited, or they had been born at the mission itself. The other half of those selected had come from a large range of villages: La Soledad, La Punta, Valle San Luis, Santa Mónica, La Perla, San Miguel, Río Oso, Jupai, Techa, Yguai, Captijua, Otai, Pomo, and Tía Juana. The majority of the population had been Christians for ten to twenty years and some since birth. Others had spent as many as thirty to forty years at the mission. Despite that length of time, all participated in a vision of emancipation that involved returning to their territories and repossessing their ancestral land. Short of that, they wanted to stay within the mission where they and their relatives had cultivated and irrigated the land and created lives.

Of those who had been selected but did not leave the mission, around one hundred adults and eighty-three children, the men held a range of skills that would have been common in any town. Thirty-two laborers made up the largest group.

Five cowboys, two fishermen, a carpenter, a stockman, two blacksmiths, a chocolate maker, a cook, a shoemaker, and an alcalde defined some of the many skills people possessed and the Indigenous figures of governance that could be found among the mission population. Most were married. At least half of the men were forty years old or older, while less than half of the women had reached that age.[53] They remained at the mission that they had begun to forge into a community nearly sixty years earlier, some time after the San Diego revolt of 1775.

In San Luis Rey, Argüello selected 449 people, nearly half of the mission population, to form two pueblos at Santa Margarita and Las Flores.[54] The same Indigenous politics prevailed among this large group. Only four families, all born in Santa Margarita (or Topome) accepted emancipation to form a pueblo in that territory. One hundred families agreed to form a pueblo at Las Flores. They had either been born there or descended from people who claimed Las Flores as their ancestral land.

The 138 adults who remained on the list had come from ten different villages: Temecula, Cuqui, Paumega, San Dieguito (mentioned earlier), Vateqitos, San Alejo, Pyualamni, Talpay, Pumusi, and Quechinga, both of the latter were among the first village populations to affiliate to the mission. The mission had been built in the territory of Quechinga in 1798, and some of those selected had been born in the Indigenous village. Only twenty-two of the adults selected for emancipation at Mission San Luis Rey had been born and baptized at the mission proper. Five people in this select group had also been baptized at other missions, emphasizing how a web of interconnections had developed among people at the southern missions including San Juan Capistrano, San Diego, San Gabriel, and San Fernando.

Those on the list of people selected for emancipation held the skills that would have been common among the citizens of many Mexican pueblos. The two largest listed occupations were thirteen laborers and thirteen livestock tenders. The rest of the men had a range of skills: seven cowboys, two soap makers, two weavers, two fishermen, two shoemakers, a shepherd, a mason, a muleteer, a grinder, two carpenters, an alcalde, and a cantor for the church. These skills were rarely articulated in the records in the detail and variation found on these lists. A comparable sense of detail is missing for the women whom Argüello simply listed as wives. In the case of men, he selected some who were single or had been widowed, but only married women were selected for emancipation. Representing them as dependents of their husbands, without employment of their own, the census illustrates women's lack of full citizenship in Mexico.

Mission San Luis Rey had been in existence for thirty-five years, substantially fewer than Mission San Diego, which had been founded sixty-three years before. More than a third of those selected for emancipation to form the two towns had been Christians for most of their lives. The group tended to be more evenly distributed by age than those selected at San Diego (though here, too, as at San Diego, wives tended to be younger than their husbands). The largest group of men ranged between thirty and forty years old. Most couples had children: eighteen couples had one child, twenty-two couples had two, fourteen couples had three children, and seven couples had four or more children. These figures are important because they provide some sense of the nature of the communities that survived through the mission period.

Despite the differences in the populations selected at Missions San Diego and San Luis Rey, both expressed the same ideas about what they wanted from emancipation. Argüello found this out when he announced the formation of the two Indian pueblos to the selected group at Mission San Luis Rey. He recounted his "surprise when an undercurrent of voices began to spread throughout the crowd and the interpreter said they wanted to speak to me." They told Argüello they did not want to leave their mission. One by one, they made it clear they wanted something different from the plan he announced: they wanted to return to their territories or be given possession of the mission proper.

Argüello harangued the crowd for their refusal to form the pueblos. He spoke of the liberal principles of the state and the importance of towns, offering the example of Los Angeles, which he called a flourishing city. He spoke of settlers who had gone to faraway territories and founded them, and of the wealth they had attained. He tried to convince the crowd that "they would never amount to anything (nunca serían gentes)." He said they depreciated the benefits that the government offered them when they had the opportunity to set an example and be the first among all of their friends.

But his language and logic did not move the agitated crowd. Only four couples remained silent, he noted. Afterward, they took up the offer for their emancipation and stated their willingness to form part of the Indian pueblo at Santa Margarita, although they had not originally come from there.[55] Despite his threats and promises of modernity, neither Santa Margarita nor the Pueblo de las Flores, where a mission *estancia* already existed, became self-governing towns until 1835. On May 8, 1835, the missionaries created an Indian pueblo and placed Las Flores under the leadership of an elected Indian alcalde.[56]

At San Juan Capistrano in September 1833, the military officer, Captain Portillo, called a similar meeting with those selected for emancipation and citizenship, and here he proposed to form an Indian pueblo at the mission's Rancho San Mateo. He thought this might work, because no one expressed overt resistance when they went with him to San Mateo so that he could show them where they would build their houses and the plots of land they would be given. He encouraged them to make their houses before the rains, but said he could not yet supply them with horses, as horses needed to be rounded up.[57]

Shortly thereafter, however, a group of alcaldes who had accompanied Argüello came to Portillo to express their opposition and propose that the mission itself be turned into a pueblo. Around the mission proper, they argued, "everyone has their piece of land on which they raise crops, and they have an abundance of water, and already have their homes" and common land.[58] San Mateo, they argued, did not have the abundance of water that existed at the mission. In response, Portillo wrote Figueroa to see if this could be done, but Figueroa suspended the provisional emancipation before the distribution.[59] In the letter, Portillo also spoke up for the many *emancipados* who received their emancipation papers earlier but had returned to the missions and remained landless. He insisted that they too receive a portion of mission land together with the rest of their compatriots at San Juan Capistrano, San Luis Rey, and San Diego.[60]

The claim to "our mission" would be repeated during this provisional emancipation period. It reflected the legal rights that Indigenous people had under Spanish law to land they improved, and it acknowledged the more recent history in which the speaker, if not two or three generations of his ancestors, had built the mission and improved the land with fields, irrigations systems, and orchards. The claim to their specific territories also reflected their rights to return to their *patrias* or homelands under Spanish law.

As Portillo came to understand, the population's mobilization to implement emancipation arose from their own understanding of what emancipation meant. He called it "their confusion" over the law's objectives. In discussing the plan with the alcaldes and other Indigenous leaders, Portillo learned that the native population thought emancipation would bring a total redistribution of land and that everyone would be able to return to their *patria*. This, he said, arose from their social order whereby they "don't form a nation." Separated by villages or tribes, they claimed different lands, spoke different languages, and had different leaders. At the mission proper, they had created wealth shared in common, spoke their own languages, and, at Mission San Juan Capistrano, spoke the common language of "Aerto." They also maintained differences among themselves of a social, political, and cultural nature, he emphasized.[61]

But, unlike Portillo, Argüello expressed his conviction that Indigenous people at the missions needed to be brought into civilization. Although he had listed the many skills that the Indigenous population possessed, and he had witnessed the creation of mission wealth, Argüello argued that mission Indians worked very little at the mission because they received clothing and had their necessities met. Echoing the colonial ideas that would persist in the nation, he attributed their refusal to agree to the government's mandates to their uncivil intentions, and concluded that the likely outcome of emancipation would be flight to the mountains, where they would "convert themselves again into barbarous savages" and thieves.[62]

EMANCIPATION AND SECULARIZATION, 1834

This history of Indigenous responses to the government's plans for emancipation and citizenship expressed a native politics shared by vastly different populations.

Indigenous people at three missions resisted the government's idea that they form Indian pueblos on the ancestral lands of other people. They wanted to return to their own ancestral spaces. Short of that, they envisioned claiming the missions, where they had created self-sustaining situations and shared elements of culture. The population at the missions shared a space forged through generations of labor. They kept their ancestral homelands, leadership, lineages, and language present while at the missions.

The Emancipation and Secularization Decree of 1834 failed to reflect native visions. It took the Territorial Legislature more than a year to work out the final terms of emancipation and secularization under Figueroa's leadership. The final decree allowed for a general emancipation of self-supporting Christians, but restricted their access to land, and mandated that they continue to labor on the undivided lands of the mission to support the public good. The law placed an administrator at each mission to govern the secularized spaces. It also gave former neophytes the formal right to receive an unspecified amount of land and goods from the assets of the missions. The missions were nominally, but not exclusively, envisioned as Indian pueblos. A central problem the government continued to debate was how to fund the pueblos, especially how to pay the elementary school teachers and the priests whom they wanted to hire "to ensure that the new pueblos are stable." Although the governing officials considered the Spanish missionaries in California to be declared enemies of the Mexican state, they continued to work with them in order to expedite the execution of the law.[63] Governor Figueroa placed José María Echeandía in charge of the Mexican colonization of the territory and raised his salary.

The decree ended the condition of *neófia* but restricted the freedom of those emancipated by placing controls over their labor, ease of movement, and community life at the missions. Curtailing liberties further, the law called for a non-Indian administrator to oversee the missions, in contrast to earlier plans that called for elected Indigenous leaders to take charge of the Indian pueblos and secularized missions. The "public good" that the labor of former neophytes supported included producing enough to provide for the salary of the mission administrators and other salaried supervisors. They were to support the schools, the church, the cult of the saints, and government projects. This expectation that Indigenous workers support the public good would be extended to the towns as well.

The administrators appointed by the governor supervised all affairs except spiritual matters, a job left to the missionaries. Punishment remained a central point of contention between liberal and conservative officials and between native people and their administrators. The government allowed lashings to continue to be administered to those who failed to follow orders.

The Emancipation and Secularization Decree of 1834 initiated an era in which Indigenous people along the coast negotiated their conditions of life under new terms. Between 1834 and the early 1840s, most of the mission land would begin to be divided among Californio soldiers, settlers, and new colonists from Mexico and elsewhere. Indigenous citizens privately cultivated portions of mission land, and some aided in supporting mission populations with food and seeds. Despite the persistence of colonial thought and relations, a new range of possibilities emerged, as did an Indigenous peasantry of small property holders near the former missions.

EMANCIPATED MISSION COMMUNITIES

The workers no longer recognize the voice of the de razón, even that of authority. They refuse to work, insisting that they are a "free nation." ... In one voice they yell "we are free, we don't want to obey, we don't want to work."[64]

—FROM SAN LUIS REY, PORTILLA Á FIGUEROA

The distribution of mission goods among Indigenous communities remained halting, uneven, and was a promise that went largely unfulfilled even as the mission populations continued to assert their rights according to law. They frequently demanded the distribution of land and goods that the 1834 Emancipation and Secularization Law promised. At Mission San Juan Bautista, the administrator made a one-time distribution of goods, crops, and seeds in 1835. Those things amounted to 8,439.75 pesos in value, or 6 percent of the mission's total inventory.[65]

At Mission Santa Cruz, the administrator Ignacio del Valle gave a last name to each member of the Indian pueblo that had been formed on one of the mission's farms. During the next year, the pueblo received more than 10,000 pesos in goods and money to enable its citizens to keep the farm productive.[66] At Santa Cruz and San Juan Capistrano, the government eventually deeded mission buildings and rooms to prominent Indian families. But only a limited distribution of goods took place at most missions, and the government failed to distribute most of the mission land and significant portions of the livestock among former neophytes.

Emancipated communities working at the missions received little compensation for their labor; payment remained marginal and generally came in the form of necessities that mission administrators purchased with the hides, tallow, and horns the workers produced. Yet, the clothing itself and other distributed items speak to the changes underway. Between 1835 and 1838, for example, Administrator José Joaquín Ortega reported distributing 439 shirts, 673 skirts, 202 petticoats, and a certain quantity of corn, wheat, beans, and barley among the mission population at San Diego.[67] In 1839, Juan Bandini distributed ready-made clothing of common wool and cotton and handkerchiefs and shawls among the 233 men and women at Mission San Gabriel. He established its value at $1,615.00.[68]

In 1839, Administrator Francisco Cota asked permission to kill three hundred head of young cattle to pay the Indians who he said had not been compensated since 1837.[69] Cota distributed cloth and garments that replicated things worn during the colonial period and introduced more valuable fabrics and clothing. In November 1839 he distributed crude blankets, striped cloth, and "Indiana," fabrics common during the colonial era at the missions. He also distributed better fabrics than those made available previously to mission Indians, such as silk, corduroy, and stamped cloth, forty shawls, and four woolen jackets. He distributed 228 spools of thread to make clothing from the materials.[70]

Shawls, handkerchiefs, shirts, skirts, and jackets had not been part of Indigenous clothing in the missions but had been worn by the settlers and soldiers in the colonial era. Some of the items distributed in the late 1830s replicated the dress of Californio laborers and small ranchers. It identified a population who held greater rights than during the mission era and looked more like the growing town population.

Ortega also distributed to individual Indian families the foods that only the families of soldiers had previously received as rations at the missions. The Indigenous population generally had their food cooked for the group and served in stews and *atole,* and that tradition persisted into this era. Though still living at the mission and doing work in common, the constant conditions of surveillance and group schedules no longer prevailed. In the meantime, Indian villages and farmers began to contribute to the sustenance of these mission communities, and members of mission families started farming on portions of mission property. They also found work on the ranchos and in seasonal industries such as the round-up of cattle, production of hides, and shearing of sheep as land and livestock became increasingly monopolized by large landowners.

Those who continued to work at the missions acted to secure greater compensation for their labor. Cases abounded in each mission in which the workers refused to labor without compensation and under conditions considered unfair. At many missions, they questioned the right of administrators to high pay and scrutinized their accounts and the activities of the missionaries.

A group of people at San Fernando, for example, rigorously questioned Fray Franco Ybarra. They insisted on seeing the missionary's accounts from the previous year. They demanded that Governor Figueroa return a box of silver he had taken away. They said they would not permit the taking of seeds in case they needed them after a year of drought. They repeated their demand to see the Father's accounts, saying they knew he had left the year before with two boxes of money.[71] They also refused to obey the new administrator, Carlos Carrillo, whom the government sent in response.[72] Shortly after Carillo arrived, the Indians came and said that if they were not given clothing, "they would not work the harvest nor work in anything." They "threw in his face" that he earned 50 pesos while spending each month just watching them work. They threatened him that, if they worked the harvest, they would take it all for themselves. Carrillo said, "As much as I did to make them apply themselves, I couldn't" get them to work.[73]

At San Diego, the majority of the former mission population left the fields in ruins in 1839 and went to work elsewhere. They left fifty people at the mission while they were away: old people and the youngest, and women who fed and cared for them. The others went to Santa Clara, surrounding *ranchos,* and Los Angeles to find work.[74]

In 1840, a group at Mission San Rafael sought both the promised distribution of goods, payment for their labor, and the dissolution of the mission community. Inspector of the Missions Guillermo Hartnell represented their position. He wrote that "they no longer wanted the mission; that they have been deceived too many times; that few people were left to work and everyone was tired; that their land had been taken away." They said "they wanted their liberty" and asked that the government honor its word "and distribute the [mission] goods."[75]

Communities employed daily forms of resistance against the administrators whom they considered unfair, and they elected Indigenous alcaldes who, they thought, best represented them. When Santiago Moreno spoke against the insubordination of the alcaldes and other Indians at Mission San Luis Obispo, he expressed a common complaint among administrators. Moreno went to see the harvest at the Rancho Santa María and found that the Indigenous alcalde only pretended to correct the workers for taking wheat without his permission. Moreno asked for soldiers because he was afraid of an uprising against him that he could not contain without their help.[76] Some individuals used long-established strategies against cruel administrators. At Mission San Miguel, for example, a Yokuts man named Cannuto from the village of Fontach poisoned and killed the administrator in 1839.[77] More commonly, communities waged formal protests through elected representatives, withdrew their labor, left the missions, and negotiated for a greater exercise of their rights.

Despite the presence of Californio administrators, a high level of native self-governance existed during these years. Governor José Figueroa and some legislators had envisioned native administrators taking over the missions in one draft of the Emancipation and Secularization Decree. That provision did not become part of the law, but Figueroa repeated his observation that Indians could be administrators, saying in December 1834, "This post" of *mayordomo* should "be given to a neophyte of the mission, allotting a moderate salary. I don't see any need for a *mayordomo de razón.*"[78] Indigenous workers, however, set up by law to work "for the common good" rarely appeared among the few salaried employees of the secularized missions.

In a rare instance, four salaried Chumash men had employment at Mission Santa Bárbara in 1838. Listed only by first name, they included Vicente, the corporal of the guard, who received 144 pesos; the blacksmith Gaspar, paid 120 pesos; the doctor Nicolás, who received 100 pesos; and the sacristan Lino, who received 72 pesos. The job of *escribán*, or scribe, work performed by Manuel Ponce de León, received the pay of 120 pesos, the same amount that the Chumash blacksmith Gaspar received. The employment of these four Chumash men at Santa Bárbara, and the comparatively favorable pay, offered a rare case of a certain equality in status if judged by compensation.[79] In contrast to the range of annual wages made by workers of various backgrounds, the administrator Manuel Cota's salary included 480 pesos and additional goods. The *mayordomo*, José María Valenzuela, received 240 pesos, and the mission allotted 500 pesos for "the cult of the saint" that included money to care for the church and hold celebrations. The range in these annual amounts suggests the vast differentiation in wealth and public expenditure. When given a salary, Indigenous workers tended to receive less, although some people found work that paid within the range of compensation given to Californios.

Deep forms of colonial relationships persisted at the missions. They were present in the liberties given to *gente de razón* to take loans from the missions. Many Californios maintained accounts with the missions and accumulated debts they owed for goods made there, or purchased by the missionaries and administrators and then sold and traded with the surrounding populations. At Santa Ines, this included cloth made at the missions and purchased from ships, and mission products such as soap, flour, beans, meat, corn, and *manteca* (fat for cooking and candles). Sometimes individuals owed the mission money that they had borrowed.[80] Similar debts plagued Mission San Fernando throughout this era, with tremendous wealth lost to the mission through unpaid debts. In response to the escalation of this pattern of unpaid loans, Guillermo Hartnell, as mission overseer, imposed rules prohibiting people from borrowing if they did not settle their accounts.[81] But, in contrast to the Californios, the native population did not have open access to the mission goods their labor created, or to loans and credit.

UNSTABLE RIGHTS

After Emancipation and Secularization began in California, the discussion of Indigenous citizenship and equality virtually ceased. The law freed people from the condition of *neófia* but defined persistent coercive labor relations. It required that emancipated individuals work at the mission and for the public good. It placed most of the mission land in the hands of the state and severed the association of the land to historic Indigenous territories. The history of citizenship would continue to unfold, and conditions would begin to vary more widely for Indigenous individuals and communities. A whole generation of Indigenous youth received some schooling during the 1820s and 1830s, and they saw their elders engaged in political action. The opportunities to move beyond the restrictions of their colonial status remained uneven, however. For example, in 1835, two Indigenous students named José and Mariano, still identified as neophites, went to study at a school in San José. Their mission paid half the expenses, and the government the other half. That included two semesters of tuition, paper, pens, a chalkboard for each student, and shoes.[82] Poverty remained endemic among those emancipated, and the status of *neófio* hovered as a social and legal category.

The history of Indigenous politics of emancipation began with the first petitions in 1826, but the unstable conditions of leaving the mission with the status of being "disaffiliated," and without land or goods, and their ancestral lands and community, brought many back to the vicinity of the missions. Native conceptions of freedom included visions of return to their territories and being granted the missions where they had established flourishing economies. Yet a systematic distribution of mission land to their Indigenous populations never occurred. The one-time distribution of mission goods remained partial. Native populations petitioned for and organized around attaining their new rights, but their legal and social condition remained unsettled in Mexican California.

6

Indigenous Landowners and Native Ingenuity on the Borderlands of Northern Mexico

Documents produced from 1834 to 1846 referred to the Indigenous population as *indios* or *indígenas* and frequently continued to employ the colonial term *neófito*. But a broader set of references also existed that reflected the expanded Indian peasantry and citizenry that emerged after 1826. Some Indians would be referred to, or referred to themselves, as Mexican citizens and as *gente de razón*. Others referred to themselves as *segregados, emancipados,* and *licenciados,* legal statuses that set them outside the control of missionaries and administrators. The settler population tended to be the ones who received the designation *ciudadano* or *vecino,* and the colonial term *gente de razón* also persisted.

A reversal in Indigenous rights began in Mexico in 1833, with the rise of a conservative, centralist regime in Mexico. The erosion occurred as many state constitutions began to limit citizenship to literate individuals who held land and property.[1] In California, the reversal began when Governor José Figueroa himself, who, at one point, had ordered Indigenous votes be guaranteed, ended universal emancipation in 1835. Once again, individuals had to apply for it. Until they had the license, they remained legal minors.

In 1836 Governor Mariano Chico published a decree that further undermined the promise of universal citizenship when he established the penalties to which Indians would be subject if they left their respective Indian pueblos or missions without a license to do so.[2] These changes left a man named Felipe, who was referred to as a neophyte of San Diego, without legal rights in the early 1840s. Fined 6 pesos for killing an ox, the judge ruled that "since he is congregated and still considered a minor, he cannot be fined." Instead, the judge sent him back to the mission for punishment he deserved "according to the custom."[3]

The courts and government officials enforced the rights that native people could access in a sporadic fashion. The continuation of beating Indian servants and Indians at the missions particularly emphasized how severe inequities remained. In 1836 the state brought a case to trial against Francisco M. Alvarado for whipping an Indigenous servant in his household. The court imposed a fine of 45 pesos on Alvarado. In his legal defense, Alvarado emphasized that whipping constituted a general "custom recognized here, although forbidden by law."[4]

With the beginning of liberal reform in the late colonial period, and again upon independence, the government declared corporal punishment prohibited by law. Accompanying almost every written decree that arrived in California against corporeal punishment was a written statement that the practice could continue though often modified to a particular number of lashes.[5] When the inspector of the missions, Guillermo Hartnell, drew up regulations that defined the rights and responsibilities of the administrators of each mission in 1839, he limited punishment to a maximum of twenty-five lashes per flogging against any single individual.[6] Though an inhumane number, the limits were frequently exceeded. At San José in 1839, the population of 589 persons complained that the administrator sometimes applied between fifty and one hundred lashes and was known to take people by the hair and throw them on the ground. Subject to violence and forced labor, the Indian community lacked many things they needed for basic living. They received distributed goods only once a year, and the mission administrators and alcaldes did not distribute them evenly. The community complained. They also continued to dance and take recourse in Indigenous practices.[7]

For his part, the administrator at Mission San José desperately requested some remedy from Hartnell to stop the population from their "superstitious" dancing. He especially wanted to know how to end the nocturnal dancing. Hartnell told him to consult the missionaries who were familiar with the constant practice of dance at the missions. Hartnell wrote general rules to which he made additions or modifications to address the specific conditions at each mission. For Mission San José he emphasized: no killing of cattle or other work on Sundays; no more than twenty-five lashes against a single individual; no sale of mission goods until a better redistribution of the proceeds was in place. Hartnell also insisted that Californios repay their debts to the mission without exception.[8]

In the ensuing years, administrators of the missions and missionaries alike insisted on their right to use the whip and inflict physical punishment to keep order and to make people follow the rules. In 1841 the administrator Rafael Gonzales at Mission San Buenaventura responded to the complaints against him for the kind of punishment he administered. He said he only gave those punishments for severe crimes like "robbery, abductions, men and women cohabiting without being married, and other crimes of the same class." He didn't believe there was another way, and he threatened to resign his job if his disciplinary measures were not accepted.[9] Gonzalez articulated what many other administrators and missionaries also said.

Gonzalez dictated these ideas to a scribe; many Californio administrators could not write and hired scribes for their correspondence and accounting. They had little access to read the new rights that Indigenous people held. Instead, older traditions prevailed, such as the custom of inflicting physical violence that Francisco Alvarado described earlier.

INDIAN LAND GRANTS: NATIVE LANDOWNERS AND INDIGENOUS PUEBLOS

To you I ask and plea . . . give me a title to said land.
—SEFERINO DE JESÚS, *SEGREGADO* FROM THE EX-MISSION OF
SAN GABRIEL, APRIL 17, 1843

Indigenous people in the missions persisted in seeking their rights under the law even as they often experienced grueling conditions and conflict with mission administrators. Allotments of mission land had been made informally to Indigenous people since the Emancipation and Secularization Decree passed in 1834 that enabled small groups and independent families of landholders to emerge around each mission. By the 1840s, their requests were framed around the argument that they had a right to a parcel of mission land because of the work they or their families had done at the mission. Yet the decision to grant the land often relied on laws formulated in the language of Mexican federal law of the 1820s, not California legislation.[10]

People were again emancipated without land after 1835, making it imperative to apply for grants or be left without a means for a stable existence. Typical of the earliest days of emancipation, Governor Juan Bautista Alvarado emancipated Augustín from Mission San Luis Rey, in 1841. He wrote that the *Indígena* of the Mission of San Luis Rey, called Agustín, asked to be emancipated "because he feels capable of maintaining himself in honest work." Alvarado approved the license so that Augustín could "find his means of subsistence with his family wherever it best suits him."[11]

Small farms and small lots constituted an important part of the society that emerged in the Mexican period. The grants situated Indigenous people alongside presidio soldiers, widows, and poorer *vecinos* from the towns, who similarly applied for small grants. Many such petitions requested lots of 200 to 400 square *varas,* or approximately 1500 to 3000 square feet. Sergeants and corporals petitioned for larger parcels of land, as did men and women of the upper classes, who petitioned on their own behalf and on behalf of their children. The applicant had to prove that they could sustain production of farms and livestock on their grant.

A "committee on vacant land" determined whether anyone had prior claim to the parcel. The governor signed many of the approvals to grant the land, although some first went through town councils to verify its vacant status. The largest portion of lands granted during these years went to a relatively few families in the region, but the number of grants made was extensive. A few Indigenous applicants would also be granted lucrative ranchos, farms, and orchards.

Many of the Indigenous petitioners referred to their long histories of labor at the mission as they sought land. From Mission San Diego a woman named Maria Inés claimed, "Since my childhood, I as well as my two husbands have contributed our labor to the mission." Fray Vicente Olivos wrote a note that testified Maria Inés had been ill and was no longer of service to the mission, but that her husband had been a sacristan for seven years, and two of her sons had worked at the mission. She was granted part of the land for her cattle. The son of Maria Inés, Francisco Aherez, signed the petition made by his mother and in the name of his brothers and took it to Monterey. She was granted part of the land for her cattle, but not all that she requested. According to Olivos, mission livestock still grazed on the land.[12]

In nearly of all the missions from San Diego northward, Indigenous people who remained at the missions in the 1830s would begin to cultivate allotments that became small farms and ranchos. These parcels enabled people to remain in well-irrigated and established areas. In San Diego, many Kumeyaay remained in what became known as Mission Valley, a luxuriant area with streams, living in allotments up and down the valley. Others moved to communities near the bay and ocean. Those who lived in their villages to the east and south, such as El Cajón, Jamacha, and Otay, often remained there.[13]

At Mission San Luis Rey, where Luiseño people had long remained in some of their historic territories like La Jolla, Pauma, Rincón, and Temecula, those communities persisted. Indigenous people from the village of Temecula formed one of the autonomous Indian communities that remained in Luiseño territory. It contributed to the mission population's sustenance by sending seeds and other goods. But when they heard that their lands might be encroached upon by a Californio, they sent word that they were armed and would resist through the alcalde of Pala, Nepomuceno, who conveyed their unanimous sentiment. They wanted the authorities to know that all the people in Temecula possessed arms. They said they did not intend the statement to threaten the authorities at the mission, but that they would defend themselves against the unauthorized use of their land. In an effort to make clear that they still served the mission with valuable contributions, they asked, Nepomuceno to remind the authorities that the rancho of Temecula gave the best seeds to the mission.[14]

Big communities continued to live and work at Pala and the mission of San Luis Rey. Individuals and groups also cultivated their own plots and small ranchos. Some individual petitioners received grants of Mission San Luis Rey land during the 1830s and 1840s, but most of the ancestral and mission land remained undeeded to the Luiseño population. A man named Felipe of the Mission of San Luis Rey, for example, had begun to cultivate some land in 1836 upon his emancipation. He had a small number of livestock with which he supported his family, and he petitioned for the land based on his merit "as a native of the mission, where I have spent so much labor."[15]

Another Luiseño petitioned for a Mexican grant to Guajome that had a small farm belonging to the mission. Andrés and José Manuel, a father and son, asked for the land of Guajome that had 140 bearing vines, 22 pear trees, 14 peach trees, other fruit trees, and agricultural land where Andrés and José Manuel already grew beans, vegetables, and other crops. Andrés based his request on being a "native of this mission, where I have spent so much labor."[16] They received the rancho. Pablo Apis, who signed his full name, asked for a tract of land to support his large family on the rancho of Temecula as a native of San Luis Rey. [17]

In San Juan Capistrano the Achachemem population received almost two acres of mission land in small plots granted around the mission.[18] The grant provided for about two dozen fair-sized lots of 3,000 square feet. As San Juan became a town its population expanded in the 1840s, and many Achachemem remained in the vicinity of the mission but without formal title. The best lands that the mission offered and some mission buildings went to long-established Indigenous families, as did some of the mission property. When the mission was sold to Juan Forster, the government first allotted some of its buildings to more elite Indian families who had served at the mission.[19] But without title, their positions remained precarious. Others could easily petition for their property.

Around Mission San Gabriel a large group of Indigenous people petitioned for grants of the land they already occupied or worked. In this elaboration of small and larger grants that formed near the mission, its significance as a site of tribal and family history and of Indigenous politics is sometimes diminished.[20] Seferino de Jesús wrote and signed a petition for land as a person "segregated from the ex-mission." He requested about 1,500 square feet of land for a vineyard and an orchard of fruit trees. He received the grant in May 1843 and enlarged it immediately thereafter.[21] In 1845 he petitioned to enlarge his grant.[22] Hugo Reed petitioned for the Rancho Santa Anita of Mission San Gabriel and received title "in reward for the services rendered to this mission by his [Gabrieliño] wife and by her late husband Pablo," also a Gabrieliño man.[23] He and another man, Santiago Leyba, a *vecino* of Los Angeles who asked for land as "a poor man responsible for a family and married to a neophyte of the mission," both received land.[24]

The Indígena Emilio Joaquin said he had given his service to San Gabriel Mission for more than forty years and asked in his petition that the land office "do me the justice" of giving him a piece of land of about 1,500 square feet for a house and an orchard.[25] I. Ramón Rosauaro Valueria, who called himself "an emancipated

Parking Permit

4311 Melrose Ave. Los Angeles, CA 90029

"Temporary Staff"

OCTOBER 2019

2 0 1 9

All Day – Lot #4

Hollywood

Work Source

CALIFORNIA

Indian of the Mission San Gabriel," asked for a grant of land for himself, his father Valencia, and his brother Pablo, all of the mission. They had possessed it for a long time and built an orchard and a vineyard there.[26] The Indians Simeón, José le Dessuan, Felipe, and Próspero all petitioned for and were granted lots for fields, houses, and orchards.[27] The grants varied in size between roughly 1,500 and 3,000 square feet.

An Indigenous *mayordomo* Manuel Antonio at Mission San Gabriel petitioned for land of the mission that he had cultivated since 1834. He continued to work for the mission as a *mayordomo* during the subsequent eleven years, even as he grazed stock on his land and cultivated his fields. In his petition for title, Manuel Antonio complained about not having been granted the land that pertained to him under the terms of the 1834 Emancipation and Secularization Decree. Instead, the land was opened up to others, he said, "who have not the same right, nor as much stock" as himself. He included a map; most Indigenous petitions did not. He asked for title to the land mapped as "Diseño del Potrero Grande de Misión Vieja." About one-third of an acre, it was bordered on two sides by the lands of San Gabriel.[28] His grant subsequently appeared as "land of the Indian Antonio" that would constitute the southern border of a grant requested by Doña María Antonia Domínguez de Cabalero "to support her cattle." Tomás Olvera's rancho bordered her requested land on the west and that of Julian Forster to the southwest.[29]

Sometimes more ample distributions of livestock and land took place. At Mission San Fernando in 1839, Mission Inspector Guillermo Hartnell called for a distribution of 8,547 head of livestock, including cattle and sheep, 280 hides, and small parcels of land so that the Fernandiños could engage in commerce and be self-supporting.[30] Many Indigenous allotments to land were granted as well. Indians spread out on lands that some held as a collective group and others as individual families. Tiberio Román sought title with others to land at San Fernando to which the missionaries had given them provisional title. Writing on behalf of the group, he said that "having spent much of our lives in San Fernando in the service of the establishment," they wanted a large grant of land called Rancho Encino. Their families already resided there, and they grazed their stock on the land.[31] In 1843, another collective grant allotted thirty-nine Indians title to an allotment.[32] Others petitioned separately or in smaller groups.

Samuel petitioned for formal title to land he had cultivated since his emancipation in 1838. He had built a house made of stakes and had a wheat field and land prepared for corn and beans. He continued to "assist my Mission," he explained. He gave "a part of what I raise every year" to help sustain the missionary and the community that resided there. Samuel grew wheat, corn, beans, peas, peaches, and other vegetables and fruits, but like many native petitioners, he did not submit a map to accompany the petition. Nonetheless, the governor granted Samuel 2,750 square feet.[33] By 1843 three men—Urbaniso, Odon, and Manuel—petitioned for El Escorpion. Urbaniso also wrote a petition to be emancipated that he alone signed. Married and with children, he had given twenty-five years of service in the mission.[34]

In San Buenaventura the population spread out in allotments along the river and in good lands of the mission. In 1844, when Pio Pico decided to sell the mission, the alcaldes José Antonio, Juan de Jesús, José Bunis, Faustino, and Simplícito appeared and verified their approval of the sale based on the guarantee in writing that the allotments to the community would not be disturbed in any way.[35] Some still petitioned to get title to their claims when they learned of their impending dispossession, as did both Juan de Jesús and José Gabriel. They petitioned as married men and sought a grant of land on which, they said, they cultivated every year for the support of their families.[36] Another man from San Buenaventura named Lino had been "emancipated from the service of the mission in the year 1834 by Governor Figueroa." Exempt from service since his emancipation, he lived on a plot of land near the mission and sought title for it.[37] Others farmed without title to their land.

In Santa Bárbara no formal grants to the Indigenous population were recorded, but the Indigenous community from that mission formed at least two pueblos and held separate allotments as well. Chumash islanders who came in later to the mission formed two settlements: one near San Buenaventura named Kamexmey and further north Qwaʼ. They built tule houses, sweat lodges, acorn granaries, and other traditional buildings using historic architecture. Practices that had persisted at the mission now flourished under full native authority. People fished, built canoes, made bead money, and persisted with the dances and ceremonies they had practiced at the missions. Another Indian pueblo formed at the historic village of Cienguita, and smaller farms existed on or near mission land that had been granted to family and relatives of de la Guerra y Noriega, military commander and merchant.[38]

At Missions Santa Inés and La Purísima the Indigenous populations received grants of mission land. At Santa Inés many in the community received sixteen small tracts of land in 1844. Marcelino Cuinait, recognized as the chief of the Santa Inés band in 1843 (but only referred to as "marcelino, neófito de Santa Inés" in his petition) secured Rancho Alamo Pintado.[39] Antonino Silimunajait, from a coastal village and initially baptized at Mission Santa Bárbara, had helped found Santa Inés in 1804. He received Rancho Saca on the upper Zaca Creek near the mission.[40] In 1850 the Santa Inés population elected four alcaldes and persisted as a community.[41]

The Santa Inés community had the advantage of employment in the Seminario de Guadalupe established at the mission to train priests in 1845. This brought work apart from labor at the mission. The seminary hired a *tortilla* maker and a cook; paid people to plant, tend, and harvest the fields, and keep up the irrigation ditches. The Chumash cooks made a *jacal* for cooking.[42] The seminary petitioned for a rancho, and they hired Indian *vaqueros* to tend the livestock.[43] This employment augmented work on surrounding ranchos and subsistence production of food and livestock on Indigenous property.

At nearby Mission La Purísima the community remained at the mission tending their own plots until a devastating epidemic of smallpox killed a large portion of the population in 1844. Elesario and Pastor wrote and signed a petition for a large grant of land. They described themselves as having been faithful in their service to the mission. Administrator Juan Moreno verified that they had survived smallpox and said they deserved the land. They were granted a medium sized lot of about 2,200 square feet.[44]

At Mission San Miguel the allotments of land to Indians remained in shadows, engulfed with little trace by the applications and maps of the *de razón* who sought mission land. In one land grant petition made by Inocente García, the administrator did try to protect Indigenous property, arguing that Indigenous people at the missions occupied the land García sought. Rather than bare, it was occupied "with the goods of these neophytes. Sheep, cattle and smaller livestock, and almost all the fields for harvest on which these neophytes subsist."[45] The same obscurity characterized Indigenous allotments in a map of Mission San Luis Obispo. A land map of the mission simply recorded "land of the Indians" without giving names or lot sizes.[46]

In some rare instances Indigenous people received title to substantial portions of land for ranchos. Steven Hackel reports the case of Cristina Salgado, an Indian woman whose parents had come from Mission San Borja in Baja California, who became a large landowner. She had married Esselen Indian Gaspar María Talatis at Mission San Carlos in 1819. Allowed to leave Mission San Carlos and move to San José, where Talatis worked as a carpenter, they eventually moved to the Salinas Valley, where Salgado applied for Rancho Ríncon de las Salinas with 2,200 acres at the mouth of the Salinas River, and which she received in 1834. She had bonds with Californios who had different municipal posts and who testified on her behalf as to her decency and industry. She built a house and a sawmill and raised four orphans. In 1835, María Bernarda Panna from the ex-mission of Santa Clara moved into her household with her seven children, three of whom had been orphaned. The two women cultivated the land and engaged in the hide and tallow trade.[47]

At Santa Clara, where a population of 800 still lived at the mission in 1834, very few grant applications were made to secure and map the mission's farms and orchards. Rather than smaller grants to Indigenous individuals and groups, three large grants were made to Indigenous people from mission lands for a total of 12,000 acres.[48] In contrast, a man named Roberto petitioned for Los Broches, his ancestral land that had become a mission sheep ranch. He only received permission to occupy it on a temporary basis.[49] A man named Íñigo from Mission San José had been in possession of Posita de las Ánimas since 1839, when he was emancipated. He won a case to keep land in 1843 against the conflicting claim of Francisco Estrada. Íñigo received title to the rancho in 1844.[50] Allotted a significant grant of 3,042 acres, he also proved exceptional in that he successfully litigated the grant in the American courts at a later date.[51]

When Indian pueblos and allotments around the missions did not receive legal titles, they remained subject to being plotted onto the rancho grants of others, as happened at Missions San Juan Capistrano, Santa Bárbara, San Miguel, San Luis Obispo, San Buenaventura, and Carmel. Though some Indigenous families were given land and some mission buildings in the redistribution of goods, they generally lacked title to the property. Their arrangements were unstable. Over time, only a title could verify landownership. As many as a quarter of rancho grants had a simple sign "∧" to denote Indigenous communities, but they remained without title to the land.

The idea, discussed between 1816 and 1833, of forming Indian pueblos as self-sustaining communities had subsided, and the pueblos formed during the early years of emancipation too often had tentative legal status. The pueblo of San Dieguito, which had been reinhabited by people from Mission San Diego who had been born there, became part of the Rancho San Dieguito, granted to Juan María Osuña, the first Mexican mayor of San Diego. Having been granted the rancho at an earlier date, Osuña wanted the Indian pueblo included in his grant. The rancho map has "pueblo of San Dieguito" written on the bottom right-hand corner: otherwise there would be little trace of the pueblo's legal existence.[52] Without actual ownership, those from the *pueblito* did not have access to the rights as citizens. Osuña, in contrast, lived as a *"vecino* de San Diego" with all the rights entailed of belonging to the town. The Osuña grant would be remembered in subsequent histories, but the ancient Indigenous territory and Indian pueblo is often forgotten.[53]

MOVING BETWEEN WORLDS: CRESPÍN AND POLICARPIO

People relocated. Many remained at or near the missions. Others moved about for work.[54] Some traveled, as did José María Crespín and Policarpio, who left Pala at Mission San Luis Rey and the Mission San Juan Capistrano, respectively, to travel the Old Spanish Trail to Abiquiu, New Mexico, where they lived in different towns before traveling together to El Paso.[55] They left the coastal territories separately between 1833 and 1834, at the height of the political moment of emancipation and secularization.

José María Crespín had been born in 1816 and baptized one year later at a large baptism of children at Pala under the name Crespín Colacleux. He received baptism with his brother and twenty-eight other children from Pala, Cuca (Portero), and Palma. The mission population at San Luis Rey was undergoing sustained expansion during that time. Most families in the interior remained in their villages rather than move into the mission. He would have been raised in the interior, perhaps at Pala, where a Luiseño village had thrived through traditional economies and by incorporating the Spanish economy of farming and livestock raising. He would have grown up speaking Luiseño and Spanish. In 1834, Crespín left his wife, a Luiseño woman named Romualda, behind in Pala, in a community that included Romualda's father, Feliciano Atoula, and her mother, Feliciana Thosobal, both of whom had been baptized at Pala. Crespín also left his mother and father, Maria Colachuix and Estevan Colacolix, and other relatives in Pala. [56]

Crespín's family remained in Pala, a village with precolonial origins that had also grown during the mission era. It was a center of cultivation with the painted chapel, discussed in chapter 3, forming part of the mission settlement within a changing Luiseño town. Both men left missions where people had defiantly called for the emancipation of the community. Many had refused to work under the old terms. Crespín left because he was "bothered by his master," meaning, in 1834, the Califiornio administrator of the mission properties. [57]

Policarpio also grew up in a Luiseño village at least until the age of ten and perhaps into his adulthood. His father, Mumathuihujac, and his mother, Nacquenem, had him baptized with the given name of Policarpo at Mission San Juan Capistrano just after his birth on January 25, 1811 (the latter appears as Policarpio). They did not affiliate to the mission themselves; Policarpio's closest familial connection there seems to have been his godparents, José del Carmen Buibaison and Pancarasi Buibaison.

In 1833, around the age of twenty-two, Policarpio left Mission San Juan Capistrano to travel to Abiquiu, New Mexico. Months later, at the same age, José María Crespín left Pala with a trader from New Mexico named Juan Lucero who had been at Mission San Luis Rey to do business. Lucero promised to treat Crespín "as if he were his son," saying that "he wouldn't lack for anything." [58]

The Santa Fe Trail had grown in importance for trade with California settlements during the 1820s. Juan Lucero took Crespín with him, while Policarpio traveled the trail with another Indian named Pablo Martín. As Lucero and Crespín passed through Mexican settlements and Indigenous villages in California, they stole horses and mules and purchased some livestock. [59] Thus they engaged in a small part of the raiding, trading, and horse wrestling business that was pervasive in the larger region.

Both Policarpio and Crespín arrived at the pueblo of Abiquiu. Policarpio left Pablo Martín in Abiquiu and moved to the pueblo of Santo Domingo, a Keresan-speaking pueblo town, and then went on to the pueblo of Ysleta. Crespín remained in Abiquiu for more than a year. [60] The pueblo of Abiquiu stood at the crossroads of

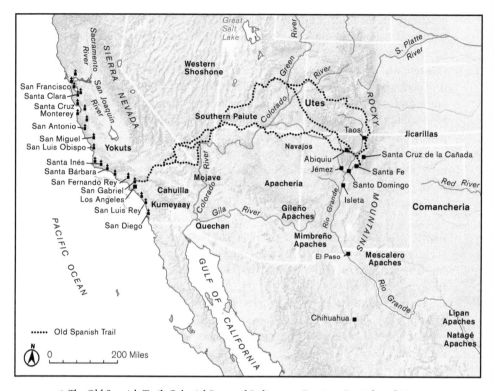

MAP 6. The Old Spanish Trail: Colonial Sites and Indigenous Empires. Spanish and Mexican settlements in New Mexico and California created colonial orbits on an Indigenous borderlands in which Indian empires like that of the Comanche, and powerful groups like the Utes and Apache, held dominance well into the nineteenth century. Drawn by Benjamin Pease.

trade and warfare, and had been abandoned and reestablished as a village in 1754.[61] The *vecinos* included many *genízaros* (detribalized Indigenous people) who had been held in servitude in New Mexican households and then released upon becoming Christians and adults. The population of detribalized people in New Mexico grew because of trade in human captives that predominated throughout the region. The Crown granted *genízaros* and lower-status settlers land throughout the eighteenth century in order to create buffer zones between nomadic raiding and the colonial towns, including those of Pueblo Indians, such as Santo Domingo and Ysleta. The Navajos to the west of Abiquiu had become suppliers in the slave trade and brought captives and goods to trade fairs in Abiquiu through the late 1850s. Comanches also traded furs and captives at trade fairs in Abiquiu and Taos, New Mexico.[62]

When Crespín and Policarpio arrived, a regional peace had been negotiated for a period between and among Indigenous groups and New Mexicans. The relative calm had encouraged expansion of New Mexican settlements, and some people from Abiquiu would migrate during this period to found Guadalupe in southern Colorado.[63] Meanwhile, Abiquiu remained a prominent place on the trail, and during his stay Crespín noted that other California Indians passed through and resided in Abiquiu. Their passage on the Old Santa Fe trail had become part of the more vigorous connections that developed between California and other parts of Mexico's north during the 1820s.

After living in Abiquiu for more than a year, Crespín left in December 1835, stating that he did not want to be in the company of Lucero any longer, and he moved to the Pueblo Indian town of Ysleta. A precolonial pueblo, Ysleta had a different history and social structure than Abiquiu. It formed part of the pastoral economy of sheep raising that was widespread throughout the region. Crespín would live there for another year, and Policarpio lived there for two years. It seems they knew each other before and, when they saw each other in the pueblo, they decided to travel south together toward El Paso.

Crespín and Policarpio left Ysleta together in August 1836, for El Paso, a six-day journey to the south. Subsequent court records show that they had a horse and carried two sacks of gunpowder, one of bullets, and a shipment of serapes. Crespín and Policarpio each gave a different reason for leaving Ysleta. Crespín said they left with the objective of "eating a lot of just ripened fruit" in El Paso, and to "travel around and have a good time."[64] Policarpio said José María Crespín invited him to El Paso "to find work." Policarpio testified that they met up with strangers en route to the Gila River to trade horses with the Apaches, and that they got away from the Americans in El Paso. When questioned again by the judge, Crespín agreed, reversing his previous testimony. They traveled with the Americans until they arrived at the place of Fray Cristóbal in El Paso, where they found refuge.

El Paso lay at the southern tip of New Mexico and was a town of Indigenous people and settlers, and a crossroads of the trade routes between Chihuahua and the New Mexican and Texas territories. A small community of settlers and Manso Indians lived around the mission the Franciscans had built on the south side of the river, in the present-day city of Juárez, in 1659. People migrated south to El Paso during the Pueblo Revolt of 1680, and the town of El Paso had a military presidio and a population of well over 3,000 settlers, more than half of whom were *genízaros* and Pueblo Indians, by the late eighteenth century. Trade brought many to the region, like the Americans with whom Crespín and Policarpio traveled and who offered them horses and money if they would accompany the traders to the Gila River. The Americans would later be arrested in Chihuahua for trading gunpowder, bullets, and serapes for horses and mules with the Río Gilas and Apaches.[65]

In El Paso, a military sergeant arrested Crespín and Policarpio on September 23, 1836. He took possession of their horse, gunpowder, bullets, and serapes. An official stated that they appeared clandestinely in El Paso and seemed to be involved in the illegal trade with *indios bárbaros* (savage or wild Indians), and as another consideration "they didn't have any kind of pass."[66] In order to determine whether or not José María Crespín and Policarpio had committed a crime, the court held a hearing at which both men gave testimonies, as did three soldiers, two of whom knew them from various interactions in the pueblos of New Mexico.

The two soldiers had previously met the men when they lived in Abiquiu and Ysleta. Bernardo Abeisa came from the old colonial city of Santa Cruz de la Cañada. He testified to having known them and spoke favorably on their behalf.[67] Juan Otero, from Pueblo de Valencia, said he only knew them by sight.[68] Their testimonies were favorable to both men, and emphasize the ability of Crespin and Policarpio to move between worlds.

The third soldier, Francisco Martínez, who identified himself as a citizen and soldier from Taos, testified against them. He was the only one who had not met them previously. Martínez was stationed in El Paso, and he reiterated the common stereotypes against Indians engaged in the economy of raiding and trading. Martínez said they had been "with the Apaches of the Río de Gila," and at one point, he called them Gileños (Gila Indians). He also called them "clever thieves" *(coyoteros)*. He said that "they didn't fear anything, not even the devil."[69] But because Martínez had no hard evidence to support his accusations, and their proximity to popular stereotypes in the region, the judge dismissed Martínez's testimony as a lone voice against the defendants.

The judge determined that Crespín and Policarpio didn't appear to be criminals, yet "the confession that José María Crespín made about having fled the service of his master" spoke against him, as did "his vagrancy" when he left his pueblo of residence without a motive. Policarpio fell under this same suspicious behavior. Their insubordinate actions of moving about freely, without passes, made their case worth carrying to trial.[70]

But the case never went forward because Crespín and Policarpio escaped from the jail. The abilities that Crespín and Policarpio had demonstrated to move across cultures and among different language groups would have made them valuable to traders on this borderlands of Indigenous nations and settlers. They seemed to have escaped the Americans with whom they traveled, or perhaps completed their business. In all, they had succeeded in leaving California, finding a way to live for years in distinctive communities of Indigenous citizens in New Mexico, and finally, they had eluded trial and imprisonment.

Perhaps the guards, like the soldiers who testified on their behalf during the hearing, and who had gotten to know them or recognized them by sight when they lived among Pueblo people, were also Indigenous citizens. They may have felt sympathy for Crespín and Policarpio. The fact that they were able to flourish in an interethnic Indigenous and settler society in which the category of barbarous Indians persisted alongside Indigenous citizens in *genízaro* and Pueblo communities suggests they possessed tremendous skills as translators, negotiators, and mediators. Those qualities would have also been useful to the Americans as they engaged in trade and with whom they traveled.

Crespín and Policarpio disappeared from public record at that point. They may have gone back to California, or they may have remained within this region for a long period. On December 27, 1836, three months after their arrest, the military commander in El Paso sent their case back to headquarters, explaining that José María Crespín and Policarpio could not be found. He asked to close the case, although the military still attempted to find a trace of José María Crespín and Policarpio for the next few months.[71] Their ability to avoid recapture demonstrates their skill at moving between worlds undergoing drastic change.

INDIGENOUS BORDERLANDS

Whereas colonial society had formed in the context of tribal lands and colonial centers, the story of José María Crespín and Policarpio suggests how the reference points shifted in the Mexican era toward a greater connection to Mexico's north. In most of California, as in the rest of northern Mexico, Indigenous societies had found ways to flourish and held dominion over much of the region. A large portion had been called the *Comanchería*, and in California, the missionaries spoke of the feared *Apachería*.[72] James Brooks defined the vigorous pastoral, mountain, and plains economies that developed in this Indigenous borderlands and the intersection of Indigenous tribes and settlers around the vigorous practices of raiding, trading, and human captivity and exchange.[73]

As Julianna Barr showed, in most places in this vast region, Spaniards had to "accommodate themselves to native systems of control if they wished to form viable relationships" with Indigenous societies.[74] The boundaries of established discourse about the colonial north seemed broken as historians found these Indigenous societies to be thriving centers of the regional economy. After Mexican independence, the federal government made explicit efforts to make peace with distinct Indigenous nations in the north. But these agreements tended to be eroded, and the economy of trading, raiding, and captivity, produced violence on all sides. It created, by the mid-nineteenth century, what Brian Delay called "a fragmented landscape of deserts," with settlements depopulated, impoverished, and often in ruins.[75]

The dominant position certain tribes attained in this economy entailed being involved in a colonial web of violence no less devastating because Indigenous people exercised authority and control. Ned Blackhawk emphasizes the suffering created by violence when discussing this era. "While Utes did indeed become dominant actors in the Spanish borderlands, they often did so at the expense of their neighbors." Blackhawk points to the particular vulnerability of Indigenous people without horses, who paid a "high and deadly" cost when in contact with equestrian raiding groups that thrived in the "expanding orbit" of New Mexico's economy.[76]

This study has traced how Yokuts became part of California's colonial orbit. From a crossroads of Indigenous trade, Yokuts territory became the *Apachería* the Spanish had feared. In 1826 Jedediah Smith initiated the Anglo-American fur trade in the Central Valley. An international group of traders soon moved through the area. They often found Indigenous Spanish-speaking guides on horseback from among the many who returned to their territories or found refuge from the missions among Yokuts.[77] New Mexicans also traded with Yokuts people. They began to arrive in large numbers in the 1830s on the Old Spanish Trail from Abiquiu to Los Angeles. By the end of the 1830s, sub-branches of the trail extended from San Diego to San Jose northward, and across the bay to San Rafael.

To supply the traders, Yokuts persisted in ever more systematic raiding of the missions By the 1830s the rates of horse stealing from towns and ranchos had reached unprecedented proportions. The Yokuts were not alone. San José lost almost all their horses to raids in 1832. Violence against Yokuts increased. Governor José Figueroa allowed citizens to mount their own expeditions against horse thieves, greatly augmenting violence against Yokuts populations during the mid-1830s.[78] Few officials contained the civilian violence; indeed, they supported it in their raids against villages they considered to have instigated hostilities or harbored thieves.

In 1833, trappers from the Hudson's Bay Company brought malaria to Miwok and Yokuts territories in the Central Valley that killed "an estimated twenty thousand." Illness virtually depopulated particular territories.[79] Malaria became endemic in the many waterways of the region. It produced a decline in raiding between 1833 and 1835, but the raiding resumed in 1835. Those who remained in their territories in the valley, or who moved as fragmented groups to ally with others, kept Mexican society from expanding very far beyond the parameters that existed during the colonial era.

The cycles of violence and revenge, trading and illness, made conditions so difficult that some Yokuts people resumed their affiliations with particular missions. In the year or so before 1824 and the Chumash War, affiliations to the missions from Yokuts territories had almost ceased. But due to the increasingly difficult conditions in the valley, the missions offered a refuge that couldn't be found elsewhere. The 1830s migrations from Yokuts territories went especially to Missions San Juan Bautista, San Miguel, and Soledad. Some Yokuts turned to family and village connections established at particular missions when they confronted a time of little choice.

At Mission San Juan Bautista, Yokuts people from Hoyima affiliated through a continuous stream of migration between 1828 and 1840, but especially in 1830 and again in 1832. People from Chauchila came in their majority between 1820 and 1822, but again between 1835 and 1839 in a scattered fashion. Mission San Miguel would again rebuild a mission population that had declined to 658 persons by 1832 from its height of 1,076 in 1814, when people from Bubal, Wowol, and Auyame had constituted the majority of Yokuts at the mission. People from the village of Wowol, that had maintained its close and precarious relationship to San Miguel, began to affiliate to the mission again around 1834, after having nearly ceased to do so for a decade. Many people also went to San Miguel from villages that had never sent affiliates to that mission prior to the 1830s.

A large affiliation of people from Suntachi, allies to the Chumash in the 1824 revolt, affiliated to Mission San Miguel between 1834 and 1835 and again in 1838. From Youelmani, some affiliated to the mission between 1834 and 1838. People from Tachi and Nutunutu, villages that Chumash leaders had contacted in the 1824 revolt, had not affiliated with San Miguel previously, but did so in 1834 and 1835, which seems to point to the physical and economic devastation of their villages. A handful also came in from Tulamni, and others in few numbers from villages in a region suffering under violence and illness by 1833.

New groups also went to Mission Soledad. They included people from Vechegot, with a sizable affiliation of forty. The majority affiliated during the year of crisis when malaria set into the valley in 1833. The major Yokuts group at Soledad had been from Pitkachi, but their affiliations had virtually ceased until about twenty people again affiliated in 1830 and 1831. People from Tachi, who fled Soledad in large numbers in 1819, again affiliated in 1833 and 1834.[80]

In California, the borderlands of independent tribes often began on the missions' eastern boundaries. In 1827 at Mission San Fernando, for example, the boundaries of the mission's ranchos were contiguous with the lands of autonomous native societies identified as the "land of the Gentiles."[81] In 1836, the city of Los Angeles had a specific convergence of Indigenous people from independent groups of Apache, Paiutes, Serrano, and Cahuilla tribes, among others.[82] Independent Indigenous societies and the settled spaces of Mexican society would increasingly converge during this era.

A HISTORY IN SHADOWS

Emancipation and the granting of land created a new status and condition for all those who had been neophytes, but the governor reimposed the colonial status for those still living at the missions in 1835. Violence and beatings persisted. Compensation remained negligible. In March 1845 the governor of California recommended that the Indigenous populations at the missions be allowed to have their "liberty" and be made into Indian pueblos. He suggested some of the mission goods be distributed among them.[83] This came late in the Mexican era, and the colonial Indian pueblo promised little hope of restoring ancestral land rights. The proposal also arrived after more than a decade in which individuals had created the best conditions they could. Many already lived on grants they petitioned for and received in the vicinity of their missions. They formed a landed group with various degrees of rights within the Mexican countryside. They received relatively small grants, generally the size allotted to poorer soldiers and widows, with variation as to their demonstrated ability to farm and raise livestock. Some petitioned collectively for grants. A few Indigenous men and women received large grants.

These grants marked important gains from the condition of landlessness that emancipation and secularization produced, yet they also represented loss: a loss that came from the absence of a systematic redistribution of mission land among their Indigenous populations, and one compounded by the absence of an official memory of the Indigenous geography of California. The federalization of Indigenous lands succeeded in California, with the Californios gaining title to most of the *missions'* Indigenous lands after 1834. The development of Indigenous land ownership occurred within a context of persistent violence and unfreedom that Indigenous people continued to experience at the missions. It is one of two stories told in this chapter. The other concerns California's greater proximity to the Indigenous borderlands of northern Mexico during these years. They had long been structured around violent relations of raiding, trading, and human captivity.

The experiences of Crespín and Policarpio emphasized the tentative nature of Indigenous rights at this time. Jailed for not having a pass from their masters, as Indigenous men from missions they were suspect for freely moving about and for appearing to engage in illicit trade. Their story emphasizes the ingenuity and humor they brought to their circumstances, and their ability to move between worlds. But the history of their communities, and the Indigenous geographies that defined the region, remained largely obscured in the official documents and patterns of landownership that had emerged by 1846.

Conclusion

Indigenous Archives and Knowledge

An important group of Indigenous citizens emerged in California during the Mexican era, but the California state constitution effectively revoked their citizenship rights after the region became part of the United States in 1848. When the California constitutional convention debated Indian suffrage in 1849, José de la Guerra y Noriega, the representative from Santa Bárbara, spoke through a translator against excluding Indigenous people from the vote. He argued that they had done "all the work that was seen in California. . . . If they were not cultivated and highly civilized, it was because they had been ground down and made slaves of." The citizen should endeavor "to elevate them and better their condition in every way, instead of seeking to sink them still lower."

José de la Guerra y Noriega requested that an exception be made for Indians "who were the holders of property and had therefore exercised all the rights and privileges of freemen." He asked that they "might still be permitted to continue in the exercise of those rights." As delegates expressed their fears that wealthy Mexican ranch owners would be able to buy those votes and swing elections, de la Guerra y Noriega pointed out the comparatively small size of the potential electorate. He calculated that "all the Indians in the entire Territory who owned land and were entitled to vote, under the laws of Mexico, were not more than two hundred."[1]

Had de la Guerra y Noriega's objections been upheld, the regional history of Indigenous equality, and the political visions held by native communities, might have become part of the story of California's past. Although he pointed to the small number of two hundred Indigenous citizens and voters, their significance spread far beyond that in their families and communities. The exclusions placed on Indigenous citizenship in California helped to obscure the native geographies and tribal and colonial histories that are the subject of this book. The act of taking away Indigenous citizenship rights denied the political past of Indigenous communities.

Indigenous exclusion from the rights of citizen in 1849 placed a large social group outside the position assigned to the modern individual. It opened Indian "lives and lands to the visitations of various breeds of primitivism."[2] It allowed the nation-states of the United States and Mexico to vent epistemic violence on native populations during the nineteenth century, and attribute it to the natives' position "as victims of modernity."[3] For too long, the absence of citizenship and notions of primitivism meant that Indigenous people were too rarely considered political subjects in California history.

Local and global discourses about Indigenous and human rights, colonialism, and genocide have contested these national and regional imaginings.[4] Native sources, categories, and concerns have enabled this book to establish Indigenous people as political subjects and actors.[5] Interdisciplinary approaches have offered material to capture native visions, with attention to visual history, Indigenous knowledge, and narrative form.

The creation of the primitive subject that left native lives and lands open to various kinds of misrepresentation and appropriation began, in this book, with colonialism. Colonial thinking influenced the way that documents were written, and ultimately left much of the knowledge about this past within Indigenous memory and communities. It became "Indigenous knowledge," the substance of which was sometimes left in traces in the colonial archive, but remembered more fully, and differently, in native communities.

In bringing that knowledge into the writing of colonial history, this book has placed a greater focus on tribal geography both within and beyond colonial settlement. Spanish documents mapped the Indigenous geographies of the regions they settled. Documents provided the names of villages and their leadership, and size of the population, as in 1796 in Santa Bárbara, and in 1798, during the exploration to find a site for Mission Santa Inés. But once Chumash and other people went into the missions, that tribal geography became lost. An erasure began almost immediately in official documents and became pronounced in the Mexican era, when mission land ultimately became the patrimony of the state and was redistributed sparingly to those who sought land grants.

As native communities made clear, they wanted to return to their lands or stay at the missions. At Missions San Diego and San Luis Rey, they refused to move to land seen as belonging to other Indigenous people. At San Juan Capistrano, communities preferred to claim the missions where they cultivated plots and could sustain livelihoods. The missions had become part of an Indigenous geography of California, and in those sites the histories of one or more generations of people from specific families and villages transpired. Indigenous people and their relatives had built the infrastructure and produced the wealth of institutions they subsequently claimed, just as the Ineseño and Purísimeño population had run Mission La Purísima for nearly a month during the Chumash War in 1824.

The book has also placed emphasis on the ways people within the missions moved between worlds with particular agility, and the enormous capacity of Indigenous translators, interpreters, and tribal historians to make colonial society intelligible. The story of José María Crespín and Policarpio suggests that the two men had learned to negotiate distinctive societies in the towns of New Mexico, and on the Indigenous borderlands, from their Luiseño upbringing during the colonial era.

Part of that ability to survive came from the way Indigenous leaders and communities influenced how Catholicism and Spanish practices would be understood. At Santa Inés, Indigenous godparents, often recently affiliated themselves, played important roles in the induction of their relatives and villages into the mission. At San Luis Rey, elders translated Catholicism and gave meaning to the religion. They named the new practices of dressing and sought redress from the humiliations and sorrows they confronted at the mission. They became weavers of the garments they wore; generations came to possess an enormous range of skills related to the new economy and remained engaged in different aspects of traditional economies.

Elders passed down versions of the histories of their political defeat that later emerged in the writing of Pablo Tac and in oral testimonies. They imparted various kinds of Indigenous knowledge at the missions, and they addressed the reality of the moment through their narrations produced in painting, sculptor, and in dance, song, and ritual. With their bodies and voice, they used Indigenous means to rectify conditions. Drawing on native logic, they brought new elements into their society that influenced Indigenous cultural practices and produced a relationship to new things, such as the horse, that fostered the communities' well-being.

Indigenous theorists Maria Brave Heart and Philip Gone emphasize the particularly important role narration plays in overcoming the hold of traumatic experience produced in colonial encounters, and their ideas suggest another dimension of the significance of native authority and knowledge systems within the missions. Both argue that, in healing from historical and generational trauma, it is important to reclaim Indigenous heritage, identity, and spirituality.[6] Gone points to the distinctive cultural psychologies of space and place commonly found in native and Western thought, and to the importance of Indigenous spaces to establish individual and collective well-being.[7] When Indigenous leaders and communities created Indigenous spaces, practice, and authority within the missions, they helped sustain people's health in the face of the great losses, sorrow, and fragmentation that colonialism produced.

The exclusion from citizenship that began to affect Indigenous people in the Mexican era in California seems to have cast a veil over native political history. Lifting it, this book treats the political as both daily acts and those larger movements that are meant to change relationships to the state. Within this, it has been important to note how, for example, the elite at Mission La Purísima learned Spanish in order to better define how new concepts entered the language. Painting meant engaging in the politics of the image and enabled Indigenous artisans to influence the visual narratives presented in the missions. Politics sometimes meant dance and at other times meant major actions, such as the Chumash War of 1824. The war relied on a coordinated Indigenous leadership. Indigenous thought and means of alliance fostered its success. Native politics also involved writing petitions, making claims, and standing up for labor compensation. But those demands held their greatest promise between 1822 to 1834, when discussions of Indigenous citizenship created a greater range of possibilities.

The political terrain of Indigenous action narrowed substantially when the egalitarian ideas of the early republic began to lose force in state and local politics in Mexico after 1833. Shortly after the Emancipation and Secularization Decree passed in 1834, the whole discussion of Indigenous citizenship virtually ended in California. The promise of equality and citizenship had produced important changes, however, and many Indigenous people and communities acted to define and extend their new political rights in the Mexican era. But the rights of Indigenous citizens remained on highly unstable grounds after 1834 in California.

Throughout this book Indigenous sources have contributed to a multivocal explanation of what was at stake and for whom in colonial and Mexican California. The historical imaginaries reflected in the records of the settlement of Mission San Luis Rey, for example, show incommensurate approaches to the event. European and Indigenous descriptions of dance varied markedly, and without the latter, its significance would be difficult to determine. Indigenous painting suggests how the European stories of Catholicism took on meaning in native culture. The Chumash War, and ideas expressed about freedom, formed different aspects of native politics. In all of these cases, native narrations offered critical ways to understand the significance of events.

INDIGENOUS ARCHIVES

The Indigenous archives, by which I mean material made, represented, and/or saved by native communities, have been crucial to the story of power and colonial rule examined herein. Native archives for this period are not in one place; they include material in the colonial archives and museums of California, Mexico, and in European collections. They contain varied materials, and often work with translated knowledge and form. They belay reference points and meaning not commonly found in archival materials written by missionaries, the military, and settlers.

The Santa Ynez band, who retained portions of mission land granted to their leaders and families during the 1840s, kept records of tribal history during the colonial and Mexican eras. Rafael Solares, one of the many Indigenous *sacristáns* or wardens of the church, lived at Santa Inés since his birth in the spring of 1822. He moved to the nearby Indian community toward the end of the Mexican period and lived there until his death in 1884, at the age of sixty-two. Solares acted as the keeper of church vestments, books, and other objects.[8] Able to speak Latin and sing entire masses, he assisted at religious events. A leader within the church, Solares also led Chumash ceremony. He was one of the last members of the historic 'Antap politico-religious organization at Santa Inés. As a leader within this community, Solares carried on a tradition common in Chumash territory since colonization. Those most knowledgeable in Indigenous culture and language also often held prominent positions within the church. As leaders, they could give their own meaning to the missions as sites of Indigenous experience.

Rafael Solares later acted as a principal consultant on Chumash culture for the French ethnographers and linguists Léon de Cessac and Alphonse Pinart, whom he met in 1874.[9] Cessac developed a dictionary of some twelve hundred words through his work with Solares. Cessac built a collection of thousands of objects, and Solares helped him collect Chumash objects in the proximity of Santa Ines. Acquired by the Musée del Homme in Paris, these vast quantities of Chumash objects constituted a substantial addition to the archive of world civilizations.[10] Yet this very act of preservation further removed elements of a cultural legacy from Chumash communities. Perhaps Solares felt that, under the circumstances of genocidal violence against Indigenous people in California from 1849 through the early 1870s, Pinart and Cessac could better guarantee the survival of cultural memory represented in these objects.[11]

At Santa Inés, the community also contributed to the preservation of the Chumash painting of the Archangel Raphael and of other valued mission goods. Within the Santa Inés community, Indian choristers and the older population sang mission-era songs at mass for generations. The Chumash orchestra at Mission Santa Inés produced mission-era music through the first decades of the twentieth century, and elders, both women and men, sang from positions around the side altars for mass.[12] The painting remained entwined with the history of this community whose relatives had once burned the mission to the ground during the 1824 war.

In the late nineteenth century, almost three generations later, when Santa Inés did not have a regular priest living at the mission and the objects could not be protected, the Ineseño Chumash community saved the painting of the Archangel Raphael.[13] Someone had taken it out of its frame and folded it to store it. In contrast, some of the mission's other paintings fared poorly, such as a painting of Saint Francis, which had been simply crumpled under a water tank.[14] The community also saved the extravagant collection of vestments that the priests had ordered, and that had been woven and sewed at the mission to match altar cloths also made in mission textile and work rooms. They protected the collection of unique song-books written by the missionaries and used by the native choir and orchestra at Santa Inés.[15]

After being keepers of Chumash goods and moving them into the world market, Ineseños and other California Indian people told their tribal histories to J. P. Harrington, who worked for the Smithsonian Institute. Harrington settled in Santa Bárbara and worked with Chumash consultants until the end of his life.[16] The event-based histories of the Chumash War that Harrington gathered had been kept by families for generations. They emerged from the oral histories told by relatives who had been involved in the war and who passed down the stories told to them.

But by the end of the twentieth century, this community still had no presence at the mission as a historical group with a patrimony to it as their historical site. In some places, as in a mass of reconciliation held recently in which Franciscans acknowledged the losses and pain suffered by the Amah Mutsun tribe, historical trauma is being addressed. But often, the loss of tribal and historical patrimonies persists in the present. To regain full access to cultural patrimony, and to officially valorize this history, often depends, in California, on tribal recognition.[17] The full recovery of an Indigenous archive forms part of the ongoing restoration of tribal sovereignty over the sites and implications of this colonial and Mexican past.

APPENDIX

Population Data for Five Colonial Missions

TABLE 1 Mission San Luis Obispo, 1772–1846

Year	Baptisms	Deaths	Indigenous Men	Indigenous Women
1772	1	1	—	—
1773	41	—	—	—
1774	95	5	—	—
1775	146	11	—	—
1776	216	20	—	—
1777	280	38	—	—
1778	334	50	—	—
1779	402	65	—	—
1780	477	79	—	—
1781	528	92	—	—
1782	585	113	—	—
1783	625	124	—	—
1784	645	160	—	—
1785	700	187	—	—
1786	738	203	—	—
1787	769	227	—	—
1788	843	246	—	—
1789	877	270	—	—
1790	924	292	—	—
1791	1,057	348	—	—
1792	1,157	392	—	—
1793	1,192	412	—	—
1794	1,282	447	—	—
1795	1,339	499	—	—
1796	1,400	554	384	430
1797	1,437	602	—	—
1798	1,486	659	388	404
1799	1,546	738	386	400

(*continued*)

TABLE 1 (*Continued*)

Year	Baptisms	Deaths	Indigenous Men	Indigenous Women
1800	1,599	815	373	351
1801	1,652	894	366	331
1802	1,734	962	374	325
1803	2,009	1,033	439	385
1804	2,074	1,091	—	—
1805	2,131	1,128	508	453
1806	2,162	1,216	458	372
1807	2,192	1,280	—	—
1808	2,218	1,324	416	346
1809	2,246	1,378	—	—
1810	2,265	1,420	399	312
1811	2,296	1,475	378	308
1812	2,325	1,519	395	282
1813	2,376	1,579	392	271
1814	2,402	1,631	385	253
1815	2,427	1,682	367	243
1816	2,447	1,720	351	241
1817	2,463	1,757	343	227
1818	2,489	1,807	328	218
1819	2,518	1,845	313	218
1820	2,537	1,890	304	200
1821	2,557	1,919	290	192
1822	2,562	1,955	293	174
1823	2,286	1,984	289	173
1824	2,599	2,023	277	146
1825	2,606	2,066	249	146
1826	2,612	2,103	232	129
1827	2,616	2,129	229	115
1828	2,620	2,149	218	110
1829	2,627	2,175	210	100
1830	2,631	2,203	195	88
1831	2,640	2,230	184	81
1832	2,644	2,268	161	70
1846	3,000	2,598	—	—

SOURCE: Zephyrin Engelhardt, *Mission San Luis Obispo in the Valley of the Bears* (1963).

TABLE 2 Mission San Buenaventura, 1782–1843

Year	Baptisms	Deaths	Indigenous Men	Indigenous Women
1782	3	—	—	—
1783	—	—	—	—
1784	69	3	—	—
1785	133	13	—	—
1786	199	25	—	—
1787	311	49	—	—
1788	407	68	—	—
1789	—	—	—	—
1790	534	115	—	—
1791	642	151	—	—
1792	696	192	—	—
1793	759	195	—	—
1794	815	267	—	—
1795	897	308	—	—
1796	1,121	359	—	—
1797	1,157	382	378	358
1798	1,213	412	392	374
1799	1,257	475	388	359
1800	1,291	534	381	341
1801	1,455	634	380	391
1802	1,669	693	436	502
1803	1,885	781	—	—
1804	2,012	879	523	584
1805	—	—	—	—
1806	2,306	1,126	544	615
1807	2,464	1,253	—	—
1808	2,648	1,332	611	679
1809	2,741	1,426	—	—
1810	2,834	1,511	616	679
1811	2,875	1,586	605	655
1812	2,912	1,673	593	618
1813	2,958	1,761	582	587
1814	3,071	1,836	623	584
1815	3,144	19,32	628	558
1816	3,367	2,013	700	628
1817	3,415	2,111	677	600
1818	3,471	2,233	653	556
1819	3,508	2,307	634	538
1820	3,547	2,391	617	510
1821	3,583	2,462	599	493
1822	3,608	2,608	551	422
1823	3,648	2,687	533	402
1824	3,676	2,740	513	395
1825	3,698	2,799	489	376
1826	3,724	2,849	474	378

(continued)

TABLE 2 (*Continued*)

Year	Baptisms	Deaths	Indigenous Men	Indigenous Women
1827	3,741	2,883	467	366
1828	3,763	2,949	447	342
1829	3,788	3,000	436	329
1830	3,805	3,053	418	308
1831	3,825	3,098	410	293
1832	3,843	3,150	392	276
1833	—	—	—	—
1834	3,924	3,216	—	—
1842	—	—	—	—
1843	—	—	—	—

SOURCE: Zephyrin Engelhardt, *San Buenaventura, The Mission by the Sea* (1930).

TABLE 3 Mission La Purísima Concepción, 1787–1846

Year	Baptisms	Deaths	Indigenous Men	Indigenous Women
1787	—	—	—	—
1788	95	—	—	—
1789	162	7	—	—
1790	308	25	—	—
1791	488	51	—	—
1792	598	86	—	—
1793	663	113	—	—
1794	804	138	—	—
1795	935	181	—	—
1796	997	226	383	373
1797	1,132	266	—	—
1798	1,229	307	448	472
1799	1,301	364	—	—
1800	1,380	420	460	501
1801	1,472	516	—	—
1802	1,581	557	457	571
1803	2,033	610	—	—
1804	2,214	707	685	835
1805	2,328	800	—	—
1806	2,360	1,020	533	633
1807	2,394	1,108	—	—
1808	2,425	1,170	502	582
1809	2,453	1,243	—	—
1810	2,495	1,312	500	520
1811	2,534	1,399	480	498
1812	2,595	1,443	489	510
1813	2,680	1,518	507	497
1814	2,729	1,586	496	486
1815	2,846	1,675	510	509

1816	2,920	1,755	515	503
1817	2,955	1,846	486	472
1818	2,991	1,915	481	456
1819	3,019	1,980	468	420
1820	3,046	2,054	452	388
1821	3,075	2,112	435	373
1822	3,099	2,172	413	351
1823	3,121	2,243	496	326
1824	3,138	2,324	366	296
1825	3,163	2,370	300	232
1826	3,173	2,446	234	287
1827	3,183	2,486	201	270
1828	3,199	2,527	193	252
1829	3,213	2,561	170	236
1830	3,224	2,563	179	234
1831	3,244	2,549	180	224
1832	3,255	2,633	227	145
1833	3,266	2,658	—	—
1834	3,325	2,688	—	—
1835	3,334	2,732	—	—
1836	3,342	2,760	—	—
1837	3,347	2,781	—	—
1838	3,350	2,805	—	—
1839	3,357	2,821	—	—
1840	3,361	2,839	—	—
1841	3,364	2,860	—	—
1842	3,371	2,880	—	—
1843	3,375	2,894	—	—
1844	3,377	2,964	—	—
1845	3,381	2,972	—	—
1846	3,386	—	—	—

SOURCE: Zephyrin Engelhardt, *Mission la Concepción Purísma de María Santísima* (1932).

TABLE 4 Mission Santa Inés, 1804–1850

Year	Baptisms	Deaths	Indigenous Men	Indigenous Women
1804	112	—	116	109
1805	—	—	—	—
1806	371	118	229	341
1807	412	154	—	—
1808	445	186	272	315
1809	487	210	—	—
1810	546	245	286	342
1811	591	301	280	331
1812	626	338	288	323
1813	664	378	294	313

(*continued*)

TABLE 4 (*Continued*)

Year	Baptisms	Deaths	Indigenous Men	Indigenous Women
1814	695	412	277	311
1815	807	473	306	330
1816	992	524	377	391
1817	1,033	609	366	354
1818	1,063	680	353	328
1819	1,095	743	333	314
1820	1,140	789	331	304
1821	1,170	850	318	286
1822	1,193	895	306	276
1823	1,223	944	301	263
1824	1,235	997	254	262
1825	1,250	1,026	245	255
1826	1,271	1,061	234	253
1827	1,286	1,085	233	244
1828	1,299	1,118	—	—
1829	1,313	1,140	218	210
1830	1,326	1,159	—	—
1831	1,335	1,190	205	183
1832	1,345	1,227	196	164
1833	1,366	1,231	—	—
1834	1,372	1,262	—	—
1835	1,398	1,288	—	—
1836	1,411	1,302	—	—
1837	1,431	1,334	—	—
1838	1,447	1,359	—	—
1839	1,460	1,385	—	—
1840	1,472	1,403	—	—
1841	1,492	1,427	—	—
1842	1,501	1,446	—	—
1843	1,523	1,473	—	—
1844	1,541	1,506	—	—
1845	1,558	1,528	—	—
1846	1,574	1,546	—	—
1847	1,586	1,573	—	—
1848	1,608	1,600	—	—
1849	1,622	1,620	—	—
1850	1,631	1,632	—	—

SOURCE: Zephyrin Engelhardt, *Mission Santa Inés, Virgen y Martir, and Its Ecclesiastical Seminary* (1932).

TABLE 5 Mission Santa Bárbara, 1782–1846

Year	Baptisms	Deaths	Indigenous Men	Indigenous Women
1782	—	—	—	—
1783	—	—	—	—
1784	—	—	—	—
1785	—	—	—	—
1786	3	—	—	—
1787	188	6	—	—
1788	336	29	—	—
1789	475	50	—	—
1790	520	102	—	—
1791	662	141	—	—
1792	729	209	—	—
1793	775	235	—	—
1794	815	263	300	249
1795	870	298	305	264
1796	1,023	372	325	321
1797	1,215	425	403	379
1798	1,301	493	411	385
1799	1,395	588	402	390
1800	1,541	662	431	433
1801	1,844	812	495	527
1802	1,997	894	521	572
1803	2,829	1,026	833	959
1804	3,092	1,186	823	960
1805	3,217	1,315	836	931
1806	3,279	1,529	738	865
1807	3,328	1,641	705	834
1808	3,380	1,748	691	786
1809	3,419	1,846	665	748
1810	3,450	1,936	644	711
1811	3,498	2,014	690	635
1812	3,560	2,100	659	645
1813	3,615	2,189	647	622
1814	3,732	2,271	663	637
1815	3,837	2,340	659	581
1816	3,961	2,437	663	596
1817	4,011	2,517	645	581
1818	4,088	2,610	646	553
1819	4,147	2,708	633	526
1820	4,194	2,780	624	508
1821	4,233	2,913	574	465
1822	4,288	2,997	522	458
1823	4,325	3,081	532	430
1824	4,360	3,155	508	415
1825	4,382	3,220	490	395
1826	4,412	3,267	485	382

(continued)

TABLE 5 *(Continued)*

Year	Baptisms	Deaths	Indigenous Men	Indigenous Women
1827	4,436	3,316	485	372
1828	4,464	3,419	425	337
1829	4,495	3,475	407	330
1830	4,517	3,522	391	320
1831	4,546	3,582	371	308
1832	4,563	3,637	343	285
1833	4,577	3,688	324	266
1834	4,593	3,722	307	249
1835	4,602	3,772	284	222
1836	4,616	3,797	270	211
1837	4,629	3,832	—	—
1838	4,635	3,875	—	—
1839	4,650	3,922	—	—
1840	4,660	3,964	—	—
1841	4,676	3,997	—	—
1842	4,680	—	—	—
1843	4,699	—	—	—
1844	4,703	—	—	—
1845	4,712	—	—	—
1846	4,715	—	—	—

SOURCE: Zephyrin Engelhardt, *Santa Bárbara Mission* (1923).

NOTES

INTRODUCTION: SAINTS AND INDIGENOUS CITIZENS

1. Harrington 2005: 107.

2. See the Early California Population Project, an online database from the Huntington Library that has digitized the sacramental records and made them readily available.

3. Santiago Argüello, 1 Agosto 1833 San Diego. Lista de los Neófitos de la Mision de San Diego, y Lista de los Neófitos de la misión de San Luis Rey que pueden salir de la Neofia, Vallejo C-B 31 pt. 1: 115, 123; "Padrón de los Neófitos de esta Misión de San Carlos." No. 2353 Manuscript Collection of Alexander Taylor, Huntington Library (hereafter HL).

4. The longue durée is a concept developed by historians Marc Bloch and Lucien Febvre in the interwar years and associated with the French Annales School. Fernand Braudel develops the approach in his classic *The Mediterranean and the Mediterranean World in the Age of Philip II* (1972). Iain Chambers reflects on the Mediterranean's "many voices" in *Mediterranean Crossings* (2008): 1–22.

5. See Hinton 1994: 83. Hinton notes that few maps can convey the significant social divisions between Indigenous peoples, and only a few of the names on the map have any relation to what groups called themselves at the time of contact. See p. 157.

6. Golla 2011: 1.

7. Erlandson 1994: 47–48.

8. Gamble and King 1997: 63.

9. The Colorado Desert formed one of the most ethnically, linguistically, and situationally diverse regions of California. It included the Mojave Desert. Uto-Aztecan speakers began to occupy to western part of the Mojave Desert about 5,000 years ago. Over three millennia, they diversified as linguistic families and came to occupy much of southern and eastern California and the Mojave Desert. See Schaefer and Laylander 2007.

10. Hinton 1994: 85 and Sutton, Basgall, Gardner, and Allen 2007: 243. See the language map in Chartkoff and Chartkoff 1984: 200 and the mapping of ethnohistorical groups on 202.

11. Millikin et al. 2007: 118.

12. Fagan 2003: 270. See the map on 270: the end point of the rivers is at Buena Vista Lake; see map on 298 too for southern California.

13. Rosenthal, White, and Sutton 2007: 149.

14. Johnson, 1989; and Millikin 1995; Hackel 2005, esp. chapter 3.

15. Stoler 2002: 9–10 and 2006.

16. James Sandos (2004) makes an excellent analysis of the Indian choristers and the role of song in teaching about the Catholic religion; conversion, understood in the sense of learning about the religion from a Spanish perspective, took place among relatively few people. In this book, I refer to being placed on the baptismal role as "conversion" without assuming particular beliefs. I argue, instead, for examining the process of translation and religion in practice.

17. Hackel 1997 (staff, a/b).

18. Haas 2011.

19. Gruzinski 1992, 1993.

20. Salomon 1990; Adorno 2001: 39; Adorno 2007: 40; and Dean 1999 and Timberlake 1999.

21. Haskett 1998; see Adorno 1986, and 1998: 137–65.

22. Wood 2003.

23. Lockhart 1992.

24. On the visions that peacemakers came to share on the Philadelphia frontier, see Merrill 1999. On translators who moved between worlds see Karttunen 1994.

25. See Johnson 2001 and 2007. See Barbara Voss (2008) on the processes of ethnogenesis among the Californio population at the Presidio of San Francisco.

26. Hackel 2005, esp. pt. 2.

27. See Sandos 2004 and Caywood 2012.

28. See Lightfoot 2005 and Peelo 2010, 2011.

29. See, for example, Recopilación de leyes, tomo 2, 1943: 41; Recopilación de leyes, tomo 2, 1943: 44.

30. Seed 2001: 76.

31. Lomnitz-Adler 1992: 3, 23.

32. Scott 2005 and 1998. Scott's work has formed an important part of this literature.

33. Cooper, Holt, and Scott 2000: 2.

34. Muñoz and López 1998: 60–61.

35. See Mallon 1995: 9.

36. Horcasitas 2000: 13, and Guardino 1996.

37. Hämäläinen 2008. Also see Barr 2007.

38. Brooks 2002.

39. Blackhawk 2006.

40. Costo and Costo 1987: 23–24 and 131–70.

41. Smith 1999: 33.

42. Mihesuah 2004:145.

43. Lonetree 2012.

44. Deloria 2004: 50; and Guidotti-Hernández 2011: 176.

45. White 1987: 41.

46. Ibid.: 57.

1. COLONIAL SETTLEMENTS ON INDIGENOUS LAND

1. In planned revolts at Mission Santa Gertrudis (Antigua California) and San Juan Capistrano, native leaders spoke of the absence of seeds, and of the humiliations they had experienced, among their causes for rebellion. In both places the defiant killing and eating of livestock formed part of their warring against the missions. See Sargento Francisco de Aguilar por orden del Capitan de Rivera y Moncada, 12 Deciembre 1777, Santa Gertrudis, C-A 1: 297–99, BL; and José Francisco de Ortega Teniente y Comandante, *Informe*, 1 Mayo 1778, San Diego, C-A 1: 288–93, BL.

2. Killing horses was common in all actions of war against and resistance to the missions. The Spanish reacted violently to any threat against their livestock.

3. See Millikin 1995: 115–36. Millikin presents each chapter by identifying "Spanish actions" and "Tribal actions" and posits different periods, including a period of mutual accommodation followed by a very poignant era of social transformation. For the Indigenous population at Mission Dolores, this was especially true for the difficult years 1793 to 1795.

4. Hackel 2005: 65 and all of chapter 3 is relevant to this discussion.

5. See Johnson, 1989b. Peelo 2009b: 620. Peelo emphasizes that "change in every aspect of their economic, social, political, and religious lives" ultimately explained the movement of the Salinan population into Mission San Antonio.

6. Santiago 1998: 114–15, 126. See map on 12.

7. Larson, Johnson, and Michaelsen 1994: 278.

8. Johnson 2000: 316.

9. Geiger 1965: 10.

10. Duggan 2000: esp. 22–24 emphasizes the negotiations that many village leaders made with the Spanish prior to their settlement.

11. Johnson 2001: 55.

12. Perissinotto 1998: 75, 129, 213, 231.

13. Diego de Borica al Virey, Informe sobre conversión de indios gentiles, 1769 (n.d.), C-A 50: 226–33, 230, BL.

14. Diego de Borica al Virey, ibid. 230, BL.

15. Felipe Goycoachea, 31 Diciembre 1798, Presidio de Santa Bárbara, Misiones y Pueblos de la Jurisitición del Real Presidio de Santa Bárbara. C-A 50:265–68, 268, BL.

16. Fray Juan Cortés y Estevan Tapis a Fray Francisco de Lasuén, Informe, 30 Octubre 1800, Santa Bárbara, CMD 497, SBMAL.

17. Duggan 2004: 12.

18. Fray Cortés y Tapis a Fray Francisco de Lasuén, Informe, 30 Octubre 1800, Santa Bárbara, CMD 497, SBMAL.

19. Johnson 1988: esp. 83–181. Johnson argues that the interconnections between villages within Chumash territory and the role of beads influenced the movement into the missions.

20. McRae 1999: 37.

21. Ibid.: 38.

22. Fray Estevan Tapis a Fray Presidente Lasuén, 23 Octubre 1798, Santa Bárbara, CMD 404, SBMAL.

23. Ibid.

24. Larson, Johnson, and Michaelsen 1994: 85.

25. Johnson 1989c.

26. Engelhardt 1923: 9–10.

27. Sacramental Register of Baptism, Mission Santa Inés, Nos. 1–12, SBMAL.

28. Ibid., Nos. 13–27, SBMAL.

29. Ibid., No. 28, 24 Septiembre 1804, SBMAL.

30. Ibid., Nos. 29–36, 24 Septiembre 1804, SBMAL.

31. Ibid., No. 37, 4 Octubre 1804, SBMAL.

32. Ibid., No. 39, 22 Octubre 1804, SBMAL.

33. Ibid., Nos. 47–79, ending 22 Diciembre 1804, SBMAL.

34. Ibid., Nos. 43 and 46, SBMAL.

35. *Informes* 31 Diciembre, 1806 Mission Santa Ines 1804–06, SBMAL.

36. Ibid.

37. Sacramental Register of Baptism, Mission Santa Ines, No. 569, SBMAL.

38. Libros de Misión, Archivo de la Misión de Santa Inés, Libros y Documentos, C-C 53:12, BL.

39. Sacramental Register of Baptism, Mission Santa Ines; see among those baptized from No. 723 to No. 1098, SBMAL.

40. *Informes*, 31 Diciembre, 1818 Mission Santa Ines, SBMAL.

41. Estado de las Misiones, 1793–94 13 Julio 1795 C-A 50: 165–66.

42. Crespí 2001: 275.

43. As noted earlier, the diverse language families in California broke down into languages and dialects that often became identified with the missions where an Indigenous lingua franca emerged. Hinton 1994: 83–85.

44. Crespí 2001: 279.

45. Ibid.: 293.

46. Fray Juan Mariner of Mission San Diego, *Diario,* 26 Agosto 1795, SBMAL; and Engelhardt 1921: 3–5.

47. Fermín Francisco de Lasuén to Governor Diego de Borica, 28 Marzo 1797, No. 117, Collection of Alexander Taylor, HL.

48. Fermín Francisco de Lasuén to Fray Pedro Callejas, 21 Octubre 1797, San Diego, in Kenneally 1965, vol. 2: 51.

49. Shipek 1977: 43.

50. Fermín Francisco de Lasuén, "Diary," October 1797, in Kenneally 1965, vol. 2: 53.

51. Fermín Francisco de Lasuén to Don Diego de Borica from Mission San Buenaventura, 14 Abril 1798, in Kenneally 1965, vol. 2: 78; and Fermín Francisco de Lasuén, 14 Abril 1798, No. 133, Collection of Alexander Taylor, HL.

52. Fermín Francisco de Lasuén to Fray Miguel Lull, 17 Abril 1798, Mission San Buenaventura, in Kenneally 1965, vol. 2: 79.

53. Haas 2011: 183.

54. Shipek 1977: 67–68.

55. See Johnson and O'Neil 2001: 28.

56. Fermín Francisco de Lasuén to Don Diego de Borica, 13 Junio 1798, in Kenneally 1965, vol. 2: 84–85.

57. Don Diego de Borica to Fermín Francisco de Lasuén on the founding of Mission San Luis Rey, 12 Junio 1798, CMD 379, SBMAL; Lasuén, 13 Junio 1798, No. 143, Collection of Alexander Taylor Collection, HL.

58. Menocal 2002 and Catlos 2004.

59. For a longer discussion of this, see Haas 2011: 26.

60. Fermín Francisco de Lasuén to Don Diego Borica, 20 Junio 1798, in Kenneally 1965, vol. 2: 87.

61. Fray Gerónimo Boscana wrote the one ethnography produced by a missionary in California during the early 1820s. See Harrington 2005.

62. Fray Francisco de Lasuén to Don Diego Borica, 20 Junio 1798, in Kenneally 1965, vol. 2: 87.

63. Engelhardt 1921: 16.

64. Fray Francisco de Lasuén to Fray Pedro Lull, 4 September 1798, in Kenneally 1965, vol. 2: 92.

65. Johnson and O'Neil 2001: 7–8.

66. Fray Francisco de Lasuén a Gobernador Diego de Borica, 28 Marzo 1797, No. 117, Collection of Alexander Taylor, HL.

67. See Johnson and Crawford 1999, esp. the map on 85. See McCawley 1995.

68. True, Meighan, and Crew 1974: 125; Shipek 1977: 99–100.

69. Engelhardt 1921: 222.

70. Shipek 1977: 180–81.

71. Engelhardt 1921: 36.

72. Shipek 1977: 166–72.

73. I've calculated 1 league as 3 geographic miles, but the league does not conform exactly to the mile.

74. Johnson and Crawford 1999: 87.

75. Johnson and O'Neil 2001: 24–26; and for Mexico, see Horn 1997.

76. Johnson and O'Neil 2001: 19–23.

77. Engelhardt 1921: 35.

78. Johnson and O'Neil 2001: 33–35.

79. Ibid.: 35–36.

80. Ibid.: 40.

81. Ibid.:8. The first *padrón* or census (1811–19) of the mission devoted forty-six pages of entries to people living away from the mission in their respective towns. The last third of the second *padrón* (1819–35) lists families living in interior villages affiliated with San Antonio de Pala. See Johnson and Crawford 1999: 91.

82. Engelhardt 1921: 43–44. (From the *Diario* of Father Sánchez at the Santa Barbara Mission Archive.)

83. Fray Antonio Peyri and Fray Francisco Suñer, *Preguntas y Respuestas,* San Luis Rey, 12 Diciembre 1814, PRA-18, SBMAL.

84. Ibid.

85. Duhaut-Cilly 1997: 114–15.

86. Described in detail by Fray Antonio Peyri and Fray Francisco Suñer, *Preguntas y Respuestas,* San Luis Rey, 12 Deciembre 1814, PRA-18, SBMAL.

87. Fray Antònio Peyri al Superior Gobierno de este Terratoreo, 23 Diciembre 1827, San Luis Rey, PRA-18, SBMAL.

88. Engelhardt 1920: 300–301.

89. Shipek, 1977: 76 and 172; Lightfoot (2005) compares the two southern missions to the rest with these statistics, keeping in mind the greater survival of pre-contact villages and landholding among Luiseño and Diegeño tribes and people.

90. Fray Mariano Payeras a Gobernador Solá, 30 Junio 1819, Soledad, No. 946, Collection of Alexander Taylor, HL.

91. "Lista de Neofitos," 1818, No. 962, Collection of Alexander Taylor, HL.

92. Mariano Payeras a Gobernador Solá, 30 Junio 1819, No. 946, Collection of Alexander Taylor, HL.

93. Cook 1962: 245–47. George Phillips (1993) plots these expeditions and the growing violence and resistance in the region.

94. Cutter 1995: 131.

95. Gobernado Pedro Fages a Francisco de Lasuén, 20 Agosto 1787, CMD 64, SBMAL. (Lasuén's response to Fages's letter is written in the margins on August 21, 1787.)

96. Francisco de Lasuén a Gobernador Pedro Fages, 23 Agosto 1787, CMD 65.

97. On the autonomous societies to the south and east of colonial California and the Old Spanish Trail, see Zappia 2008.

98. Cutter 1995: 184–85.

99. Ibid.: 185.

100. Early California Population Project (ECPP) Online Data Base for Mission Soledad. Until 1818, the baptismal registry of Mission Soledad did not identify the specific villages from which Yokuts emerged, and one needs to rely upon written material in the archives to identify them.

101. See Jackson and Castillo 1995: 54–55.

102. ECPP Online Data Base. Huntington Library.

103. Engelhardt 1931: 127.

104. Engelhardt offers the larger statistics while the tribal designations and specific territorial groups have been derived from the California Population Data Base for Mission San Miguel.

105. ECPP Online Data Base. The Huntington Library, Research for Mission San Miguel with the research assistance of Sarah Peolo, archeologist.

106. Engelhardt 1971: 60.

107. Fray Pedro Cabot a Fray Vicente Francisco de Sarría, 1 Junio 1816, No. 491, Collection of Alexander Taylor, HL.

108. See Phillips 1993: 61.

109. Cook 1962: 181–93, 184.

110. ECPP Online Data Base The Huntington Library, Mission San Miguel. Within the mission the population married other Yokuts villagers and Salinan people.

111. Fray Mariano Payeras, Report entitled "Fled from La Purísima," 2 Enero 1818, in Cutter 1995: 143–44.

112. Fray Mariano Payeras to Captain José de la Guerra, 4 Mayo 1818, Purísima, in Cutter 1995: 149.

113. Fray Mariano Payeras to Captain and Commander of the Presidio and Jurisdiction of Santa Bárbara, 4 Mayo 1818, in Cutter 1995: 149. (This was one of two letters Payeras wrote on May 4, 1818.)

114. Fray Mariano Payeras to José de la Guerra, 12 Octubre 1818, in Octubre 1995: 157.

115. Payeras, "Fled from La Purísima."

116. Fray Luís Antonio Muños a Gobernador Pablo de Solá, 30 Mayo 1816, San Luis Obispo, No. 479, Collection of Alexander Taylor Collection, HL.

117. Arkush 1993; see 620 and trade map on 621.

118. Ibid.: 622–24.

119. Gobernador a Comandante de Santa Bárbara, 12 Septiembre 1807, San Antonio, CA-26: 121, BL; Gobernador a Comandante de Santa Bárbara, 21 Junio 1808, Monterey, CA-26: 128, BL; Gobernador a Comandante de Santa Bárbara, 18 Agosto 1808, Monterey, CA-26: 128, BL; and Gobernador a Comandante de Santa Bárbara, 26 Agosto 1808, Monterey, CA-26: 129, BL.

120. "Military Report Noting Contemplated Attack on San Gabriel," 2 Marzo 1811, No. 377, Taylor Collection, HL; and "An 1811 Letter Soliciting More Military Force at San Gabriel," No. 386, Taylor Collection, HL.

121. Informe 13 Abril 1813, No. 398, Collection of Alexander Taylor, HL.

122. Gobernador Solá a José de la Guerra, 14 Mayo 1816, Monterey, CA-26: 35, BL.

123. The report, 30 Mayo–3 Junio 1819, No. 943, Collection of Alexander Taylor Collection, HL.

124. "Interogatorio," 24 Marzo 1821, CA-13: 290–91, BL.

125. José María Estudillo a Gobernador Solá, 24 Marzo 1821, San Diego, CA-13: 290–91, BL. See also Cook 1962: 161. José María Estudillo expressed the same fears as traders approached Mission San Gabriel in 1822, see José María Estudillo a Pablo Vicente de Solá, 3 Noviembre 1822, CA-27: 10, BL.

126. See Cutter 1995: 184–85.

127. Fray Mariano Payeras a Gobernador Solá, 30 Junio 1819, No. 946, Collection of Alexander Taylor, HL.

128. Arróm 1986: 15.

129. Report from Mission San Antonio, 18 Marzo 1799, No. 186, Collection of Alexander Taylor, HL.

130. Fray Estevan Tapis al Gobernador, 3 Junio 1806, No. 304, Taylor Collection, HL. Tapis worried that many soldiers on the expedition would leave the presidio and Mission San Luis Rey vulnerable to attack.

131. Both reports from Fray Ramón Abella to the Governor, 28 Febrero 1807, No. 317, Collection of Alexander Taylor, HL; and Ygnacio Martínez, "Declaraciones Contra Indios Ladrones," 17 Mayo 1827, CA-18: 236, BL.

132. Fray Ruis a Capitán Antonio Luis Argüllo, 17 Marzo 1822, CA-27: 11, BL.

133. Fray Martínez, 2 Marzo 1827, CA-18: 236, BL.

134. José Romero a José María Echeandía, "Sobre fuga de los Yndios Cocomaricopas," 4 Diciembre 1825, C-A 27: 355–56, BL.

2. BECOMING INDIAN IN COLONIAL CALIFORNIA

1. Gregorio Fernández (Rúbrica), *Preguntas y Respuestas*, 11 Noviembre 1800, PRA-2, SBMAL.

2. Radding 1997: 118, 256. Cynthia Radding discusses the Apache peace camps set up near several presidios in the northeastern portion of Sonora.

3. Hageman and Ewing 1991.

4. Butzer 2001: esp. 14–16.

5. Martínez 2007: 202, 213.

6. For studies of the vivid representation and significance of *casta* categories and painting, see Katzew and Deans-Smith 2009.

7. See Beltrán 1981: 233.

8. See ibid. and Trey 2006. Also see R. Anderson 1988 and Carroll 2001; Menard and Schwartz 1993: 101.

9. Restall 2006: 147–74, and see the tables on 155 and 161.

10. Beltrán 1981: 271, 278. Beltrán's work made the discussion of colonial slavery in Mexico come alive, but public intellectual discussion of African descent slavery in Mexico did not began until the 1990s. See one of the first exhibits at the Museo de Arte Popular in Coyoacán, Mexico City, 1991.

11. See Castañeda 1990.

12. Mason 1998: 50.

13. Pubols 2009: 27.

14. 31 Julio de 1782, Reál Presidio de Monterrey, C-A 50: 5–6, BL; Hermengildo Sal, 19 Diciembre 1790, Reál Presidio de Monterrey, C-A 50: 22–26, BL; Joséph Francisco de Ortega, 23 Mayo 1791, Reál Presidio de Monterrey, C-A 50: 11–13, BL. Note that as late as 1813 the Monterey Padrón still counted the *casta* designation, noting on 278, "Habitantes con distinción de castas en 1813," C-A 50: 225–52, BL; Lista de la Compañía, 31 Agosto 1782, Reál Presidio de San Francisco, 1790, C-A 50: 3–4, BL; Fray Pedro Benito Cambón y José Argüello, 2 Octubre 1790, Reál Presidio de San Francisco, C-A 50: 2–4, BL.

15. Voss 2008: esp. 83–97.

16. Hackel 2005: 55–62.

17. José de Zúñiga, 20 Mayo 1782, Reál Presidio de San Diego, C-A 50: 7–8, BL; 10 Diciembre 1783, Reál Presidio de San Diego, C-A 50: 9–10, BL; José de Zúñiga y Fray Hilario Tórrez, Año de 1790, Reál Presidio de San Diego, C-A 50: 17–21, BL.

18. Felipe de Goycoachea, 31 Diciembre 1785, Reál Presidio de Santa Bárbara, C-A 50: 5–10, BL; Felipe de Goycoachea y Fray Antonio Paleña, 21 Agosto 1790, Reál Presidio de Santa Bárbara, C-A 50:10- 15, BL.

19. Fray Ramón Olbes, *Preguntas y Respuestas,* Misión de Santa Bárbara, 31 December 1813, PRA-3, SBMAL.

20. Fray Torres de la Peña, 5 Octubre 1790, San José de Guadalupe Afaliu de Porros, C-A 50: 6–8, BL.

21. 31 Diciembre 1781, Pueblo de la Reyna de Los Angeles, C-A 50: 1–2, BL; Fray António Cruzado y Felipe de Goycochea, 17 Agosto 1790, Pueblo de la Reyna de Los Angeles, C-A 50:45–49, BL.

22. Mason 1998.

23. Tanghetti 2004: 25.

24. Castañeda 1990: 215.

25. Tanghetti 2004: 26.

26. Lepowsky 2004: 4–5.

27. Ibid.: 52; Sandos 2007: 7.

28. Fages á Lasuén y respuesto de Lasuén, 10 Junio 1788, Monterey, CMD 79, SBMAL; and Fages á Lasuén, 15 Junio 178, Monterey, CMD 80, SBMAL.

29. Johnson 2007: 34.

30. Wroth 1999: 86–88.

31. Fray Estevan Tapis a Fray Francisco Xavier Uría, *Preguntas y Respuestas,* Misión de Santa Ynez, 8 Marzo 1814, PRA-8; Fray Juan Cortés y Estevan Tapis to Francisco Lasuén, *Informe* 30 Octubre 1800 CMD 497, SBMAL. In 1800 they discussed *taparrabos* of *manta poblana* woven at the mission. This remained the dress throughout the mission period.

32. Frays Estevan Tapis y Fray Francisco Xavier Uría, *Preguntas y Respuestas* Misión de Santa Ynez, 8 Marzo 1814, PRA-8, SBMAL

33. António Peyri y Francisco Suñar, *Preguntas y Respuestas,* San Luis Rey, 12 Diciembre 1814, PRA-18; Fray José Sánchez, *Preguntas y Respuestas,* San Diego 23 Diciembre 1814, PRA-19 SBMAL.

34. Fray Ramón Olbés, *Preguntas y Respuestas,* Misión de Santa Bárbara, 31 Diciembre 1813, PRA-3, SBMAL.

35. Salvucci 1988: 30; and on backstrap weaving, see Sayer 2002: 15.

36. Fray Vicente Fuster al gobernador Diego de Borica, 31 Marzo 1797, Misión San Juan Capistrano, CMD 319, SBMAL.

37. See Salvucci 1988: esp. 104–12; and on the attempts to regulate and reform the *obrajes,* see 130.

38. Salvucci 1988: 98.

39. Fernández (Rúbrica), *Preguntas y Respuestas,* (Copy of La Purísima Provincias Internas, 11 Noviembre 1800, Misión de la Purísima, Tomo 216 AGN.)

40. Fray Juan Cortés y Fray Esteven Tapis a Fray Francisco de Lasuén, *Informe,* 30 Octubre 1800, Santa Bárbara, CMD 497, SBMAL.

41. Fray Juan Cortés y Fray Esteven Tapis a Fray Francisco de Lasuén, *Informe,* 30 Octubre 1800, Santa Bárbara, CMD 497, SBMAL.

42. Salvucci 1988: 136.

43. Duggan 2000: 329–30; and San Diego de Alcalá, 1774, Kurt Baer Archive, SBMAL.

44. Wroth 1999: 10–11.

45. Fray Mariano Payeras, 1810, La Purísima, C-C 4: 215, BL.

46. Ibid.

47. Wroth 1999: 15. *Sarape* appeared in Spanish dictionaries only in the mid-nineteenth century as a Mexicanism and spelled *zarape* or *serape.*

48. Fray Mariano Payeras a José de la Guerra, 26 Junio 1818, Purísima, in Cutter 1999: 153–54.

49. See, for example, Fray Pedro Cabot a Gobernador Argüello, 29 Junio 1825, Misión San Antonio, CMD 2783, SBMAL, and Fray Pedro Cabot a Herrera, 25 Febrero 1827, Misión San Antonio, CMD 3022, SBMA.

50. Perissinotto 1998: 48–51.

51. Ibid.: 56–61.

52. Salvucci 1988: 98.

53. Perissinotto 1998: vol. 1796, 275; vol. 1797, 282–84; vol. 1810, 355.

54. See Salvucci 1988: 19. Many operations couldn't withstand the competition with the Britain price of cotton falling 70 percent between 1780 and 1812. Contraband significantly challenged Mexico's internal market. See 155–57.

55. At Mission Santa Ines, the color and textiles made at the mission for the altar and priests' garments often complemented exquisite imported clothes and vestments, as discussed in chapter 3.

56. Perissinotto 1998: 52.

57. Perissinotto 1998: 75, 129, 213, 231.

58. Simpson 1961: 55.

59. See Von Langsdorff 1813–14: 61, 105–7.

60. Deetz 1991: 166.

61. Frays Estevan Tapis y Fray Uría commented on how beads remained the only currency among the population at Santa Ines in 1814. Fray Esteven Tapis á Fray Francisco Javier Uría, Mision de Santa Ynez, 8 de Marzo de 1814, *Preguntas y Respuestas,* PRA-8, SBMA. They remained important gift items in native systems of generating alliances. During the 1824 war, leaders from Santa Ines and from La Purisima sent beads to Yokuts villages to create alliances.

62. Hudson and Blackburn 1985: vol. 3: 297.

63. Ibid.: 298.

64. King 1974: 90–91.

65. Beeler 1967: 40–42.

66. Allen 1992: esp. 31; and 1998.

67. Harrington 2005: 48.

68. Shipek 1991: 40.

69. See Lockhart 1992 and 1994 on the Náhuatl legal and historical documents; see Stephanie Wood on the histories that Indigenous communities produced in Mexico, Wood 2003; and see Adorno 2007.

70. Richard Konetzke 1962: 11. (He cites Recopilación de Leyes de las Indias 15, título 13, libro 1 y la 18, título 1 del libro 6.)

71. Konetzke 1962: 79.

72. Felipe de Goycoachea, 10 Marzo 1795, C-A 8: 102, 267.

73. Fray Vicente Francisco Sarría, 9 Julio 1827, Mission San Carlos, No. 1941, Collection of Alexander Taylor, HL.

74. José María de Echeandía, Estado sobre escuelas primarias, 19 Mayo 1829, C-A 51: 2–3, BL.

75. See Jan Timbrook 2009: 329. Timbrook notes that Zelia Nuttall found two of the baskets in a shop in Mexico City in 1920. One was obtained by the Santa Barbara Natural History Museum and another by the Bancroft Library. A tray done by Juana Basilia with similar design was also found in the shop at that time. The inscription on the basket reads in Spanish: "Maria Marta noefita de la mission de el serafico doctor san buenaventura me hizo an." (Perhaps she intended *an* to become *año.*) Zelia Nuttall is especially known for her work on the Mixtec Codex Zouche-Nuttall.

76. Fray Gregorio Fernández y Fray José António Calzada, 31 Diciembre 1798, C-C 4: 216, BL.

77. Fray Mariano Payeras, 1810, La Purísima, C-C 4: 215, BL.

78. Fray José de la Cruz al Señor Gobernador, Misión de Nuestra Purísima, 5 Febrero 1799, No. 182, Collection of Alexander Taylor, HL.

79. Ibid.

80. Memoirs and accounts about this era often talk about how the rudiments of formal education were provided in small schools and at the missions. The shifting nature of conditions is apparent. See, for example, the *testimonio* of Apolinaria Lorenzana in Beebe and Senkewicz 2006: 165–92.

81. After 1833, the administrators of the missions often came from California, and some employed an *escriván* to write their documents. Elsewhere in Mexico, the *escribano* forms part of a cultural tradition of public writing and reading.

82. Fray Estevan Tapis a Fray Francisco Xavier Uría, *Preguntas y Respuestas,* Misíon de Santa Ynez, 8 Marzo 1814, PRA- 8, SBMAL.

83. Raymond White 1976: 356.

84. Harrington 2005: 18.

85. Raymond White 1976: 357 and 360.

86. Shipek 1977: 34 and 41. On pay, see Harrington 2005.

87. Shipek 1977: 97.

88. See Raymond White 1976 and Harrington 2005.

89. Harrington 2005: xv.

90. As an epidemic swept through Chumash territory in 1801, for example, a woman at Mission Santa Bárbara had a prophecy that people would die if they accepted baptism. The movement spread along the coast, into the still-independent villages of the interior, and on the islands, but seems to have died out. Missionary Tapís wrote about it in 1805. See Lepowsky 2004; Engelhardt 1923: 82–83; Heizer 1941.

91. Harrington 2005: 29 and 34.

92. Ibid.: 29 and repeated on 30.

93. See ibid., esp. 45–51, and 56–57.

94. Ibid. 2005: 37–40.

95. See DuBois 1908: 75.

96. Shipek 1977: 98.

97. Laylander 2004: 118.

98. Haas, 2011: 238, 22–23, 221–22.

99. See Hudson 1979b; and Hudson, Timbrook, and Rempe 1978 for a discussion of the Brotherhood of the Canoe, esp. 162–63.

100. Hudson, Blackburn, Curletti, and Timbrook 1977: 19–26.

101. Fray Mariano Payeras, 1810, La Purísima, C-C 4: 215, BL.

102. Ibid.

103. See Kelsey 1979: 13. This is the most complete doctrine and confessional that exists for the California missions. Each mission had bilingual editions of the doctrine, confessional, and other prayers, but few exist in archives today.

104. Beeler 1967: 30.

105. Ibid.: 25.

106. Ibid. Beeler published the entire work with some facsimile pages. The original is at the Santa Barbara Mission Archives.

107. Harrington 2005.

108. Johnson 1982.

109. See Von Langsdorff 1813-14: 61, 105-7. On an expedition in 1816 Louis Choris discusses dance, gambling, and tattoos among distinct tribal groups at Mission San Francisco. Choris 1822: 4-5.

110. Goellner and Murphy 1995: xii. Foster (1995) discusses this in her essay. Many scholars are interested in writings that "return bodily experience *as a form of consciousness and understanding* to a central place" in ethnography and other writing (italics in quote). Ness 1992: 239, n. 4.

111. Kaeppler (1993: 7) shows the transformations of the hula *pahu*, a sacred dance, under the nineteenth-century court of the Kalakaua era.

112. Nunnis 1977: 103, n. 46.

113. Browning (1995: 69) offers vivid descriptions of how the divine come down to inhabit their own, very specific choreographies in *candomblé* dance and ritual in Brazil.

114. Harrington 2005: 30.

115. Ibid.: 34. This is the coastal version. In the mountain version, two of the names for Chinigchinich are different.

116. Raymond White 1953: 577.

117. Haas 2011: 193-94.

118. Missionary Peyri discusses this process in Fray Antonio Peyri and Fray Francisco Suñer, *Preguntas y Respuestas,* San Luis Rey, 12 Diciembre 1814, PRA-18, SBMAL.

119. See Field et al. 2008: 25-26, 31 on the von Langsdorff expedition in northern California in 1806, the two abalone necklaces he collected, and related questions. Also see Blackburn and Hudson, 1990.

120. Hudson 1983 and Dawson 1965.

121. Luisa Ignacio Harrington—Barbareño slipfile—690520-021. 0033 Smithsonian Archives (microfilm).

122. Nunnis 1977: 106, no. 82.

123. Ibid.: 71.

124. Hudson et al. 1977: 79.

125. Nunnis 1977: 84-85.

126. Ibid.: 89.

127. Haas 2011: 143-44.

128. That is the first version of dance in Tac's manuscript on folios 61 and 62. The second version states, "But the California Indians do not dance just for festivals but also before starting a war; in grief, because they have been defeated; in remembrance of the grandparents, uncles and aunts, and parents now dead. Now that we are Christians, we dance ceremonially." Haas 2011: 193.

129. Goellner and Murphy 1995: x.

130. Raymond White 1976: 374.

131. Haas 2011: 194-95.

132. Ibid.: 195-96.

133. Desmond (1997: xii) describes dance as a kind of "cultural record keeping."

134. Haas 2011: 195.

135. See, for example, Z. Mendoza 2000. She, as others, argue that in the Andes dance has been an arena for "conflicts over power and ethnic/racial identity" since colonial times.

136. See Von Langsdorff 1813–14: 100, 105–7. The painting hangs in the Bancroft Library.

137. Hudson et al. 1977: 83.

138. Ibid.: 69–71.

139. Ibid.: 79.

140. Hudson 1979b.

141. Ibid.: 73–74.

142. Haas 2011: 243.

143. Elliott 1999: 252–53.

144. Comandante Maitorena a Comandante General Echeandía, "Sumaria," 26 Abril 1829, C-A 18: 394–399, BL.

3. THE POLITICS OF THE IMAGE

1. Gruzinski 1992: 79.

2. Freedberg 1989 and Mitchell 2005.

3. Invoice for 1807, San Buenaventura. Notebook on San Luis Obispo and San Buenaventura, Kurt Baer Collection, SBMAL.

4. Invoices for 1774 and 1778, San Luis Obispo. Notebook on San Luis Obispo and San Buenaventura, Kurt Baer Collection, SBMAL.

5. Baer Collection: 21.

6. See Neuerburg 1985. The material on these paintings is from Kinkead (1984) who examines 1,509 paintings—the known total of Sevillian paintings—either sent to or destined for the New World open markets between 1647 and 1665. In the fifty years between 1650 and 1700, Seville exported at least 24,000 paintings to the Americas.

7. See Taylor 1987 and Christian 1981.

8. Cummins 2011, 225.

9. Duggan 2000: 212, 214, 219–22.

10. See the catalog from a recent exhibition on the missions of northern Mexico, including California. Bargellini and Komanecky 2009; the essay by William Merrill is particularly interesting. Merrill 2009.

11. Reese 1985: 75. See Boone 2000.

12. See Deans-Smith 2009: 49.

13. Baer (1956: 227) evaluated the painting of the Archangel Raphael as "harsh, crude, though exceedingly sincere."

14. Dean 1999: 161–62; Umberger and Cummins 1995.

15. Taylor 2011: 19.

16. Baer 1956: 227–28; he identifies the painting on 224 as "oil on canvas, early 19'th c. Indian Neophyte painting." Hackel 2005: 168 discusses the image.

17. Evaluation of the work is drawn largely from comments by art historian Carolyn Dean, who accompanied the author to view the painting at Mission Santa Ines, March 23, 2002.

18. Hudson and Blackburn 1986, vol. 4: 195–97. [Volume 4 of *The Material Culture of the Chumash* is published in 1986 with the subtitle: *Ceremonial Paraphernalia, Games and Amusement.*]

19. Walker and Hudson 1993: esp. 55.

20. Rather than adopt a form of Western framing of geography and the representation of space, itself undergoing reconsideration during these years, maps made in central Mexican communities draw on non-Western representations of space, as would seem likely in the case of Chumash painting. See Wood 1991b and Haskett 1998.

21. Ms. 89/95, Inventorio—Cuentas de los bienes, 24 January 1846, Mission Santa Inés Miguel Cordero, SBMA.

22. Grant 1993: 74.

23. Hudson and Blackburn 1986, vol. 4: 67–74.

24. Haas 2011: 173.

25. DuBois 1908: 96.

26. The same painter may have also done a painting of the Archangel Michael that is said to have hung at Mission Santa Bárbara. In both paintings the archangels stood on clouds, whereas Michael usually stands on a serpent. Neither work had underpainting, highly trained brushwork, nor the three-dimensional perspective of European work. Neither painting was signed. When Kurt Baer saw the painting in 1959 it was "severely damaged, torn and even rotten in places." Baer 1991: 95.

27. Hudson, Blackburn, Curletti, and Timbrook 1977: 43. The festival at San Buenaventura began during the mission era and continued into the late nineteenth century.

28. See Gruzinski 1992 and 1993; Boone and Cummins 1998: 95. For the competing narratives painted during the sixteenth century, see Terraciano 2011, 75.

29. For a discussion of the pre-Columbian visual world of New Spain and its influence on colonial art, see Fields and Zamudio-Taylor 2001. For a discussion of the Virgin of Guadalupe who initially served as a local virgin venerated by the Spanish around Mexico City and Nahua communities, see Taylor 1987; and Poole 1995.

30. Pierce 1996: 61.

31. See, for example, Lara 2004.

32. See the collection in the National Museum, Mexico City (2001).

33. Sullivan 1996: 36.

34. Damian 1995a: 39.

35. Gomar 2004.

36. Lockhart (1992: 235) studied colonial Mexico through Nahua sources in contrast to the earliest studies that used only Spanish documents, including Gibson 1964 and Ricard 1966. In the genre of historiography that uses native writing, see Horn 1997 and Wood 2003.

37. Lockhart 1992: 289.

38. Burkhart 1997: 34.

39. Lockhardt 1992: 279.

40. See Wood 1991a.

41. Taylor 2005: 967.

42. Ibid.: 963–64.

43. Damian 1995: 40; Mesa and Gisbert 1981:1, 137. Mesa and Gisbert date the birth of the school in 1688, when a virtual separation of the Spanish and Andean artists took place.

44. See Gisbert, Mesa, Querejazu, and Plata 1994.

45. See Damian 1988: 22; Phipps 1996.

46. Cummins 1994: 192–94 and 1998: 95.

47. Damian 1995b: 30.

48. See Gisbert 1992; de Mesa, Querejazu, and Álvarez Plata 1994; and Brett 1991.

49. These anonymous paintings were displayed in the Museo y Convento de Santo Domingo in Cuzco, Peru (June 2003).

50. Timberlake 1999: 565.

51. For an excellent discussion of this see Dean 1996a and 1993.

52. Dean 1999, esp. 97–178.

53. Gisbert and Mesa 1979. Examples of this work are displayed in the Museo Inka in Cuzco, Peru.

54. Phipps 1996: 154. See Gisbert and Mesa 1979; Museo Inka for Cuzqueño portraiture, the rebellion, and its aftermath; Church of Santo Domingo for Cuzqueño religious art; and the Museo de Arte Religioso for Spanish style work. All are situated in Cuzco, Peru.

55. See Neuerburg 1997: 5.

56. Works sent to found Mission San Diego, given by the King, 1769 in San Diego and Santa Cruz Notebooks, Kurt Baer Collection, SBMAL.

57. Tibesar 1966: 241–43 [Monterey, 1774 year-end inventory].

58. Taylor 1987: 19.

59. Von Langsdorff 1814, pt. II: 44–45.

60. Tibesar 1966, vol. I: 223 [6/20/71].

61. Mission San José, Notebook: 7, Kurt Baer Collection, SBMAL. In contrast, Steven Hackel proposes that the "principle value" of religious objects "resided in their ability to capture the Indians' attention." See Hackel 2005: 148.

62. Tibesar 1966, vol. II: 319 [8/22/75].

63. Tibesar 1966, vol. III:91 [February 26, 1777].

64. Pierce, Gomar, and Bargellini 2004:66, 217.

65. Cutter 1995:132.

66. Tibesar 1966, vol. II: 477.

67. Ibid.: 237 "two cassocks of blue cloth . . . for the sacristans" and four of the same in red for big feast days. Inventory at San Antonio de Padua de los Robles, December 1774.

68. Ibid.: 319 [8/22/75].

69. Tibesar 1966, vol. III: 91 [February 26, 1777]; he repeats this again in vol. I: 221 [6/20/71]. He asks for "Our Father Saint Francis receiving the stigmata, or as Your Reverence may prefer, so long as they do not paint him in blue." And vol. II: 319, Serra notes that paintings with blue habits had already arrived in California.

70. Ibid.: 229 [8/19/78].

71. Ibid.: 227, 229 [8/19/78] and Hackel 2005: 153–54.

72. Ibid. and Hackel 2005: 153–54.

73. Tibesar 1996, vol. 1: 187 [June 12, 1770].

74. Ibid.: 155 [February 10, 1770]. In vol. 1: 369 [May 21, 1773] Serra noted, "Concerning this mission to which I am now alluding, I can only say that the entire ranchería, which made war on us on the Feast of the Assumption of Our Lady 1769, is now Christian."

75. Tibesar 1996, vol. 1: 187 [July 2, 1770].

76. Ibid.: vol. 1:189 [July 2, 1770].

77. Ibid.: vol. 2: 431 [April 13, l776].

78. Hudson and Blackburn 1984, vol. 3: 322. Another Chumash consultant mentioned here defined them as black, white, and red spots.

79. Whitley 1994a: 92. From the 1950s on, scholars have talked about the shamanic quality of these sites, although the idea that they formed part of hunting magic or astrology may account for some of the painting. See Hedges 1992. Raymond White (1963) depicts visionary images.

80. Grant 1993.

81. Hudson and Underhay 1978: 52. The authors discuss the meaning of the sun in Chumash cosmology.

82. Applegate 1978: 42.

83. Walker and Hudson 1993: esp. 55.

84. Whitley 1996: 22 and 1992: 91.

85. See Smith and Turner 1975: esp. 15 on ground painting; and Cohen 1987.

86. DuBois 1908: 87.

87. See Waterman 1910: 300–304.

88. Notebooks for Missions San Diego, San Juan Capistrano, and San Gabriel, Baer Collection, SBMAL.

89. Neuerburg 1989: 7.

90. Neuerburg and Lee 1989: 473.

91. Neuerburg 1989: 54.

92. Whitley 1994b: vol. 1: 14, 23.

93. Invoices for 1774 and 1778, San Luis Obispo and San Buenaventura notebook, Baer Collection, SBMAL.

94. Ibid.

95. Ben Wood (artist) and Eric Blind (archaeologist) photographed and projected this *reredo* on the Basilica Dome at Mission Dolores in January and February of 2004.

96. Documentary Catalog of Mission Dolores, ms., October 25, 2002 (printed spreadsheet from the Archive at Mission Dolores).

97. Bargellini 2009: 196. See the painted and gilded tabernacle from the Philippines, c. 1780, at Mission Dolores. See Fisher 2009, esp. 185 on codes about dress.

98. See Mendoza 2009: 8, and Mendoza, 2005.

99. Geiger 1965: 42.

100. Ibid.: 46- 47.

101. See Schuetz-Miller 1994. This study compiles the names of foreign and native artisans at the missions by their occupation and according to the names published in Bancroft's large history. It isn't comprehensive for Indigenous artisans, who are more difficult to trace.

102. Neuerburg 1980.

103. Webb 1945.

104. Neuerburg 1989: 20. Neuerburg notes that hand-painted Chinese wallpaper was used to cover the walls of the baptistry at Mission Santa Clara by 1795, and rolls of wallpaper appeared in the inventories of Missions Santa Barbara and San José.

105. Baer 1991: 88 and San Miguel Notebook, Baer Collection, SBMA. The painted interior remained virtually the same until recently. Some of the description is from on-site viewing, 2001.

106. Baer 1956: 225. Baer found most of the imported paintings of "mediocre quality," 140.

107. Pedida, 1806–07, Mission Santa Inés, Kurt Baer Collection, SBMAL.

108. Notebook Santa Inés, Kurt Baer Collection, SBMAL.

109. See Sandos (2004) on the importance of music and the choristers to every performance of the sacred in the churches and to create a hierarchy among individuals within the missions.

110. See Durán's frequent requests for specific Indian musicians from Santa Ines.

111. *Informes,* Notebook Santa Inés, December 1819, Kurt Baer Collection, SBMAL.

112. *Informes,* 31 Diciembre 1823, La Purísima, BANC MSS C-C 216, BL.

113. Francisco Palou, ms: 3, 1913, SBMAL.

114. Notebook Santa Inés, Kurt Baer collection, SBMAL; and see Neuerburg 1989: 25–28; Webb 1945: 143. On page 99 Webb cites an 1861 observation that "the church was highly painted." G. Wharton James found the church to be "covered with unmeaningful designs" in what he called "foolish colors" in 1905. He again emphasizes the lack of Western color when he notes the painters did "not yet [have] the slightest appreciation of color harmony" on page 331. He would have preferred everything "left in the rough, or plastered and whitewashed. Using this logic, churches that had Indigenous painting and color schemes were whitewashed when "restored" in the early twentieth century.

115. Francisco Palou, ms: 4, 1913, SBMAL.

116. Engelhardt, *San Fernando Rey* 1927: 145 [Engelhardt published an eyewitness account, 1846]; *Informes,* 1797–1834, Mission San Fernando, SBMAL.

117. San Fernando Notebook, Baer Collection, SBMAL.

118. In his article on these paintings, Neuerburg (1997) noted that the originals probably derived from the set of prints in the Mission San Fernando's inventory in 1808 and have since been lost. The article is extremely valuable.

119. Francis Weber 1965: 10. Weber cites Arthur Woodward, curator of history of the Los Angeles County Museum of Art, who placed the paintings on display at LACMA c. 1940. Neuerburg (1997) says that the clothing of the soldiers resembled a typical male costume worn by Spanish and Mexican men during the period, but only "very few" resemble the military uniforms that would have been worn in that era.

120. Phillips (2007) engages in controversy with Neuerburg around the issue of whether the painters were expressing resistance to Spanish colonialism. The controversy otherwise raises interesting points. In this study I've followed art historians who situate their questions within a larger understanding of Indigenous colonial work. See the entire set of fourteen paintings printed in color following Phillips's article on 81–87 in the same issue of the *Boletín.*

121. Phillips, George Harwood, 2007.

122. See Barbolla 1992.

123. For the *recuerdos* of Eulalia Perez and Apolinaria Lorenzana, see Beebe and Senkewicz 2006: 95–117 and 165–92.

124. Taylor 1994: 157.

125. Ibid.: 160.

126. Elliott (1999) placed this word in his dictionary of Luiseño and offered a more in-depth interpretation of its significance.

127. Whitley 1994a: 92.

4. "ALL THE HORSES ARE IN THE POSSESSION OF THE INDIANS": THE CHUMASH WAR

1. Fray Juan Cabot to Gobernador Argüello, 28 Febrero 1824 Misión. C-A 1.

2. See the forthcoming book of David Sartorius.

3. On the significance of this body to Mexican national law, see N. L. Benson 1966: 3–9, and Calero 1995.

4. See Rieu-Millán 1990 and de Armellada 1979.

5. Garza 1966: 48 n. 12. The measure passed, and two subsequent ones reinforced the exclusion to Spanish status for people of African descent.

6. Cutter 1995: 292; and Payeras's response in Cutter 1995: 301. Payeras writes about this in 1821, after the Spanish king restored the Constitution of Cádiz from 1820 to 1823, and the Mexican nation decided to adhere to aspects of that constitution until they had formulated their own.

7. Cutter 1995: 340.

8. Ibid.: 341.

9. Ibid.:339.

10. Listed by mission and name on 19 Noviembre 1822, in Cutter 1995: 337–38; see Osío 1996: 55 for quote "devil followers."

11. *Informes,* 31 Diciembre 1824, Santa Inés, SBMAL.

12. 15 Julio 1825, CA-18: 149–50, BL. When they couldn't get compensation for their lost items from the church, the soldiers and families took their demands for compensation to the military court. The government held a hearing about the losses suffered by the soldiers and their families on Febrero 24, 1825.

13. Fray Sarría a José Maríano Estrada, 27 Febrero 1824, CMD 2579, SBMAL.

14. John Johnson, manuscript on eleven villages of the Santa Barbara Backcountry, Santa Barbara (undated): 10.

15. *Interrogatorio de los Indios,* 1–3 Junio 1824, Santa Bárbara, FAC 667, De la Guerra Collection, SBMAL.

16. Ibid.

17. Ibid. Pelagio, from Mission San Fernando, had also been at the lake. He reported that people took steam baths day and night. During the day they dug walls for defense. They played cards and games of chance.

18. Cook 1962: 155.

19. Fray Luis Antonio Martínez a Gobernador Argüello 27 Febrero 1824, No. 2579, Collection of Alexander Taylor, HL.

20. José (Marianno) Estrada Quartel General de La Purísima, 19 Marzo 1824, CMD 2960, SBMAL.

21. José de la Guerra y otros, *Sentencia contra Indios rebeldes,* 23 Marzo 1824, Misión de La Purísima, C-A 18: 188–89. BL

22. José de la Guerra a Roberto Pardo, 21 Abril 1824, No. 174, De la Guerra Collection, SBMAL; and Roberto Pardo's response to José de la Guerra y Noriega, 27 Abril 1824, No. 174, De la Guerra Collection, SBMAL.

23. Roberto Pardo a José de la Guerra y Noriega, 27 Abril 1824, No. 179, De la Guerra Collection, SBMAL.

24. Fray Estevan Tapis a Fray Francisco Xavier Uría, Misión Santa Ynez, 8 Marzo 1814, PA-8, SBMAL.

25. Fray L. A. Martínez a Luis Antonio Argüello, 19 Marzo 1824, CMD 2586, SBMAL.

26. Ignacio Vallejo, 16 Abril 1824, San Luis Obispo, C-A 18:121–23, BL.

27. Fray L. A. Martínez a Luis Antonio Argüello, 19 Abril 1824, CMD 2601, SBMAL.

28. Fray L. A. Martínez, 30 Abril 1824, CMD 2609, SBMAL.

29. Fray L. A. Martínez a Luis Antonio Argüello, 1 Mayo 1824, CMD 2611, SBMAL.

30. Fray Sarría a Luis Antonio Argüello, 30 Abril 1824, CMD 2610, SBMAL.

31. Fray Gil y Taboada a Luis Antonio Argüello, 5 Abril 1824, Santa Cruz, CMD 2581, SBMAL. He again wrote Argüello complaining about whites giving Indians liberal ideas. See Fray Gil y Taboada a Luis Antonio Argüello, 19 Abril 1824, Santa Cruz, CMD 2600, SBMAL. Also see Fray Durán to Gobernador Argüello on fugitives at San Emigdio who had a Russian with them, 3 Marzo 1824, CMD 2596, SBMAL; and a letter from Santa Inés about the danger of an Indian attack from Rancho San Emigdio, 26 Marzo 1824, CMD 2593, SBMAL.

32. Fray Blas Ordaz, 26 Marzo 1824, CMD 2593, SBMAL; and Narciso Durán a Luis Antonio Argüello, 31 Marzo 1824, San José, CMD 2598, SMBAL. The second letter conveys the same sentiment.

33. I am adapting Zygmunt Bauman's (2006) concept that he used to describe the creation and use of fear in contemporary society.

34. Gobernador Luís Antonio Argüello al Gobierno Mexicano, 21 Abril 1824, CMD 2960, SBMAL.

35. Fray Sarría a Luis Antonio Argüello, 14 Mayo 1824, CMD 2618, SBMAL; and Fray L. A. Martínez a José de la Guerra 6 Mayo 1824, CMD 2613, SBMAL.

36. Fray Antonio Ripoll a Fray Sarría (seven handwritten pages), 5 Mayo 1824, CMD 2612, SBMAL. On fear in Indigenous and Spanish colonial writing, see Haas 2012.

37. Ibid.; and Fray Ripoll, CMD 1599, SBMAL.

38. See a third request from Fray Vicente Sarría a Luis Antonio Argüello, 27 Mayo 1824, CMD 2623, SBMAL. This was written from Santa Barbara as they prepared for the expedition to extend the pardon. See letters from the pueblo in the de la Guerra collection, SBMAL.

39. Fray Sarría a Gobernador Argüello, 18 Mayo 1824, San Luís Obispo, CMD 2621, SBMAL.

40. Fray L. A. Martínez a Gobernador Argüello, 6 Mayo 1824, San Luís Obispo, CMD 2613, SBMAL.

41. Pablo de la Portillo, "Diario de la Expedición," 27 Junio 1824, C-A 27: 41–51, BL. Also translated in Cook 1962: 154–56.

42. Ibid.: 41–51, 45.

43. Ibid. 51, 47.

44. Pablo de la Portillo, "Diario de la Expedición," 27 Junio 1824, C-A 27: 41–51 BL.

45. Pablo de la Portillo a Luis Antonio Argüello, 27 Junio 1824, Santa Bárbara, 51–52. SBMAL.

46. The annual reports for the missions offer the best evidence. Also see the population statistics in Engelhardt 1923: 293.

47. L. A. Martínez a Argüello, Junio 1824, San Luis Obispo, 2631a, SBMAL.

48. Fray Sarría a Argüello [reporting a letter from Ripoll of Santa Barbara on the return of twelve fugitives from the Tulare], 23 Junio 1825, No. 2781, SBMAL.

49. Luís Antonio Argüello a José de la Guerra y Noriega, 23 Julio 1824, C-A 18: 99, BL.

50. Fray Vicente Sarría a Luis Antonio Argüello, 23 Junio 1825, CMD 2781, SBMAL.

51. All three Chumash consultants worked with John P. Harrington, who did most of his ethnographic work among the Chumash between 1912 and 1928. At that time he was working with Luisa Ignacio, her daughter Lucretia Garcia, and Maria Solares. All three multilingual women spoke Chumash, Spanish, and English. They did not place accents over their Spanish names. Harrington's work is broadly referenced and widely known.

52. Rappaport 1998: 11.

53. Maria Solares, Microfilm 690520, reel 007, frames 0011–20 1914 Harrington Papers, Smithsonian. See also Blackburn 1975: 223–27. Also see Sandos (1985), who brings these stories about the revolt together into one narrative, where I have emphasized the significance of their difference.

54. Lucrecia Garcia, Microfilm 690520, reel 55, frames 108–11, Harrington Papers, Smithsonian.

55. Lucrecia Garcia, Barbareño informants reading Ineseño, Microfilm 690520, reel 26, frames 756–57, Harrington Papers, Smithsonian.

56. See Applegate 1978.

57. Lucrecia Garcia, Microfilm 690520, reel 55, frames 108–11, Harrington Papers, Smithsonian.

58. Luisa Ignacio, 1914, Microfilm 690520, frames 0027–28, typescript pages 1–3, Harrington Papers, Smithsonian.

59. Ibid. The published version is edited to offer a different sequence of events than recounted by Luisa Ignacio. See Hudson 1980: 123–25.

60. Luisa Ignacio, Microfilm 690520, frames 1127–28, typescript pages 1–3, Harrington Papers, Smithsonian.

61. See, for example, Léon-Portilla 1962: 69 and Lockhart 1993.

62. Lepowsky 2004, and see the role of spirit possession in the Boxer Rebellion in China. Taking those ideas seriously, Cohen (1997) questions what "truth" is in a historical sense, especially 212.

63. Ripoll writes, "On Sunday the soldiers killed one Indian riding a mule carrying a basket full of wheat, with grotesque sadism." On Monday, the soldiers killed four neophytes from Dos Pueblos who had come from a *milpas* (field) to see what was going on. See Fray Antonio Ripoll, No. 1599, Collection of Alexander Taylor, HL.

64. Luisa Ignacio, Microfilm 690520, frames 0027–28, typescript pages 1–3, Harrington Papers, Smithsonian. [1914]

65. Gobernador Argüello al Gobierno Mexicano, 21 Abril 1824, CMD 2960, SBMAL.

66. Ibid.

67. Fray Sarría to Luis Antonio Argüello, 25 Febrero 1824, CMD 2578, SBMAL.

68. Fray Antonio Ripoll, No. 1599, Collection of Alexander Taylor, HL.

69. Geiger 1980: 11.

70. Beebe and Senkewicz 1996: 278.

71. Beebe and Senkewicz 2000: 281.

72. Vallejo, *Recuerdos* I, 351–69, C-D 17, California Collection, BL.

73. Morton 2005: 2 and chap. 3. Also see Padilla 1993: 81.

74. Johnson, 1989a.

75. Vallejo, *Recuerdos* I: 351–69, 352, C-D 17, BL.

76. Ibid.: 353–54, C-D 17, BL.

77. See Juan Bautista Alvarado's *Historia de California* (5 vols.), Bancroft Library, C-D 1–5, BL. See Morton 2005: 24 and chap. 3.

78. Johnson 1989b.

79. Pacomío a Gobernador José Figueroa, answered by Gobernador Manuel Victoria, 26 November 1833, No. 2162, Collection of Alexander Taylor, HL. Pacomío and his wife died in the 1844 smallpox epidemic in Monterey.

80. An Ohlone woman named María Viviana Soto saw Pacomío sing and dance when she was a child and recorded two of his songs in 1902 for Alfred Kroeber, a major figure in anthropological studies of Indigenous California. See Johnson 1989a.

81. Osío 1996: 55.

82. On its history and significance as a manuscript, and on its value as an account meant to offer stories of an entire people through oral tradition and personal testimony, see the introduction to Osío 1996: 17.

83. Rappaport 1998: 21.

84. Smith 1999: 33.

85. Nandy 1995: 63.

5. "WE SOLICIT OUR FREEDOM": CITIZENSHIP AND THE *PATRIA*

1. See, for example, Caplan 2010.

2. For a translation of the decree, see Engelhardt 1912, vol. 3: 379–402.

3. José María Echeandía, Agosto de 1826, Addenda 1, Box 9, Collection of Alexander Taylor, HL.

4. Petition with the signature "No sabe firmar," 4 Abril 1826, No. 1817, Collection of Alexander Taylor, HL.

5. Note on the margins of the above petition signed "Echeandía," 21 Abril 1826, No. 1817, Collection of Alexander Taylor, HL.

6. Fray Fernando Martín y Fray Vicente Oliva, 30 Abril 1826, No. 1817, Collection of Alexander Taylor, HL.

7. Hackel 2005: 381–82.

8. Across a wide geographic area of the English-speaking Americas, the celebration of West India Day, August First, and Emancipation Day enabled people to construct and articulate cultural identities and histories around liberty and citizenship. See Kerr-Ritchie 2007.

9. Hackel 2005: 378; see Lillian Smith 1982: 63–64. Fray José Señan sold hides, blankets, otter pelts, lard, tallow, and baskets to foreign ships. They had long been traded between the

island and mainland. He sent them as gifts to the College of San Fernando in Mexico City; one of the gift baskets is represented in chap. 2, Fig. 2.

10. Hackel 2005: 377–81.

11. José María Echeandía, 2 Marzo 1829, San Diego, No. 2053, Collection of Alexander Taylor, HL.

12. Fray Martínez y Fray Vicente I, 3 Marzo 1829, San Diego, No. 2053, Collection of Alexander Taylor, HL.

13. Petition signed by Fray Ramón Abella, 30 Octubre 1826, No. 1837, Collection of Alexander Taylor, HL.

14. Petition written by Manuel Ventura, 24 Septiembre 1828, No. 2034, Collection of Alexander Taylor, HL.

15. Letter of Santiago Argüello, 27 Septiembre 1833, Vallejo Collection, vol. 31, pt. 1:108; and Pablo de la Portillo a Figueroa, 27 Septiembre 1833, Vallejo Collection, vol. 31, pt.1: 113.

16. Among the excellent studies on emancipation that focus on these processes through the compilation of documents, see Berlin, Fields, Glymph, Reidy, and Rowland 1985 and Holt 1992. Rebecca Scott (1985 and 1988) poses the question about the meaning of freedom with tremendous effect.

17. Vicente Juan y Gaspar, 31 Mayo 1827, No. 1939, Collection of Alexander Taylor, HL. "Que Soliciamos de la Generosa Vondad de Usted Para Quedar Libres."

18. Fray Xavier Uría, 2 Junio 1827, Soledad, No. 1939, Collection of Alexander Taylor, HL.

19. Fray José Sánchez, 21 Octubre 1829, Mission San Gabriel, No. 2073, Collection of Alexander Taylor, HL; see No. 2048 in the same collection, which is a report from Mission San Francisco; it simply recorded those soliciting emancipation and went on to discuss the right of the mission to particular lands being sought by settlers.

20. The petition written by Patricio appears to be extant. This is the response of Marco Antonio de Vitoria, 8 Febrero 1830, No. 2082, Collection of Alexander Taylor, HL.

21. 21 Noviembre 1833, for both documents. Not signed by name, they were dated and sent from Monterey to Fray Vicente Oliva at Mission San Luis Rey and to Fray Estenaga at Mission San Gabriel. See Nos. 2160 and 2161, Collection of Alexander Taylor, HL.

22. Fray Juan Cabot, 12 July 1834, No. 2177, Collection of Alexander Taylor, HL.

23. Fray Sarría, 15 July 1834, No. 2180, Collection of Alexander Taylor, HL.

24. Pablo de la Portillo a José Figueroa, Fall 1833, C-B vol. 31: 113, Vallejo Collection, BL.

25. Fray Narciso Durán, 8 Febrero 1828, No. 2037, Collection of Alexander Taylor, HL.

26. Fray Narciso Durán, 1 Marzo 1829, No. 2052, Collection of Alexander Taylor, HL.

27. Fray Viader, 20 Agosto 1829, No. 2065, Collection of Alexander Taylor, HL.

28. Fray Peyri al Comisionado "Qué cantidad de tierras reconoce por propias cada Misión . . .," 12 and 22 Octubre 1822, San Luis Rey, CMD 2316 (listed as Noviembre on the document), SBMAL.

29. Fray Peyri al Comisionado, 22 Noviembre 1822, San Luis Rey, CMD 2316, SBMAL.

30. Fray José Zalvidea a Fray José Barona, 22 Dieciembre 1827, San Juan Capistrano, CMD 3113, SBMAL.

31. Fray Felipe Arroyo de la Cuesta y Fray Juan Moreno, "Relación de las tierras que ocupa esta Misión de San Juan Bautista," 7 Enero 1828, CMD 3125, SBMAL—"sitio originario y nativo de varios de los Indios."

32. For a political history of this era from the perspective of the politically powerful José de la Guerra family in Santa Barbara, see Pubols 2009, esp. 175–240.

33. "The window of the General of California's room, when he comes to the mission." Haas 2011:175.

34. Tomás Tajochi a José María de Echeandía, 6 Febrero 1833, No. 2123, Collection of Alexander Taylor, BL.

35. Echeandía's response is scrawled on the back of the letter, no date, No. 2123, Collection of Alexander Taylor, BL.

36. Santiago Argüello a José Figueroa, 8 Febrero 1833, No. 2124, Collection of Alexander Taylor. Here he notes he had neither paper nor money to buy it. Also see No. 2140, Collection of Alexander Taylor.

37. Ygnacio del Valle a José Figueroa, 10 Febrero 1833, C-A 28: 90, BL.

38. Santiago Argüello a José Figueroa, 15 Junio 1833, C-A 28: 117–118, BL.

39. Santiago Argüello a José Figueroa, 22 Junio 1833; and Argüello a Macedonio González, 20 Junio, 1833, C-A 28: 119, BL.

40. Santiago Argüello a José Figueroa, 1 Julio 1833, C-A 28: 123, BL. On the arrest and the sentencing, see José Figueroa, 22 Noviembre 1833, Monterey, C-A 19, 370–373, BL.

41. From July 1833 through December 16, 1834, frequent reports of feared attacks were peppered throughout the archive. See C-A 28: 123–205, BL.

42. Fray Narciso Durán a José Figueroa, 19 Julio 1833, No. 2151, Collection of Alexander Taylor, HL.

43. José Figueroa a Sus Soldados (proclama en borrador), 12 Noviembre 1832, La Paz, Mexico, C-A 28, 59–62 BL. See Fields and Zamudio-Taylor 2001: 5.

44. José María Echeandía a los Californios, 28 Julio 1832, San Diego, C-A 28, 64–66, BL.

45. José Figueroa a José María Echeandía, 14 Enero 1833, C-A 18: 78, BL.

46. José Figueroa, Bando sobre celebración cívica, 20 Abril 1833 [archive]. On these celebrations and building of patriotism elsewhere in the north, see Reséndez 2005.

47. "Actas provisionales para la emancipación de los indios," José Figueroa, 15 Julio 1833, C-B 31, pt. 1: 72–81, 74, Vallejo Collection, BL.

48. "Actas provisionales," José Figueroa, 15 Julio 1833, C-B 31, pt. 1: 70, Vallejo Collection, BL.

49. Argüello a José Figueroa, 18 Febrero 1833, C-B 31, pt.1: 71, Vallejo Collection, BL. See Holt (1992).

50. Ibid.:105–6, Vallejo Collection, BL.

51. Argüello a José Figueroa 27 Septiembre 1833, C-B 31, pt. 1:112, Vallejo Collection, BL.

52. Lista de los del rumbo de San Dieguito que solicitan salir de la neofía y emanciparse y pasar a Poblar con Ligeric María Yeulec, 12 Agosto 1833, Vallejo Collection, C-B 31, pt. 1:119.

53. Santiago Argüello, "Lista de los Neófitos de la Misión de San Diego que pueden salir de la Tulela(?) segun sus circunstancias," 1 Agosto 1833, San Diego, C-B 31, pt. 1:115–18, Vallejo Collection, BL.

54. [no date] "Lista de los Neófitos de la Misión de San Luis Rey que pueden salir de la neofía por ser emancipados según sus circunstancias," C-B 31, pt. 1:123–26, Vallejo Collection, BL.

55. 27 Septiembre 1833, C-B 31, pt. 1:107–14, Vallejo Collection, BL.

56. 8 Mayo 1835, and 8 Julio 1836, C-A 51: 286, BL.

57. Pablo de la Portillo a José Figueroa, 21 Septiembre 1833 (dated 12 Octubre 1833), C-B 31:128–29, Vallejo Collection, BL.

58. Pablo de la Portillo a José Figueroa, 12 Octubre 1833, C-B 31, pt. 1:130–31, Vallejo Collection, BL.

59. José Figueroa a Pablo Portillo, 25 Octubre 1833, C-B 31, pt. 1:132, Vallejo Collection, BL. When the final decree passed the following year, many of the former neophytes still asked for, and sometimes received, plots of mission land, and occasionally they received rooms or a building of the mission.

60. Pablo de la Portillo a José Figueroa, 12 Octubre, 1833, C-B 31, pt. 1:113, Vallejo Collection, BL.

61. Pablo de la Portillo 12 Octubre, 1833 C-B 31, pt. 1:113, pt. 1:111–12, Vallejo Collection, BL.

62. Santiago Argüello to José Figueroa, C-B 31, pt. 1:109–110, Vallejo Collection, BL.

63. Juan B. Alvarado, 3 Junio 1834, C-A 60, tomo ii: 100–105. BL.

64. Pablo de la Portillo a José Figueroa, 23 Enero 1835, San Luis Rey, C-A 51: 327, BL.

65. Decree without author, 1835, C-A 51: 18, BL.

66. Ignacio del Valle a Juan González (about Santa Cruz), 1 Diciembre 1835, C-A 51: 244, BL.

67. José Joaquín Ortega, "Administración de cosas hechas a los indios de esta mision en los años 1835–1838," 1838, C-A 51: 38, BL.

68. Juan Bandini to Hartnell, "Distribución de ropa hecha entre los indios de San Gabriel," 23 Marzo 1840, C-A 51: 42, BL.

69. Franco Cota a Manuel Jimeno, 30 Abril 1839, C-A 51: 179, BL.

70. Franco Cota, "Lista de la distribuciones de los efectos hechos a los indígenas en los días 3 y 4 de Noviembre," Noviembre 1839, C-A 51: 60, BL.

71. Antonio del Valle a José Figueroa, 5 Julio 1835, C-A 51: 281, BL.

72. Juan María Ybarra a José Figueroa, nd. 1835, C-A 51: 281, BL.

73. Santiago Carrillo al gobierno, 16 July 1838, C-A 51: 214, BL.

74. José Joaquín Ortega a José Figueroa, 4 Febrero 1839, C-A 51: 214, BL.

75. Guillermo Hartnell recommends the dissolution of the emancipated community at San Rafael, 14 Mayo 1840, C-A 51: 290, BL.

76. Santiago Moreno al Gobernador Juan Bautista Alvarado, 5 Octubre 1838, C-A 51: 253, BL.

77. Inocente García a Jimeno, 24 Agosto 1839, C-A 51: 277, BL.

78. José Figueroa a Manuel Crespo. 20 Deciembre 1834 C-A 51: 157, BL.

79. Manuel Cota, "Sueldos," 31 Diciembre 1838, C-A 51: 135, BL.

80. Santa Inés account book began by Father Blas Ordaz, SBMAL. See, for example, the entries for debts taken on between January and April 1833, pp. 11–12, 27, 38–39. Many of the pages of this book don't have numbers and the accounts tend to be out of order.

81. Mission San Fernando account book, SBMAL.

82. Guillermo Hartnell, "Seminario de San José," 8 Julio 1835, C-A 51, p. 39, BL.

6. INDIGENOUS LANDOWNERS AND NATIVE INGENUITY ON THE BORDERLANDS OF NORTHERN MEXICO

1. Bárcenas 2002: 15; Ohmstede 1993.

2. Band from Governor Mariano Chico, 30 Mayo 1836, C-E 69: 133, BL.

3. Prefect Argüello to José Antonio Estudillo 12 Mayo 1841, C-E 69: 137, BL.

4. Francisco M. Alvarado, 28 Marzo 1836, C-E 69: 132, BL.

5. The Mexican nation had prohibited whipping Indians in 1822. Fray Martínez grumbled about it upon reporting the new regulation. See Fray Martínez a Fray Payeras, 27 Febrero 1823, CMD 2393, SBMAL. See Guillermo Hartnell, "Instruciones a que debe sujetarse el Administrador de la Misión," 28 Agosto 1839, C-A 51: 229, BL.

6. Hartnell, "Instruciones," 2 Agosto 1839, C-A 51: 142–45.

7. Guillermo Hartnell, 29 Agosto 1839, C-A 51: 271.

8. Hartnell, "Instruciones," 28 Agosto 1839, C-A 51: 229.

9. Rafael González, 6 Diciembre 1841, C-A 51: 229.

10. See, for example, the cases of Simeón, No. 563, Reel 4; No. 443, Reel 4; Reel 4 (no maps); Felipe, 11 Abril 1845, No. 446, Reel 7; Próspero, No. 533, Reel 4, Spanish Archives, BL. The governor cited the law of 18 de Agosto de 1824 and the Reglamento de 21 de Noviembre de 1828.

11. Governor Juan Bautista Alvarado, 28 Julio 1841, Monterey, C-E 69: 52, BL.

12. Francisco Aherez, 1 Marzo 1841, Monterey No. 242, Reel 5 Spanish Archives, BL.

13. See Shipek 1991: 9.

14. Joaquín de los Ríos y Ruis, 15 Noviembre 1840, San Luis Rey, C-A 51: 260, BL.

15. Felipe, Mission San Luis Rey, No. 456, (n.d.) Spanish Archives, Reel 7, BL.

16. Andrés and José Manuel, 28 Junio 1843, San Luis Rey, No. 459, Reel 7. Spanish Archives, BL

17. Valle de Temecula, No. 331, Reel 9, Spanish Archives, BL; Pablo Apis, 10 Julio 1843, No. 448, Reel 7 Spanish Archives, BL.

18. Hackel 2005: 390, n. 36.

19. On the history of the mission pueblo see Haas 1995, esp. chap. 3.

20. Chávez-García 2004: 60–63, 75–78.

21. Seferino de Jesús, 17 Abril 1843, No. 527, Reel 4, Spanish Archives, BL. Governor. Argüello sent the petition back to San Gabriel to Estenaga to get approval from the administrator on May 6, 1843. Argüello then approved the petition on May 12, 1843 (no map).

22. Seferino de Jesús, 1845, No. 486, Reel 7, Spanish Archives, BL.

23. P. Hugo Reid signed in the presence of Felipe Reid, who signed with a cross, 2 Junio 1843, No. 436, Reel 7, Spanish Archives, BL.

24. Santiago Leyba, (n.d.) No. 538, Reel 4. Spanish Archive, BL.

25. Emilio Joaquín, No. 530, Reel 4, Spanish Archives, BL.

26. I. Ramón (rosauaro) Valeuria, San Gabriel No. 434, Reel 4, Spanish Archive, BL.

27. Simeón, No. 563, Reel 4; José le Dessuan, No. 443, Reel 4; (no maps); Felipe, 11 Abril 1845, No. 446, Reel 7; Prospero, No. 533, Reel 4, Spanish Archives, BL.

28. Manuel Antonio (signed) 17 Mayo 1845, No. 439, Reel 4, Spanish Archives, BL. And the map, Reel 9, Spanish Archives, BL.

29. Doña Domínguez de Cabalero, No. 442, Reel 4, Spanish Archives, BL. And the map, Reel 9, Spanish Archives, BL.

30. Guillermo Hartnell, *Razón,* 23 Junio 1839, San Fernando, C-A 51: 51, BL.

31. Tiberio Román, 2 Mayo 1843, No. 458, Reel 7 Spanish Archives, BL (no map).

32. See Johnson 1997: 260–61, for a table of five grants at Mission San Fernando including a list of those who applied for each grant.

33. Samuel, 21 Abril 1843, No. 427, Reel 7, Spanish Archives, BL.

34. Urbano, Odón and Manuel, 5 Abril 1843, No. 461, Reel 7, Spanish Archives, BL.

35. Johnson 1997: n. 16, p. 15.

36. Juan de Jesús and José Gabriel, 12 Abril 1845, San Buenaventura, No. 460, Reel 7, Spanish Archives, BL.

37. Lino, San Buenaventura, No. 466, Reel 7, Spanish Archives, BL. He signed his own name. (No date, no map.)

38. Johnson 1995: 7. He cites a number of ethnographic studies about the village of Kamexmey and discusses Cienguita.

39. Marcelino, "Neófito de esta mision," 12 Agosto 1843, No. 309 [No 62], Reel 5: 420, Spanish Archives, BL. See the Diseño of Santa Ynes and a grant on the other side of the river, No. 395, Reel 9.

40. Johnson 1995: 5.

41. Account Book of Santa Inés, 1850, C-C 53: 37, BL.

42. Ibid., Diciembre de 1848, C-C 53: 36, BL.

43. Seminario de Guadalupe, Santa Inés, Date, No. 540, Reel 4, Spanish Archives, BL.

44. Elesario and Pastor 2 Noviembre 1845, and 14 Noviembre (certification), No. 480, Reel 7, Spanish Archives, BL (no map).

45. Inocente García, 11 Febrero 1838, San Miguel, No. 32, Reel 4. Spanish Archives, BL.

46. Mapa 406, San Luis Obispo, No. 406, Reel 9: Spanish Archives, BL.

47. Hackel 2005: 391–97 relates the story of Salgado and of Baldomero José, also a former neophyte at San Carlos who received and expanded his rancho land, protected it from encroachment, and engaged in the hide and tallow trade.

48. Marcelo, Pico, Conslotal, 22 Mayo 1846, No. 450, Reel 9, Spanish Archives, BL. (Includes a map for the lands of Ulistae. Here again the governor referred to the law of 18 Agosto 1824, and Article 5 of a regulation passed 21 Agosto 1828 to grant the land.)

49. Roberto, 30 Septiembre 1840, 9 Octubre 1840, No. 210, Reel 5: 326, Spanish Archives, BL.

50. Indian Iñigo, No. 422, Reel 7: 155–56, Spanish Archives. See the map on 108, Reel 9, Spanish Archives, BL. Also see Posolmi: Posita de las Animas, No. 410, Reel 9 (n.d.), Spanish Archives, BL; see Diseño, No. 353, Reel 9, Spanish Archives, BL. In the upper right corner of this map see a note "Terreno del indio Iñego," and see map No. 422 (n.d.), "Terreno de . . . Yñigo" (with Mission Santa Clara to the south and other grants to the north).

51. Shoup and Millikin 1999: 117.

52. Juan María Osuña No. 529, Reel 4, Spanish Archives, BL. And see Juan María Osuña Rancho de San Dieguito, No. 463, Reel 9, the *diseño* or map.

53. The Indian pueblo of San Dieguito dropped out of subsequent histories, but the Osuña family would be remembered as owners. Their land had been reduced by 1906 to "about two hundred acres surrounding the original adobe home." The Santa Fe Railroad purchased that and other lands Anglo ranchers owned to reassemble the original grant. Ed

Fletcher subdivided the land and created the Spanish theme development of Rancho Santa Fe. See Phoebe S. Kropp's excellent book; Kropp 2006: 161, and the whole of chap. 4.

54. See Silliman, 2004.

55. "Criminal Proceedings against Natives of California allegedly engaged in ammunition trade with hostile tribes [José María Crespín and Carpio]," 7 October 1836, El Paso, Reel 22, frames 461–97, Mexican Archives of New Mexico. I thank Andrés Reséndez for pointing this case out to me.

56. Padrón, 1836 Mission San Luis Rey, #2304–30. I worked with John Johnson's database compiled from the Padrón [census record] of Mission San Luis Rey.

57. "Criminal Proceedings," Reel 22, frame 487, Mexican Archives of New Mexico. I thank Andrés Reséndez for pointing this case out to me.

58. Padrón, 1836 Mission San Luis Rey.

59. "Criminal Proceedings," Reel 22, frame 487, Mexican Archives of New Mexico.

60. Frank 2000; de la Teja and Frank 2005. For an earlier period, see especially Sheridan 2005 and Cuello 2005.

61. Brooks 2002: 108. On Mexican policy in this frontier region, see Ramos 2004.

62. Brooks 2002: 153. Hämäläinen, 2008 79. The map on 79 locates the trading and raiding zone of the Comanchería in relationship to the New Mexican settlements of Abiquí and El Paso. It offers a good sense of the trading and raiding zone in the late eighteenth century.

63. Deutsch 1987: 17.

64. "Criminal Proceedings," Reel 22, frames 486–90, Mexican Archives of New Mexico.

65. Ibid., frame 496. "Asking on behalf of the *Jefe Politico* of New Mexico" the letter requested authorities in Chihuahua to send back the three Americans who had been apprehended and were accused of trading with the Apaches," January 1837, El Paso, Reel 22, Mexican Archives of New Mexico.

66. Ibid., frame 466, Mexican Archives of New Mexico. (The entry is made on 29 September 1836.)

67. Ibid., frames 482–83, Mexican Archives of New Mexico.

68. Ibid., frames 484–86, Mexican Archives of New Mexico.

69. Ibid., frames 479–82, Mexican Archives of New Mexico.

70. Ibid., frame 494, Mexican Archives of New Mexico.

71. Criminal Proceedings," 27 December 1836, El Paso, Reel 22, frame 463, Mexican Archives of New Mexico, and the letter about this and the trade in "Criminal Proceedings," 14 February 1837, Reel 22, frames 474–77, Mexican Archives of New Mexico.

72. See Hämäläinen (2008) especially chaps. 4 and 5 to see the emergence of the *Comancherhía* or Comanche Empire.

73. Brooks 2002. See especially chaps. 3, 4, and 5; and Hämäläinen (2008) for an excellent discussion of this process. Also see the assessment of contemporary borderlands by Pekka Hämäkäinen and Samuel Truett, and the special section on borderlands history that reflects the kinds of scholarship of interest here. See Hämäläinen and Truett 2001: 338–61.

74. Barr 2007: 15. Barr presents an excellent history of the Texas borderlands. She especially analyzes the role of women and girls who formed the majority of the captives in the trade in human captives.

75. Delay 2008:109 and map on page 256.

76. Blackhawk 2006: 27.

77. Hurtado 1988: 39. See the map on 33 for what he calls the international region.

78. Phillips 1993: 83; and see Zappia 2008: 135–72.

79. Phillips 1993: 108–9; and Hurtado 1988: 46–47.

80. Here, as with the other work in the database, I am extremely grateful for my collaboration with Sarah Ginn, archaeologist, whose own work on California promises to open a greater understanding of these relationships and their implications. All material from the Early California Population Project, but spellings of the tribal groups varied.

81. Fray Ibarra, 24 Noviembre 1827, SBMAL.

82. See González 2005. "Indians" form an important part of González's story, but the book is not a history of Indigenous people in Los Angeles during this era.

83. Gobernador Micheltorena a Diputados Antonio Carrillo y Ygnacio del Valle, 18 Marzo 1845, Monterey, C-A 51: 334, BL.

CONCLUSION: INDIGENOUS ARCHIVES AND KNOWLEDGE

1. Browne 1850: 307.

2. Deloria 2004: 50.

3. Guidotti-Hernández 2011: 176.

4. Madley 2008: 303–4.

5. Mallon 2012: 1–19.

6. Maria Brave Heart-Jordan 1995, Gone 2009, 2010 [and on space and place, 2008].

7. Gone 2008.

8. Church records document with some detail Rafael Solares's baptism and death. Marie Walsh discusses "Rafael," but it isn't the same person, because Walsh arrived to Santa Inés in 1904. She worked with her uncle, Father Bucker, on directing the restoration of the mission while he was stationed there from 1904 to 1917. Working with the Ineseño community and other artisans, they completed the restoration by the spring of 1912. See Walsh 1930: 60, 62.

9. See Hudson, Blackburn, Curletti, and Timbrook 1977: 123–25; Heizer, ed. 1952.

10. Reichlen and Heizer 1964.

11. On the genocidal violence against Indigenous populations that preceded this era, see Lindsay 2012. It is interesting to note that at this same time Mariano Vallejo was encouraging Californios to give their objects to Hubert H. Bancroft, from whom Vallejo initially kept his distance. By the mid-1770s, after losing most of his land and seeing the losses experienced by other Californios, Vallejo considered the records safer with Bancroft. Those donations to Bancroft's library formed part of the very material consulted to write this history.

12. Walsh 1930: 65, 73–74.

13. Those who saved the painting, vestments, and songbooks probably formed part of the *cofradía* at Santa Ines, a confraternity or ritual lay organization composed of members of the parish. Dedicated to the spiritual and material interests of its members, the group also had the responsibility for maintaining and protecting particular religious objects in their mission church or parish.

14. Abbott 1961: 67–68, and Baer 1956: 302.

15. F. J. Weber 1965: 114.

16. See Walsh 1976.

17. Field 2008: 25.

BIBLIOGRAPHY

Abbott, Mamie Goulet. *Santa Ines Hermosa: The Journal of the Padre's Niece.* Santa Barbara: Sunwise Press, 1951.

Adorno, Rolena. *Guaman Poma: Writing and Resistance in Colonial Peru.* Austin: University of Texas Press, 1986.

———. *Coloniales del Centro de México.* Zamomra, Michoacán: El Colegio de Michoacán, 1998.

———. *Guaman Poma and His Illustrated Chronicle from Colonial Peru: From a Century of Scholarship to a New Era of Reading.* Copenhagen: Museum Tusculanum Press, 2001.

———. *The Polemics of Possession in Spanish American Narrative.* New Haven: Yale University Press, 2007.

Allen, Rebecca. "Use of Shellfish and Shell Beads at Santa Cruz Mission." *Pacific Coast Archaeological Society Quarterly* 28, no. 2 (1992): 18–34.

———. *Native Americans at Mission Santa Cruz, 1791–1834.* Los Angeles: Institute of Archaeology, UCLA, 1998.

Anderson, Arthur, Frances Berdán, and James Lockhart. *Beyond the Codices: The Nahua View of Colonial Mexico.* Los Angeles: University of California Press, 1976.

Anderson, M. Kat. *Tending the Wild: Native American Knowledge and the Management of California's Natural Resources.* Berkeley: University of California Press, 2005.

Anderson, Rodney. "Race and Social Stratification: A Comparison of Working-Class Spaniards, Indians, and 'Castas' in Guadalajara, Mexico, in 1821." *Hispanic American Historical Review* 68, no. 2 (May 1988): 209–43.

Applegate, Richard. *Atishwin: The Dream Helper in South-Central California.* Socorro, NM: Ballena Press, 1978.

Arias de Greiff, Jorge. "Las Cortes de Cádiz y la Emancipación." *Boletín de Historia y Antigüedades* 90, no. 823 (Octubre—Diciembre 2003): 669–88.

Arkush, Brooke. "Yokuts Trade Networks and Native Culture Change in Central and Eastern California." *Ethnohistory* 40, no. 4 (1993): 619–40.

Arnold, Jeanne. "The Chumash in World and Regional Perspectives." In *The Origins of a Pacific Coast Chiefdom: The Chumash of the Channel Islands,* edited by Jeanne Arnold, 1–19. Salt Lake City: University of Utah Press, 2001.

Arnold, Jeanne, and Anthony Graesch. "The Evolution of Specialized Shellworking among the Island Chumash." In *The Origins of a Pacific Coast Chiefdom: The Chumash of the Channel Islands,* edited by Jeanne Arnold, 71–112. Salt Lake City: University of Utah Press, 2001.

Arróm, José Juan. *Cimarrón.* Santo Domingo: Fundación García-Arévalo, 1986.

Baer, Kurt. *The Treasures of Mission Santa Ines: A History and Catalogue of the Paintings, Sculpture, and Craft Works.* Fresno: Academy of California Church History, 1956.

———. "California Indian Art (1959)." In *Spanish Borderlands Sourcebook: The Archaeology of Alta California,* vol. 15, 81–110. New York: Garland, 1991.

Barbolla, Diane E. "Alta California Troops: Acculturation and Material Wealth in a Presidio and Mission Context, 1769–1810." PhD diss., University of California, Riverside, 1992.

Bárcenas, Francisco López. *Legislación y Derechos Indígenas en el México del Siglo XIX.* Tlanepantla, Mex.: Centro de Estudios Antropológicos, 2002.

Bargellini, Clara. "Asia at the Missions of Northern New Spain" 191–200. Bargellini, Clara, and Michael Komanecky. *The Arts of the Missions of Northern New Spain, 1600–1821.* Mexico City: Antiguo Colegio de San Ildefonso/Mexico City, 2009.

Barr, Julianne. *Peace Came in the Form of a Woman: Indians and Spaniards in the Texas Borderlands.* Chapel Hill: University of North Carolina Press, 2007.

———. "Geographies of Power: Mapping Indian Borders in the 'Borderlands' of the Early Southwest." *William and Mary Quarterly* 68, no.1 (January 2011): 5–46.

Basso, H. *Wisdom Sits in Places: Landscape and Language among the Western Apache.* Albuquerque: University of New Mexico Press, 1996.

Bauman, Zygmunt. *Liquid Fear.* Cambridge, UK: Polity Press, 2006.

Bean, Lowell J., ed. *Mukat's People: The Cahuilla Indians of Southern California.* Berkeley: University of California Press, 1972.

———. "Social Organization in Native California." In *Native Californians: A Theoretical Retrospective,* edited by Lowell J. Bean and Thomas Blackburn, 99–124. Menlo Park, CA: Ballena Press, 1976a.

———. "The Artist and Shamanic Tradition (1985)." In *Ethnology of the Alta California Indians II: Postcontact,* edited by Lowell J. Bean, David H. Thomas, and Sylvia Brakke Vane, 963–70. New York: Garland, 1991.

———. *California Indian Shamanism.* Menlo Park, CA: Ballena Press, 1992a.

———. "Power and Its Applications in Native California." In *California Indian Shamanism,* edited by Lowell J. Bean, 21–32. Menlo Park, CA: Ballena Press, 1992b.

———. *The Ohlone, Past and Present: Native Americans of the San Francisco Bay Region.* Menlo Park, CA: Ballena Press, 1994.

Bean, Lowell J., and Thomas C. Blackburn. *Native Californians: A Theoretical Retrospective.* Menlo Park, CA: Ballena Press, 1976b.

Bean, Lowell J., and Harry W. Lawton. "Some Explanations for the Rise of Cultural Complexity in Native California with Comments on Proto-Agriculture and Agricul-

- **Textbook Packages without CDs, Cassettes or Codes:** A $5.00 fee is charged to rewrap the package. All pieces must be returned and in new condition (un-opened).
- **Study Guides, and Supplemental Course Materials:**
  - **With Shrink-Wrap:** Full-refund if shrink-wrap is unopened.
  - **Without Shrink-Wrap:** Not refundable.
- **Trade Books, Dictionaries, Thesaurus, Paperback Novels:**
  - Defective books will be exchanged(within publisher's guidelines), not refunded.
  - Refundable if you are enrolled in a class requiring a specific dictionary, thesaurus, or paperback novel and the book is new condition as determined by LACC Cubstore (free of any markings or cover damage) To qualify for a refund you must show the original receipt and your Registration / Fee Receipt showing that you have dropped the class. NO REFUND ON BARCHARTS.
- **Calculators, Tape Recorders, Electronic and Electrical Devices, Computer Software, Laboratory Tool Kits and Supplies:** Exchanges only on defective items if returned to LACC Cubstore within 24 hours of purchase.
- **Clothing:** Refundable **only if unworn** with original packaging/tags attached and returned within 24 hours of purchase.

---

24 HOUR RETURN / EXCHANGE NOTIFICATION REQUIREMENT

If you cannot make it back to the store within 24 hours of purchase, you must contact us within that time period and notify our Customer Service Desk of the problem. Phoning does not guarantee a refund or exchange but it can extend your timeline.
See *How to Contact LACC Cubstore* at the bottom of this page for details.

- **Goggles and Other Items Governed by California Health Laws:** Not refundable.
- **Special Orders:** Not refundable
- **Rental Books:** Please refer to your Rental Contract.
4. **REFUND PAYMENTS:** Refunds are processed according to the purchase payment method. Refunds may not be processed for individuals with a dishonored check until the bad debt is cleared at the Business Office.

REFUND PAYMENT PROCESSING		
Payment By	Refund By	Timeline
Cash	Cash	Immediate
Credit/Debit Card	Credit to Your Charged Account	Store process at the end of business day; Actual credit to account determined by bank
Check- No personal, sponsored only	Check(sponsored only)	Sponsored – funds returned to agency NOTE- BOOKS MUST BE RETURNED BY REFUND DEADLINES
Voucher	Credit to Voucher Account	Immediate

DO NOT LOSE YOUR RECEIPT!!! WE ARE UNABLE TO CREATE DUPLICATES!!!
ANY REFUNDS GIVEN OUTSIDE THE PARAMETERS OF THIS POLICY ARE SUBJECT TO A RESTOCKING FEE.

HOW TO CONTACT BOOKS N' MORE

Location: Phone: (323) 953-4000 Ext. 2140/2141   Visit us on the web at:
Los Angeles City College   Fax: (323) 953-4042   www.laccbookstore.com
Student Union   Bookstore Email: bookstore@lacitycollege.edu
          Store Hours: Mon-Thurs: 7:30 AM – 7:00 PM   Fri: 7:30 AM – 3:00 PM
                    CHECK WWW.LACCBOOKSTORE.COM FOR SPECIAL HOURS/HOLIDAY HOURS

RETURN AND REFUND POLICY

LAST DATE FOR A FULL REFUND: SEE ATTACHED RECEIPT

1. Textbooks and supplementary classroom material purchased for the **current academic term** may be returned for refund during **specified time limits** and providing refund requirements are met. Books not accepted for return may be sold at Buy Back. See Buy Back Policy for details.

2. **TIME LIMITS:** Full refunds on textbooks and textbook rentals are allowed for each academic term as specified below. Books purchased after the specified refund time limit are non-refundable or exchangeable. *No refunds or exchanges are permitted during the last ten (10) days of classes and during final exam periods.*

   - *Fall / Spring Semesters:* First (10) days of semester.
   - *Summer / Winter Inter-Session:* First five (5) days of session.
   - *Short-Term Classes/ITV:* First five (5) days of session.
   - *After Time Limit Specified Above:* 24 hour limit if wrong book or defective.
     (may exchange incorrect book for correct book only-NO REFUNDS)!!
   - *8 DAY CLASSES: SAME DAY AS START OF CLASS (1 DAY)!!*

3. **REQUIREMENTS:** Refunds are allowed only when the following conditions are met.

   - A photo ID and **original** cash register receipt must be presented during the current semester/session time limit specified above. **No exceptions.**
   - Proof of enrollment may be required for some transactions.
   - Books must be in the same condition as when purchased. LACC Cubstore reserves the right to judge the condition of the returned item.
   - *New Textbooks:* Must be in New Saleable Condition-No signs of being read or erased. No marks, writing, Creases, bends, wrinkles etc. "New" books that have **any** signs of the above will not qualify for full refund.
     NO LIQUID damaged books!

SAVE &
SHOW YOUR
RECEIPT!

> **Do not write in your books or open shrink-wrapped books** until you have gone to class and are certain the book you purchased is correct. LACC Cubstore cannot be responsible for incorrect title purchases.

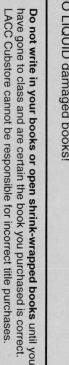

   - *Used Textbooks:* Returnable at used book purchase price providing book is in saleable condition as determined by LACC Cubstore Staff.
   - *Textbooks with CDs, Cassettes, or Codes:* No refund if shrink-wrap is damaged, open, or missing.

(over) →→→→

ture." In *Before the Wilderness: Environmental Management by Native Californians*, edited by Thomas Blackburn and M. Kat Anderson, 27–54. Menlo Park, CA: Ballena Press, 1993.

Beebe, Rose Marie, and Robert Senkewicz. "The End of the 1824 Chumash Revolt in Alta California: Father Vicente Sarría's Account." *Americas* 53, no. 2 (1996): 273–84.

———. "Uncertainty on the Mission Frontier: Missionary Recruitment and Institutional Stability in Alta California in the 1790s." In *Francis in the Americas: Essays on the Franciscan Family in North and South America*, edited by John F. Schwaller. Berkeley, CA: Academy of American Franciscan History, 2005.

———, eds. *Testimonios: Early California through the Eyes of Women, 1815–1848*. Berkeley, CA: Heydey Books, 2006.

Beeler, Madison, ed. *The Ventureño Confesionario of José Señan, O.F.M.* Berkeley: University of California Press, 1967.

Beilharz, Edwin. *Felipe de Neve: First Governor of California*. San Francisco: California Historical Society, 1971.

Beltrán, Gonzalo Aguirre. "The Slave Trade in Mexico." *Hispanic American Historical Review* 24, no. 3 (August 1944): 412–31.

——— *La Población Negra de México, 1519–1810: Estudio Etnohistorico*. Mexico City: SRA-CEHAM, 1981.

Benson, Nettie Lee, ed. *Mexico and the Spanish Cortes, 1810–1822*. Austin: University of Texas Press, 1966.

Berlin, Ira, Barbara Fields, Thavolia Glymph, Joseph P. Reidy, and Leslie Rowland, eds. *The Destruction of Slavery*, Series I, vol. 1 of *Freedom: A Documentary History of Emancipation, 1861–1867*. Cambridge: Cambridge University Press, 1985.

Bernard, Julienne. "Status and the Swordfish: The Origins of Large-Species Fishing among the Chumash." In *Foundations of Chumash Complexity*, edited by Jeanne Arnold, 25–51. Los Angeles: UCLA Costen Institute of Archaeology, 2004.

Blackburn, Thomas. "The Chumash Revolt of 1824: A Native Account." *Journal of California Anthropology* 2 (1975): 223–27.

Blackburn, Thomas, and M. Kat Anderson, eds. *Before the Wilderness: Environmental Management by Native Californians*. Menlo Park, CA: Ballena Press, 1993.

Blackburn, Thomas, and Travis Hudson, *Time's Flotsam: Overseas Collections of California Indian Material Culture*. Menlo Park, CA: Ballena Press, 1990.

Blackhawk, Ned. *Violence over the Land: Indians and Empires in the Early American West*. Cambridge, MA: Harvard University Press, 2006.

Boone, Elizabeth H., ed. *Stories in Red and Black: Pictorial Histories of the Aztecs and Mixtecs*. Austin: University of Texas Press, 2000.

Boone, Elizabeth H., and Tom Cummins, eds. *Native Traditions in the Post Conquest World*. Washington, DC: Dumbarton Oaks, 1998.

Boone, Elizabeth H., and Walter Mignolo, eds. *Writing without Words: Alternative Literacies in Mesoamérica and the Andes*. Durham, NC: Duke University Press, 1994.

Brave Heart-Jordan, Maria Yellow Horse. "The Return to the Sacred Path: Healing from Historical Trauma and Historical Unresolved Grief among the Lakota: a Dissertation based upon an Independent Investigation." PhD diss.: Smith College School for Social Work, 1995.

Braudel, Fernand. *The Mediterranean and the Mediterranean World in the Age of Philip II.* 2 vols. New York: Harper and Row, 1972.

Brett, Guy. "Being Drawn to an Image: Depiction of Angels in Post-Conquest Art." *Oxford Art Journal* 14, no. 1 (1991): 3–9.

Brooks, James F. *Captives and Cousins: Slavery, Kinship, and Community in the Southwest Borderlands.* Chapel Hill: University of North Carolina Press, 2002.

Brown, Laura. "Not Outside the Range." In *Trauma: Explorations in Memory,* edited by Cathy Caruth. Baltimore: Johns Hopkins University Press, 1995, 100–112.

Browne, J. Ross. *Report of the Debates in the Convention of California on the Formation of the State Constitution, September and October, 1849.* Washington, DC: John T. Towers, 1850.

Browning, Barbara. *Samba: Resistance in Motion.* Bloomington: Indiana University Press, 1995.

Burkhart, Louise. "Mexica Women on the Home Front: Housework and Religion in Aztec Mexico." In *Indian Women of Early Mexico,* edited by Susan Schroeder, Stephanie Wood, and Robert Haskett, 25–54. Norman: University of Oklahoma Press, 1997.

———. *Before Guadalupe: The Virgin Mary in Early Colonial Nahuatl Literature.* Albany, NY: Institute for Mesoamerican Studies, University at Albany, 2001.

Butzer, Elisabeth. *Historia Social de una Comunidad Tlaxcalteca—San Miguel de Aguayo, 1686–1820.* Tlaxcala, Tlax.: Instituto Tlaxcalteca de la Cultura, 2001.

Calero, Manuel Chust. "De Esclavor, Encomenderos y Mitayos: El Anticolonialismo en las Cortes de Cádiz." *Mexican Studies/Estudios Mexicanos* 11, no. 2 (Summer 1995): 179–212.

Caplan, Karen. *Indigenous Citizens: Local Liberalism in Early National Oaxaca and Yucatán.* Stanford, CA: Stanford University Press, 2010.

Carrico, R. L. *Strangers in a Stolen Land: American Indians in San Diego County from Prehistory to the New Deal.* San Diego: Sunbelt Publishers, 2008.

Carroll, Patrick J. *Blacks in Colonial Veracruz: Race, Ethnicity and Regional Development.* Austin: University of Texas Press, 2001.

Caruth, Cathy, ed. *Trauma: Explorations in Memory.* Baltimore: Johns Hopkins University Press, 1995.

———. *Unclaimed Experience: Trauma, Narrative, and History.* Baltimore: Johns Hopkins University Press, 1996.

Casas, María Raquel. *Married to a Daughter of the Land: Spanish-Mexican Women and Interethnic Marriage in California, 1820–1880.* Reno: University of Nevada Press, 2007.

Castañeda, Antonia I. "Presidarías y Pobladoras: Spanish-Mexican Women in Frontier Monterey, Alta California, 1770–1821." PhD diss., Stanford University, 1990.

———. "Sexual Violence in the Politics and Policies of Conquest: Amerindian Women and the Spanish Conquest of Alta California." In *Building with Our Hands: New Directions in Chicana Studies,* edited by Adela de la Torre and Beatríz Pesquera, 15–33. Berkeley: University of California Press, 1993.

Castillo, Edward. "An Indian Account of the Decline and Collapse of Mexico's Hegemony over the Missionized Indians of California." *American Indian Quarterly* 13, no. 4 (1989): 391–408.

———. "The Assassination of Padre Andrés Quintana." *California History* 68, no. 3 (Fall 1989): 391–408.

———. "The Other Side of the 'Christian Curtain': California Indians and the Missionaries." *Californians* 10, no. 2 (1992): 8–17.

Catlos, Brian. *The Victors and the Vanquished: Christians and Muslims of Catalonia and Aragón, 1050–1300*. New York: Cambridge University Press, 2004.

Caywood, Margaret. "Missions and Transmissions: Music and the Spanish Missions of Alta California from 1769." PhD diss, University of California, Davis, 2012.

Certeau, Michel de. *The Writing of History*. New York: Columbia University Press, 1988.

Chambers, Iain. *Mediterranean Crossings: The Politics of an Interrupted Modernity*. Durham, NC: Duke University Press, 2008.

Chartkoff, Joseph, and Kerry Kona Chartkoff. *The Archaeology of California*. Stanford, CA: Stanford University Press, 1984.

Chávez-García, Miroslava. *Negotiating Conquest: Gender and Power in California, 1770s to 1880s*. Tucson: University of Arizona Press, 2004.

Chávez-Hita, Adriana Naveda. *Esclavos Negros en las Haciendas azucareras de Córdoba, Veracruz, 1690–1830*. Jalapa: Universidad Veracruzana, 1987.

Choris L. *Voyage Pittoresque autour du monde, avec des portraits de sauvages d'amérique, d'asie, d'afrique, et des iles du grand coean; des paysages, des vue maritimes, et plusieurs objets d'histoire natureel*. Paris: L'Imprimerie de Firmin Didot, 1822.

Christian, William. *Apparitions in Late Medieval and Renaissance Spain*. Princeton: Princeton University Press, 1981.

Colston, S. A. *Approaches to Historical Archaeology: The Case of the Royal Presidio of San Diego*. San Diego: San Diego History Research Center, San Diego State University, 1982.

Cohen, Bill. "Indian Sandpaintings of Southern California." *Journal of California and Great Basin Anthropology* 9, no. 1 (1987): 4–34.

Cohen, Paul. *History in Three Keys: The Boxers as Event, Experience, and Myth*. New York: Columbia University Press, 1997.

Cook, Sherburne. "Colonial Expeditions to the Interior of California: Central Valley, 1800–1820." *University of California Anthropological Records* 16, no. 6 (1960): 239–92.

———. "Expeditions to the Interior of California, Central Valley, 1820–1840." *University of California Anthropological Records* 20, no. 5 (1962): 151–214.

Cooper, Frederick, Thomas Holt, and Rebecca Scott. *Beyond Slavery: Explorations of Race, Labor, and Citizenship in Post Emancipation Societies*. Chapel Hill: University of North Carolina Press, 2000.

Costello, Julia G. *California Historical Archaeology: Santa Inés Mission Excavations: 1986–1988*. Salinas, CA: Coyote Press, 1989.

Costello, Julia G., and Phillip L. Walker. "Burials from the Santa Barbara Presidio Chapel." *Historical Archaeology* 21, no. 1 (1987): 3–17.

Costo, Rupert, and Jeanette Henry Costo, eds. *The Missions of California: A Legacy of Genocide*. San Francisco: Indian Historian Press, 1987.

Craig, S. "Ethnographic Notes on the Construction of Ventureño Chumash Baskets." *Archeological Survey of the University of California* 8 (1966): 197–214.

———. "The Basketry of the Ventureño Chumash." *Archaelogical Survey Annual Report* 9 (1967): 78–149.

Crespí, Juan. *A Description of Distant Roads: Original Journals of the First Expedition into California, 1769–1770,* edited and translated by Alan Brown. San Diego: San Diego State University Press, 2001.

Crosby, Harry W. *Antigua California: Mission and Colony on the Peninsular Frontier, 1697–1768.* Albuquerque: University of New Mexico Press, 1994.

Cuello, José. "Racialized Hierarchies of Power in Colonial Mexican Society: The Sistema de Castas as a Form of Social Control in Saltillo." In *Choice, Persuasion, and Coercion: Social Control on Spain's North American Frontiers,* edited by Jesús F. de la Teja and Ross Frank, 201–26. Albuquerque: University of New Mexico Press, 2005.

Cummins, Tom. "Representation in the Sixteenth Century and the Colonial Image of the Inca." In *Writing without Words: Alternative Literacies in Mesoamerica and the Andes,* edited by Elizabeth Boone and Walter Mignolo, 188–219. Durham, NC: Duke University Press, 1994.

———. "Let Me See! Reading Is for Them: Colonial Andean Images and Objects In *Native Traditions in the Post Conquest World,* edited by Elizabeth Boone and Tom Cummins. Washington, DC: Dumbarton Oaks, 1998.

———. "The Indulgent Image: Prints in the New World" in Ilona Katzew, ed., *Contested Visions,* (Los Angeles: Los Angeles Museum of Art, 2011) 203–225.

Cummins, Tom, and Emily G. Umberger, eds. *Native Artists and Patrons in Colonial Latin America.* Tempe: Arizona State University Press, 1995.

Cutter, Donald P., ed. *The Writings of Mariano Payeras.* Santa Barbara: Bellerophon Books, 1995.

Damian, Carol. "The Survival of Inca Symbolism in Representations of the Virgin in Colonial Peru." *Athanor* 7 (1988): 21–31.

———. "Artist and Patron in Colonial Cuzco: Workshops, Contracts and a Petition for Independence." *Colonial Latin American Historical Review* 4, no. 1 (1995a): 25–53.

———. *The Virgin of the Andes: Art and Ritual in Colonial Cuzco.* Miami Beach: Grassfield, 1995b.

Davis, James T. "Trade Routes and Economic Exchange among the Indians of California." *Reports of the University of California Archaeological Survey* 54 (1961): 5–75.

Dawson, A. D. "A Corpus of Chumash Basketry." *University of California Archaeological Survey* 7 (1965): 193–275.

Dean, Carolyn. "Ethnic Conflict and Corpus Christi in Colonial Cuzco." *Colonial Latin American Review* 2, no. 1/2 (1993): 93–120.

———. "Copied Carts: Spanish Prints and Colonial Peruvian Paintings." *Art Bulletin* 78, no. 1 (1996a): 98–110.

———. "The Renewal of Old World Images and the Creation of Colonial Peruvian Visual Culture." In *Converging Culture: Art and Identity in Spanish America,* edited by Diane Fane, 171–82. Brooklyn: Brooklyn Museum Press, 1996b.

———. *Inka Bodies and the Body of Christ: Corpus Christi in Colonial Cuzco, Peru.* Durham, NC: Duke University Press, 1999.

Deans-Smith, Susan. "The (Racial) Politics of Painting." In Ilona Katzew and Susan Deans-Smith, eds., *Race and Classification: The Case of Mexican America,* 43–72. Stanford, CA: Stanford University Press, 2009.

De Armellada, Cesáreo. "La Causa Indigena Americana en Las Cortes de Cádiz." *Montalbán* 9 (1979): 497–564.

Deetz, James. "Archaeological Investigations at La Purísima Mission (1963)." In *The Archaeology of Alta California,* edited by Leo Barker and Julia Costello, 139–99. New York: Garland, 1991.

DeJohn Anderson, Virginia. "King Phillip's Herds: Indians, Colonists, and the Problem of Livestock in Early New England." In *American Encounters: Natives and Newcomers from European Contact to Indian Removal, 1500–1850,* edited by Peter C. Mancall and James H. Merrell, 246–68. New York: Routledge, 2007.

De La Perouse, Jean Francois. *Life in a California Mission: The Journals of Jean Francois de la Perouse, Monterey in 1786.* Berkeley, CA: Heydey Books, 1989.

de la Teja, Jesús F., and Ross Frank, eds. *Choice, Persuasion, and Coercion: Social Control on Spain's North American Frontiers.* Albuquerque: University of New Mexico Press, 2005.

Delay, Brian. *War of a Thousand Deserts: Indian Raids and the U.S.-Mexican War.* New Haven: Yale University Press, 2008.

Deloria, Philip J. *Indians in Unexpected Places.* Lawrence: University of Kansas Press, 2004.

Desmond, Jane C., ed. *Meaning in Motion: New Cultural Studies of Dance.* Durham, NC: Duke University Press, 1997.

Deutsch, Sarah. *No Separate Refuge: Culture, Class, and Gender on an Anglo-Hispanic Frontier in the American Southwest, 1880–1940.* New York: Oxford University Press, 1987.

DuBois, Constance Goddard. "The Religion of the Luiseño Indians of Southern California." *University of California Publications in American Archaeology and Ethnology* 8, no. 3 (June 1908): 69–186.

Duggan, Marie C. "Market and Church on the Mexican Frontier: Alta California, 1769–1832." PhD diss., New School University, 2000.

———. *The Chumash and the Presidio of Santa Barbara: Evolution of a Relationship, 1782–1823.* Santa Barbara: Santa Barbara Trust for Historic Preservation, 2004.

Duhaut-Cilly, Auguste. *A Voyage to California, the Sandwich Islands, and Around the World in the Years, 1826–1829,* translated by August Fruge and Neal Harlow. Berkeley: University of California Press, 1997.

Du Plessis, Robert "Cotton's Consumption in the Seventeenth-and Eighteenth-Century North Atlantic." In *The Spinning World: A Global History of Cotton Textiles, 1200–1850,* edited by Giorgio Riello and Prasannan Parthasarathi. New York: Oxford University Press, 2009.

Elliott, Eric. "Dictionary of Rincón Luiseño." PhD diss., University of California, San Diego, 1999.

Engelhardt, Fray Zephyrin. *Missions and Missionaries of California.* Vol. 2–4 San Francisco: James H. Barry Co., 1912.

———. *San Diego Mission.* San Francisco: James H. Barry Co., 1920.

———. *San Luis Rey Mission.* San Francisco: James H. Barry Co., 1921.

———. *San Juan Capistrano Mission.* Los Angeles: Standard Printing Company, 1922.

———. *Santa Barbara Mission.* San Francisco: James H. Barry Co., 1923.

———. *San Gabriel Mission and the Beginnings of Los Angeles.* San Gabriel: Mission San Gabriel, 1927.

———. *The Missions and Missionaries of California, vol. 1: Lower California.* Santa Barbara: Mission Santa Barbara, 1929.

————. *Mission San Juan Bautista: A School of Church Music*. Santa Barbara: Mission Santa Barbara, 1931.

————. *San Miguel, Arcangel*. Ramona, CA: Acoma Books, 1971a.

————. *The Franciscans in California*. Harbor Springs, MI: Holy Childhood Indian School, 1971b.

————. *Mission San Fernando* (1912). Reprinted as *Mission San Fernando Rey: The Mission of the Valley*. Ramona, CA: Ballena Press, 1973.

————. *Mission Santa Ines: Virgen y Martir and its Ecclesiastical Seminary*. Santa Barbara: McNally and Loftin, 1986.

Erlandson, Jon. *Early Hunter-Gatherers of the California Coast*. New York: Plenum Press, 1994.

————. "The Middle Holocene on the Western Santa Barbara Coast." In *The Origins of a Pacific Coast Chiefdom: The Chumash of the Channel Islands*, edited by Jeanne Arnold, 91–109. Salt Lake City: University of Utah Press, 2001.

Fagan, Brian. *The Royal Presidio of Santa Barbara: Archaeology of the Chapel Site*. Santa Barbara: Santa Barbara Trust for Historic Preservation, 1976.

————. *Before California: An Archaeologist Looks at Our Earliest Inhabitants*. Lanham, MD: Rowman and Littlefield, 2003.

Fane, Diane, ed. *Converging Cultures: Art and Identity in Spanish America*. Brooklyn: Brooklyn Museum, 1996.

Farris, G. "Recognizing Indian Folk History as Real History: A Fort Ross Example." *American Indian Quarterly* 13, no. 4 (1989): 471–81.

Farris, G., and John R. Johnson. *Prominent Indian Families at Mission La Purisima Concepción as Identified in Baptismal, Marriage, and Burial Records*. San Diego: California Mission Studies Association, 1999.

Ferrer Benimeli, J. A. "Las Cortes de Cádiz: America y la Masonería." *Cuaderno Hispanoamérica* 460 (1988): 7–34.

Field, Les W., with Cheryl Seidner, Julian Land, Rosemary Cambra, Florence Silva, Vivien Hailstone, Darlene Marshall, Bradley Marshall, Callie Lara, Merv George Sr., and the Cultural Committee of the Yurok Tribe. *Abalone Tales: Collaborative Explorations of Sovereignty and Identity in Native California*. Durham, NC: Duke University Press, 2008.

Fields, Virginia, and Victor Zamudio-Taylor. *Road to Aztlán: Art from a Mythic Homeland*. Los Angeles: Los Angeles County Museum of Art, 2001.

Fisher, Abby Sue. "Trade Textiles: Asia and New Spain." In *Asia and Spanish America: Trans-Pacific Artistic and Cultural Exchange, 1500–1850*, edited by Donna Pierce and Ronald Otsuka, 175–90. Denver: Denver Art Museum, 2009.

Foster, Susan. "Textual Evidences." In *Bodies of the Text: Dance as Theory, Theory as Dance*, edited by Ellen Goellner and Jacqueline Shea Murphy, 231–47. New Brunswick, NJ: Rutgers University Press, 1995.

Frank, Ross. *From Settler to Citizen: New Mexican Economic Development and the Creation of Vecino Society, 1750–1820*. Berkeley: University of California Press, 2000.

Freedberg, David. *The Power of Images: Studies in the History and Theory of Response*. Chicago: University of Chicago Press, 1989.

Gamble, Lynn, and Chester King. "Middle Holocene Adaptations in the Santa Monica Mountains." In *Archaeology of the California Coast during the Middle Holocene*, edited by

Jon Erlandson and Michael Glassow, 61–72. Los Angeles: Institute of Archaeology, UCLA, 1997.

Garza, David. "Mexican Constitutional Expression in the Cortes of Cádiz." In *Mexico and the Spanish Cortes*, edited by Nettie Lee Benson, 43–58. Austin: University of Texas, 1966.

Gayton, A. H. "Estudillo among the Yokuts, 1819." In *Essays in Anthropology: Presented to A. L. Kroeber in Celebration of His Sixtieth Birthday*, edited by Robert H. Lowie, 67–85. Berkeley: University of California Press, 1936.

Geiger, Maynard, OFM. *Franciscan Missionaries in Hispanic California: 1769–1848, A Biographical Dictionary*. San Marino: Huntington Library, 1969.

———. *Mission Santa Barbara, 1782–1965*. Santa Barbara: Franciscan Fathers of California, 1965.

———. *Fray Antonio Ripoll's Description of the Chumash Revolt at Santa Barbara in 1824*. Santa Barbara: Mission Santa Barbara Archive Library, 1980.

Gibson, Charles. *The Aztecs under Spanish Rule*. Stanford, CA: Stanford University Press, 1964.

Gisbert, Teresa. "Andean Painting." In *Gloria in Excelsis: The Virgin and Angels in Viceregal Painting of Peru and Bolivia*, edited by Barbara Duncan and Teresa Gisbert, 22–31. New York: Center for Inter-American Relations, 1986.

———. "La Imagen del Paraíso en la Pintura Cuzqueña." *Boletín Museo Instituto Camón Aznar* 48/49 (1992): 115–39.

Gisbert, Teresa, and José de Mesa. "Los Incas en la Pintura Virreinal del Siglo XVIII." *América Indígena* 39, no. 4 (1979): 749–72.

Gisbert, Teresa, José de Mesa, Pedro Querejazu, and Marisabel Álvarez Plata. *Bolivian Masterpieces: Colonial Painting*. Bolivia: Secretaria de Cultura, 1994.

Glassow, Michael. "Identifying Complexity during the Early Prehistory of Santa Cruz Island, California." In *Foundations of Chumash Complexity*, edited by Jeanne Arnold, 17–24. Los Angeles: Costen Institute of Archaeology, UCLA, 2004.

Goellner, Ellen, and Jacqueline Shea Murphy, eds. *Bodies of the Text: Dance as Theory, Theory as Dance*. New Brunswick, NJ: Rutgers University Press, 1995.

Golla, Victor. "Linguistic Prehistory." In *California Prehistory: Colonization, Culture, and Complexity*, edited by Terry L. Jones and Kathryn A. Klar, 71–82. New York: Rowman and Littlefield, 2007.

———. *California Indian Languages*. Berkeley: University of California Press, 2011.

Gomar, Rogelio Ruíz. "Unique Expressions: Painting in New Spain." In *Painting a New World: Mexican Art and Life, 1521–1821*, edited by Rogelio Ruíz García, Donna Pierce, and Clara Bargellini, 66–67. Denver: Denver Art Museum, 2004.

Gone, Joseph Philip. "'So I Can Be Like a Whiteman': The Cultural Psychology of Space and Place in American Indian Mental Health." *Culture and Psychology* 14, no. 3 (2008): 369–99.

———. "A Community-Based Treatment for Native American Historical Trauma: Prospects for Evidence-Based Practice." *Journal of Consulting and Clinical Psychology* 77, no. 4 (2009): 751–62, 752.

———. "Psychotherapy and Traditional Healing for American Indians: Exploring the Prospects for Therapeutic Integration." *Counseling Psychologist* 38, no. 2 (2010): 182–83.

González, Michael J. *This Small City Will Be a Mexican Paradise: Exploring the Origins of Mexican Culture in Los Angeles, 1821–1846*. Albuquerque: University of New Mexico Press, 2005.

Grant, Campbell. *The Rock Paintings of the Chumash: A Study of a California Indian Culture*. Santa Barbara: Santa Barbara Museum of Natural History, 1993.

Grizzard, M. "Four Eighteenth-Century Mestizo Paintings form Cuzco." *University of New Mexico Art Museum Bulletin* 13 (1980): 3–8.

Gruzinski, Serge. *Painting the Conquest: The Mexican Indians and the European Renaissance*. Paris: Flammarion, 1992.

———. *The Conquest of Mexico: The Incorporation of Indian Societies into the Western World, 16th-18th Centuries*. Malden, MA: Blackwell, 1993.

Guardino, Peter. *Peasants, Politics, and the Formation of Mexico's National State: Guerrero, 1800–1857*. Stanford, CA: Stanford University Press, 1996.

Guha, Ranajit. "Introduction." In *A Subaltern Studies Reader, 1986–1995*, edited by R. Guha, ix—xxii. Minneapolis: University of Minnesota Press, 1997.

Guidotti-Hernández, Nicole M. *Unspeakable violence: Remapping U.S. and Mexican National Imaginaries*. Durham, NC: Duke University Press, 2011.

Gutiérrez, Ramón. *When Jesus Came, the Corn Mothers Went Away: Marriage, Sexuality, and Power in New Mexico, 1500–1846*. Stanford, CA: Stanford University Press, 1991.

Gutiérrez, Ramón, and Richard J. Orsi, eds. *Contested Eden: California before the Gold Rush*. Berkeley: University of California Press, 1997.

Haas, Lisbeth. *Conquests and Historical Identities in California, 1769–1936*. Berkeley: University of California Press, 1995.

———. *Pablo Tac, Indigenous Scholar Writing on Luiseño Language and Colonial History, c. 1840*. Berkeley: University of California Press, 2011.

———. "Fear in Colonial California and Along the Borderlands." In *Facing Fear: The History of an Emotion in Global Prespective*, edited by Michael Laffan and Max Weiss. Princeton University Press, 2002.

Hackel, Steven. "Land, Labor, and Production: The Colonial Economy of Spanish and Mexican California." In *Contested Eden: California before the Gold Rush*, edited by Ramón Gutiérrez and Richard J. Orsi, 111–46. Berkeley: University of California Press, 1997.

———. "The Staff of Leadership: Indian Authority in the Missions of Alta California." *William and Mary Quarterly* 54 no. 2 (1997): 347–77.

———. *The Children of Coyote, Missionaries of Saint Francis: Indian-Spanish Relations in Colonial California, 1769–1850*. Chapel Hill: University of North Carolina Press, 2005.

———, ed. *Alta California: Peoples in Motion, Identities in Formation, 1769–1850*. Berkeley: University of California Press, 2010.

Hageman, Fred C., and Russell C. Ewing. *An Archeological and Restoration Study of Mission La Purisima Concepción*. Santa Barbara: Santa Barbara Trust for Historic Preservation, 1991.

Hämäläinen, Pekka. *The Comanche Empire*. New Haven, CT: Yale University Press, 2008.

Hämäläinen, Pekka, and Samuel Truett. "On Borderlands" *Journal of American History* 98, no. 2 (September 2001): 338–61.

Harrington, John P. "The Mission Indians of California." In *Explorations and Field-Work*, 198–204. Washington, DC: Smithsonian Institution, 1928.

————. "Field-work among the Mission Indians of California." In *Explorations and Field-work*, 85–90. Washington, DC: Smithsonian Institution, 1933.

————, ed. and anno. *Father Gerónimo Boscana's Chinigchinich: Historical Account of the Belief, Usages, Customs and Extravagancies of the Indians of the Mission of San Juan Capistrano Called the Acagchemem Tribe*. Banning, CA: Malki Museum Press, 2005.

Haskett, Robert. "El Legendario Don Toribio en Los Títulos Primordiales de Cuernavaca." In *De Tlacuilos y Escribanos: Estudios Sobre Documentos Indígenas*, edited by Xavier Noguez and Stephanie Wood, 137–65. Zamora, Michoacán: El Colegio de Michoacán, 1998.

Hedges, Ken. "Shamanistic Aspects of California Rock Art." In *California Indian Shamanism*, edited by Lowell J. Bean, 67–88. Menlo Park, CA: Ballena Press, 1992.

Heizer, Robert F. "A California Messianic Movement of 1801 among the Chumash." *American Anthropologist* 43 (1941): 128–29.

————, ed. *Mission Indian Vocabularies of Alphonse Pinart*. Berkeley: University of California Press, 1952.

————, ed. *California Indian Linguistic Records: The Mission Indian Vocabularies of H. W. Henshaw*. Berkeley: University of California Press, 1955.

Hemond, Aline, and Pierre Ragon, eds. *L'image au Mexique: Usages, Appropriations et Transgressions*. Paris: Harmattan, 2001.

Hildebrant, W. R. *Xonxon'ata, in the Tall Oaks: Archaeology and Ethnohistory of a Chumash Village in the Santa Ynez Valley*. Santa Barbara: Santa Barbara Museum of Natural History, 2004.

Hinton, Leanne. *Flutes of Fire: Essays on California Indian Languages*. Berkeley, CA: Heyday Books, 1994.

Holt, Thomas. *The Problem of Freedom: Race, Labor, and Politics in Jamaica and Britain, 1832–1938*. Baltimore: Johns Hopkins University Press, 1992.

Horn, Rebecca. *Postconquest Coyoacán: Nahua-Spanish Relations in Central Mexico, 1519–1650*. Stanford, CA: Stanford University Press, 1997.

Horcasitas, Beatríz Urías. *Indígena y Criminal: Interpretaciones del Derecho y la Antropología en México, 1871–1921*. México, DF: Universidad Iberoamericana, 2000.

———— "A Rare Account of Gabrielino Shamanism from the Notes of John P. Harrington." *Journal of California and Great Basin Anthropology* 1, no. 2 (1979a): 356–62.

————. *Breath of the Sun: Life in Early California as Told by a Chumash Indian, Fernando Librado*. Banning, CA: Malki Museum Press, 1979b.

Hudson, Travis. "The Chumash Revolt of 1824: Another Native Account from the Notes of John P. Harrington." *Journal of California and Great Basin Anthropology* 2, no. 1 (1980): 123–25.

————. "The Kunstkammer's Chumash Baskets." *Bulletin of the Santa Barbara Museum of Natural History* 66 (1983): 3.

Hudson, Travis, and Thomas Blackburn. *The Material Culture of the Chumash Interaction Sphere*, vols. I–III. Ramona, CA: Ballena Press, 1979–87.

Hudson, Travis, Thomas Blackburn, Rosario Curletti, and Janice Timbrook, eds., *The Eye of the Flute: Chumash Traditional History and Ritual as Told by Fernando Librado Kitsepawit to John Harrington*. Santa Barbara: Santa Barbara Museum of Natural History, 1977.

Hudson, Travis, A. Labbe, and C. Moser. *Skywatchers of Ancient California.* Santa Ana, CA: Bowers Museum, 1983.

Hudson, Travis, Janice Timbrook, and Melissa Rempe, eds. *Tomol: Chumash Watercraft as Described in the Ethnographic Notes of John P. Harrington.* Menlo Park, CA: Ballena Press/Santa Barbara Museum of Natural History Cooperative Publication, 1978.

Hudson, Travis, and Ernest Underhay. *Crystals in the Sky: An Intellectual Odyssey Involving Chumash Cosmology, Astronomy, and Rock Art.* Socorro, NM: Ballena Press, 1978.

Hurtado, Albert. *Indian Survival on the California Frontier.* New Haven: Yale University Press, 1988.

———. "California Indian Demography, Sherburne F. Cook, and the Revision of American History." *Pacific Historical Review* 58, no. 3 (1989): 323–44.

———. *John Sutter: A Life on the North American Frontier.* Norman: University of Oklahoma, 2006.

Jackson, Robert H. "Disease and Demographic Patterns at Santa Cruz Mission, Alta California." *Journal of California and Great Basin Anthropology* 5, no. 1/2 (1983): 33–57.

———. "Patterns of Demographic Change in the Missions of Southern Baja California." *Journal of California and Great Basin Anthropology* 9, no. 2 (1987): 251–79.

———. *Missions and the Frontiers of Spanish America: A Comparative Study of the Impact of Environmental, Economic, Political, and Socio-cultural Variations on the Missions in the Rio de la Plata Region and on the Northern Frontier of New Spain.* Scottsdale, AZ: Pentacle Press, 2005.

Jackson, Robert H., and Edward Castillo. *Indians, Franciscans, and Spanish Colonization: The Impact of the Mission System on California Indians.* Albuquerque: University of New Mexico Press, 1995.

Jackson, T. "Reconstructing Migrations in California Prehistory." *American Indian Quarterly* (Fall 1989): 359–68.

James, G. Wharton. *In and Out of the Old Missions of California.* Boston: Brown and Co., 1905.

Johnson, John R. "The Trail to Fernando." *Journal of California and Great Basin Anthropology* 4, no. 1 (1982): 132–38.

———. "Chumash Social Organization: An Ethnohistoric Perspective." PhD diss., University of California, Santa Barbara, 1988.

———. *Pacomío's Chumash Dancing Songs.* Unpublished manuscript, 1989a.

———. "Pacomío's Chumash Dancing Songs." *Bulletin of the Santa Barbara Museum of Natural History* 134 (December 1989b): 1.

———. "The Chumash and the Missions." In *Columbian Consequences: Archaeological and Historical Perspectives on the Spanish Borderlands West,* edited by David Hurst Thomas, vol. 1, 365–76. Washington, DC: Smithsonian University Press, 1989c.

———. "The Indians of Mission San Fernando." *Southern California Quarterly* 79, no. 3 (1997): 249–90.

———. "Social Responses to Climate Change among the Chumash Indians of South-Central California." In *The Way the Wind Blows: Climate, History, and Human Action,* edited by Roderick J. McIntosh, Joseph A. Tainter, and Susan Keech McIntosh, 301–26. New York: Columbia University Press, 2000.

———. "Ethnohistoric Reflections of Cruzeño Chumash Society." In *The Origins of a Pacific Coast Chiefdom: The Chumash of the Channel Islands,* edited by Jeanne E. Arnold, 53–70. Salt Lake City: University of Utah Press, 2001.

———. "Toypurina's Descendants: Three Generations of an Alta California Family." *Boletín: The Journal of the California Mission Studies Association* 24, no. 2 (2007): 31–55.

Johnson, John R., and Dinah Crawford. "Contributions to Luiseño Ethnohistory Based on Mission Register Research." *Pacific Coast Archaeological Society Quarterly* 35, no. 4 (Fall 1999): 79–102.

Johnson, John R., and David D. Earle. "Tataviam Geography and Ethnohistory." *Journal of California and Great Basin Anthropology* 12, no. 2 (1990): 191–214.

Johnson, John R., and Sally McLendon. "The Social History of Native Islanders Following Missionization." *Proceedings of the Fifth California Islands Symposium,* vol. 2, 646–53. Santa Barbara: Santa Barbara Museum of Natural History, 2002.

Johnson, John R., and S. O'Neil. *Final Report: Descendants of Native Communities in the Vicinity of Marine Corps Base Camp Pendleton.* Santa Barbara: Santa Barbara Museum of Natural History, 2000.

Johnston, Francis J. "Two Southern California Trade Trails." *Journal of California and Great Basin Anthropology* 2, no. 1 (1980): 88–96.

Jones, Terry. "Marine-Resource Value and the Priority of Coastal Settlement: A California Perspective." *American Antiquity* 56, no. 3 (1991): 419–43.

Kaeppler, Adrienne. *Hula Pahu: Hawaiian Drum Dances.* Honolulu: Bishop Museum Press, 1993.

Karttunen, Frances. *Between Worlds: Interpreters, Guides, and Survivors.* New Brunswick, NJ: Rutgers University Press, 1994.

Katzew, I. *New World Orders: Casta Painting and Colonial Latin America.* New York: Americas Society Art Gallery, 1996.

———, ed. *Contested Visions.* Los Angeles: Los Angeles Museum of Art, 2011.

Katzew, Ilona, and Susan Deans-Smith, eds. *Race and Classification: The Case of Mexican America.* Stanford: Stanford University Press, 2009.

Kelsey, Harry. *The Doctrina and Confesionario of Juan Cortés.* Altadena, CA: Howling Coyote Press, 1979.

Kenneally, Finbar. *Writings of Fermín Francisco de Lasuén,* vol. 2. Washington, DC: Academy of American Franciscan History, 1965.

Kennett, D. J. *The Island Chumash: Behavioral Ecology of a Maritime Society.* Berkeley: University of California Press, 2005.

Kerr-Ritchie, J. R. *Rites of August First: Emancipation Day in the Black Atlantic World.* Baton Rouge: Louisiana State University Press, 2007.

Kimbro, E. *Cómo la sombra huye la hora: restoration research: Santa Cruz Mission Adobe: Santa Cruz Mission State Historical Park.* Davenport, CA: Historical Investigations, 1985.

King, Chester D. "Chumash Inter-Village Economic Exchange." In *Native Californians: A Theoretical Perspective,* edited by Lowell J. Bean, 289–318. Menlo Park, CA: Ballena Press, 1976.

———. "The Names and Locations of Historic Chumash Villages." *The Journal of Anthropology* 2, no 2 (1975): 171–179.

———. "The Explanation of Differences and Similarities among Beads Used in Prehistoric and Early Historic California." In *Antap: California Indian Political and Economic Orga-*

nization, by edited Lowell John Bean and Thomas F. King, 77–91. Ramona, CA: Ballena Press, 1974.

Kinkead, Duncan. "Juan de Luzón and the Sevillian Painting Trade with the New World in the Second Half of the Seventeenth Century." *Art Bulletin* (June 1984): 303–10.

Knaak, Manfred. *The Forgotten Artist: Indians of Anza-Borrego and Their Rock Art.* Borrego Springs, CA: Anza-Borrego Desert Natural History Association, 1988.

Konetzke, Richard, ed. *Colección de documentos para la historia de la formación social de Hispanoamérica, 1493–1810.* Madrid: Consejo Superior de Investigaciones Científicas, 1962.

Kroeber, Alfred L. "A Mission Record of the California Indians." *University of California Publications in American Archaeology and Ethnology* 8, no. 1 (1908): 1–27.

———., José Francisco de Paula Señán, and Vicente Francisco Sarría. *A Mission Record of the California Indians, from a Manuscript in the Bancroft Library.* Berkeley: University of California Press, 1908.

———. Yokuts Dialect Survey *University California Anthropological Records* 11 (1963): 177–251.

Kropp, Phoebe S. *California Vieja: Culture and Memory in a Modern American Place.* Berkeley: University of California Press, 2006.

Langellier, John Phillip, and Daniel B. Rosen. *El Presidio de San Francisco: A History under Spain and Mexico, 1776–1846.* Denver: National Park Service, 1992.

Lara, Jaime. *City, Temple, Stage: Eschatological Architecture and Liturgical Theatrics in New Spain.* Notre Dame, IN: University of Notre Dame Press, 2004.

Larson, Daniel O., John R. Johnson, and Joel C. Michaelsen. "Missionization among the Coastal Chumash of Central California: A Study of Risk Minimization Strategies." *American Anthropologist* 96, no. 2 (1994): 263–99.

Latta, F. F. *Handbook of Yokuts Indians.* Bakersfield, CA: Kern County Museum, 1949.

Laylander, Don. "Inferring Settlement Systems for the Prehistoric Hunter-Gatherers of San Diego County." *Journal of California and Great Basin Anthropology* 19, no. 2 (1997): 179–96.

———, ed. *Listening to the Raven: The Southern California Ethnography of Constance Goddard DuBois.* Archives of California Prehistory. Salinas, CA: Coyote Press, 2004.

León-Portilla, Miguel. *The Broken Spears: The Aztec Account of the Conquest of Mexico.* Boston: Beacon Press, 1962.

Lepowsky, María. "Indian Revolts and Cargo Cults: Ritual Violence and Revitalization in California and New Guinea." In *Reassessing Revitalization Movements: Perspectives from North America and the Pacific Islands,* by M. E. Harkin, 1–60. Lincoln: University of Nebraska Press, 2004.

Lightfoot, Kent. *Indians, Missionaries, and Merchants: The Legacy of Colonial Encounters on the California Frontiers.* Berkeley: University of California Press, 2005.

Lindsay, Brendan. *Murder State: California's Native American Genocide, 1846–1873.* Lincoln: University of Nebraska Press, 2012.

Lockhart, James. *The Nahuas after the Conquest: A Social and Cultural History of the Indians of Central Mexico, Sixteenth through Eighteenth Centuries.* Stanford, CA: Stanford University Press, 1992.

———, ed. *We People Here: Náhuatl Accounts of the Conquest of Mexico.* Berkeley: University of California Press, 1993.

Loendorf, Lawrence L., Christopher Chippindale, and David S. Whitley, eds. *Discovering North American Rock Art.* Tucson: University of Arizona Press, 2005.

Lomnitz-Adler, Claudio. *Exits from the Labyrinth: Culture and Ideology in the Mexican National Space.* Berkeley: University of California Press, 1992.

Lonetree, Amy. *Decolonizing Museums: Representing Native America in National and Tribal Museums.* Chapel Hill: University of North Carolina Press, 2012.

Lope Blanch, J. "The Cortes of Cádiz and America. The Earliest Spanish and Mexican Vocabulary of Liberalism." *Revue de Linquistique Romane* 63, no. 249–50 (1998): 281–82.

Luomala, Katherine. "Flexibility in Sib Affiliation among the Diegueño." In *Native Californians: A Theoretical Retrospective,* edited by Lowell J. Bean and Thomas C. Blackburn, 245–70. Menlo Park, CA: Ballena Press, 1976.

Madley, Benjamin "California's Yuke Indians: Defining Genocide in Native American History." *Western Historical Quarterly* 39, no. 3 (Autumn 2008): 303–32.

Mallon, Florencia. *Peasant and Nation: The Making of Postcolonial Mexico and Peru.* Berkeley: University of California Press, 1995.

———, ed. *Decolonizing Native Histories: Collaboration, Knowledge, and Language in the Americas.* Durham, NC: Duke University Press, 2012.

Martínez, María Elena. "Interrogating Blood Lines: 'Purity of Blood,' the Inquisition, and Casta Categories." In *Religion in New Spain,* edited by Susan Schroeder and Stafford Poole, 196–217. Albuquerque: University of New Mexico Press, 2007.

Martínez Quinteiro, M. E. *Los grupos liberales antes de las Cortes de Cádiz.* Madrid: Narcea, 1977.

Mason, William Marvin. *The Census of 1790: A Demographic History of Colonial California.* Menlo Park, CA: Ballena Press, 1998.

Mathes, W. Michael. *Vizcaíno and Spanish Expansion in the Pacific Ocean, 1580–1630.* San Francisco: California Historical Society, 1968.

McCarthy, Helen. "Managing Oaks and the Acorn Crop." In *Before the Wilderness: Environmental Management by Native Californians,* edited by Thomas Blackburn and M. Kat Anderson, 213–28. Menlo Park, CA: Ballena Press, 1993.

McCawley, W. *Ethnohistoric Report: Camp Pendleton, San Diego County, California.* Irvine: LSA Associates, 1995.

———. *The First Angelinos: The Gabrielino Indians of Los Angeles.* Banning, CA: Malki Museum Press/Ballena Press Cooperative Publication, 1996.

———. "From Ranchería to Rancho: The Ethnohistory of Topomai-Rancho Santa Margarita." Paper presented at the annual meeting of the Society for California Archaeology, Bakersfield, 1996.

McLendon, Sally, John Johnson, Chester King, Archeology and Ethnography Program (U.S.), and Santa Barbara Museum of Natural History. *Cultural Affiliation and Lineal Descent of Chumash Peoples in the Channel Islands and the Santa Monica Mountains.* Washington, DC: National Park Service, 1999.

McRae, Kaylee Stallings. "'Soxtonokmu': An Analysis of Artifacts and Economic Patterns from a Late Period Chumash Village in the Santa Ines Valley." Master's thesis, University of Texas at San Antonio, 1999.

Menard, Russell, and Stuart Schwartz. "Why African Slavery? Labor Force Transitions in Brazil, Mexico and the Carolina Low Country." In *Slavery in the Americas,* edited by Wolfgang Binder, 89–114. Wurzburg, Germany: Konigshausen & Neumann, 1993.

Mendoza, Rubén G. "Sacrament of the Sun: Eschatological Architecture and Solar Geometry in a California Mission." *Boletín: The Journal of the California Mission Studies Association* 22, no.1 (2005): 88–110.

———. "Presidio Light: A Midwinter Solstice Event at the Presidio Chapel of Santa Bárbara." *La Compana* (Fall 2009): 1–11.

Mendoza, Zoila. *Shaping Society through Dance: Mestizo Ritual Performance in the Peruvian Andes.* Chicago: University of Chicago Press, 2000.

Menocal, María Rosa. *The Ornament of the World: How Muslims, Jews, and Christians Created a Culture of Tolerance in Medieval Spain.* Boston: Little, Brown, 2002.

Merrill, James H. *Into the American Woods: Negotiators on the Pennsylvania Frontier.* New York: Norton, 1999.

Mesa, José de, and Teresa Gisbert. *Historia de la Pintura Cuzqueña.* Lima: Fundación Augosto N. Wiese, 1981.

———. "Angelic Ways: Bolivian Angels with Extracts from the Books of Enoch." *FMR: The Magazine of Franco Maria Ricci* 85 (1997): 17–40.

Mignolo, Walter. "Misunderstanding and Colonization: The Reconfiguration of Memory and Space." *South Atlantic Quarterly* 92, no. 2 (1993): 209–61.

Mihesuah, Devon Abbott. "American Indian History as a Field of Study." In Devon Abbott Mihesuah and Angela Cavender Wilson, eds., *Indigenizing the Academy: Transforming Scholarship and Empowering Communities,* 143–60. Lincoln: University of Nebraska Press, 2004.

Millikin, Randall. *A Time of Little Choice: The Disintegration of Tribal Culture in the San Francisco Bay Area: 1769–1810.* Menlo Park, CA: Ballena Press, 1995.

Millikin, Randall, Richard T. Fitzgerald, Mark G. Hylkema, Thomas Origer, Randy Groza, Randy Wiberg, Alan Leventhal, David Bieling, Andrew Gottsfield, Donna Gillette, Viviana Bellefemine, Eric Strother, Robert Cartier, and David A. Fredrickson. "Punctuated Culture Change in the San Francisco Bay Area." In *California Prehistory: Colonization, Culture, and Complexity,* edited by Terry L. Jones and Kathryn A. Klar, 99–123. New York: Rowman and Littlefield, 2007.

Miranda, Daborah. *Bad Indians: A Tribal Memoir.* Berkeley: Heyday Press, 2012.

Mitchell, W. J. T. *Iconology: Image, Text, Ideology.* Chicago: University of Chicago Press, 1986.

———, ed. *Landscape and Power.* Chicago: University of Chicago Press, 1994.

———. *What Do Pictures Want? The Lives and Loves of Images.* Chicago: University of Chicago Press, 2005.

Monroy, D. *Thrown among Strangers: The Making of Mexican Culture in Frontier California.* Berkeley: University of California Press, 1990.

Moratto, M. J. *California Archaeology.* Orlando: Academic Press, 1984.

Moriarty, James Robert, and Brian Smith. "Historic Site Archaeology at Mission San Diego de Alcala." *Masterkey* 43, no. 3 (1969): 100–108.

———. "Discovery and Interpretation of Intaglio Impressions Mission San Diego de Alcalá." *Pacific Coast Archaeological Society Quarterly* 13, no. 4 (1977): 67–72.

Morton, Michelle. "Utopian and Dystopian Visions of California in the Historical Imagination." PhD diss., University of California, Santa Cruz, 2005.

Muñoz, Manuel Ferrer, and María Bono López. *Pueblos Indígenas y Estado Nacional en México en el Siglo XIX.* México: Universidad Nacional Autónoma de México, 1998.

Nandy, Ashis. "History's Forgotten Doubles." *History and Theory* 34, no. 2 (1995): 44–66.

Ness, Sally Ann. *Body, Movement, and Culture: Kinesthetic and Visual Symbolism in a Philippine Community*. Philadelphia: University of Philadelphia Press, l992.

Neuerburg, Norman. "Indian Carved Statues at Mission Santa Barbara." *Masterkey* 51, no. 4 (1977): 147–51.

———. "The Indian Via Crucis from Mission San Fernando: An Historical Exposition," *Southern California Quarterly* 79 (Fall 1997): 329–382.

———. "Indian Sculpture at Mission Santa Barbara." *Masterkey* 54, no. 4 (1980): 150–53.

———. "Indian Pictographs at Mission San Juan Capistrano." *Masterkey* 56, no. 2 (1982): 55–58.

———. "The Function of Prints in the California Missions." *Southern California Quarterly* 67 (Fall 1985): 263–280.

———. *The Decoration of the California Missions*. Santa Barbara: Bellerophon Books, 1989.

Neuerburg, Norman, and Georgia Lee. "The Alta California Indians as Artists before and after Contact." In *Columbian Consequences*, edited by David H. Thomas, vol. 1, 467–80. Washington, DC: Smithsonian Institution Press, 1989.

Oak, H. *A Visit to the Missions of Southern California in February and March 1874*. Los Angeles: Southwest Museum, 1981.

O'Hara, Matthew. "*Miserables* and Citizens: Indians, Legal Pluralism, and Religious Practice in Early Republican Mexico." In *Religious Culture in Modern Mexico*, edited by Martin A. Nesvig, 14–34. Lanham, MD: Rowman and Littlefield, 2007.

Ohmstede, Antonio Escobar. "Los Condueñázgos Indígenas en las Huastecas Hidalguense y Veracruzana: ¿Defensa del Espacio Comunal?" In *Indio, Nación y Comunidad en el México del Siglo XIX*, edited by Antonio Escobar Ohmstede and Patricia Lagos Preisser, 171–88. México, DF: Centro de Estudios Mexicanos y Centroamericanos, 1993.

Ohmstede, Antonio Escobar, and Patricia Lagos Preisser, eds. *Indio, Nación y Comunidad en el México del Siglo XIX*. México, DF: Centro de Estudios Mexicanos y Centroamericanos, 1993.

Osío, António María. *The History of Alta California: A Memoir of Mexican California*, edited by Rose Marie Beebe and Robert Senkewicz. Madison: University of Wisconsin Press, 1996.

Oxendine, Joan. "The Luiseno Girls' Ceremony." *Journal of California and the Great Basin Anthropology* 2, no. 1 (1980): 37–50.

———. "The Luiseño Village during the Late Prehistoric Era." PhD diss., University of California, Riverside, 1983.

Padilla, Genaro. *My History, Not Yours: The Formation of Mexican American Autobiography*. Madison: University of Wisconsin Press, 1993.

Peelo, Sarah M. Ginn. "Creating Community in Spanish California: An Investigation of California Plainwares." PhD diss., University of California, Santa Cruz, 2009a.

———. "Baptism among the Salinan Neophytes of Mission San Antonio de Padua: Investigating the Ecological Hypothesis." *Ethnohistory* 56, no. 4 (Fall 2009b): 589–624.

———. "The Creation of a Carmeleño Identity: Marriage Practices in the Indian Village at Mission San Carlos Borromeo del Río Carmel." *Journal of California and Great Basin Anthropology* 20, no. 2 (2010): 117–139.

———. "Pottery-Making in Spanish California: Creating Multi-Scalar Social Identity through Daily Practice." *American Antiquity* 76, no. 4 (2011): 642–64, 642.

Peralta, Rina Ortíz. "Inexistentes Por Decreto: Disposiciones Legislativas Sobre Los Pueblos de Indios en el Siglo XIX: El Caso de Hidalgo." In *Indio, Nación y Comunidad en el México del Siglo XIX*, edited by Antonio Escobar Ohmstede and Patricia Lagos Preisser, 153–70. México: Centro de Estudios Mexicanos y Centroamericanos, 1993.

Perissinotto, Giorgio, ed. *Documenting Everyday Life in Early Spanish California: The Santa Barbara Presido, Memorias y Facturas, 1779–1810*. Santa Barbara: Santa Barbara Trust for Historic Preservation, 1998.

Peterson, Jeanette F. *Synthesis and Survival: The Native Presence in Sixteenth-Century Murals of New Spain*. Tempe: Arizona State University Press, 1995.

Phillips, George Harwood. "Indian Painting from Mission San Fernando: An Historical Interpretation." *Journal of California Anthropology* 3, no. 1 (1976): 94–114.

———. *Indians and Intruders in Central California, 1769–1849*. Norman: University of Oklahoma Press, 1993.

———. *"Bringing Them under Subjugation": California's Tejón Indian Reservation and Beyond, 1852–1864*. Lincoln: University of Nebraska Press, 2004.

———. "The Stations of the Cross Revisited, Reconsidered, and Revised (sort of)." *Boletín: The Journal of the California Mission Studies Association* 24, no. 2 (2007): 76–80.

Phipps, Elena. "Textiles as Cultural Memory: Andean Garments in the Colonial Period." In *Converging Cultures: Art and Identity in Spanish America*, edited by Diane Fane, 144–56. Brooklyn: Brooklyn Museum, 1996.

Pierce, Donna. "From New Spain to New Mexico: Art and Culture on the Northern Frontier." In *Converging Cultures: Art and Identity in Spanish America*, edited by Diane Fane, 59–68. Brooklyn: Brooklyn Museum, 1996.

Pierce, Donna, R. R. Gomar, and Clara Bargellini, eds. *Painting a New World: Mexican Art and Life, 1521–1821*. Denver: Denver Art Museum, 2004.

Poole, D. *Vision, Race, and Modernity: A Visual Economy of the Andean Image World*. Princeton: Princeton University Press, 1997.

Poole, Stafford. *Our Lady of Guadalupe: The Origins and Sources of a Mexican National Symbol, 1531–1797*. Tucson: University of Arizona Press, 1995.

Prakash, Gyan. "Writing Post-Orientalist Histories of the Third World: Perspectives from Indian Historiography." In *Mapping Subaltern Studies and the Postcolonial*, edited by Vinayak Chaturvedi, 163–90. London: Verso, 2000.

Preston, William. "Serpent in Eden: Dispersal of Foreign Diseases into Pre-Mission California." *Journal of California and the Great Basin Anthropology* 18, no. 1 (1996): 2–37.

Pubols, Louise. "Fathers of the Pueblo: Patriarchy and Power in Mexican California, 1800–1880." In *Continental Crossroads: Remapping U.S.-Mexico Borderlands History*, edited by Samuel Truett and Elliott Young, 67–93. Durham, NC: Duke University Press, 2004.

———. *The Father of All: The de la Guerra Family, Power, and Patriarchy in Mexican California*. Berkeley: University of California Press, 2009.

Radding, Cynthia. *Wandering Peoples: Colonialism, Ethnic Spaces, and Ecological Frontiers in Northwestern Mexico, 1700–1830*. Durham, NC: Duke University Press, 1997.

———. "Cultural Dialogues: Recent Trends in Mesoamerican Ethnohistory." *Latin American Research Review* 33, no. 1 (1998): 193–211.

———. "Crosses, Caves, and Matachinis: Divergent Appropriations of Catholic discourse in Northwestern New Spain." *The Americas* 55, no. 2 (1998): 177–203.

Raibon, P. *Authentic Indians: Episodes of Encounter from the Late-Nineteenth-Century Northwest Coast.* Durham, NC: Duke University Press, 2005.

Ramos, Raúl. "Finding the Balance: Béxar in Mexican/Indian Relations." In *Continental Crossroads: Remapping U.S.-Mexico Borderlands History,* edited by Samuel Truett and Elliott Young, 35–66. Durham, NC: Duke University Press, 2004.

Rappaport, Joanne. *The Politics of Memory: Native Historical Interpretation in the Colombian Andes.* Durham, NC: Duke University Press, 1998.

Ray, Arthur. "Anthropology, History, and Aboriginal Rights: Politics and the Rise of Ethnohistory in North America in the 1950s." In *Pedagogies of the Global: Knowledge in the Human Interest,* edited by Arif Dirlik, 89–111. Boulder: Paradigm, 2006.

———."Kroeber and the California Claims: Historical Particularism and Cultural Ecology in Court." In *Central Sites, Peripheral Visions: Cultural and Institutional Crossings in the History of Anthropology,* edited by Richard Handler, 148–247. Madison: University of Wisconsin Press, 2006.

Real y Supremo Consejo de las Indias. *Recopilación de leyes de los reynos de las Indias,* tomo 1 and 2. Madrid: Graficas Ultra, 1943.

Reed, N. "Juan de la Cruz, Venancio Puc, and the Speaking Cross." *The Americas* 53, no. 4 (1997): 497–523.

Reese, Thomas, ed. *Studies in Ancient American and European Art: The Collected Essays of George Kubler.* New Haven, CT: Yale University Press, 1985.

Reichlen, Henry, Heizer, R. "Scientific Expedition of Leon de Cessac to California, 1877–1879." *University of California Archaeological Survey* (1964): 5–22.

Reséndez, Andrés. *Changing National Identities at the Frontier: Texas and New Mexico, 1800–1850.* New York: Cambridge University Press, 2005.

Restall, Matthew. "Manuel's Worlds: Black Yucatan and the Colonial Caribbean." In *Slaves, Subjects, and Subversives: Blacks in Colonial Latin America,* edited by Jane Landers and Barry Robinson, 147–74. Albuquerque: University of New Mexico Press, 2006.

Reyes, Bárbara O. "Race, Agency, and Memory in a Baja California Mission." In *Continental Crossroads: Remapping U.S.-Mexico Borderlands History,* edited by Samuel Truett and Elliott Young, 97–120. Durham, NC: Duke University Press, 2004.

Richard, Robert. *The Spiritual Conquest of Mexico.* Berkeley: University of California Press, 1966. Translated from *La Conquete Spirituelle du Mexique,* 1933.

Richmond, D. "The Legacy of African Slavery in Colonial Mexico, 1519–1810." *Journal of Popular Culture* 35, no. 2 (2001): 1–16.

Rieu-Millán, Marie Laure. *Los diputados americanos en las Cortes de Cádiz (Igualdad o independencia).* Madrid: Consejo Superior de Investigaciones Científicas, 1990.

Rosenthal, Jeffrey, Gregory G. White, and Mark Q. Sutton. "The Central Valley: A View from the Catbird's Seat." In *California Prehistory: Colonization, Culture, and Complexity,* edited by Terry L. Jones and Kathryn A. Klar, 147–63. New York: Rowman and Littlefield, 2007.

Ross, Frank. *From Settler to Citizen: New Mexican Economic Development and the Creation of Vecino Society, 1750–1820.* Berkeley: University of California Press, 2000.

Salomon, Frank. *Nightmare Victory: The Meaning of Conversion among Peruvian Indians (Huarochiri, c. 1608).* College Park: University of Maryland: Department of Spanish and Portuguese, 1990.

Salomon, Frank, and George Urioste, *The Huarochirí Manuscript: A Testament of Ancient and Colonial Andean Religion*. Austin: University of Texas Press, 1991.

Salvucci, Richard. *Textiles and Capitalism in Mexico: An Economic History of the Obrajes, 1539–1840*. Princeton: Princeton University Press, 1988.

Sandos, James. "Levantamiento! The 1824 Chumash Uprising Reconsidered." *Southern California Quarterly* 67, no. 2 (1985): 109–33.

———. "Junipero Serra's Canonization and the Historical Record." *American Historical Review* 95, no. 5 (1988): 1253–58.

———. "Christianization among the Chumash: An Ethnohistoric Perspective." *American Indian Quarterly* 15, no. 1 (1991): 65–90.

———. *Converting California: Indians and Franciscans in the Missions*. New Haven, CT: Yale University Press, 2004.

———. "Toypurina's Revolt: Religious Conflict at Mission San Gabriel in 1785." *Boletín: The Journal of the California Mission Studies Association* 24, no. 2 (2007): 4–14.

Sanneh, Lamin O. *Translating the Message: The Missionary Impact on Culture*. Maryknoll, NY: Orbis, 1989.

Santiago, Mark. *Massacre at the Yuma Crossing: Spanish Relations with the Quechans, 1779–1782*. Tucson: University of Arizona Press, 1998.

Sarris, G., ed. *The Sound of Rattles and Clappers: A Collection of New California Indian Writing*. Sun Tracks: An American Indian Literary Series. Tucson: University of Arizona Press, 1994.

Sayer, Chloë. *Textiles from Mexico*. Seattle: University of Washington Press, 2002.

Schaefer, Jerry, and Don Laylander. "The Colorado Desert: Ancient Adaptations to Wetlands and Wastelands." In *California Prehistory: Colonization, Culture, and Complexity*, edited by Terry L. Jones and Kathryn A. Klar, 247–59. New York: Rowman and Littlefield, 2007.

Schuetz-Miller, Mardith K. *Building and Builders in Hispanic California, 1769–1850*. Tucson: Southwestern Mission Research Center; Santa Barbara, CA: Santa Barbara Trust for Historic Preservation, 1994.

Scott, Rebecca. *Slave Emancipation in Cuba: The Transition to Free Labor, 1860–1899*. Pittsburgh: University of Pittsburgh Press, 1985.

———. "Exploring the Meaning of Freedom: Post-Emancipation Societies in Comparative Perspective." *Hispanic American Historical Review* 68, no. 3 (1988): 407–60.

———. *Degrees of Freedom: Louisiana and Cuba after Slavery*. Cambridge, MA: Harvard University Press, 2005.

Seed, Patricia. *American Pentimento: The Invention of Indians and the Pursuit of Riches*. Minneapolis: University of Minnesota Press, 2001.

Shackley, M. S., ed. *The Early Ethnography of the Kumeyaay*. Berkeley: Phoebe Hearst Museum of Anthropology, University of California, Berkeley, 2004.

Sheridan, Cecilia. "Social Control and Native Territoriality in Northeastern New Spain." In *Choice, Persuasion, and Coercion: Social Control on Spain's North American Frontiers*, edited by Jesús F. de la Teja and Ross Frank, 121–48. Albuquerque: University of New Mexico Press, 2005.

Shipek, Florence Connolly. "A Strategy for Change: The Luiseño of Southern California." PhD diss., University of Hawaii, 1977.

———. *Pushed into the Rocks: Southern California Indian Land Tenure, 1769–1986*. Lincoln: University of Nebraska Press, 1988.

———. "Mission Indians and Indians of California Land Claims." *American Indian Quarterly* 13, no. 4 (1989): 409–20.

———. *Delfina Cuero: Her Autobiography, An Account of Her Last Years and Her Ethnobotanic Contributions*. Menlo Park, CA: Ballena Press, 1991.

Shoup, Laurence H., and Randall T. Millikin. *Inigo of Rancho Posolmi: The Life and Times of a Mission Indian*. Menlo Park, CA: Ballena Press, 1999.

Silliman, Stephen. *Lost Laborers in Colonial California: Native Americans and the Archaeology of Rancho Petaluma*. Tucson: University of Arizona Press, 2004.

Simpson, Lesley Byrd, ed. *Journal of José Longinos Martínez: Notes and Observations of the Naturalist of the Botanical Expedition in Old and New California and the South Coast, 1791–1792*. San Francisco: J. Howell Books, 1961.

Skowronek, R. K. "Sifting the Evidence: Perceptions of Life at the Ohlone Missions of Alta California." *Ethnohistory* 45, no. 4 (1998): 675–88.

Smith, Gerald, and Wilson Turner. *Indian Rock Art of Southern California with Selected Petroglyph Catalog*. Redlands, CA: San Bernardino County Museum Association, 1975.

Smith, Lillian. "Three Inscribed Chumash Baskets with Designs from Spanish Colonial Coins." *American Indian Art Magazine* 7, no. 3 (1982): 62–68.

Smith, Linda Tuhiwai. *Decolonizing Methodologies: Research and Indigenous Peoples*. London: Zed, 1999.

Sota, A. "Mission San Luis Rey, California—Excavations in the Sunken Gardens." *Kiva* 26, no. 4 (1961): 34–43.

Stern, P. "Gente de Color Quebrado: Africans and Afromestizos in Colonial Mexico." *Colonial Latin American Historical Review* 3, no. 2 (1994): 185–205.

Stoler, Anne, ed. *Carnal Knowledge and Imperial Power: Race and the Intimate in Colonial Rule*. Berkeley: University of California Press, 2002.

———, ed. *Haunted by Empire: Geographies of Intimacy in North American History*. Durham, NC: Duke University Press, 2006.

Sullivan, Edward. "European Painting and the Art of the New Colonies." In *Converging Cultures: Art and Identity in Spanish America*, edited by Diane Fane, 28–41. Brooklyn: Brooklyn Museum, 1996.

Sutton, Mark Q., Mark E. Basgall, Jill K. Gardner, and Mark W. Allen. "Advances in Understanding Mojave Desert Prehistory." In *California Prehistory: Colonization, Culture, and Complexity*, edited by Terry L. Jones and Kathryn A. Klar, 229–45. New York: Rowman and Littlefield, 2007.

Tanghetti, Rosamaría. "Intimate Unions: Conquest and Marriage in California, 1769–1890." PhD diss., University of California, Davis, 2004.

Taylor, E., and William Wallace. *Mohave Tattooing and Face-Painting*. Los Angeles: Southwest Museum Leaflets, 1947.

Taylor, William B. "The Virgin of Guadalupe in New Spain: An Inquiry into the Social History of Marian Devotion." *American Ethnologist* 14 (February 1987): 9–33.

———. "Santiago's Horse: Christianity and Indian Resistance." In *Violence, Resistance, and Survival in the Americas*, edited by William B. Taylor and Franklin Pease. Washington, DC: Smithsonian Institution Press, 1994.

———. *Magistrates of the Sacred: Priests and Parishioners in Eighteenth-Century Mexico.* Stanford, CA: Stanford University Press, 1996.

Taylor, William B., and Franklin Pease, eds. *Violence, Resistance, and Survival in the Americas: Native Americans and the Legacy of Conquest.* Washington, DC: Smithsonian Institution Press, 1994.

———. "Two Shrines of the Cristo Renovado: Religion and Peasant Politics in Late Colonial Mexico." *American Historical Review* 110, no. 4 (October 2005): 945–74.

———, "Introduction." In *Contested Visions in the Spanish Colonial World,* edited by Ilona Katzew, 15–27. New Haven: Yale University Press and Los Angeles: Los Angeles County Museum of Art, 2011.

Terraciano, Kevin. "Competing Memories of the Conquest of Mexico." In *Contested Visions in the Spanish Colonial World,* edited by Ilona Katzew, 55–78. Los Angeles: Los Angeles County Museum of Art, 2011.

Tibesar, Antonine, ed. *Writings of Junipero Serra.* Washington DC: Academy of American Franciscan History, 1966.

Timberlake, Marie. "The Painted Colonial Image: Jesuit and Andean Fabrication of History in Matrimonio de García de Loyola con Nuesta Beatriz." *Journal of Medieval and Early Modern Studies* 29, no. 3 (1999): 563–98.

Timbrook, Jan. "Native American Arts in the Spanish Missions: Chumash Basketry." In *The Arts of the Missions of Northern New Spain, 1600–1821,* edited by Clara Bargellini and Michael Komanecky. Mexico City: Antiguo Colegio de San Ildefonso/Mexico City, 2009: 327–332.

Trey, Frank. "Gender and the Manumission of Slaves in New Spain." *Hispanic American Historical Review* 86, no. 2 (May 2006): 309–36.

True, D. L., Clement W. Meighan, and Harvey Crew. *Archaeological Investigations at Molpa, San Diego County, California.* Berkeley: University of California Press, 1974.

Umberger, Emily, and Tom Cummins, eds. *Native Artists and Patrons in Colonial Latin America.* Tempe: Arizona State University Press, 1995.

Valdes, Carlos Manuel, and Ildefonso Dávila. *Esclavos Negros en Saltillo Siglos XVII-XIX.* Coahuila: Universidad Autónoma de Coahuila, 1988.

Valdes, D. "The Decline of Slavery in Mexico." *The Americas* 44, no. 2 (1987): 167–94.

Vancouver, G. *A Visit to the Santa Barbara Royal Presidio in 1793.* Santa Barbara: Bellerophon Books, 1986.

Van Young, Eric. "Rebelión Agraria Sin Agrarismo: Defensa de la Comunidad, Significado y Violencia Colectiva en la Sociedad Rural Mexicana de Fines de la Época Colonial." In *Indio, Nación y Comunidad en el México del Siglo XIX,* edited by Antonio Escobar Ohmstede and Patricia Lagos Preisser. Mexico: Centro de Estudios Mexicanos y Centroamericanos, 1993.

Venegas, Miguel. *Histoire naturelle et civile de la Californie, contenant une description exacte de ce pays: les moeurs de ses habitans, leur religion, leur government.* Paris: Durand, 1767.

Von Barghahn, B. "Cuzco Colonial Painting: Vision and Variation." *Latin American Art* 4, no. 3 (1992): 72–75.

Von Langsdorff, G. H. *Voyages and Travels in Various Parts of the World during the Years 1803, 1804, 1805, 1806, and 1807.* London: Henry Colburn, 1813–14.

Voss, Barbara L. *The Archaeology of Ethnogenesis: Race and Sexuality in Colonial San Francisco.* Berkeley: University of California Press, 2008.

Wagner, Henry R. "The Voyage to California of Sebastián Rodríguez Cermeño in 1595." *California Historical Quarterly* (1924): 3–24.

Walker, Philip, and Travis Hudson. *Chumash Healing: Changing Health and Medical Practices in an American Indian Society.* Banning, CA: Malki Museum Press, 1993.

Walker, Philip, and John Johnson. "Effects of Contact on the Chumash Indians." In *Disease and Demography in the Americas,* edited by John Verano and Douglas Ubelaker, 127–39. Washington, DC: Smithsonian Institution, 1992.

Walsh, Jane MacLaren. *John Peabody Harrington: The Man and his California Indian Field Notes.* Ramona, CA: Ballena Press, 1976.

Walsh, Marie T. *The Mission of the Passes, Santa Ines: An Intimate Historical Study Relating to the Founding and Subsequent Existence of This Lovely Old Mission.* Los Angeles: Times-Mirror, 1930.

Washburn, D. "The Neighbor Factor: Basket Designs in Northern and Central California." *Journal of California and Great Basin Anthropology* 9, no. 2 (1987): 146–73.

Waterman, T. T. "The Religious Practices of the Diegueno Indians." *University of California Publications in American Archaeology and Ethnology* 8, no. 6 (1910): 271–358.

Webb, Edith. "Pigments Used by the Mission Indians of California." *The Americas* 2, no. 2 (October 1945): 137–50.

Weber, David. *Bárbaros: Spaniards and Their Savages in the Age of Enlightenment.* New Haven, CT: Yale University Press, 2005.

Weber, Francis J. "The Stations at Mission San Fernando." *Masterkey* 39, no. 1 (1965): 7–12.

White, Hayden. *The Content of the Form: Narrative Discourse and Historical Representation.* Baltimore: Johns Hopkins University Press, 1987.

White, Raymond C. "Two Surviving Luiseno Indian Ceremonies." *American Anthropologists* 55 (1953): 569–78.

———. "Luiseno Social Organization." *University of California Publications in American Archaeology and Ethnology* 48, no. 2 (1963): 91–194.

———. "Religion and Its Role among the Luiseño." In *Native Californians: A Theoretical Retrospective,* by Lowell J. Bean and Thomas Blackburn, 335–78. Menlo Park, CA: Ballena Press, 1976.

Whitehead, R. S., ed. *Citadel on the Channel: The Royal Presidio of Santa Barbara, Its Founding and Construction, 1782–1798.* Santa Barbara: Santa Barbara Trust for Historic Preservation and Arthur Clark Co., 1996.

Whitley, David. "Shamanism and Rock Art." *Cambridge Archaeological Journal* 2, no. 1 (1992): 89–113.

———."Ethnography and Rock Art in the Far West: Some Archaeological Implications." In *New Light on Old Art: Recent Advances in Hunter-Gatherer Rock Art Research,* by David Whitley and L. L. Loendorf, Monograph 36, 81–93. Los Angeles: UCLA Institute of Archaeology, 1994a.

———. "Shamanism, Natural Modeling, and the Rock Art of the Far Western North American Hunters and Gatherers." In *Shamanism and Rock Art in North America,* edited by S. Turpin, vol. 1, 1–43. San Antonio: Rock Art Foundation, Inc., 1994b.

————. *A Guide to Rock Art Sites: Southern California and Southern Nevada.* Missoula, MT: Mountain Press Publishing Company, 1996.

————. *The Art of the Shaman: Rock Art of California.* Salt Lake City: University of Utah Press, 2000.

Williams, J. S. "Adobe Ramparts: Archaeology and the Evolution of the Presidio of San Diego." *Pacific Coast Archaeological Society Quarterly* 33, no. 4 (1997): 29–56.

Wood, Stephanie. "Adopted Saints: Christian Images in Nahua Testaments of Late Colonial Toluca." *The Americas* 47, no. 3 (1991a): 259–94.

————. "The Cosmic Conquest: Late Colonial Views of the Sword and the Cross in Central Mexican Títulos." *Ethnohistory* 38, no. 2 (1991b): 176–95.

————. *Transcending Conquest: Nahua Views of Spanish Colonial Mexico.* Norman: University of Oklahoma Press, 2003.

Wroth, William. *Sarape Textiles from Historic Mexico, The Mexican Sarape: A History.* Saint Louis: Saint Louis Art Museum, 1999.

Zappia, Natale. *The Interior World: Trading and Raiding in Native California, 1700–1863.* Ph. D. dissertation, University of California, Santa Cruz, 2008.

INDEX

CPSIA information can be obtained
at www.ICGtesting.com
Printed in the USA
FSHW012031080119
54916FS